# ARTIFICIAL INTELLIGENCE

## APPLICATIONS THROUGHOUT THE REAL ESTATE INDUSTRY

**ARTIFICIAL INTELLIGENCE APPLICATIONS**

THROUGHOUT THE REAL ESTATE INDUSTRY

By Gilbert H. Castle, III and Srikant "Steve" Hemmady

ISBN: 979-8-3283411-1-0

Cover: Nada Orlic
Editorial Design: Luca Funari

Printed in United States of America
First Edition: July 2024

# ARTIFICIAL INTELLIGENCE

## APPLICATIONS THROUGHOUT THE REAL ESTATE INDUSTRY

Where We Have Been,
Where We Are Now, and
Where We Are Going

GILBERT H. CASTLE, III
SRIKANT "STEVE" HEMMADY

# CONTENTS

# PREFACE

Welcome to "Artificial Intelligence Applications Throughout the Real Estate Industry: Where We Have Been, Where We Are Now, and Where We Are Going." This book aims to provide an in-depth exploration of the intersection between artificial intelligence (AI) and the real estate industry. We will examine the evolution of AI technology, its current applications in real estate, and the future prospects and trends that lie ahead.

Worldwide interest in and adoption of AI technologies have been increasing exponentially in the last few years, including in the real estate industry. Undoubtedly the real estate industry is about to be fundamentally transformed by AI. Accordingly, the co-authors of this book believe that now is a critical time to inform our real estate colleagues of all the benefits and disbenefits inherent in that forthcoming AI transformation.

The co-authors and the members of the Technical Advisory Panel are all real estate professionals. Collectively we have been actively monitoring the evolution of AI since the early 1990s. Most of us have an additional specialty in Geographic Information Systems (GIS) and other geospatial technologies. We have come to believe that artificial intelligence combined with GIS – that is, GeoAI – holds far more potential for the real estate industry than has yet been widely recognized. Accordingly, GeoAI is a featured part of this book.

Collectively we also have a special interest in AI real estate applications in the United States and India, generally regarded as the second and fifth largest real estate markets in the world respectively. India's real estate market has been booming, with the potential to surpass the fourth largest country (United Kingdom) or even third largest (Japan) in the near future.

In this book, we will begin by establishing a foundational understanding of AI, and exploring its different types and classifications. We will discuss the historical context of AI, including its early developments and notable examples within the real estate domain. Additionally, we will delve into the current applications of AI in the real estate industry, focusing on how it is being utilized in areas such as automated property valuation, property search and recommendation, predictive analytics, customer service, personalized marketing, property management, and more. Notably, we will highlight the significance of geographic information systems (GIS) in the context of AI applications.

Furthermore, this book will provide insights into the future direction of AI in real estate. Through a comprehensive review of literature, research studies, and expert predictions, we will explore the potential advancements and opportunities that AI can bring to the industry. We will examine various segments of the real estate market, including commercial, residential, finance, data providers, government, and others, to understand the specific implications and anticipated developments.

It is important to note that this book does not aim to be an exhaustive technical manual but rather a comprehensive guide for professionals, industry stakeholders, and enthusiasts seeking to understand the current state and future potential of AI in real estate. It combines theoretical knowledge with practical examples, case studies, and expert insights to provide a holistic view of the subject matter.

We would like to express our gratitude to the researchers, practitioners, and organizations whose work and contributions have helped shape the content of this book. Their dedication to advancing AI technology and its application in the real estate industry has been instrumental in driving progress and innovation.

We hope that this book will serve as a valuable resource for readers, inspiring further exploration, discussion, and implementation of AI applications in the real estate industry. It is our belief that by embracing and leveraging the power of AI, the real estate industry can unlock new levels of efficiency, accuracy, and customer satisfaction, ultimately shaping the future of this dynamic and evolving sector.

Enjoy your journey through the fascinating world of AI applications in the real estate industry!

Gilbert H. Castle, III

Srikant G. Hemmady

July 2024

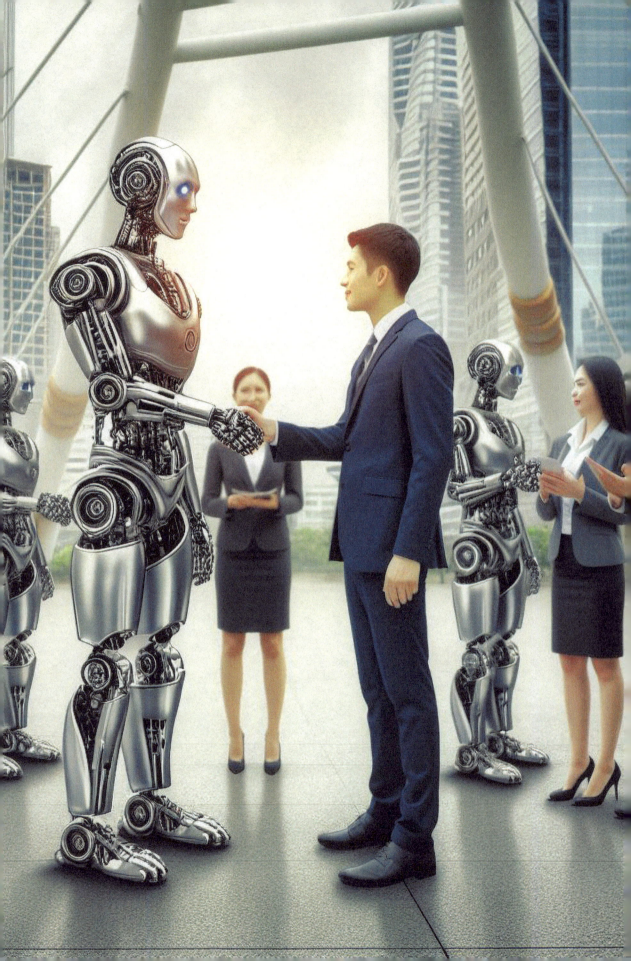

# PART I

# WHAT IS AI?

Learn from yesterday,
live for today, hope for tomorrow.
The important thing is not to stop questioning.

**– Albert Einstein**

# CHAPTER 1
# EVOLUTION OF AI
# CONCEPTS AND
# DEFINITIONS

## 1.1.  HOW YOU WILL BENEFIT FROM READING
## THIS CHAPTER

We begin by exploring widely used definitions of artificial intelligence (AI). You will thereby gain a solid foundation for exploring the specific applications, challenges, and opportunities of AI in the real estate industry discussed throughout this book.

Learning about a highly advanced, dynamic technology like AI is complicated enough without further lacking the basic vocabulary. According to the Merriam-Webster Dictionary, a "definition" is: "a statement expressing the essential nature of something… the action or the power of describing, explaining, or making definite and clear." Definitions are thus our all-important starting point.

During the course of reading this book, you will become conversant in what AI is and is not at present. This will enable you to competently follow the literature on AI; engage in useful discussions with others interested in the field; and especially zero in on which aspects of AI hold the greatest potential value for you.

Along the way you are also in for many surprises, which hopefully you will find entertaining as well as enlightening.

## 1.2.  EMERGENCE OF AI CONCEPTS, DATING BACK
## TO ANCIENT GREECE

Speaking of surprises, most people don't know that AI concepts can be traced back at least as far as 700 B.C. In this section we will briefly describe approximately 50 milestones in AI's evolution to date. The milestones not only provide a context for the AI definitions later in this chapter but also foreshadow future discussions of how multi-faceted the technology has become.

The milestones are presented in three chronologic groups:

- Milestones occurring from antiquity through the 1940s,
- Milestones occurring from 1950 to 2023, and
- Real estate-specific milestones.

### 1.2.1. Methodology and Main Sources

Before turning to the milestones, a comment about how we compiled all the information in this book is appropriate. All sources cited in the References at the end of each chapter are publicly available via the Internet. This is in the interests of transparency, reliability, and replicability should any of our readers wish to pursue additional research on any given topic.

Adhering to sound journalism practices, all information presented in this book has typically been verified from at least two recognized, independent sources. For example, the milestones in this chapter have all been cited by at least two sources and sometimes as many as four sources. Such overlapping has also been useful in filtering out the most important milestones since any given source might describe dozens of milestones – and one encompasses over 300 milestones.

Finally, one of the most important roles of our Technical Advisory Panel has been to corroborate this book's information in its entirety, not only in terms of credibility but also comprehensiveness.

### 1.2.2. Antiquity through the 1940s Milestones

In the next section we will see that after 1 was a pivotal year for AI development, in many ways a "tipping point", and hence the bifurcation of AI's chronologic milestones into pre- and post-1950. That said, the 2,650 years of AI milestones leading up to 1950 encompass numerous essential contributions to AI's evolution. Many have been readily apparent, as in the case of robotics, one of the pillars of AI literally from the beginning (Hesiod in 700 B.C.). Other contributions have been more in the background, including:

- The development of theories of logic that are indispensable to AI programming, beginning with Aristotle in 384 B.C.;

- The invention in 1672 of the binary numeral system, the core of all computer software, by Gottfried Wilhelm Leibniz;
- Four years later, his invention of the chain rule essential to Deep Learning, arguably the most important technology pillar of AI at present; and
- The positing of AI moral and ethical issues, first raised by Mary Wollstonecraft Shelley with her publication of *Frankenstein; Or, The Modern Prometheus* in 1818.

Table 1.1 presents the AI milestones from 700 B.C. to 1949.

TABLE 1.1

| YEAR | EVENT |
| --- | --- |
| 700 B.C. | The Greek poet Hesiod recites the myth of Talos, the first recorded conception of a robot. Talos was a giant bronze man commissioned by Zeus and built by Hephaestus, to defend Crete. Three times daily Talos would traverse the island's perimeter, throwing boulders at any invading ships. |
| 384 B.C. – 322 B.C. | Aristotle develops theories of logic, especially syllogism, which had an unparalleled influence on Western thought for more than 2,000 years. Syllogism is foundational to the deductive reasoning built into artificial intelligence programming. |
| 1st Century A.D. | Heron (Hero) of Alexandria, a Greek prolific mathematician and inventor, creates groups of automatons powered by the first steam-powered engine. |
| 1206 | Ebru İz Bin Rezzaz (Ismail) al-Jazari, sometimes called the "father of robotics", creates numerous automatons including a mechanical humanoid waitress that served drinks. |
| 1620 | Francis Bacon develops an empirical theory of knowledge acquisition. "Empiricism" subsequently contributed to the development of scientific method and to the Machine Learning (ML) facet of artificial intelligence. |
| 1642 | Blaise Pascal designs the first digital calculating machine. He made public his device three years later after building 50 prototypes. |

| YEAR | EVENT |
|------|-------|
| 1672 | Gottfried Wilhelm Leibniz invents the binary numeral system, the basis of today's computer programming. Four years later he developed the chain rule which is essential to artificial neural networks – especially the backpropagation algorithm for Deep Learning. |
| 1726 | Jonathan Swift publishes *Gulliver's Travels* in which he describes The Engine, a machine "for improving speculative Knowledge by practical and mechanical Operations" whereby "the most ignorant Person at a reasonable Charge, and with a little bodily Labour, may write Books in Philosophy, Poetry, Politicks, Law, Mathematicks, and Theology, with the least Assistance from Genius or study." |
| 1763 | Thomas Bayes' *An Essay Towards Solving a Problem in the Doctrine of Chances* lays the foundations of Bayes' Theorem, which has become fundamental to reasoning about the probability of events in Machine Learning (ML). |
| 1818 | At age 20, Mary Wollstonecraft Shelley publishes *Frankenstein; Or, The Modern Prometheus*. Among the AI issues raised for the first time by the book are the morality and ethics of artificially creating an intelligent being, and the prospect of AI turning on its creator *a.k.a.* the Singularity. |
| 1854 | George Boole, believing that logical reasoning can be systematized in the same manner as solving mathematical equations, invents Boolean algebra -- which has become a cornerstone of Machine Learning (ML). |
| 1914 | Leonardo Torres y Quevedo builds the first automaton for chess endgames, playing without human intervention. He has been called "the 20th century's first AI pioneer". |
| 1923 | Czech writer Karel Čapek coins the word "robot" (from the word "robota", to work) in his theater play *Rossum's Universal Robots*. |
| 1941 | Konrad Ernst Otto Zuse invents the world's first programmable computer. The same year he begins producing the Z4, the world's first commercial computer. Zuse is regarded by some as the father of the modern computer. |
| 1943 | Warren Sturgis McCulloch and Walter Pitts publish "A Logical Calculus of the Ideas Immanent in Nervous Activity", the first mathematical description of an artificial neural network. The paper leads to the creation of computer-based "neural networks" and later "deep learning". |

## 1.2.3. 1950 to 2023 Milestones

Most AI historians say that the AI discipline truly began with the Dartmouth College Summer AI Conference in the mid-1950s – including John McCarthy coining the term "artificial intelligence". As captured in Table 1.2, many other famous milestones occurred in the 1950s, which in turn set the stage for the explosion of AI activities that continues to this day.

TABLE 1.2

| YEAR | EVENT |
| --- | --- |
| 1950 | Alan Turing publishes *Computing Machinery and Intelligence*, in which he introduces the Turing Test which analyses a machine's ability to exhibit intelligent behavior that is indistinguishable from a human's.<br>The Turing Test remains the most famous AI benchmark to the present day. |
| 1950 | Isaac Asimov publishes his often-cited Three Laws of Robotics in *I, Robot*: "(1) A robot may not injure a human being or, through inaction, allow a human being to come to harm. (2) A robot must obey the orders given it by human beings except where such orders would conflict with the First Law. (3) A robot must protect its own existence as long as such protection does not conflict with the First or Second Law." |
| 1951 | The first working AI programs are written, running on a Ferranti Mark 1 machine: Christopher Strachey's checkers-playing program and Dietrich Prinz's chess-playing program. |
| 1955 | Arthur Samuel develops the first computer program to learn on its own (playing checkers) on IBM's first commercial computer, the IBM 701. Four years later he popularizes the term "Machine Learning". |
| 1955 | The Dartmouth College Summer AI Conference is proposed by John McCarthy (Dartmouth College), Marvin Minsky (Harvard University), Nathaniel Rochester (IBM), and Claude Shannon (Bell Telephone Laboratories). The workshop takes place in July and August 1956 and is seen as the official birthdate of the artificial intelligence field. |
| 1955 | John McCarthy coins the phrase "artificial intelligence" in the proposal for the Dartmouth College Summer AI Conference. |

| YEAR | EVENT |
| --- | --- |
| 1956 | The Logic Theorist (LT) software program for solving mathematical problems is written by Allen Newell, J.C. Shaw, and Herbert A. Simon. The program is considered to be the first artificial intelligence system. |
| 1958 | John McCarthy and Marvin Minsky establish the Massachusetts Institute of Technology Artificial Intelligence Laboratory. |
| 1959 | John McCarthy develops the programming language Lisp (an acronym for list processing) which becomes the most widely used programming language in artificial intelligence research. |
| 1961 | George Devol invents the first industrial robot, named Unimate, which starts working on an assembly line in a General Motors plant in New Jersey. That same year Devol with his business partner Joseph Engelberger launch the world's first robot manufacturing company, Unimation. |
| 1964 | Joseph Weizenbaum develops ELIZA, an interactive software program that carries on a dialogue in the English language on any topic. ELIZA is most famously known for simulating a psychotherapist of the Rogerian school. ELIZA is one of the first chatterbots ("chatbots") and one of the first programs seriously subjected to the Turing Test. |
| 1964 | Edward Feigenbaum, Bruce G. Buchanan, Joshua Lederberg, and Carl Djerassi begin work on DENDRAL at Stanford University -- the first expert system. A ten-year project, DENDRAL replicates the decision-making process and problem-solving behavior of organic chemists. |
| 1964 | Shakey the Robot is developed at the Artificial Intelligence Center of Stanford Research Institute (SRI). Encompassing research in robotics, computer vision, and natural language processing, Shakey becomes the first general-purpose mobile robot to combine logical reasoning and physical action. |
| 1973 | The (James) Lighthill Report on the state of artificial intelligence research in the UK concludes that "in no part of the field have discoveries made so far produced the major impact that was then promised," leading to severely curtailed government spending for AI research and contributing directly to the "AI Winter" of 1974 to 1980. |

| YEAR | EVENT |
| --- | --- |
| 1978 | Herbert A. Simon wins the Nobel Prize in Economics for his work on decision-making in the absence of perfect and complete information -- one of the cornerstones of artificial intelligence known as "satisficing". |
| 1982 | The Japanese Ministry of International Trade and Industry launches an $850 million "Fifth Generation Computer" project. The project's objectives directly support AI development, i.e., build parallel computers that can conduct conversations, translate languages, interpret pictures, and reason like human beings. |
| 1986 | As with Japan's 1982 initiative, the Indian government launches the AI-centric Knowledge-Based Computing Systems (KBCS) program under the umbrella of the Indian Fifth Generation Computer Systems (FGCS) research program. |
| 1986 | The first driverless *a.k.a.* robotic car is built by Ernst Dickmanns' team at Bundeswehr University in Munich. The Mercedes-Benz van, equipped with cameras and sensors, drives up to 55 mph on empty streets. |
| 1992 | Japan's Fifth Generation Project ends, having spent less than $320 million of its $850 million budget. As was not uncommon with AI projects at the time, arguably expectations greatly exceeded realistic possibilities. The termination is a bellwether of the 1987-1993 "AI Winter". |
| 1997 | IBM's "Deep Blue" supercomputer becomes the first computer chess-playing program to defeat a reigning world chess champion, Garry Kasparov. The match was held under tournament conditions. |
| 1997 | A description of the deep learning method a.k.a. long short-term memory (LSTM) is published in Neural Computation by Sepp Hochreiter and Juergen Schmidhuber. LSTM becomes widely used in handwriting recognition, speech recognition, machine translation, speech activity detection, robot control, video games, and healthcare. |
| 2000 | Cynthia Breazeal's MIT dissertation describes a robot named Kismet that can recognize and simulate human emotions. [In the present day Kismet is one of the very few operational examples of a highly advanced type of AI called Artificial General Intelligence.] |

| YEAR | EVENT |
| --- | --- |
| 2002 | The company iRobot begins marketing Roomba®, a robot that vacuums floors while autonomously identifying and avoiding obstacles. Roomba® is arguably one of the first and certainly one of the most widely sold domestic robots to date. |
| 2004 | The first Defense Advanced Research Projects Agency (DARPA) sponsors its first Grand Challenge, a prize competition for autonomous vehicles navigating a 150-mile route in the Mojave Desert. No competitor came even close to successfully finishing the course. However, five vehicles successfully completed a 132-mile route in the 2005 DARPA Grand Challenge. |
| 2009 | Google begins developing a driverless car which, in 2014, becomes the first autonomous vehicle to pass a U.S. state (Nevada) self-driving test. |
| 2011 | IBM's "Watson", a natural language question-answering computer, defeats the television game show Jeopardy! champions Brad Rutter and Ken Jennings. |
| 2011–2014 | Three natural language smartphone apps that answer questions, make recommendations, and perform various actions come to market: Apple's Siri (2011), Google's Google Now (2012), and Microsoft's Cortana (2014). |
| 2016 | DeepMind's "AlphaGo" program (later purchased by Google) defeats Lee Sodol, the world Go champion, 4 games to 1. Lee Sedol is a 9th dan professional Korean Go player who won 27 major tournaments from 2002 to 2016. |
| 2022–2023 | OpenAI debuts ChatGPT in November 2022. By January 2023 ChatGPT has more than 100 million users. The AI chatbot triggers worldwide public discourse on the pros and cons of artificial intelligence. OpenAI releases ChatGPT-4 in March 2023 with much-lauded improvements, though still plagued by some of the earlier version's problems. As one test of ChatGPT-4's comparative "intelligence", OpenAI claims that the program achieved a score of 1410 on the SAT (94th percentile) and 298 on the Uniform Bar Exam (90th percentile). |

## 1.2.4. Real Estate-Specific Milestones

The real estate industry has not been one of the earliest to embrace AI technology. Nonetheless, as will become self-evident in Part II of this book, the industry in recent years has undeniably been making up for lost time. According to an InData Labs report, real estate businesses using AI soared by 270% from 2015 to 2019, and the pace may well be accelerating. Table 1.3 provides a sampling of when various real estate companies incorporated AI into their business offerings.

TABLE 1.3

| YEAR | COMPANY – TYPE OF PRODUCT OR SERVICE |
|---|---|
| 2013 | Canoe – Management of Investment Data |
| 2014 | Locate AI – Retail Site Selection<br>GeoPhy – Two Products, Evra and Apprise, Addressing Multifamily Commercial Investments<br>Quantarium – A Range of Products Including TerraIndex (Home Price Index), TerraLook, and TerraPlot |
| 2015 | Kavout – Building Investment Portfolios<br>Particle Space – "Tenant" Chabot for Assisting Property Managers<br>Deepblocks – Development Site Selection<br>LocalizeAI – "Hunter" Chatbot for Multiple Types of Home Buyer Interactions<br>Restb.ai – Image Analyses for Assisting Brokers |
| 2016 | TRIGIGA – Property Management<br>Propic – Two Products, "Propic Concierge" and "Propic Insights", for Sales Management<br>RoofAI – Customer Relations<br>Enodo – Underwriting Multifamily Commercial Investments |
| 2017 | Silverwork Solutions – Mortgage-Related Operations<br>Doma – Title and Escrow Management<br>SkylineAI – Optimization of Property and Portfolio Investments |

| YEAR | COMPANY – TYPE OF PRODUCT OR SERVICE |
|------|--------------------------------------|
| 2018 | Zillow – First Zillow AI Forum (Continuing to Be Held Annually)<br>FoxyAI – Property Valuation<br>Entera – Investing in Income-Generating Single-Home Properties<br>AI Home Solutions – Smart Home Devices<br>Trulia – "Trulia Neighborhoods" Product for Assisting Home Buyers<br>Hydro – Tenant Management |
| 2019 | STAN AI – Property Management<br>Homebase AI – Smart Home Devices |
| 2021 | Zumper – "PowerLeads AI" Product for Tenant Management<br>Frigate – Property Security Devices |
| 2022 | Diffe.rent – Tenant Management<br>CREX Capital – Financing and Risk Assessment |

## 1.3. SALIENT DEFINITIONS ARISING FROM 1950 TO THE PRESENT DAY

Again, collectively the above milestones provide a context for our further investigation of AI. We now shift from anecdotal descriptions to rigorous definitions.

### 1.3.1. Seminal Definitions

As noted, John McCarthy coined the phrase "artificial intelligence" in 1955 in the proposal for the Dartmouth College Summer AI Conference. In the proposal, the very first definition of artificial intelligence was this: "**…the artificial intelligence problem is taken to be that of making a machine behave in ways that would be called intelligent if a human were so behaving.**"

Marvin Minsky was another of the four AI pioneers who organized and attended the Dartmouth College Summer AI Conference. McCarthy and Minsky subsequently co-founded the Massachusetts Institute of Technology Artificial Intelligence Laboratory.

In 1968 Minsky offered this enduring definition: "**Artificial intelligence is the science of making machines do things that would require intelligence if done by men**."

Probably the most frequently cited definition from the AI field's early years was penned by John McCarthy in a 2007 paper entitled *What Is Artificial Intelligence?* McCarthy wrote: "**It is the science and engineering of making intelligent machines, especially intelligent computer programs. It is related to the similar task of using computers to understand human intelligence, but AI does not have to confine itself to methods that are biologically observable**."

## 1.3.2. Definitions Today

We begin appropriately enough with the definition of "artificial intelligence" in multiple dictionaries and encyclopedias. Though inevitably redundant, the multiple sources in Table 1.4 do show a consensus while also providing a few interesting variations.

TABLE 1.4

| DICTIONARY DEFINITIONS | | |
| --- | --- | --- |
| Merriam Webster | 1. | A branch of computer science dealing with the simulation of intelligent behavior in computers. |
| | 2. | The capability of a machine to imitate intelligent human behavior. |
| Cambridge | | The study of how to produce machines that have some of the qualities that the human mind has, such as the ability to understand language, recognize pictures, solve problems, and learn. |
| Collins | | A type of computer technology concerned with making machines work in an intelligent way, similar to the way that the human mind works. |
| Oxford | | The study and development of computer systems that can copy intelligent human behaviour. |
| MacMillan | | The use of computer technology to make computers and other machines think and do things in the way that people can. |

| | |
|---|---|
| Dictionary.com | 1. The capacity of a computer, robot, or other programmed mechanical device to perform operations and tasks analogous to learning and decision making in humans, as speech recognition or question answering. |
| | 2. The branch of computer science involved with the design of computers or other programmed mechanical devices having the capacity to imitate human intelligence and thought. |

**ENCYCLOPEDIA DEFINITIONS**

| | |
|---|---|
| Encyclopedia Britannica | Artificial intelligence (AI) is the ability of a computer or a robot controlled by a computer to do tasks that are usually done by humans because they require human intelligence and discernment. |
| Stanford University Encyclopedia of Philosophy | Artificial intelligence (AI) is the field devoted to building artificial animals (or at least artificial creatures that – in suitable contexts – appear to be animals) and, for many, artificial persons (or at least artificial creatures that – in suitable contexts – appear to be persons). |
| Wikipedia | Artificial intelligence (AI) is intelligence—perceiving, synthesizing, and inferring information—demonstrated by machines, as opposed to intelligence displayed by humans or by other animals. Example tasks in which this is done include speech recognition, computer vision, translation between (natural) languages, as well as other mappings of inputs. |
| Investopedia | Artificial intelligence (AI) refers to the simulation of human intelligence by software-coded heuristics. Nowadays this code is prevalent in everything from cloud-based, enterprise applications to consumer apps and even embedded firmware. |

Next, to gauge definitions utilized in the private sector, Table 1.5 quotes the definitions offered by the world's largest management and IT consulting firms, together with those of the world's largest AI-focused technology companies.

TABLE 1.5

## WORLD'S LARGEST MANAGEMENT AND IT CONSULTING COMPANIES
*[All Have Offices in India]*

| | |
|---|---|
| Deloitte | The theory and development of computer systems able to perform tasks that normally require human intelligence, such as visual perception, speech recognition, decision-making, and translation between languages. |
| EY | Artificial intelligence (AI) is not a single technology but a set of methods and tools with sub-domains applied to countless situations. |
| McKinsey & Company | Artificial intelligence is a machine's ability to perform the cognitive functions we usually associate with human minds. |
| Accenture | AI is a collection of technologies that can enable a machine or system to sense, comprehend, act, and learn. Training a system through machine learning or deep learning is a core part of what makes it intelligent—and can be incredibly powerful. |
| Price Waterhouse Coopers (PwC) | In our broad definition, AI is a collective term for computer systems that can sense their environment, think, learn, and take action in response to what they're sensing and their objectives. Forms of AI in use today include digital assistants, chatbots, and machine learning amongst others. |
| Gartner | Artificial intelligence (AI) applies advanced analysis and logic-based techniques, including machine learning, to interpret events, support and automate decisions and take action. |
| Booz Allen Hamilton | Artificial intelligence (AI) is not a single technology breakthrough. It is a complex integration of people, processes, and technology that empowers organizations to focus on their missions. |

## WORLD'S LARGEST AI-FOCUSED TECHNOLOGY COMPANIES

| | |
|---|---|
| Amazon *[Via Forbes]* | The field of computer science is dedicated to solving cognitive problems commonly associated with human intelligence, such as learning, problem-solving, and pattern recognition. |

31

| | |
|---|---|
| Alphabet<br>*a.k.a.* Google<br>*[Via Forbes]* | Create smarter, more useful technology and help as many people as possible" from translations to healthcare to making our smartphones even smarter. |
| Meta<br>*a.k.a.* Facebook<br>*[Via Forbes]* | Advancing the file of machine intelligence and creating new technologies to give people better ways to communicate. |
| Microsoft | Artificial intelligence is the capability of a computer system to mimic human-like cognitive functions such as learning and problem-solving. |
| IBM | Artificial intelligence leverages computers and machines to mimic the problem-solving and decision-making capabilities of the human mind. |
| General Electric | AI research is practiced as a multidisciplinary exercise at GE, where insights from data-driven machine learning are fused with domain-specific knowledge drawn from areas such as materials, physics, biology, and design engineering, to amplify the quality as well as causal-veracity of the predictions derived—what we call hybrid AI. |
| Baidu | AI technologies encompass deep learning, image recognition, computer vision, robotics, collaborative systems, machine learning, and natural learning process, among other things. Through the years, Baidu has accelerated its AI resourcefulness under the umbrella of Baidu research through its Big Data Lab, Institute of Deep Learning, and Silicon Valley AI Lab. |

Finally, for real estate-specific definitions, in Table 1.6 we look to those offered by real estate professional societies in the United States and India. (These tend to read more like descriptions and commentary than the previous definitions.)

TABLE 1.6

| LEADING REAL ESTATE PROFESSIONAL SOCIETIES IN THE UNITED STATES | |
|---|---|
| National Association of Realtors | Artificial intelligence is already powering a number of real estate technology tools, but it's still an emerging technology that has an opportunity to change the industry, |

| | |
|---|---|
| Counselors of Real Estate (CRE) | Technology Acceleration and Innovation was listed as the #2 issue in the 2021-22 Top Ten Issues Affecting Real Estate® by The Counselors of Real Estate®.<br><br>Technology once again makes our Top Ten list but under different conditions and with more short-term implications. Constant themes like artificial intelligence (AI), machine learning (ML), the Internet of Things (IoT), and cybersecurity remain part of the landscape. They have moved from "new" to "how we do things now." This year the news is not about new tech but about our acceptance of it. |
| Society of Industrial and Office Realtors (SIOR) | "PERSONALIZED. TARGETED. RELEVANT. Using the power of Artificial Intelligence (AI), SIOR Weekly is a customized aggregation of CRE industry news and SIOR blog posts and highlights that are most relevant to you, delivered right to your inbox. The more you read, the more targeted the content is to your personal and professional interests." |
| Building Owners and Managers Association (BOMA) | 2020 Vision: Predicting the Future of PropTech Investment - "Now we are applying artificial intelligence (AI) and machine learning to data sets. In the future, real-time data gathering from a multitude of sources means faster and more advanced platforms will be making decisions for us." |
| Institute of Real Estate Management (IREM) | We continue to hear that artificial intelligence (AI) is changing every aspect of our daily lives. While we are all aware of how it is utilized in making "suggestions" as to what TV shows we should watch and what products we should buy, it is not always fully understood as to what artificial intelligence brings to the table in property management. |
| International Association of Assessing Officers (IAAO) | It is an amorphous term even for professionals in the field. The term originated in the 1950s and was used to describe a range of intelligence and learning possibilities in machines, including approximating human language; storing and utilizing input they receive; asking questions and creating insights; showing adaptability and pattern identification in new contexts; recognizing speech; and displaying the ability to manipulate objects. Even among today's data science and AI professionals, a precise and meaningful definition is still elusive. |

**LEADING REAL ESTATE PROFESSIONAL SOCIETIES IN INDIA**

| | |
|---|---|
| National Association of Realtors - India | AI Needs Thoughtful Regulation to Prevent Catastrophe Artificial intelligence … is advancing so rapidly that the real estate industry is behind on figuring out its most equitable uses. |
| Confederation of Real Estate Developers' Associations of India (CREDAI) | CREDAI and Venture Catalysts, India's first and largest incubator and accelerator for start-ups, have partnered to set up a $100 million proptech fund. The proposed fund will be investing in start-ups bringing innovative disruption in the real estate sector. It will invest in early to growth stage start-ups that have the potential to transform the real estate industry through technology, data analytics, blockchain, *artificial intelligence (AI)* and augmented reality. |

### 1.3.3. A Comprehensive Definition of AI is Actually Much More Complicated

Pithy definitions and descriptions of AI are a useful starting point, but not sufficient preparation for understanding the real estate-specific AI applications discussed in Part II of this book. Chapters 2 and 3 will delineate the numerous, important technological branches of AI that have evolved from 1950 to the present. For now, this section will provide a heads-up on just how broad and complex AI has become.

*European Commission Report*

This report underscores the challenges of trying to reduce AI to a singular definition. The European Commission is the principal executive body of the European Union. Its responsibilities include instigating and implementing the EU's policies. Toward that end, the European Commission publishes comprehensive reports pertaining to possible policy initiatives, AI being one example. In 2020 it published a **90-page report** *[emphasis added]* entitled *Defining Artificial Intelligence: Towards an Operational Definition and Taxonomy of Artificial Intelligence,* prepared by six authors and innumerable contributors from the EU's 27 member countries.

The report's conclusion states that "The AI definition adopted by the High Level Expert Group on Artificial Intelligence (HLEG) in 2019 is used as a baseline definition.

It is selected based on the review of **55 relevant documents** *[emphasis added]* covering AI policy and institutional reports (including standardisation efforts, national strategies, and international organisations reports), research publications and market reports…As AI is a dynamic field, we propose an iterative method that can be updated over time to capture the rapid AI evolution."

The referenced High Level Expert Group on AI definition in the report is this: "Artificial intelligence (AI) systems are software (and possibly also hardware) systems designed by humans that, given a complex goal, act in the physical or digital dimension by perceiving their environment through data acquisition, interpreting the collected structured or unstructured data, reasoning on the knowledge, or processing the information, derived from this data and deciding the best action(s) to take to achieve the given goal. AI systems can either use symbolic rules or learn a numeric model, and they can also adapt their behaviour by analyzing how the environment is affected by their previous actions."

Though in the end the European Commission did manage to settle on one definition, obviously a tremendous number of different perspectives had to be considered.

### AI Is Comprised of Many Distinct Technologies

Artificial intelligence is not a single technology but rather encompasses a multitude of highly diverse technologies. Accordingly, any reasonably adequate understanding of AI requires consideration of AI's complexities. The next chapter will underscore that currently there are at least seven salient, recognized types of AI in two broad categories.

The situation is not unlike the Indian parable of The Six Blind Men and the Elephant. In the parable, six blind men encounter an elephant for the first time. They each feel a different part of the elephant, and come to widely divergence conclusions on what an elephant is:

> The first one happened to put his hand on the elephant's side. "Well, well!" he said, "now I know all about this beast. He is exactly like a wall."
>
> The second felt only of the elephant's tusk. "My brother," he said, "you are mistaken. He is not at all like a wall. He is round and smooth and sharp. He is more like a spear than anything else."
>
> The third happened to take hold of the elephant's trunk. "Both of you are wrong," he said. "Anybody who knows anything can see that this elephant is like a snake" … and so on.

Similarly, any given individual's perspective on what constitutes artificial intelligence will be heavily informed by which applications of AI most interest that individual. For example, consider the differences in even a few of the early AI systems (all of which will be described in detail in the next chapter) between the following:

Robotics – In 1961 the first industrial robot, Unimate, starts working on a General Motors assembly line.

Natural language processing (NLP) including speech recognition – In 1965 at MIT Joseph Weizenbaum builds ELIZA, an interactive program that carries on a dialogue in the English language on any topic, a precursor to ChatGPT et al.

Computer vision – In the late 1960s, computer vision began at universities that were pioneering artificial intelligence and was meant to mimic the human visual system. Fast forwarding, computer vision continues to be widely used in such diverse applications as medical diagnostics (e.g., detecting breast cancers in mammograms), steering self-driving vehicles, quality control inspections on factory assembly lines, and so on.

Expert systems – In 1974 Ted Shortliffe's Ph.D. dissertation at Stanford on the MYCIN software program demonstrated a very practical rule-based approach to medical diagnoses (dubbed "The Internist-I").

### Note the HUNDREDS of Terms Encountered in AI Glossaries

A person might reasonably expect that any subject matter that has its own glossary of even a few dozen words is probably somewhat complicated – much less the hundreds of terms encompassed by these AI glossaries:

- Google for Developers | Machine Learning – 460 terms
- Expert.ai – 106 terms
- Dataconomy – 99 terms
- Wikipedia – 357 terms.

Not to belabor the point, but Table 1.7 is a mere **2%** sample of the 460 terms defined in the Google for Developers | Machine Learning glossary.

TABLE 1.7

| TERM | DEFINITION |
| --- | --- |
| Artificial Intelligence | A non-human program or model that can solve sophisticated tasks. For example, a program or model that translates text or a program or model that identifies diseases from radiologic images both exhibit artificial intelligence. |
| Bayesian Neural Network | A probabilistic neural network that accounts for uncertainty in weights and outputs. A standard neural network regression model typically predicts a scalar value; for example, a standard model predicts a house price of 853,000. In contrast, a Bayesian neural network predicts a distribution of values; for example, a Bayesian model predicts a house price of 853,000 with a standard deviation of 67,200. |
| Crash Blossom | A sentence or phrase with an ambiguous meaning. Crash blossoms present a significant problem in natural language understanding. For example, the headline Red Tape Holds Up Skyscraper is a crash blossom because an NLU model could interpret the headline literally or figuratively. |
| Dynamic Model | A model that is frequently (maybe even continuously) retrained. A dynamic model is a "lifelong learner" that constantly adapts to evolving data. A dynamic model is also known as an online model. Contrast with static model. |
| Earth Mover's Distance | A measure of the relative similarity between two documents. The lower the earth mover's distance, the more similar the documents. |
| Feature Set | The group of features your machine learning model trains on. For example, postal code, property size, and property condition might comprise a simple feature set for a model that predicts housing prices. |
| Ground Truth | The thing that actually happened. For example, consider a binary classification model that predicts whether a student in their first year of university will graduate within six years. Ground truth for this model is whether or not that student actually graduated within six years. |

| TERM | DEFINITION |
|------|------------|
| Hallucination | The production of plausible-seeming but factually incorrect output by a generative model that purports to be making an assertion about the real world. For example, if a dialog agent claims that Barack Obama died in 1865, the agent is hallucinating. |
| Incompatibility of Fairness Metrics | The idea that some notions of fairness are mutually incompatible and cannot be satisfied simultaneously. As a result, there is no single universal metric for quantifying fairness that can be applied to all Machine Language (ML) problems. |
| Keypoints | The coordinates of particular features in an image. For example, for an image recognition model that distinguishes flower species, keypoints might be the center of each petal, the stem, the stamen, and so on. |

Hence, relying on the KISS Principle is probably not the best way to proceed when dealing with AI.

## 1.4. KEY TAKEAWAYS

- Artificial intelligence is far from being an 11th-hour phenomenon, given that AI concepts have been evolving steadily for more than 2,700 years.
- As of seventy years ago AI has been perceived as a technology with vast potential, and since the beginning of the 21st Century has been recognized as even a possible societal game-changer.
- For the real estate industry, the starting gun was fired around 2014.
- Regarding what AI is, short definitions consistently refer to computer systems or machines that mimic human intelligence and perform tasks that typically require human cognitive abilities, such as problem-solving, decision-making, and learning.

- That said, it is vitally important to recognize that short definitions are not sufficient when investigating how best to use AI concepts and tools in real-world situations, notably in real estate industry applications.

- As will be elaborated upon in the next chapter, AI is a rapidly evolving field that encompasses a wide diversity of highly sophisticated technologies, including but decidedly not limited to machine learning, natural language processing, computer vision, and expert systems.

## 1.5.  REFERENCES *[in the same order as they appear above]*

- Principal sources for Tables 1.1 and 1.2:
  - Mijwil, M. M. (2015). History of artificial intelligence. ResearchGate. Retrieved from *https://www.researchgate.net/ publication/322234922_History_of_Artificial_Intelligence*
  - Press, G. (2021, May 19). 114 milestones in the history of artificial intelligence (AI). Forbes. Retrieved from *https://www.forbes.com/sites/gil-press/2021/05/19/114-milestones-in-the-history-of-artificial-intelligence-ai/?sh=469a97b974bf*
  - Wikipedia. (n.d.). Timeline of artificial intelligence. Retrieved November 22, 2023, from *https://en.wikipedia.org/wiki/Timeline_of_artificial_intelligence*
  - *IBM Corporation. (n.d.). What is artificial intelligence (AI)? Retrieved from https://www.ibm.com/topics/artificial-intelligence*
- Pedersen, M. (2022, July 7). The use of artificial intelligence in real estate. InData Labs. Retrieved from *https://indatalabs.com/blog/ artificial-intelligence-real-estate*
- Principal source for Tables 1.3: Ascendix. (2023, July 7). AI in real estate: Top companies revolutionizing real estate with AI solutions. Retrieved from *https://ascendixtech.com/ai-real-estate-solutions/*
- McCarthy, J. (2007, November 12). What is artificial intelligence? Retrieved from *https://www-formal.stanford.edu/jmc/whatisai.pdf*
- European Commission Joint Research Centre. (2020). Defining artificial intelligence: Towards an operational definition and taxonomy of artificial intelligence. Retrieved from *https://op.europa.eu/en/publication-detail/-/publication/6cc0f1b6-59 dd-11ea-8b81-01aa75ed71a1/language-en*

- AI Glossaries:
  - Google for Developers. (n.d.). Machine learning glossary. Retrieved from
    *https://developers.google.com/machine-learning/glossary*
  - Expert.ai. (n.d.). Glossary of AI terms. Retrieved from
    *https://www.expert.ai/glossary-of-ai-terms/*
  - Dataconomy. (2022, April 23). Artificial intelligence terms:
    AI glossary. Retrieved from
    *https://dataconomy.com/2022/04/23/artificial-intelligence-terms-ai-glossary/*
  - Wikipedia. (n.d.). Glossary of artificial intelligence. Retrieved from
    *https://en.wikipedia.org/wiki/Glossary_of_artificial_intelligence*

# CHAPTER 2
# TYPES OF AI FROM THE BEGINNING YEARS (1950S) TO THE PRESENT

## 2.1. HOW YOU WILL BENEFIT FROM READING THIS CHAPTER

Chapter 1 analogized AI to the Indian parable of The Six Blind Men and the Elephant. In this chapter you will be able to visualize the entire AI elephant.

In doing so, you will not only become conversant in the spectrum of AI technologies but also move closer to confidently determining which aspects of AI are most relevant to your particular real estate interests.

## 2.2. EVOLUTIONARY SUMMER-WINTER CYCLES

The AI industry has experienced several upturn years and downturn years which have become known as AI Summers and Winters respectively.

AI Summers are characterized by widespread interest in and generous funding for AI research and development (R & D). Media buzz contributes to high public and corporate expectations.

The opposite happens during AI Winters, which typically occur when:

- R & D promises are not met;
- AI initiatives prove significantly more complicated than expected;
- AI products and services that do come to market fall short of commercial viability; and
- Correspondingly the collective herd mentality shifts from being enthusiastic to derogatory.

Exhibit 2.1 is a timeline of AI's three Summers (in yellow) and two Winters (in blue). The exhibit includes several notable Milestones from Chapter 1 that personify each cycle.

EXHIBIT 2.1

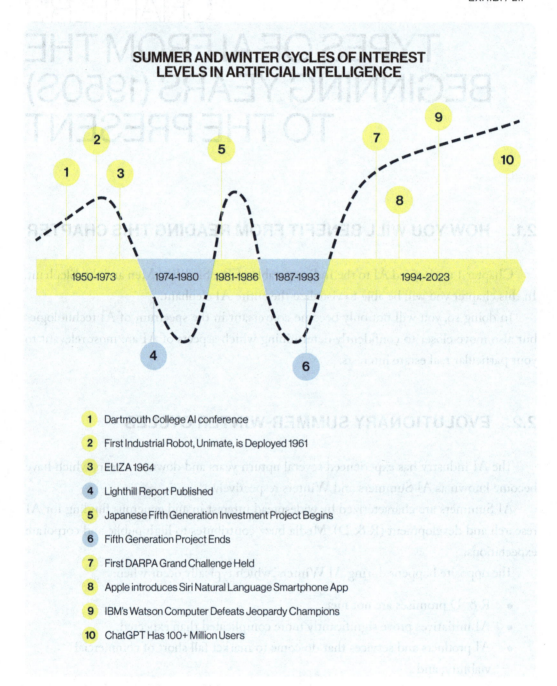

# SUMMER AND WINTER CYCLES OF INTEREST LEVELS IN ARTIFICIAL INTELLIGENCE

1950-1973    1974-1980    1981-1986    1987-1993    1994-2023

1  Dartmouth College AI conference

2  First Industrial Robot, Unimate, is Deployed 1961

3  ELIZA 1964

4  Lighthill Report Published

5  Japanese Fifth Generation Investment Project Begins

6  Fifth Generation Project Ends

7  First DARPA Grand Challenge Held

8  Apple introduces Siri Natural Language Smartphone App

9  IBM's Watson Computer Defeats Jeopardy Champions

10  ChatGPT Has 100+ Million Users

Despite periodic speculation on whether an AI Winter is forthcoming, the AI industry continues to be in a Summer cycle including in the real estate industry, as will become self-evident in Part II of this book.

## 2.3.  INITIAL, FOUNDATIONAL TYPES OF AI SYSTEMS

Six types of AI systems emerged in the early years of AI development, as illustrated in Exhibit 2.2. These initial types laid the groundwork for all AI advancements and applications over the last seven decades. In this section we will describe these initial, foundational types of AI systems and provide notable examples, including in the real estate industry. In the next section we will discuss the seven types of AI systems recognized today.

EXHIBIT 2.2

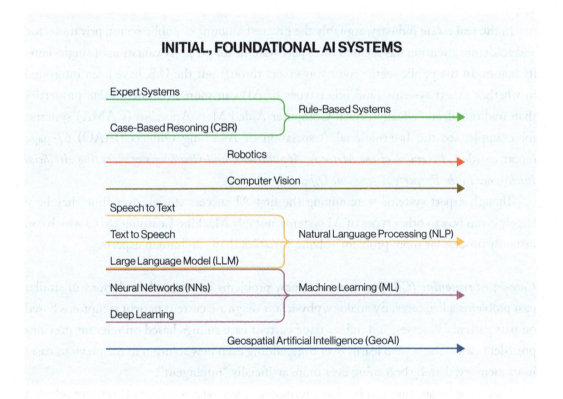

### INITIAL, FOUNDATIONAL AI SYSTEMS

## 2.3.1. Rule-Based Systems

As illustrated in the above exhibit, two types of AI systems comprise Rule-Based Systems.

*Expert systems*, among the earliest forms of AI, mimic the decision-making abilities of human experts for performing specific tasks. Experts are interviewed on how they solve

43

given problems. Their answers are captured in a series of "If–Then" rules (and sometimes "If–Then–Why" rules for more comprehensive system documentation purposes). Expert systems consist of a "knowledge base" which stores factual information and rules, and an "inference engine" which uses that knowledge to make decisions or provide recommendations.

As previously noted in Table 1.1, the first expert system was begun in 1964 at Stanford University, a multi-year project to capture the decision-making process and problem-solving behavior of organic chemists. Another notable early example was developed in 1974 by Ted Shortliffe in his Stanford Ph.D. dissertation; he demonstrated a rule-based approach to medical diagnoses despite diagnostic uncertainties. His expert system contributed directly to the rapid growth of expert systems in the late 1970s and 1980s.

In the real estate industry, arguably the greatest amount of public sector, private sector, and academic attention has focused on expert systems for property valuation of single-family homes. In the public sector county assessors throughout the U.S. have been interested in whether expert systems (and other types of AI) can more accurately value properties than traditional, statistically-driven Computer Aided Mass Appraisal (CAMA) systems; for example, see the International Association of Assessing Officers (IAAO) 67-page report entitled *A Review of the Methods, Applications, and Challenges of Adopting Artificial Intelligence in the Property Assessment Office.*

Though expert systems were among the first AI success stories, over time they have largely given way to other types of AI systems, notably Machine Learning (ML) which can instantly process far more problem-solving variables than can human experts.

*Case-based reasoning (CBR) systems* solve new problems based on the solutions of similar past problems a.k.a. cases. By analogy, physicians diagnose current patient symptoms based on past patients' illnesses, and judges issue current case rulings based on relevant previous precedent cases. The system learns over time, adding each new solution to the previous cases in its memory, thereby becoming ever more artificially "intelligent".

Case-based reasoning can be characterized as a four-step process: (1) retrieve relevant cases from memory; reuse solutions from previous cases in solving the current problem; revise the current problem solution if necessary after testing its validity; and retain the just solved case in memory for future consultations.

In real estate, case-based reasoning mirrors the valuation of a property using the "market comparables" appraisal method, and to a lesser extent the "replacement cost" appraisal method. Property valuation opportunities have been extensively explored from early on, e.g., in a 1992 article entitled "A Case-Based Reasoning Approach to Real Estate Property Appraisal" in the journal *Expert Systems with Applications.*

## 2.3.2. Robotics

Robotics combines computer science and engineering to create programmable machines – robots – that can assist humans or even supplant humans in completing specified tasks. Some robots require a human operator while other robots function autonomously. Robots can be grouped into these categories:

- *Pre-programmed robots* perform simple, monotonous tasks. An example is Unimate, the first industrial robot, that began working on a General Motors assembly line in 1961.

- *Humanoid robots* mimic human appearance and behavior. Some even have human-like faces and expressions. Two often cited examples are "Atlas" (premiered in 2013 by Boston Dynamics, which was acquired by Google that same year) and "Sophia" (debuted in 2016 by Hanson Robotics).

- *Autonomous robots* operate without a human operator. For example, NASA has sent five autonomous rovers to explore Mars, the first being Sojourner in 1997. The earliest, highly successful robot for the domestic market was iRobot's "Roomba" vacuum cleaner, available from 2002 onward.

- *Teleoperated robots* are semi-autonomous, controlled by humans via a wireless network. These robots typically work in surroundings that could be dangerous to humans, such as exploring the ocean floor at great depths, maintaining the interior of a nuclear reactor, and conducting reconnaissance on a battlefield.

- *Augmenting robots* enhance or substitute for certain human capabilities. Examples include prosthetic limbs and wearable exoskeletons for lifting heavy weights.

Among the current uses of robots in real estate are the following residential brokerage examples:

- Autonomous or remote-controlled robots can give home tours to prospective buyers, readily navigating from room to room, and providing useful information such as each room's square footage.

- Robots like those from View Labs (New York, NY) can autonomously map out a home or apartment and create a three-dimensional floor plan, thereby allowing potential buyers to virtually explore the property from a remote location.

- Chatbots are a form of robotics that can respond in real-time to a broad spectrum of questions from prospective buyers; on the other side of the coin, chatbots can ask clients questions to assist agents in qualifying those buyers.

### 2.3.3. Computer Vision

Computer vision, also known as artificial vision, focuses on enabling computers to perceive and interpret visual information. Since the late 1960s at universities researching AI possibilities, the field has concentrated on replicating human visual perception and enabling machines to analyze and understand images or videos. Today computer vision is widely used in such diverse applications as medical diagnostics (e.g., detecting breast cancers in mammograms), steering self-driving vehicles, quality control inspections on factory assembly lines, facial recognition for multiple purposes, identifying and organizing visual information into databases, and so on.

Among the most noteworthy examples of computer vision's utility in the real estate industry is contributing to estimating home prices. Zillow, Trulia, and Redfin all use computer vision to analyze high-resolution aerial photographs vis-a-vis the condition of millions of residential properties. This metadata is then combined with innumerable other data sets in Machine Learning (ML) algorithms to more accurately generate current price estimates for those millions of properties.

### 2.3.4. Natural Language Processing (NLP)

Natural Language Processing (NLP) is an interdisciplinary subfield of linguistics, computer science, and artificial intelligence that bridges the gap between humans and computers by enabling communication in natural language. These interfaces allowed users to interact with AI systems through spoken or written language, eliminating the need for complex programming languages or commands. Users can engage in conversations with AI-powered systems, ask questions, provide queries, and receive relevant responses in a conversational manner.

Natural Language Processing has three subsets: *Speech to Text* (speech input automatically converted into text output), *Text to Speech* (text input automatically converted into speech output), and *Large Language Model (LLM)* as described in section 2.3.6.

The earliest notable example is ELIZA, developed in 1965. Though ELIZA could converse on a wide range of topics, the program is remembered most for simulated conversations as a Rogerian psychotherapist. Fast forwarding to 2023, ChatGPT has become headline news worldwide, attracting 100 million users within the first two months of its debut.

Regarding NLP examples in the real estate industry, we have just seen how Chatbot-enabled robots can interact with prospective home buyers visiting a candidate property. In a prior step, from any location buyers can describe to a property search Chatbot what type of home they are looking for in as much detail as they like. The Chatbot can then instantly review all available properties in a given market; serve up detailed information on candidate homes fulfilling the buyers' criteria; repeat the process verbally with the buyers until a short list of the most promising properties emerges; and then schedule in-person visits to those properties. Foreshadowing Part II of this book, among the most popular real estate Chatbots are Brivity, MobileMonkey, and ReadyChat. (Other NLP programs were most likely instrumental in assembling, organizing, and continually updating the extensive metadata on all available properties in a market to optimize the buyers' search process, but that is another story.)

## 2.3.5. Machine Learning (ML)

Some types of artificial intelligence, notably expert systems, rely on knowledge being programmed into them. Machine Learning (ML) systems, in contrast, gain knowledge on their own. They imitate the way that humans learn, and can gradually become ever more knowledgeable on their own.

Although expert systems dominated the AI field in the 1970s and 1980s, ML systems have ever increasingly supplanted them. ML dominance has accelerated with the advent of Deep Learning, as will be described shortly.

ML systems initially were and continue to be built on *Neural Networks (NN)* Inspired by the structure and function of the human brain, Neural Networks were another significant development in early AI. Neural networks consist of interconnected nodes, or artificial neurons, organized in layers. Each node receives inputs, processes them through activation functions, and produces outputs. Through a process of training on labeled data, neural networks can autonomously identify patterns and relationships, enabling them to make predictions and classify new inputs. Just as humans can learn more and more by (say) continually reading a diversity of books, NNs become ever more knowledgeable by training on and assimilating ever larger and diverse databases.

One should note here another fundamental difference between expert systems and NNs. Expert systems are based on "if-then-why" rules, such that users can always determine the reasoning behind any given conclusion reached by an expert system. In contrast (without delving into the technicalities here), NNs reach conclusions using essentially a "black box" of so-called hidden layers of artificial neurons. Users of NNs cannot determine the reasoning behind a given conclusion. Expert systems are transparent, while Neural Networks are opaque.

*Deep Learning,* a subset of Machine Learning, began in the late 1990s to have a major impact on the AI field. Again without going into the technicalities, Deep Learning has facilitated the rapid assimilation of more types of data (e.g. unstructured data like text and images) with less human supervision of the training process. Hence, substantially more data sets can be analyzed than was previously feasible, resulting in substantially more pattern recognition opportunities and corresponding useful conclusions.

Generative AI, which has received considerable media coverage in the present day, is a manifestation of Deep Learning.

Deep Learning has accelerated the utility not only of Neural Networks but also other foundational AI systems such as Natural Language Processing and Computer Vision. For example, Deep Learning has contributed to the previously cited use of high-resolution aerial photographs by Zillow et al. in estimating home prices.

*Large Language Model (LLM)* is another subset of Machine Learning, as described in the next section.

Part II of this book delineates the many ways that AI systems are currently being used in the real estate industry. Machine Learning is present in one way or another in virtually every AI application discussed in Part II.

## 2.3.6. Large Language Model (LLM)

LLM is a type of AI system that can generate and process natural language using massive amounts of data. LLMs are a subset of both Natural Language Processing (NLP) and Machine Learning (ML) systems, and they use Deep Learning algorithms to learn from text corpora. LLMs can perform various natural language tasks, such as text summarization, translation, question answering, sentiment analysis, and text generation. LLMs are also capable of generating novel and coherent texts on any given topic, sometimes with surprising creativity and fluency. Some examples of LLMs are GPT-3, BERT, and XLNet, which are among the most advanced and widely used natural language models in the world.

LLMs have many advantages and challenges for the field of AI and society at large. On the one hand, LLMs can provide high-quality and diverse texts for various purposes, such as education, entertainment, journalism, and research. LLMs can also enhance human communication and understanding by facilitating cross-lingual and multimodal interactions. On the other hand, LLMs pose ethical and social risks, such as generating misleading or harmful information, violating privacy and intellectual property rights, and creating biases and inequalities.

In the real estate industry, LLMs have current and potential uses for various tasks and applications. For example, LLMs can generate property descriptions, answer customer queries, and create marketing content. LLMs can also help real estate professionals and clients access and analyze relevant information, such as market trends, legal regulations, and environmental factors. LLMs can also assist in the negotiation and drafting of contracts and agreements, as well as in the evaluation and optimization of real estate projects.

## 2.3.7. Geospatial Artificial Intelligence (GeoAI)

GeoAI essentially combines Geographic Information System (GIS) technologies with Artificial intelligence tools. Since the 1990s most real estate professionals have been at least somewhat familiar with GIS, given computer mapping's obvious relevance to the three most import factors in real estate – "Location, Location, Location". GeoAI, gaining prominence since approximately 2010, is like GIS on steroids.

When first exposed to GIS, the temptation of many people is to think of it as a presentation tool. People soon realize that GIS is far more than just pretty pictures, but rather can be used to efficiently and comprehensively search for real estate assets of interest. For example, "Show me the locations of all single-family homes currently for sale with a minimum of here bedrooms, a two-car garage, built no later than 1980, and not in a flood zone."

Powerful stuff already, but in truth the most important characteristic of GIS technology is as an integrator of highly diverse data sets. As we shall see shortly, GeoAI thereby can be a truly remarkable source of inputs to data-hungry Deep Learning systems.

Since 1879 the United States Geological Survey (USGS) has been the federal government's premier mapping agency. USGS defines GIS as follows: "A geographic information system (GIS) is a computer system for capturing, storing, checking, and displaying data related to positions on Earth's surface. *By relating seemingly unrelated data [Emphasis Added]*, GIS can help individuals and organizations better understand spatial patterns and relationships. GIS can use any information that includes location. The location can be expressed in many different ways, such as latitude and longitude, address, or ZIP code. Many different types of information can be compared and contrasted using GIS."

Different types of information are frequently depicted as "data layers". Exhibit 2.3 is a data layer diagram prepared by the USGS Eastern Ecological Science Center that illustrates the diversity of types of information that can easily, rapidly, and accurately be assembled and integrated into a GIS – assessor parcels, zoning, topography, and so on.

Exhibit 2.4 shows a data integration arrow passing through all the layers, collecting information from each layer on one particular location – say, a single-family home. The collected information can be fed directly into Deep Learning systems that Zillow et al. use to accurately estimate current home values.

Additional variables for the Deep Learning system to consider can be added as easily as inserting additional data layers. Note that the Deep Learning system readily accommodates data layers consisting of imagery, such as the example of high-resolution aerial photos of property conditions cited previously.

EXHIBIT 2.3                                        EXHIBIT 2.4

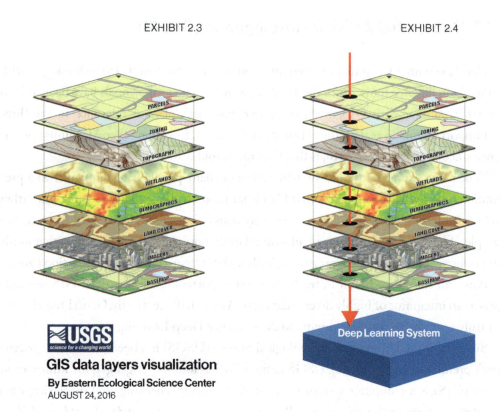

GeoAI not only provides data inputs to Deep Learning systems via vertical integration but also horizontal integration – i.e., "What is nearby?" For example, Exhibits 2.5 and 2.6 shows GeoAI inputs to a Deep Learning system estimating the value of office condo properties in downtown Los Angeles. Note that the GeoAI inputs encompass not only spatial relationships but also tabular data associated with each of the properties. The three properties circled in red satisfy these criteria: "Identify all office condo properties currently for sale that have at least 10,000 square feet *and* a cap rate below 7% *and* are within a five-minute drive time of the center of downtown Los Angeles."

EXHIBIT 2.5

EXHIBIT 2.6

| Property Address | Property Sub-type | Building Size | Asking Price | Cap Rate |
|---|---|---|---|---|
| 1   2830 I Street | Office Condo | 10,000 SF ✓ | $6,500,000 | 6% ✓ |
| 2   1375 Exposition Blvd | Office Condo | 7,000 SF | $1,200,000 | 2% |
| 3   7801 F Street | Office Condo | 8,000 SF | $3,400,000 | 3% |
| 4   2830 I Street | Office Condo | 15,000 SF ✓ | $7,700,000 | 4% ✓ |
| 5   3160 Folsom Blvd | Office Condo | 3,400 SF | $889,000 | 10% |
| 6   7273 14th Avenue | Office Condo | 6,500 SF | $1,340,000 | 2% |
| 7   1375 Exposition Blvd | Office Condo | 22,000 SF | $8,450,000 | 7% |
| 8   7801 Folsom Blvd | Office Condo | 12,000 SF ✓ | $2,376,000 | 3% ✓ |

As with the other five foundational AI systems discussed above, this characterization of GeoAI is only the tip of the iceberg of the full range of the system's capabilities – or more precisely, barely the tip of the tip of the iceberg!

## 2.4.  CURRENT TYPES OF AI SYSTEMS

AI has made remarkable advancements in recent years, leading to the emergence of various new types of AI systems. These modern types of AI leverage advanced algorithms, vast amounts of data, and powerful computing capabilities to deliver unprecedented capabilities and applications. In this chapter we will describe the current-day types of AI systems, together with real estate industry examples.

As shown in Exhibit 2.7 and described below, there are seven current-day types of AI organized into two categories.

EXHIBIT 2.7

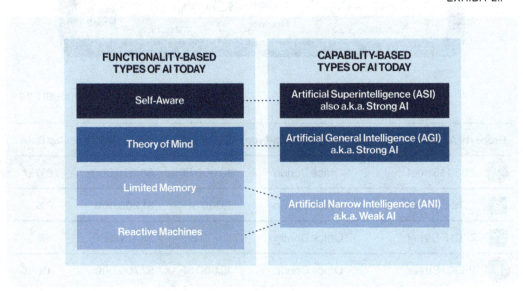

### 2.4.1. "Functionality-Based" AI Systems

The first category is the "Functionality-Based" classification of the technology. The primary objective of such systems is to perform specific functions. Based on the work of Professor Arend Hintze, this category has four types of AI systems.

*Reactive Machines* represent the most basic form of AI. These machines focus on the present moment and perform well-defined tasks. They are designed to respond to specific inputs without any memory or ability to learn from past experiences. While they can be highly intelligent in the tasks they are programmed for, they lack the ability to generalize or adapt to new situations. This kind of AI is highly reliable, consistently reacting the same way to given stimuli. Examples range from Spam filters to Chess playing supercomputers such as IBM's Deep Blue, which defeated chess world champion Garry Kasparov in 1997.

In the real estate industry, Chatbots are Reactive Machines that can perform many functions: quickly answer client questions; conduct a virtual property tour; create customized property lists; convert website visitors into leads; schedule meetings, and so on. As we have seen, Chatbots encompass multiple foundational AI systems including Natural Language Processing, Rule-Based Systems, and Robotics.

*Limited Memory Machines,* unlike Reactive Machines, retain information from past experiences and utilize this stored information to make predictions and decisions. Limited Memory Machines become ever smarter as they receive more data to train on, especially utilizing Deep Learning tools. Limited Memory Machines can monitor specific situations over time, and thus are often used in applications where historical context is essential. Self-driving cars are an often-cited example, as they employ Limited Memory Machines to recognize traffic patterns, anticipate road conditions, and navigate safely.

In real estate, Limited Memory Machines – combining such foundational AI systems as Machine Learning, GeoAI, and Computer Vision – are essential to the housing price estimates offered by Zillow, Trulia, and Redfin.

*Theory of Mind (ToM)* is a psychology term that describes humans' ability to read the emotions of others and predict future actions based on that information. Theory of Mind AI refers to systems that can understand and infer the mental states, beliefs, intentions, and emotions of humans. Since social interaction is a key part of human interaction, these AI systems can attribute thoughts and emotions to themselves and others, enabling them to interpret and respond to human behavior more accurately than is possible with existing AI systems. Although still in its early stages of development, theory of mind AI has especially promising applications in robotics.

Essentially the only examples to date – but still far from truly Theory of Mind AI systems – are the robots "KISMET" (built-in 1997 at Massachusetts Institute of Technology by Dr. Cynthia Breazeal) and "Sophia" (debuted in 2016 by Hanson Robotics). In the future, an example would be self-driving cars that can make a moral decision on whether to spare the life of a child crossing the street or put the driver's life in danger by veering off the road.

*Self-aware AI* represents the most advanced form of AI, where machines possess conscious-ness, self-awareness, emotions, and intelligence on a par with – or potentially even significantly surpassing – human beings. This type of AI is purely hypothetical at present, and AI research-ers are divided on whether Self-aware AI is actually achievable. The development of Self-Aware AI would raise philosophical and ethical considerations, as it questions the boundaries between machines and humans. Even more profound is the assertion by many AI experts that the development of Self-Aware AI could result in machines that enslave or even eliminate the entire human species; this threat is addressed in Chapter 3 in the section on "Singularity".

## 2.4.2. "Capability-Based" AI Systems

The second category is the "Capability-Based" classification, which describes AI sys-tems through specific technical competencies – for example, being able to generate credible predictions, recommendations, or decisions. The classification includes AI systems' likeness to the human mind, and their ability to "think" and perhaps even "feel" like humans. There are three types of Capability-based AI systems.

*Artificial Narrow Intelligence (ANI) a.k.a. Weak AI* mimics a limited part of the human mind, focusing on one narrow task at a time. ANI can solve complicated problems and finish tasks faster than humans. However, ANI capabilities are constrained to whatever programming it has been given, and also limited by not being able to self-program to achieve greater intelli-gence. All AI systems that presently exist are ANI systems. The other two types of Capability-based AI systems described next are still at the theoretic stage of development.

*Artificial General Intelligence (AGI) a.k.a. Strong AI* are AI systems that are comparable to human intelligence vis-à-vis being capable of thinking, comprehending, learning, and applying their intelligence to solving complex problems. Unlike any existing ANI system, AGI systems can recognize and act upon human emotions, beliefs, and desires.

*Artificial Superintelligence (ASI) also a.k.a. Strong AI* are hypothetical AI systems that sur-pass human intelligence in virtually every aspect. They can perform any task better than the most gifted human; experience human-like emotions, beliefs, and desires of their own; are self-aware; and can self-program to enhance their intelligence even further – possibly at lightning speed. As will be discussed in the next chapter under the topic of "Singularity", many AI experts worry that ASI systems will become uncontrollable by humans, possibly leading to the enslavement or even elimination of all humans on Earth.

## 2.4.3. Relationship to the Three Parts of the Human Brain

As first theorized by Dr. Paul MacLean in the 1960s and explicated in his book *The Triune Brain in Evolution*, the human brain consists of three principal components, derived from three progressive evolutionary periods:

1. The Reptilian Brain (a.k.a. Archipallium Brain, R-Complex), which includes the brain stem and the cerebellum, is the oldest brain in all animals. The functions controlled by the Reptilian Brain are related to body maintenance and physical survival – breathing, blood circulation, digestion, reproduction, aggression, stress responses, territorial instincts, ritual displays, and social dominance. Broadly speaking, the Reptilian Brain administers <u>our physical being</u>.

2. The Mammalian Brain (Paleomammalian Brain, Limbic System) consists of the septum, amygdala, hypothalamus, hippocampal complex, and cingulate cortex. Among other functions, the Mammalian Brain governs activities related to emotions and feelings – "fight or flight", reproductive behavior, parental attachment to and care of offsprings, etc. Thus, in general, the Mammalian Brain is responsible for <u>our emotional being</u>.

3. The Neocortex (Neopallium Brain, Cerebrum, Cortex), comprises two-thirds of the total brain mass in humans, takes up a much smaller portion of the brains of other mammals, and does not exist in non-mammals (reptiles, birds, fish, insects, etc.). Dr. MacLean regarded the addition of the Neocortex as the most recent step in the evolution of the human brain, conferring the ability for language, abstraction, planning, and perception. The right side of the Neocortex is more spatial, abstract, musical, and artistic, while the left side is more linear, rational, and verbal. The Neocortex, therefore, is the locale of <u>our intellectual being</u>.

Arguably these three parts of the brain align with the four Functionality-Based and three Capability-Based types of AI systems. Thus, we can "put it all together" in the manner illustrated in Exhibit 2.8.

- Reactive Machines, Limited Memory Machines, and Artificial Narrow Intelligence (ANI) systems cannot process human emotions, nor can the Reptilian Brain, thereby imposing significant Weak AI limitations on how intelligent they can become.
- Theory of Mind and Artificial General Intelligence (AGI) systems can process emotions, as can the Mammalian Brain, and thus Strong AI systems become increasingly comparable to humans in their performance potential.

EXHIBIT 2.8

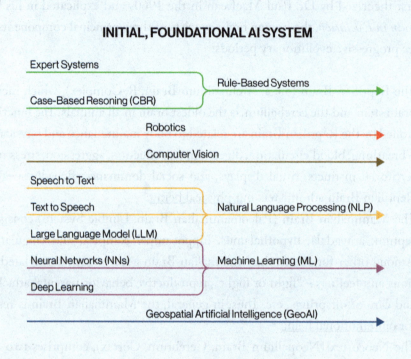

**INITIAL, FOUNDATIONAL AI SYSTEM**

- Expert Systems
- Case-Based Resoning (CBR)
  - Rule-Based Systems
- Robotics
- Computer Vision
- Speech to Text
- Text to Speech
  - Natural Language Processing (NLP)
- Large Language Model (LLM)
- Neural Networks (NNs)
  - Machine Learning (ML)
- Deep Learning
- Geospatial Artificial Intelligence (GeoAI)

- Self-Aware and Artificial Superintelligence (ASI) systems, as with the Neocortex part of the human brain, know no limits on what can be achieved – including the possibility of these AI systems rapidly becoming vastly more intelligent and accomplished than any human could ever be.

Exhibit 2.8 mirrors the Turing Test, one of Chapter 1's most widely recognized AI milestones. Proposed by Alan Turing in 1950, the test analyses a machine's ability to exhibit intelligent behavior that is indistinguishable from a human's. The test consists of a human interrogator submitting text questions remotely to two respondents, one of which is human and the other a machine. Based on the answers received, the interrogator attempts to determine which respondent is the human and which is the machine. If the interrogator cannot identify which is which, the machine passes the Turing Test. Seven decades on the Turing Test is still the most famous AI benchmark.

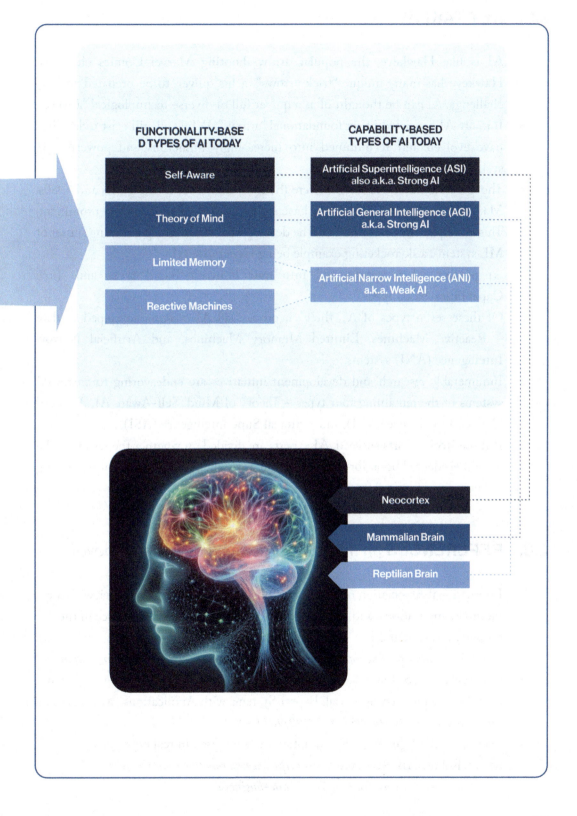

**FUNCTIONALITY-BASED TYPES OF AI TODAY**

- Self-Aware
- Theory of Mind
- Limited Memory
- Reactive Machines

**CAPABILITY-BASED TYPES OF AI TODAY**

- Artificial Superintelligence (ASI) also a.k.a. Strong AI
- Artificial General Intelligence (AGI) a.k.a. Strong AI
- Artificial Narrow Intelligence (ANI) a.k.a. Weak AI

- Neocortex
- Mammalian Brain
- Reptilian Brain

## 2.5.  KEY TAKEAWAYS

- AI is like Hawkeye, the popular arrow-shooting Marvel Comics character. Hawkeye has many unique "trick arrows" in his quiver, to be prepared for any challenge. AI can be thought of as a quiver full of diverse technological "arrows".
- Initially AI consisted of six foundational "arrows". While all still exist today, they have evolved and recombined into increasingly numerous and powerful AI systems.
- Though Rule-based AI systems were the most numerous in the 1970s and 1980s, Machine Learning (ML) systems have subsequently become the most prominent. This has especially been true with the development of the Deep Learning subset of ML systems, a skyrocketing example being Generative AI.
- At present AI is categorized into four Function-Based types and three Capabilities-based types.
- Of these seven types of AI, three encompass all AI systems developed to date – Reactive Machines, Limited Memory Machines, and Artificial Narrow Intelligence (ANI) systems.
- Innumerable research and development initiatives are endeavoring to create AI systems of the remaining four types – Theory of Mind, Self-Aware AI, Artificial General Intelligence (AGI), and Artificial Superintelligence (ASI).
- If those R&D efforts succeed, AI experts are divided on whether the result will be an unprecedented boon for humankind, an unparalleled catastrophe, or something in between.

## 2.6.  REFERENCES *[in the same order as they appear above]*

- International Association of Assessing Officers. (2022, January). A review of the methods, applications, and challenges of adopting Artificial intelligence in the property assessment office. Retrieved from *https://www.iaao.org/media/pubs/Review-of-AI-in-Property-Assessment_v2.pdf*
- Gonzalez, A. J., & Laureano-Ortiz, R. (1992). A case-based reasoning approach to real estate property appraisal. Expert Systems with Applications, 4(2), 229-246. *https://doi.org/10.1016/0957-4174(92)90115-9*
- Galvis, N. (2021, June 8). How robotics are being used in real estate businesses. RobotLAB. Retrieved from *https://www.robotlab.com/group/blog/how-robotics-are-being-used-in-real-estate-businesses*

- Cape Analytics (2023). 5 ways computer vision is revolutionizing the real estate industry. Retrieved from *https://capeanalytics.com/blog/computer-vision-real-estate/*
- Dardas, A. (2020, July 10). GeoAI series #2: The birth and evolution of GeoAI ESRI Canada. Retrieved from *https://resources.esri.ca/education-and-research/geoai-series-2-the-birth-and-evolution-of-geoai*
- Hintze, A. (2016, November 13). Understanding the four types of AI, from reactive robots to self-aware beings. The Conversation. Retrieved from *https://theconversation.com/understanding-the-four-types-of-ai-from-reactive-robots-to-self-aware-beings-67616*
- MacLean, P. D. (1990). The triune brain in evolution: Role in paleocerebral functions. Plenum Press. Retrieved from *https://pubmed.ncbi.nlm.nih.gov/17797318/*

# CHAPTER 3
# AI – FRIEND OR FOE?

## 3.1.   HOW YOU WILL BENEFIT FROM READING THIS CHAPTER

Artificial intelligence is most certainly a good-news-bad-news technology. In this chapter you will receive a briefing on the remarkable benefits AI can provide but also its disturbing – even menacing – disbenefits.

You will thereby be more fully informed for becoming:

- A proponent for adopting the technology in your business practices; or
- An opponent because the potential downside risks exceed the upside gains; or
- A cautious, highly selective experimenter with specific AI apps.

## 3.2.   AI COULD BE A GREAT FRIEND

Consistent with other sources, a 2023 article published by Forbes Advisor contains eye-popping statistics on the growth of the AI market, including these:

- AI is forecasted to have an annual growth rate of approximately 38% between 2023 and 2030;
- AI will contribute a 21% net increase to the Gross Domestic Product (GDP) of the U.S. by 2030;
- 97 out of 100 business owners anticipate that ChatGPT will benefit their business.

Obviously a great many individuals and organizations have a highly positive view of AI at present, with increasingly more jumping on the bandwagon every day. In this section we will list popular reasons given for being enthusiastic about AI.

## 3.2.1. Frequently Cited Advantages

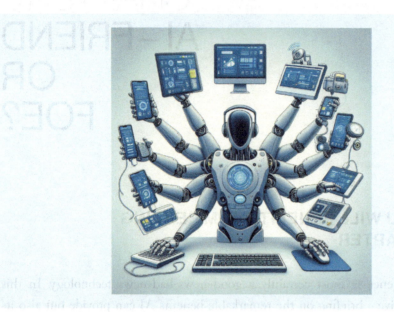

Under the right circumstances, AI systems can provide these benefits:

- Increase *efficiency and productivity* by optimizing routine processes, and supplanting human resources when appropriate;
- Improve *product quality* by eliminating human errors;
- Facilitate faster *speed of business* via quicker decisions and reduced task execution times;
- Enhance *customer relations* through better predictions of customer preferences, designing more enjoyable in-store experiences, providing more rapid and responsive customer service hotlines, etc.;
- Amplify *marketing and sales* capabilities, including developing personalized advertising channels, producing more accurate sales forecasts, optimizing product pricing, and generating higher quality sales leads, etc.;
- *Grow the business* by identifying promising new products and markets to pursue;
- Enable better *decision making* by circumventing human biases; and
- Reduce *costs* by streamlining the supply chain, lowering headcount, and so on.

## 3.2.2. Less Frequently Cited Advantages

AI systems can additionally:

- Eliminate *risks* to humans who no longer have to work in dangerous job environments;
- Strengthen *cybersecurity* defenses;
- Be available *24/7*;
- Improve *task monitoring*, complete with an audit trail;
- Create a highly scalable, *virtual workforce*;
- Capture and apply *scarce knowledge* (e.g., with expert systems);
- *Free up workers* from tedious, repetitive tasks to focus on creative assignments; and
- Assemble and evaluate *competitive intelligence*.

## 3.3.   AI COULD ALSO BE A TERRIBLE FOE

Thus far we've had the Good News. What about the Bad News?

### 3.3.1. Threats

Here is some of the Bad News:

*AI Driven Unemployment* – AI can potentially lead to substantial job losses across a broad spectrum of industries. For example, a 2018 report by the Organisation for Economic Cooperation and Development (OECD) estimates that 14% of jobs worldwide are at high risk from AI automation. This has been especially true for lower-skilled workers thus far, but increasingly highly-skilled professions appear at risk, including those with advanced university degrees (e.g., attorneys, doctors, journalists).

One hypothetical example in real estate is the replacement of human Realtors ® with virtual brokers. The References section includes a research meta study on how most people cannot distinguish AI generated faces from human faces. Link a realistic AI generated face to a sophisticated ChatBot specializing in all real estate information sources and brokerage processes, and suddenly industry job losses become a real possibility for any activity not requiring brokers and clients to be physically in the same room. The first AI company to successfully create credible, human-appearing virtual agents can of course instantly clone thousands of such virtual agents, rapidly spreading and monopolizing their availability in real estate markets throughout the nation.

*Widening Socioeconomic Inequality* – If companies fail to recognize the inherent biases that programmers intentionally or unintentionally build into AI algorithms, they may well compromise their diversity, equity, and inclusion (DEI) objectives when relying on AI-powered recruiting. As noted above, job losses due to AI-driven automation at present are more likely to affect low-skilled workers, which in turn correlates with negative impacts on racial and ethnic minorities. The most AI-centric nations (at present the United States and China) can generate wealth and political affluence at a pace outstripping nations lacking substantial AI resources.

*Social Surveillance and Privacy Violations* – AI technologies collect, assimilate and act upon large amounts of personal data without requesting permission to do so. For example, devices that work on voice commands in the home (Alexa, Google Home, Amazon Echo, etc.) can record what one does every day. Businesses can use this assembled personal consumer data to manipulate the consumer's behavior, as documented by Shoshana Zuboff in 2019. China uses facial recognition technology in offices, schools, and other venues to gather enough data to monitor a person's activities, relationships, and political views.

*Regulatory Challenges* – Governments worldwide have been slow to develop new legal frameworks and regulations to address the rapidly evolving societal risks already occurring with AI technologies. Examples include violating intellectual property rights, liability for damages suffered by individuals and organizations, blocking dangerous misinformation campaigns, combating criminal hackers and other cybersecurity threats, and ultimately ensuring that humankind does not fall victim to an AI "Singularity" (as described in the next section).

*Lack of Transparency* – Transparency is important because AI can be faulty in numerous ways. Especially given the "black box" nature of many AI systems, notably with Deep Learning models, error-ridden AI recommendations and decisions can go undetected. Input data can be poorly selected; programmers that train the AI models can inadvertently select biased data sets; business executives jealously guarding the "secret sauce" of their AI processes will thwart third-party auditing, and so on. The results can not only be faulty or even dangerous reliance on AI tools, but also widespread distrust of and resistance to using potentially beneficial AI technologies.

*Diminished Socialization and Well-Being* – Ever-increasing reliance on AI-centric communications for human interactions could have negative effects on social skills, self-esteem, and overall well-being. This is based on extrapolating the extensively researched sociological impacts of heavy reliance on social media. A research study summarized in a Harvard Business Review article, for example, found that Facebook usage is consistently detrimental to mental health.

### 3.3.2. Disasters

The Bad News is problematic enough, but worse yet is the potentially Really Bad News:

*Cybersecurity Risks* – The more sophisticated AI technologies become, the greater the risks of successful cyberattacks. Individual hackers, cybercriminal organizations, and state-sponsored cyberwarriors will all undoubtedly continue to be well-versed in AI tools available for achieving nefarious financial, political, and military objectives.

*Concentration of Power* – AI has become dominated by Big Tech companies. In 2016, for example, the Civil Liberties Union for Europe (Liberties) reported that Google, Apple, Facebook, Microsoft, and Amazon together with major Chinese competitors were responsible for 77% of the estimated $39 billion spent worldwide on AI research, development, and acquisitions. Such a concentration of power is dangerous vis-a-vis exacerbating inequalities, controlling the evolution of AI technologies and applications, and even forcing national governments to do their bidding.

*Unintended Negative Consequences* – AI systems can behave in unexpected ways leading to unforeseen consequences, including severely negative impacts on individuals, organizations, or society as a whole. For example, AI systems might: create hidden errors, such as those which cause a self-driving car to have a fatal accident; facilitate new hazards, such as providing better ransomware tools to cyber criminals; or cause a loss of control, in the extreme case leading to a Singularity (described below).

*Misinformation and Manipulation* – "Deepfakes" (Deep Learning plus fake) and other types of AI-generated content contribute directly to the spread of misinformation and the manipulation of public opinion. Social media bots pretending to be real voters, manipulated videos and images, deceptive robocalls, fabricated news stores – all are increasingly rapid and inexpensive to produce, are ever harder to detect, and are promulgated by international as well as domestic agents. Deepfakes have already been used and will increasingly be incorporated into targeted disinformation campaigns, threatening democratic processes and contributing to societal polarization.

*Financial Crises* – The financial industry is increasingly employing AI technology in the stock exchanges. One application is making thousands of trades at a pace far beyond any human's capability, with the goal of buying and then selling seconds later to accumulate a great many small profits. Such AI systems can go seriously awry, as evidenced by the 2010 Flash Crash and the 2012 Knight Capital Flash Crash. Perhaps more worrisome are the markets' vulnerabilities to direct manipulation by AI activities. In May 2023 the markets briefly dipped on AI-generated images of (non-existent) explosions at the Pentagon and White House, which presumably were not – but just as easily could have been – the handiwork of cybercriminals selling equities short just before releasing the panic-inducing disinformation.

*AI Military Weapons* – As major military powers pursue AI weapons development a global arms race becomes inevitable. Already deeply worrisome are Lethal Autonomous Weapon Systems (LAWs), which find and destroy targets with little or no human oversight; civilian deaths and other "collateral damage" due to AI errors become increasingly likely. LAWs are only one of many AI military applications being developed around the world. Adding to the potentially catastrophic dangers of their use by nations are the comparable dangers of AI weapons failing into the wrong hands. Imagine the disasters a future Osama bin Laden-like zealot might achieve with advanced AI weaponry.

*Existential Risk a.k.a. "Singularity"* – Many AI experts believe that the development of Artificial General Intelligence (AGI) could ultimately result in human enslavement or even human extinction by AI machines. The theory goes that AGI would enter a stage of unstoppable self-upgrade cycles, arising at an ever-accelerating pace, creating an AI superintelligence that far exceeds all human capabilities for controlling it. At that point AI machines might or might not view humankind as worth preserving, with humankind having no say in the final decision.

## 3.4. KEY TAKEAWAYS

- AI has pros and cons, as is true of all technologies. However, AI takes both pros and cons to potentially unprecedented levels.
- On the one hand, the rapid and continuing growth of the AI market in recent years underscores the belief by many knowledgeable observers that AI could be more beneficial to humankind than any previous technology in history.
- On the other hand, many equally knowledgeable observers fear that the misuse of AI could lead to catastrophes – and even the elimination of all human life.
- Accordingly, we all have an obligation to carefully consider how and even whether we want to proactively embrace AI systems in our lives.

## 3.5. REFERENCES

- Haan, K. (2023, April 25). 24 top AI statistics and trends in 2023. Forbes Advisor. Retrieved from https://www.forbes.com/advisor/business/ai-statistics/
- Nedelkoska, L., & Quintini, G. (2018). Automation, skills use and training. OECD Social, Employment and Migration Working Papers, No. 202. OECD Publishing. https://doi.org/10.1787/2e2f4eea-en
- Miller, Elizabeth & Steward, Ben & Witkower, Zak & Sutherland, Clare & Krumhuber, Eva & Dawel, Amy. (2023). AI Hyperrealism: Why AI Faces Are Perceived as More Real Than Human Ones. Psychological Science. Retrieved from https://doi.org/10.1177/09567976231207095
- Zuboff, S. (2019). The age of surveillance capitalism: The fight for a human future at the new frontier of power. Public Affairs.
- Shakya, H. B., & Christakis, N. A. (2017, April 10). A new, more rigorous study confirms: The more you use Facebook, the worse you feel. Harvard Business Review. Retrieved from https://hbr.org/2017/04/a-new-more-rigorous-study-confirms-the-more-you-use-facebook-the-worse-you-feel
- Arena, C. (2022, July 14). 7 disadvantages of artificial intelligence everyone should know about. Civil Liberties Union for Europe. Retrieved from https://www.liberties.eu/en/stories/disadvantages-of-artificial-intelligence/44289

# PART II

# HOW IS AI CURRENTLY BEING USED IN THE REAL ESTATE INDUSTRY?

The future depends on what you do today.

– **Mahatma Gandhi**

# CHAPTER 4

# PART II'S BENEFITS TO YOU, METHODOLOGY EMPLOYED, AND IMPLEMENATION ISSUES

## 4.1.   HOW YOU WILL BENEFIT FROM READING PART II

The real estate industry, a cornerstone of the global economy, is in the midst of a significant transformation, driven by the relentless advancement of artificial intelligence (AI). In Part II, we embark on a journey to explore the expansive landscape of AI applications within real estate. These applications span diverse functions and processes, demonstrating AI's power to reshape, rejuvenate, and redefine the industry. You will witness AI's ability to revolutionize everything from property acquisition and modification to management and disposition. The impact of AI extends beyond mere technological advancement; it is about enhancing the very core of real estate operations, making them more efficient, transparent, and ultimately, user-centric.

Part II is not just a comprehensive survey but a critical compass for professionals, researchers, and enthusiasts within the real estate sector. It unravels the multifaceted nature of AI, highlighting its disruptive potential and its role in shaping the future of real estate. Whether you're a seasoned real estate agent, an aspiring investor, or someone with a keen interest in technological innovations, understanding these categories is crucial for recognizing the dynamics that underpin AI's transformative influence.

We'll traverse various segments, from property search and acquisition to property modification, management, and disposition. Each segment encapsulates AI's impact, as it revolutionizes processes and imbues them with advanced capabilities, ensuring that they're more user-centric and efficient. The integration of AI doesn't just signal technological advancement; it's indicative of a shift towards more transparency, increased customer satisfaction, and an unwavering commitment to innovation in the real estate sector.

Part II is your gateway to comprehending the diverse applications of AI in the real estate industry. From optimizing advertising campaigns to creating predictive analytics tools, and from streamlining construction management to revolutionizing property management, AI's influence is pervasive and far-reaching. As we delve deeper into each of these categories in the ensuing chapters, you'll gain insights into the real-world applications, challenges, and future prospects that these AI-driven solutions hold.

We will be carefully examining 42 AI applications distributed among 7 broad categories. Here are the seven broad categories (with a separate chapter devoted to each):

| Chapter 5. | Search for and Acquire a Property for Purchase or Lease |
| Chapter 6. | Modify the Property as Needed for Occupancy |
| Chapter 7. | Manage the Property |
| Chapter 8. | Dispose of the Owned or Leased Property |
| Chapter 9. | Public Sector (Industry Regulators, Courtroom Officials, Etc.) |
| Chapter 10. | Education |
| Chapter 11. | Applications Overlapping Multiple Broad Categories |

Each of the seven broad categories encompasses a non-redundant subset of the 42 AI applications. For example, the first five AI applications (out of a total of 16) under the first broad category are these:

| Chapter 5. | Search for and Acquire a Property for Purchase or Lease |
| 5.1. | Home Buying and Selling |
| 5.2. | Real Estate Mortgage Automation |
| 5.3. | Commercial Real Estate Investment |
| 5.4. | Real Estate Agent Management |
| 5.5. | Investment Property Analysis |

Each of the 42 AI applications in turn will be described with a diagram and table listing companies actively involved with that application. All told, more than 800 real estate companies will be delineated.

## 4.2. METHODOLOGY EMPLOYED

In this section, we provide a comprehensive overview of the methodologies utilized to gather information and conduct research on the current usage of AI in the real estate industry. This section serves to elucidate our approach, fostering transparency and assuring readers of the reliability and accuracy of the forthcoming information. Our research design is characterized by a mixed-methods approach, fusing both qualitative and quantitative data collection and analysis techniques. The methodology consists of three integral components:

## 4.2.1 General literature review

The initial component of our methodology encompasses a thorough exploration of existing literature concerning AI in the real estate industry. Our research canvassed various sources, including academic journals, industry publications, research papers, and relevant books. To acquire a broad understanding of the historical development, current state, and future trends in AI within the industry, we employed online databases like Google Scholar, Scopus, Web of Science, and ProQuest. Keyword searches such as "artificial intelligence," "real estate," "property," "valuation," "appraisal," and others were employed to identify pertinent literature. We also employed citation tracking and snowballing techniques to extend our search into referenced sources. The literature selection was based on relevance, recency, quality, and diversity, prioritizing content directly addressing AI applications in real estate, with a focus on recency, quality, and diversity.

Key insights and trends derived from our general literature review included:

- AI's transformative impact on various real estate aspects, such as valuation, lending, investment, management, development, and planning.
- Enhanced operational efficiency, accuracy, transparency, and personalization facilitated by AI.
- New opportunities and challenges for real estate professionals, customers, regulators, and society at large.
- Influential factors like data availability and quality, technological innovation and adoption, ethical and legal considerations, and social and environmental impacts.

## 4.2.2. Focused Literature Survey of Top Real Estate Companies Worldwide

The second component of our methodology involves a targeted literature survey centered on the practices and applications of AI within the real estate industry. Our examination focused on prominent real estate companies at the forefront of AI innovation. Selection criteria encompassed market size, reputation, innovation, and impact. Our systematic search encompassed online databases, company websites, press releases, news articles, case studies, and reports. We also initiated direct contact with these companies to gather additional information and clarity. Our survey revealed key findings and recurring themes which included:

- The utilization of AI by leading real estate companies to gain competitive advantages, enhance customer satisfaction, operational efficiency and profitability.
- Diverse AI applications within these companies spanning property valuation, market analysis, site selection, risk assessment, loan underwriting, investment optimization, property management, tenant engagement, project design and urban planning.
- The integration of various AI technologies such as machine learning, natural language processing, computer vision, geospatial analysis, augmented reality.
- Challenges faced during AI implementation such as data availability and quality, technological integration and adoption, regulatory compliance, ethical considerations, social responsibility.

Some examples of top real estate companies using AI are:

- Zillow: A leading online marketplace for real estate and rental properties that offers various services such as Zestimate, Zillow Offers, and Zillow Home Loans. Zillow uses AI to provide instant home valuations, streamline the home buying and selling process, and personalize the user experience.
- Redfin: A technology-powered real estate brokerage that aims to redefine real estate in the consumer's favor. Redfin uses AI to provide accurate home valuations, personalized recommendations, and instant updates.
- Compass: A global mission to help everyone find their perfect home. Compass uses AI to power its platform that connects agents, buyers, and sellers. Compass also offers tools for marketing, CRM, analytics, and insights.

## 4.2.3. Geospatial-Specific Publications and Products

The third component of our methodology delves into geospatial-specific publications and AI products relevant to the real estate industry. This section underscores the significance of geospatial data and technologies within the industry and their harmonious coexistence with AI applications. Notable geospatial-specific AI solutions in the real estate sector were highlighted including:

- ESRI: A leading geographic information system (GIS) mapping software, location intelligence & spatial analytics technology company. ESRI uses AI to provide solutions for various real estate aspects such as site selection, market analysis, risk assessment, property management, urban planning. ESRI also uses AI to integrate imagery into geospatial workflows, create 3D GIS models and tap into the Internet of Things.
- HouseCanary: A platform offering precise and transparent property valuations and market insights for residential real estate by harnessing geospatial data.

Some examples of geospatial-specific publications that explore the role of AI in the real estate industry are:

- The Application of Artificial Intelligence in Real Estate Valuation: A Systematic Review: This paper reviews several articles published between 2020 and 2022 that use AI models and applications such as machine learning and ANN along with GIS and satellite imaging for real estate valuation. The paper identifies some challenges and opportunities for using AI in this domain.
- Geospatial Artificial Intelligence (GeoAI): This is a bibliographical entry that reviews the historical roots and recent developments of AI in geography and GIScience. The entry covers various topics of interest in the GeoAI landscape, such as spatial representation learning, spatial predictions, cartography, earth observation, social sensing, and geospatial semantics.
- Geospatial Artificial Intelligence - Special Issue of the International Journal of Geo-Information: This is a call for papers for a special issue of the journal that focuses on the applications of AI techniques in geospatial domains. The special issue invites original research articles that demonstrate the use of AI methods such as deep learning, natural language processing, computer vision, or knowledge graphs for solving geospatial problems.

## 4.3. IMPLEMENTING AI TECHNOLOGY IN YOUR ORGANIZATION

The remaining chapters in Part II will be exploring dozens of AI applications in the real estate industry involving hundreds of companies. Clearly AI usage in real estate is already highly diverse and complex, with immensely more diversity and complexity yet to come.

Accordingly, we cannot herein provide a "one size fits all" procedure for how AI technology should be implemented in any given real estate business, nor what specific expenditures will be required. We can, however, give our readers a "heads up" on typical implementation tasks, types of expenses, and cost ranges.

### 4.3.1. Typical Implementation Tasks

1. Define goals and objectives:
   - Identify areas for improvement – Analyze your current processes and identify areas where AI can streamline workflows, improve efficiency, or enhance customer service.
   - Set measurable goals – Define specific, measurable, achievable, relevant, and time-bound (SMART) goals for your AI implementation.

2. Assess your data:
   - Evaluate data quality and accessibility – Ensure your data is accurate, organized, and readily accessible for AI algorithms to utilize effectively.
   - Identify data gaps – Address any missing data points that might hinder the effectiveness of AI solutions.

3. Choose the right AI technology:
   - Explore available AI solutions – Research various AI technologies like chatbots, virtual assistants, predictive analytics, and machine learning algorithms to find solutions that align with your goals.
   - Consider budget and complexity – Choose AI solutions that fit your budget and technical capabilities.

4. Plan your implementation:
   - Identify key stakeholders – Involve relevant team members in the planning process to gain buy-in and ensure smooth integration.

- Outline a clear implementation roadmap – Develop a detailed plan outlining timelines, milestones, responsibilities, and budget allocations.

5. Pilot your AI solution:

   - Start small – Begin with a small pilot project to test the effectiveness of your chosen AI solution and gather feedback.
   - Monitor performance and iterate – Continuously monitor the results and make adjustments to your AI solution based on feedback and performance data.

6. Scale and integrate:

   - Gradually expand your AI implementation – Once the pilot project demonstrates success, gradually scale up the solution to other areas of your business.
   - Integrate AI with existing systems – Ensure seamless integration of your AI solution with existing technology and workflows.

7. Additional considerations:

   - Data privacy and security – Prioritize data privacy and security by implementing robust data protection measures and complying with relevant regulations.
   - Change management – Prepare your team for the changes AI brings by providing training and support.
   - Transparency and communication – Be transparent about your AI implementation and communicate its benefits to both employees and clients.

## 4.3.2. Types of Expenses Incurred

1. Initial AI System Set-Up

   - Software Development – Developing or acquiring AI software tailored to real estate needs involves upfront costs. This includes hiring AI implementation consultants, vendor licensing fees, and system customization.
   - Hardware Infrastructure – AI systems require robust hardware which can be expensive to set up initially, even when relying on Cloud-based AI systems.

2. Data Acquisition and Preparation:

   - Data Collection – Gathering relevant real estate data (property listings, market trends, historical prices) can incur costs. This includes purchasing data from third-party providers or creating in-house databases.

- Data Cleaning and Standardization – Preparing data for AI models involves cleaning, structuring, and ensuring consistency. Data preprocessing tools and personnel contribute to costs.

3.  Model Training:

- Training Data – High-quality data is essential for training AI models. Collecting and labeling data for supervised learning can be time-consuming and costly.
- Model Iterations – Iterative model training and fine-tuning require computational resources and expertise.

4.  Integration and Deployment:

- Integration with Existing Systems – Integrating AI into existing workflows and software may involve development efforts and compatibility checks.
- Deployment Costs – Deploying AI solutions across real estate offices (cloud or on-premises) has associated expenses.

5.  Personnel and Training:

- AI Specialists – Hiring or training AI experts to manage and optimize AI systems.
- User Training – Training real estate professionals to use AI tools effectively.

6.  Operational Costs:

- Monitoring and Support – Monitoring AI performance, addressing issues, and providing user support incur ongoing expenses.
- Maintenance and Updates – Regular model updates, bug fixes, and improvements add ongoing costs.

7.  Security and Compliance:

- Data Security – Ensuring data privacy and protection against cyber threats involves investment in security measures.
- Compliance – Meeting legal and regulatory requirements may require additional resources.

### 4.3.3. Illustrative Cost Ranges

The average cost of implementing artificial intelligence (AI) systems in real estate offices vary dramatically depending on innumerable factors, as exemplified by the many types of expenses delineated in the previous section. At one end of the spectrum, a relatively simple chatbot used by a residential broker to qualify leads will have a licensing fee ranging from $100 to $500 per month. At the other end of the spectrum, Zillow's annual AI budget may well exceed $100 million.

Accordingly, the following list of average real estate AI system costs should be considered to be rough guidelines, all the more so since the AI industry is rapidly changing:

- Pre-built/turn-key software solutions: $5,000 to $50,000+
- Custom AI development: $50,000 to $500,000 or more depending on the complexity and scope of the project
- Hardware: $5,000 to $50,000+
- Data preparation: $10,000 to $100,000 or more
- Integration with existing systems: $5,000 - $50,000+
- Training: $5,000 to $20,000+
- Data updates: $5,000 to $20,000+ annually
- Ongoing maintenance and support: 10-20% of the initial software cost per year

Considering all factors, the total cost of implementing AI systems in real estate offices can range from $30,000 to $500,000 or more over several years – or in special cases even far more, per the previously Zillow estimate.

The degree to which a real estate business is willing to invest in AI will be driven in part by the likely costs but mostly by those costs in comparison to the anticipated benefits. While cost-benefit ratios can also vary dramatically, a starting point for constructing a C-B model are the AI benefits and disbenefits previously listed in Chapter 3.

## 4.4. REFERENCES

- Soper, T. (2023, August 7). How Zillow Group is thinking about AI and the future of real estate. GeekWire. Retrieved from *https://www.geekwire.com/2023/zillow-cto-david-beitel-on-how-the-real-estate-giant-is-thinking-about-ai/*
- Wu, G. (2021, July 12). A walk-through of Redfin's powerful AI-based recommendation engines. VentureBeat. Retrieved from *https://venturebeat.com/ai/a-walk-through-of-redfins-powerful-ai-based-recommendation-engines/*

- Compass. (2019, October 9). Compass launches new consumer experience, AI capabilities. PR Newswire. Retrieved from *https://www.prnewswire.com/news-releases/compass-launches-new-consumer-experience-ai-capabilities-300934558.html*

- Esri. (n.d.). Accelerated data generation & spatial problem-solving. Retrieved from *https://www.esri.com/en-us/capabilities/geoai/overview*

- HouseCanary. (n.d.). Data and analytics. Retrieved from *https://www.housecanary.com/products/data-and-analytics/*

- Alsawan, N., & Alshurideh M. (2022). The Application of Artificial Intelligence in Real Estate Valuation: A Systematic Review. Springer. Retrieved from *https://link.springer.com/chapter/10.1007/978-3-031-20601-6_11*

- Geospatial artificial intelligence - Special issue of the International Journal of Geo-Information. (2021). ISPRS International Journal of Geo-Information, 10(4). Retrieved from *https://www.mdpi.com/journal/ijgi/special_issues/geo_ai*

- Gao, S. (2021). Geospatial artificial intelligence (GeoAI). In Oxford Bibliographies in Geography. Oxford University Press. Retrieved from *https://geography.wisc.edu/geods/wp-content/uploads/sites/28/2022/05/2021_OxfordBibliographies_GeoAI.pdf*

- Reim, Wiebke & Åström, Josef & Eriksson, Oliver. (2020). Implementation of Artificial Intelligence (AI): A Roadmap for Business Model Innovation. AI. 1. 180-191. Retrieved from DOI: 10.3390/ai1020011

# SEARCH FOR AND ACQUIRE A PROPERTY FOR PURCHASE OR LEASE

The quest for the ideal property, whether for purchase or lease, is a defining moment in any real estate journey. It involves a balance of practical considerations and emotional aspirations. Traditionally, this quest has been complex and time-consuming, with an abundance of listings and property visits, often overshadowed by uncertainty.

Enter artificial intelligence (AI). AI is revolutionizing the property search and acquisition process. It streamlines the journey by analyzing vast datasets, offering personalized recommendations, and enhancing decision-making. It provides not only efficiency but also informed and tailored experiences.

AI platforms curate property options based on criteria such as budget, location, and features, sparing seekers from countless listings and visits. AI also empowers informed choices by providing valuable property data, market trends, and neighborhood insights.

Personalization is another AI hallmark. Recommendations are fine-tuned to individual preferences, creating confidence in decision-making. Technologies like 3D modeling and augmented reality offer immersive virtual property tours.

AI doesn't just aid in searching; it simplifies transactions, from mortgage approval to title verification, making property acquisition smoother.

In this chapter, we delve into how AI transforms property searches and acquisitions, ensuring a journey that is efficient, well-informed, and tailored to individual needs.

## 5.1.  HOME BUYING AND SELLING

The home buying and selling industry involves the process of purchasing or selling residential properties, such as houses, apartments, condos, and townhouses. This industry is influenced by various factors, such as supply and demand, economic conditions, interest rates, consumer preferences, and legal regulations. The home buying and selling industry has been slow to adopt artificial intelligence (AI) in its daily business practices, compared to other industries. However, in recent years, AI has started to transform the industry, offering new opportunities and challenges for home buyers, sellers, agents, and brokers. AI can take many forms in home buying and selling, as shown in the multi-page table below and the corresponding, condensed diagram on the next page.

| AI APPLICATIONS IN HOME BUYING AND SELLING | SOLUTIONS PROVIDED BY COMPANIES | SOLUTIONS DESCRIPTIONS |
|---|---|---|
| **Property Discovery** | • PropTiger by PropTiger.com<br>• LocalizeAI by LocalizeOS<br>• Magicbricks by Magicbricks Realty Services Limited<br>• NoBroker by NoBroker Technologies Solutions Private Limited<br>• Zillow by Zillow Group, Inc.<br>• Trulia by Zillow Group, Inc.<br>• Realtor.com by Move, Inc.<br>• Redfin by Redfin Corporation<br>• Homesnap by Homesnap, Inc.<br>• Opendoor by Opendoor Labs, Inc.<br>• Knock by Knock Homes, Inc.<br>• Compass by Compass, Inc.<br>• NeighborhoodScout by CoreLogic, Inc. | • Property Discovery helps buyers find their ideal homes based on their preferences, budget, location, and lifestyle.<br>• Property Discovery uses AI algorithms to analyze millions of listings and provide personalized recommendations to buyers.<br>• These solutions also provide various features, such as virtual tours, neighborhood insights, market trends, and instant offers. |
| **Home Valuation** | • PropTiger by PropTiger.com<br>• LocalizeAI by LocalizeOS<br>• Magicbricks by Magicbricks Realty Services Limited | • Home Valuation helps sellers estimate the market value of their homes based on data and digital images. |

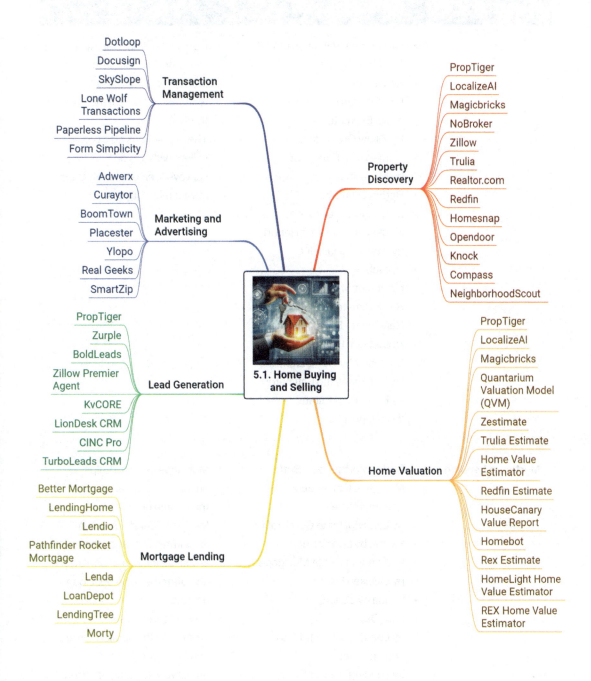

**Transaction Management**
- Dotloop
- Docusign
- SkySlope
- Lone Wolf Transactions
- Paperless Pipeline
- Form Simplicity

**Marketing and Advertising**
- Adwerx
- Curaytor
- BoomTown
- Placester
- Ylopo
- Real Geeks
- SmartZip

**Lead Generation**
- PropTiger
- Zurple
- BoldLeads
- Zillow Premier Agent
- KvCORE
- LionDesk CRM
- CINC Pro
- TurboLeads CRM

**Mortgage Lending**
- Better Mortgage
- LendingHome
- Lendio
- Pathfinder Rocket Mortgage
- Lenda
- LoanDepot
- LendingTree
- Morty

**5.1. Home Buying and Selling**

**Property Discovery**
- PropTiger
- LocalizeAI
- Magicbricks
- NoBroker
- Zillow
- Trulia
- Realtor.com
- Redfin
- Homesnap
- Opendoor
- Knock
- Compass
- NeighborhoodScout

**Home Valuation**
- PropTiger
- LocalizeAI
- Magicbricks
- Quantarium Valuation Model (QVM)
- Zestimate
- Trulia Estimate
- Home Value Estimator
- Redfin Estimate
- HouseCanary Value Report
- Homebot
- Rex Estimate
- HomeLight Home Value Estimator
- REX Home Value Estimator

| AI APPLICATIONS IN HOME BUYING AND SELLING | SOLUTIONS PROVIDED BY COMPANIES | SOLUTIONS DESCRIPTIONS |
| --- | --- | --- |
| | • Quantarium Valuation Model (QVM) by Quantarium, LLC<br>• Zestimate by Zillow Group, Inc.<br>• Trulia Estimate by Zillow Group, Inc.<br>• Home Value Estimator by Move, Inc.<br>• Redfin Estimate by Redfin Corporation<br>• HouseCanary Value Report by HouseCanary, Inc.<br>• Homebot by Homebot, Inc.<br>• Rex Estimate by REX - Real Estate Exchange, Inc.<br>• HomeLight Home Value Estimator by HomeLight, Inc.<br>• REX Home Value Estimator by REX - Real Estate Exchange, Inc. | • Home Valuation uses AI algorithms to compare properties with similar features and recent sales in the area.<br>• These solutions also provide sellers with tips on how to improve their home value and attract more buyers. |
| Mortgage Lending | • Better Mortgage by Better Mortgage Corporation<br>• LendingHome by LendingHome Corporation<br>• Lendio by Lendio, Inc.<br>• Pathfinder Rocket Mortgage by Quicken Loans<br>• Lenda by Lenda, Inc.<br>• LoanDepot by LoanDepot.com, LLC<br>• LendingTree by LendingTree, LLC<br>• Morty by Morty, Inc. | • Mortgage Lending helps buyers obtain financing for their home purchase.<br>• Mortgage Lending uses AI algorithms to assess the creditworthiness of borrowers and offer them the best loan options.<br>• These solutions also streamline the application and approval process, reducing paperwork and human errors. |

| AI APPLICATIONS IN HOME BUYING AND SELLING | SOLUTIONS PROVIDED BY COMPANIES | SOLUTIONS DESCRIPTIONS |
|---|---|---|
| **Lead Generation** | • PropTiger by PropTiger.com<br>• Zurple by Zurple, a Constellation Real Estate Group Company<br>• BoldLeads by BoldLeads<br>• Zillow Premier Agent by Zillow Group, Inc.<br>• kvCORE by InsideRE, LLC<br>• LionDesk CRM by LionDesk, LLC.<br>• CINC Pro by CINC, a Fidelity National Financial, Inc. Company<br>• TurboLeads CRM by iHOUSEweb, Inc. | • Lead Generation helps agents and brokers find potential clients who are interested in buying or selling homes.<br>• Lead Generation uses AI algorithms to identify, qualify, and nurture leads from various sources, such as websites, social media, and referrals.<br>• These solutions also help agents and brokers communicate with leads effectively and convert them into customers. |
| **Marketing and Advertising** | • Adwerx by Adwerx, Inc.<br>• Curaytor by Curaytor, LLC<br>• BoomTown by BoomTown ROI<br>• Placester by Placester, Inc.<br>• Ylopo by Ylopo, LLC<br>• Real Geeks by Fidelity National Financial, Inc.<br>• SmartZip by SmartZip Analytics, Inc. | • Marketing and Advertising helps agents and brokers promote their listings and services to potential customers.<br>• Marketing and Advertising uses AI algorithms to create and optimize ads, websites, landing pages, and email campaigns.<br>• These solutions also help agents and brokers target the right audience, measure the performance of their campaigns, and generate more leads and sales. |

| AI APPLICATIONS IN HOME BUYING AND SELLING | SOLUTIONS PROVIDED BY COMPANIES | SOLUTIONS DESCRIPTIONS |
|---|---|---|
| Transaction Management | • Dotloop by Zillow Group, Inc.<br>• DocuSign Agreement Cloud by DocuSign, Inc.<br>• SkySlope by SkySlope, Inc.<br>• Lone Wolf Transactions (zipForm Edition) by Lone Wolf Technologies<br>• Paperless Pipeline by Paperless Pipeline, LLC<br>• Form Simplicity by Florida Realtors | • Transaction Management helps agents and brokers manage the paperwork and compliance involved in buying and selling homes.<br>• Transaction Management uses AI algorithms to automate tasks, such as creating contracts, collecting signatures, storing documents, and tracking deadlines.<br>• These solutions also help agents and brokers reduce errors, save time, and ensure a smooth closing process. |

### Key Takeaways

- AI is revolutionizing the home buying and selling industry, introducing new opportunities and challenges.
- Using AI, buyers receive recommendations based on their preferences.
- AI assists sellers by providing estimates of market value and strategies to enhance property appeal.
- AI offers buyers insights into financing options, suggesting the most suitable loans.
- AI aids agents and brokers in identifying and nurturing leads from various channels.
- Through AI, agents and brokers effectively promote their listings and services to potential clients.
- AI streamlines the paperwork process for agents and brokers, ensuring transactional compliance.

## 5.2. REAL ESTATE MORTGAGE AUTOMATION

The real estate mortgage industry involves the process of lending money to individuals or businesses to purchase, refinance, or improve real estate properties. This industry is influenced by various factors, such as credit scores, interest rates, loan-to-value ratios, debt-to-income ratios, and property values. The real estate mortgage industry has been slow to adopt artificial intelligence (AI) in its daily business practices, compared to other industries. However, in recent years, AI has started to transform the industry, offering new opportunities and challenges for lenders, borrowers, brokers, and servicers. AI can take many forms in real estate mortgage automation, as shown in the multi-page table below and the corresponding, condensed diagram on the next page.

| AI APPLICATIONS IN REAL ESTATE MORTGAGE AUTOMATION | SOLUTIONS PROVIDED BY COMPANIES | SOLUTIONS DESCRIPTIONS |
| --- | --- | --- |
| **Automated Underwriting** | • LoanSnap by LoanSnap, Inc.<br>• Better Mortgage by Better Mortgage Corporation<br>• LendingHome by LendingHome Corporation<br>• Lendio by Lendio, Inc.<br>• Kabbage by Kabbage, Inc.<br>• Fundbox by Fundbox Ltd. | • Automated Underwriting reduces the time and cost of manual underwriting, improves accuracy and consistency, and enhances customer experience.<br>• Automated Underwriting helps lenders evaluate the eligibility and creditworthiness of borrowers using AI algorithms.<br>• These solutions also help borrowers compare multiple loan offers and get pre-approved faster. |
| **Risk Assessment and Fraud Detection** | • Zest AI by Zest AI<br>• DataRobot by DataRobot, Inc.<br>• FICO Falcon Platform by Fair Isaac Corporation | • Risk Assessment and Fraud Detection helps lenders identify and prevent potential losses due to default, delinquency, or fraud using AI algorithms. |

| AI APPLICATIONS IN REAL ESTATE MORTGAGE AUTOMATION | SOLUTIONS PROVIDED BY COMPANIES | SOLUTIONS DESCRIPTIONS |
|---|---|---|
|  | • SAS Fraud Management by SAS Institute<br>• Fraud.net by Fraud.net, Inc.<br>• Kount by Kount, Inc.<br>• Sift by Sift Science, Inc.<br>• Fraud Scope by Codoxo | • Risk Assessment and Fraud Detection analyzes various data sources, such as credit reports, bank statements, income verification, property appraisal, and social media to detect anomalies and irregularities.<br>• These solutions also help lenders comply with regulatory requirements and protect their reputation. |
| **Mortgage Pricing Optimization** | • Nomis Solutions by Nomis Solutions, Inc.<br>• Earnix by Earnix<br>• Zilliant by Zilliant, Inc.<br>• Pricefx by Pricefx AG<br>• Vistaar Technologies by Vistaar Technologies, Inc. | • Mortgage Pricing Optimization considers various factors, such as market conditions, customer demand, competitor pricing, borrower risk, and profitability goals.<br>• Mortgage Pricing Optimization helps lenders determine the optimal interest rates and fees for each loan product and customer segment using AI algorithms.<br>• These solutions also help lenders monitor and adjust their pricing strategies in real-time to stay competitive and profitable. |

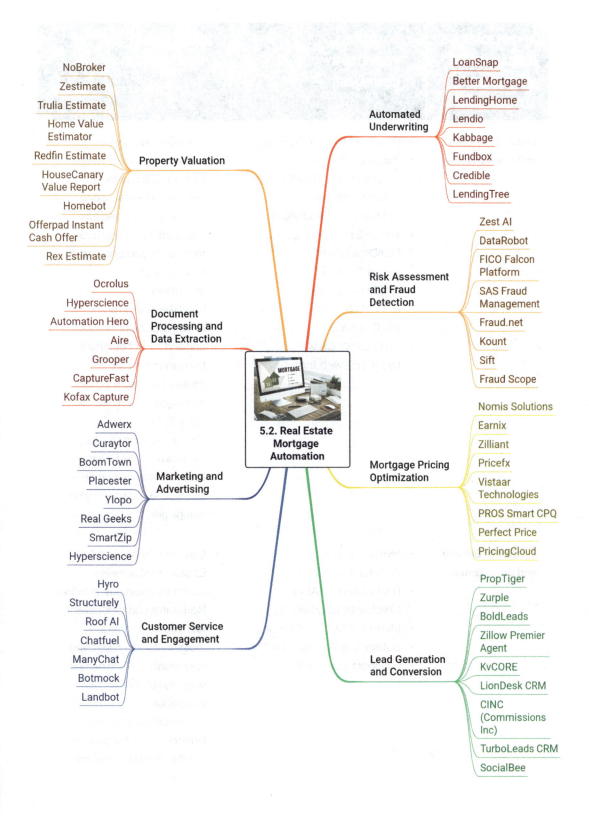

**Property Valuation**
- NoBroker
- Zestimate
- Trulia Estimate
- Home Value Estimator
- Redfin Estimate
- HouseCanary Value Report
- Homebot
- Offerpad Instant Cash Offer
- Rex Estimate

**Document Processing and Data Extraction**
- Ocrolus
- Hyperscience
- Automation Hero
- Aire
- Grooper
- CaptureFast
- Kofax Capture

**Marketing and Advertising**
- Adwerx
- Curaytor
- BoomTown
- Placester
- Ylopo
- Real Geeks
- SmartZip
- Hyperscience

**Customer Service and Engagement**
- Hyro
- Structurely
- Roof AI
- Chatfuel
- ManyChat
- Botmock
- Landbot

**5.2. Real Estate Mortgage Automation**

**Automated Underwriting**
- LoanSnap
- Better Mortgage
- LendingHome
- Lendio
- Kabbage
- Fundbox
- Credible
- LendingTree

**Risk Assessment and Fraud Detection**
- Zest AI
- DataRobot
- FICO Falcon Platform
- SAS Fraud Management
- Fraud.net
- Kount
- Sift
- Fraud Scope

**Mortgage Pricing Optimization**
- Nomis Solutions
- Earnix
- Zilliant
- Pricefx
- Vistaar Technologies
- PROS Smart CPQ
- Perfect Price
- PricingCloud

**Lead Generation and Conversion**
- PropTiger
- Zurple
- BoldLeads
- Zillow Premier Agent
- KvCORE
- LionDesk CRM
- CINC (Commissions Inc)
- TurboLeads CRM
- SocialBee

| AI APPLICATIONS IN REAL ESTATE MORTGAGE AUTOMATION | SOLUTIONS PROVIDED BY COMPANIES | SOLUTIONS DESCRIPTIONS |
|---|---|---|
| **Lead Generation and Conversion** | • PropTiger by PropTiger.com<br>• Zurple by Zurple, a Constellation Real Estate Group Company<br>• BoldLeads by BoldLeads<br>• kvCORE by InsideRE, LLC<br>• LionDesk CRM by LionDesk, LLC.<br>• CINC Pro by CINC, a Fidelity National Financial, Inc. Company<br>• TurboLeads CRM by iHOUSEweb, Inc. | • Lead Generation and Conversion sources leads from various channels, such as websites, social media, referrals, and ads, and qualifies and nurtures them using personalized communication and offers.<br>• Lead Generation and Conversion helps lenders find and attract potential borrowers who are interested in applying for a mortgage loan using AI algorithms.<br>• These solutions also help lenders track and measure the performance of their lead generation and conversion campaigns. |
| **Customer Service and Engagement** | • Hyro by Hyro, Inc.<br>• Structurely by Reinform, Inc.<br>• Roof AI by Roof AI, Inc.<br>• Chatfuel by Chatfuel, Inc.<br>• ManyChat by ManyChat, Inc.<br>• Botmock by Botmock, Inc.<br>• Landbot by Landbot | • Customer Service and Engagement answers customer questions, provides loan status updates, collects feedback, and offers cross-selling and upselling opportunities using natural language processing and generation.<br>• These solutions also help lenders improve customer satisfaction, retention, and loyalty. |

| AI APPLICATIONS IN REAL ESTATE MORTGAGE AUTOMATION | SOLUTIONS PROVIDED BY COMPANIES | SOLUTIONS DESCRIPTIONS |
|---|---|---|
| | | • Customer Service and Engagement helps lenders provide 24/7 support and guidance to their customers using AI chatbots and voice assistants. |
| Marketing and Advertising | • Adwerx by Adwerx, Inc.<br>• Curaytor by Curaytor, LLC<br>• BoomTown by BoomTown ROI<br>• Placester by Placester, Inc.<br>• Ylopo by Ylopo, LLC<br>• Real Geeks by Fidelity National Financial, Inc.<br>• SmartZip by SmartZip Analytics, Inc. | • Marketing and Advertising creates and optimizes ads, websites, landing pages, and email campaigns using data-driven insights and personalization.<br>• Marketing and Advertising helps lenders promote their loan products and services to potential customers using AI algorithms.<br>• These solutions also help lenders target the right audience, measure the effectiveness of their marketing and advertising efforts, and generate more leads and sales. |
| Document Processing and Data Extraction | • Ocrolus by Ocrolus, Inc.<br>• Hyperscience by Hyperscience, Inc.<br>• Automation Hero by Automation Hero, Inc.<br>• Aire by Aire Labs Ltd. | • Document Processing and Data Extraction reduces the manual effort, time, and errors involved in document processing, improves data quality and accuracy, and enhances compliance and security. |

| AI APPLICATIONS IN REAL ESTATE MORTGAGE AUTOMATION | SOLUTIONS PROVIDED BY COMPANIES | SOLUTIONS DESCRIPTIONS |
|---|---|---|
| | • Grooper by Grooper, Inc.<br>• CaptureFast by CaptureFast, Inc. | • Document Processing and Data Extraction helps lenders automate the collection, verification, and analysis of various documents required for mortgage applications, such as income statements, tax returns, bank statements, credit reports, property appraisal reports, etc. using AI algorithms.<br>• These solutions also help lenders streamline workflows, reduce operational costs, and improve customer experience. |
| Property Valuation | • NoBroker by NoBroker Technologies Solutions Private Limited<br>• Zestimate by Zillow Group, Inc.<br>• Trulia Estimate by Zillow Group, Inc.<br>• Home Value Estimator by Move, Inc.<br>• Redfin Estimate by Redfin Corporation<br>• HouseCanary Value Report by HouseCanary, Inc.<br>• Homebot by Homebot, Inc.<br>• Offerpad Instant Cash Offer by Offerpad, LLC<br>• Rex Estimate by REX - Real Estate Exchange, Inc. | • Property Valuation compares properties with similar features and recent sales in the area, analyzes various data sources, such as property records, listing data, neighborhood data, etc., and generates valuation reports with confidence scores and ranges.<br>• Property Valuation helps lenders estimate the market value of properties using AI algorithms.<br>• These solutions also help lenders make informed lending decisions, reduce appraisal costs and delays, and comply with valuation standards. |

## *Key Takeaways*

- AI is reshaping the real estate mortgage industry, ushering in novel opportunities and challenges.
- Through AI, lenders streamline underwriting and risk assessment processes, enhancing both accuracy and speed.
- Borrowers leverage AI to identify optimal loan options, secure competitive rates, and expedite pre-approvals.
- AI empowers lenders to refine pricing strategies through real-time adjustments and data-driven insights.
- Lenders harness AI to cultivate and convert leads via tailored communication and offerings.
- With AI integration, lenders bolster 24/7 customer engagement using chatbots and voice assistant technologies.
- AI-driven tools enable lenders to craft and fine-tune marketing campaigns based on personalization and data insights.
- AI automates document handling and data extraction for lenders, ensuring heightened data quality and regulatory compliance.
- Lenders utilize AI for precise property valuation through comprehensive data analysis and comparative methods.

## 5.3.  COMMERCIAL REAL ESTATE INVESTMENT

The commercial real estate investment industry is the field of acquiring, owning, managing, and selling income-producing properties for profit. The industry covers various types of properties, such as office, retail, industrial, multifamily, hospitality, and mixed-use. The industry faces many challenges, such as finding and evaluating potential deals, securing financing and capital, managing risks and returns, and navigating market cycles and regulations. To cope with these challenges, the commercial real estate investment industry has been adopting artificial intelligence (AI) solutions that can enhance data-driven decision making, operational efficiency, risk mitigation, and value creation. AI can take many forms in commercial real estate investment, as shown in the multi-page table below and the corresponding, condensed diagram on the next page.

| AI APPLICATIONS IN COMMERCIAL REAL ESTATE INVESTMENT | SOLUTIONS PROVIDED BY COMPANIES | SOLUTIONS DESCRIPTIONS |
| --- | --- | --- |
| **Property Valuation and Appraisal** | • HouseCanary by HouseCanary, Inc.<br>• GeoPhy by GeoPhy, a Walker & Dunlop Company<br>• Enodo by Enodo, Inc., a Walker & Dunlop Company<br>• Reonomy by Reonomy, an Altus Group Company<br>• Cherre by Cherre, Inc.<br>• Skyline AI by Skyline AI Ltd.<br>• Valcre by Valcre, LLC<br>• Bowery Valuation by Bowery Valuation, Inc. | • Property Valuation and Appraisal involves using AI to estimate the current or future value of a property based on various factors such as location, size, condition, amenities, market trends, etc.<br>• AI can use computer vision, machine learning, natural language processing, etc., to collect and analyze data from various sources such as public records, listings, images, reports, etc., and generate accurate and consistent property valuations and appraisals.<br>• These solutions help investors evaluate potential deals faster and cheaper than traditional methods. |

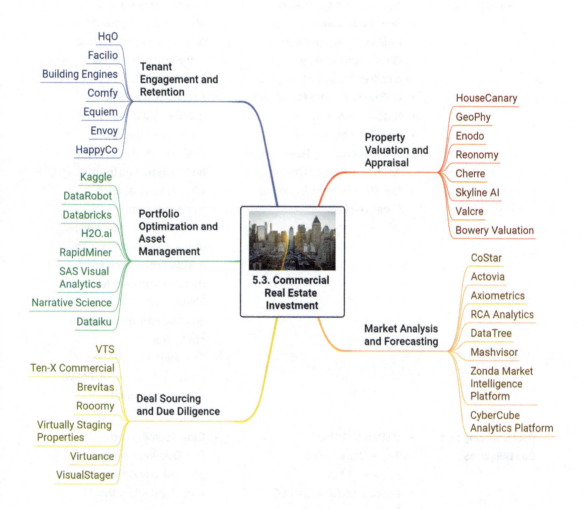

HqO
Facilio
Building Engines
Comfy
Equiem
Envoy
HappyCo

**Tenant Engagement and Retention**

Kaggle
DataRobot
Databricks
H2O.ai
RapidMiner
SAS Visual Analytics
Narrative Science
Dataiku

**Portfolio Optimization and Asset Management**

VTS
Ten-X Commercial
Brevitas
Rooomy
Virtually Staging Properties
Virtuance
VisualStager

**Deal Sourcing and Due Diligence**

**5.3. Commercial Real Estate Investment**

**Property Valuation and Appraisal**

HouseCanary
GeoPhy
Enodo
Reonomy
Cherre
Skyline AI
Valcre
Bowery Valuation

**Market Analysis and Forecasting**

CoStar
Actovia
Axiometrics
RCA Analytics
DataTree
Mashvisor
Zonda Market Intelligence Platform
CyberCube Analytics Platform

| AI APPLICATIONS IN COMMERCIAL REAL ESTATE INVESTMENT | SOLUTIONS PROVIDED BY COMPANIES | SOLUTIONS DESCRIPTIONS |
|---|---|---|
| **Market Analysis and Forecasting** | • Reonomy by Reonomy, an Altus Group Company<br>• Bowery Valuation by Bowery Valuation, Inc.<br>• GeoPhy by GeoPhy, a Walker & Dunlop Company<br>• CoStar by CoStar Group, Inc.<br>• Actovia by Actovia<br>• RealPage, Inc.<br>• RCA Analytics by Real Capital Analytics, A MSCI Company<br>• DataTree by First American Data Tree LLC | • Market Analysis and Forecasting involves using AI to understand and predict the dynamics of the commercial real estate market.<br>• AI can use machine learning, natural language processing, geospatial analysis, etc., to collect and analyze data from various sources such as transactions, leases, demographics, economics, etc., and generate insights, trends, projections, etc., that can help investors identify opportunities, assess risks, and optimize strategies .<br>• The solutions help investors gain a competitive edge in the market. |
| **Deal Sourcing and Due Diligence** | • VTS by VTS, Inc.<br>• Ten-X Commercial by Ten-X, LLC<br>• Brevitas by Brevitas, LLC<br>• RCA Analytics by Real Capital Analytics, A MSCI Company<br>• Reonomy by Reonomy, an Altus Group Company<br>• PropStream by PropStream<br>• CoStar by CoStar Group, Inc. | • Deal Sourcing and Due Diligence involves using AI to find and verify potential deals in the commercial real estate market.<br>• AI can use natural language processing, machine learning, computer vision, etc., to match properties with buyers or sellers based on their |

| AI APPLICATIONS IN COMMERCIAL REAL ESTATE INVESTMENT | SOLUTIONS PROVIDED BY COMPANIES | SOLUTIONS DESCRIPTIONS |
|---|---|---|
| | | preferences, criteria, goals, etc. It can also use natural language processing, machine learning, computer vision, etc., to verify the information, documents, images, etc., related to a property or a deal.<br>• The solutions help investors save time and money in finding and closing deals. |
| **Portfolio Optimization and Asset Management** | • Cherre by Cherre, Inc.<br>• Valcre by Valcre, LLC<br>• RCA Analytics by Real Capital Analytics, A MSCI Company<br>• Kaggle by Google LLC<br>• Databricks by Databricks, Inc.<br>• H2O.ai by H2O.ai, Inc.<br>• RapidMiner by RapidMiner, Inc. | • Portfolio Optimization and Asset Management involves using AI to optimize and manage the performance of a portfolio or an asset.<br>• AI can use machine learning, natural language processing, deep learning, etc., to optimize the allocation, diversification, and rebalancing of a portfolio or an asset based on various factors such as risk, return, liquidity, etc. It can also use machine learning, natural language processing, deep learning, etc., to monitor and manage the operations, maintenance, leasing, etc., of a portfolio or an asset.<br>• The solutions help investors maximize their returns and minimize their costs. |

| AI APPLICATIONS IN COMMERCIAL REAL ESTATE INVESTMENT | SOLUTIONS PROVIDED BY COMPANIES | SOLUTIONS DESCRIPTIONS |
| --- | --- | --- |
| **Tenant Engagement and Retention** | • HqO by HqO, Inc.<br>• Facilio by Facilio, Inc.<br>• Building Engines by Building Engines, Inc.<br>• Comfy by Comfy, Inc.<br>• Equiem by Equiem Services Pty Ltd.<br>• Envoy by Envoy, Inc.<br>• HappyCo by HappyCo | • Tenant Engagement and Retention involves using AI to improve and maintain the relationship between landlords and tenants.<br>• AI can use machine learning, natural language processing, computer vision, etc., to provide personalized and convenient services, amenities, and experiences to tenants. It can also use machine learning, natural language processing, computer vision, etc., to collect and analyze feedback, preferences, behavior, etc., of tenants and use them to enhance tenant satisfaction and loyalty.<br>• The solutions help landlords increase tenant retention and revenue. |

## *Key Takeaways*

- AI transforms commercial real estate for data-driven decisions, efficiency, risk management, and value creation.
- AI helps with property valuation and appraisal, market analysis and forecasting, deal sourcing and due diligence, portfolio optimization and asset management, and tenant engagement and retention.
- AI also creates new challenges and opportunities, such as ethical and regulatory issues, new paradigms and methods, and new forms of collaboration and competition.

## 5.4. REAL ESTATE AGENT MANAGEMENT

Real estate agent management involves the process of recruiting, training, coaching, motivating, and retaining agents who work for a real estate brokerage or agency. Real estate agents are independent contractors who represent buyers and sellers in property transactions. They earn commissions based on the sales volume they generate. Real estate agent management is crucial for the success and growth of a real estate business, as it affects the quality of service, customer satisfaction, and profitability. The real estate agent management industry has been slow to adopt artificial intelligence (AI) in its daily business practices, compared to other industries. However, in recent years, AI has started to transform the industry, offering new opportunities and challenges for managers, agents, and customers. AI can take many forms in real estate agent management, as shown below.

| AI APPLICATIONS IN REAL ESTATE AGENT MANAGEMENT | SOLUTIONS PROVIDED BY COMPANIES | SOLUTIONS DESCRIPTIONS |
|---|---|---|
| Agent Recruitment | • Sisu by Sisu, Inc.<br>• WizeHire by WizeHire, LLC<br>• ZipRecruiter by ZipRecruiter, Inc.<br>• Indeed by Indeed, Inc.<br>• LinkedIn Talent Solutions by LinkedIn Corporation<br>• Ideal by Ideal.com<br>• Real Geeks by Fidelity National Financial, Inc.<br>• BoomTown by BoomTown ROI | • Agent Recruitment helps managers find and attract qualified agents who fit their team culture and goals.<br>• Agent Recruitment uses AI algorithms to source candidates from various platforms, screen resumes and profiles, and match them with relevant opportunities.<br>• These solutions also provide various features, such as automated communication, assessment tests, video interviews, and analytics. |

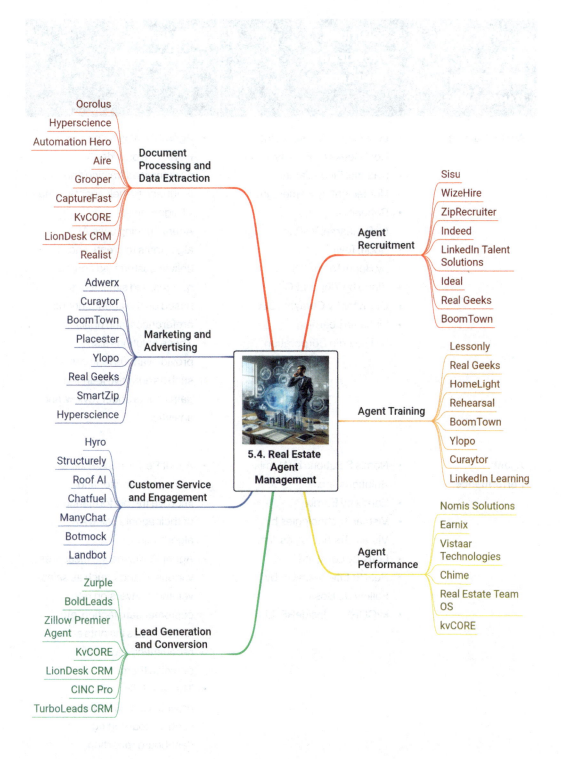

**Document Processing and Data Extraction**
- Ocrolus
- Hyperscience
- Automation Hero
- Aire
- Grooper
- CaptureFast
- KvCORE
- LionDesk CRM
- Realist

**Marketing and Advertising**
- Adwerx
- Curaytor
- BoomTown
- Placester
- Ylopo
- Real Geeks
- SmartZip
- Hyperscience

**Customer Service and Engagement**
- Hyro
- Structurely
- Roof AI
- Chatfuel
- ManyChat
- Botmock
- Landbot

**Lead Generation and Conversion**
- Zurple
- BoldLeads
- Zillow Premier Agent
- KvCORE
- LionDesk CRM
- CINC Pro
- TurboLeads CRM

**5.4. Real Estate Agent Management**

**Agent Recruitment**
- Sisu
- WizeHire
- ZipRecruiter
- Indeed
- LinkedIn Talent Solutions
- Ideal
- Real Geeks
- BoomTown

**Agent Training**
- Lessonly
- Real Geeks
- HomeLight
- Rehearsal
- BoomTown
- Ylopo
- Curaytor
- LinkedIn Learning

**Agent Performance**
- Nomis Solutions
- Earnix
- Vistaar Technologies
- Chime
- Real Estate Team OS
- kvCORE

| AI APPLICATIONS IN REAL ESTATE AGENT MANAGEMENT | SOLUTIONS PROVIDED BY COMPANIES | SOLUTIONS DESCRIPTIONS |
| --- | --- | --- |
| **Agent Training** | • Lessonly by Lessonly, Inc.<br>• Real Geeks by Fidelity National Financial, Inc.<br>• HomeLight by HomeLight, Inc.<br>• Rehearsal by Rehearsal VRP, Inc.<br>• BoomTown by BoomTown ROI<br>• Ylopo by Ylopo, LLC<br>• Curaytor by Curaytor, LLC<br>• LinkedIn Learning by LinkedIn Corporation | • Agent Training helps managers provide personalized training and feedback to their agents using AI algorithms.<br>• Agent Training uses AI algorithms to create and deliver customized courses, quizzes, and simulations based on the agents' needs, preferences, and goals.<br>• These solutions also provide various features, such as adaptive learning, gamification, peer review, and analytics. |
| **Agent Performance** | • Nomis Solutions by Nomis Solutions, Inc.<br>• Earnix by Earnix<br>• Vistaar Technologies by Vistaar Technologies, Inc.<br>• Lofty by Lofty, Inc.<br>• Real Estate Team OS by Follow Up Boss<br>• kvCORE by InsideRE, LLC | • Agent Performance helps managers monitor and improve the performance of their agents using AI algorithms.<br>• Agent Performance measures various metrics, such as sales volume, conversion rate, customer satisfaction, etc., and provides insights and recommendations to optimize them.<br>• These solutions also provide various features, such as goal setting, dashboard reporting, leaderboards, and alerts. |

| AI APPLICATIONS IN REAL ESTATE AGENT MANAGEMENT | SOLUTIONS PROVIDED BY COMPANIES | SOLUTIONS DESCRIPTIONS |
|---|---|---|
| **Lead Generation and Conversion** | • Zurple by Zurple, a Constellation Real Estate Group Company<br>• BoldLeads by BoldLeads<br>• Zillow Premier Agent by Zillow Group, Inc.<br>• kvCORE by InsideRE, LLC<br>• LionDesk CRM by LionDesk, LLC.<br>• TurboLeads CRM by iHOUSEweb, Inc.<br>• CINC Pro by CINC, a Fidelity National Financial, Inc. Company | • Lead Generation and Conversion helps agents find and attract potential buyers or sellers who are interested in transacting properties using AI algorithms.<br>• Lead Generation and Conversion sources leads from various channels, such as websites, social media, referrals, and ads, and qualifies and nurtures them using personalized communication and offers.<br>• These solutions also help agents track and measure the performance of their lead generation and conversion campaigns. |
| **Customer Service and Engagement** | • Hyro by Hyro, Inc.<br>• Structurely by Reinform, Inc.<br>• Roof AI by Roof AI, Inc.<br>• Chatfuel by Chatfuel, Inc.<br>• ManyChat by ManyChat, Inc.<br>• Botmock by Botmock, Inc.<br>• Landbot by Landbot | • Customer Service and Engagement helps agents provide 24/7 support and guidance to their customers using AI chatbots and voice assistants.<br>• Customer Service and Engagement answers customer questions, provides property information, schedules appointments, collects feedback, and offers cross-selling and upselling opportunities using natural language processing and generation. |

| AI APPLICATIONS IN REAL ESTATE AGENT MANAGEMENT | SOLUTIONS PROVIDED BY COMPANIES | SOLUTIONS DESCRIPTIONS |
|---|---|---|
| | | • These solutions also help agents improve customer satisfaction, retention, and loyalty. |
| Marketing and Advertising | • Adwerx by Adwerx, Inc.<br>• Curaytor by Curaytor, LLC<br>• BoomTown by BoomTown ROI<br>• Placester by Placester, Inc.<br>• Ylopo by Ylopo, LLC<br>• Real Geeks by Fidelity National Financial, Inc.<br>• SmartZip by SmartZip Analytics, Inc.<br>• Hyperscience by Hyperscience, Inc. | • Marketing and Advertising helps agents promote their properties and services to potential customers.<br>• Marketing and Advertising creates and optimizes ads, websites, landing pages, and email campaigns using data-driven insights and personalization.<br>• These solutions also help agents target the right audience, measure the effectiveness of their marketing and advertising efforts, and generate more leads and sales. |
| Document Processing and Data Extraction | • Ocrolus by Ocrolus, Inc.<br>• Hyperscience by Hyperscience, Inc.<br>• Automation Hero by Automation Hero, Inc.<br>• Aire by Aire Labs Ltd.<br>• Grooper by Grooper, Inc.<br>• CaptureFast by CaptureFast, Inc. | • Document Processing and Data Extraction helps agents automate the collection, verification, and analysis of various documents required for property transactions, such as contracts, deeds, titles, leases, financial statements, etc. |

| AI APPLICATIONS IN REAL ESTATE AGENT MANAGEMENT | SOLUTIONS PROVIDED BY COMPANIES | SOLUTIONS DESCRIPTIONS |
| --- | --- | --- |
| | • kvCORE by InsideRE, LLC<br>• LionDesk CRM by LionDesk, LLC.<br>• Realist by CoreLogic, Inc. | • Document Processing and Data Extraction reduces the manual effort, time, and errors involved in document processing, improves data quality and accuracy, and enhances compliance and security.<br>• These solutions also help agents streamline workflows, reduce operational costs, and improve customer experience. |

## Key Takeaways

- AI is reshaping real estate agent management, presenting new opportunities and challenges.
- Agent Recruitment uses AI for sourcing, screening, and matching qualified candidates.
- Agent Training employs AI for personalized courses, quizzes, and simulations.
- Agent Performance utilizes AI for monitoring metrics and optimizing agent effectiveness.
- Lead Generation and Conversion with AI attracts potential clients and optimizes campaigns.
- Customer Service and Engagement leverages AI chatbots and voice assistants for 24/7 support.
- Marketing and Advertising with AI optimizes ads, websites, and campaigns for targeted results.
- Document Processing and Data Extraction automates document handling, reducing manual effort.

## 5.5. INVESTMENT PROPERTY ANALYSIS

The investment property analysis industry is the field of analyzing, evaluating, and optimizing the performance and profitability of real estate investments. The industry covers various aspects, such as property selection, valuation, financing, cash flow, risk, return, and exit strategy. The industry faces many challenges, such as finding and assessing potential deals, securing and managing capital, optimizing portfolio allocation, and navigating market cycles and regulations. To cope with these challenges, the investment property analysis industry has been adopting artificial intelligence (AI) solutions that can enhance data-driven decision making, operational efficiency, investment strategy, and value creation. AI can take many forms in investment property analysis, as shown below.

| AI APPLICATIONS IN INVESTMENT PROPERTY ANALYSIS | SOLUTIONS PROVIDED BY COMPANIES | SOLUTIONS DESCRIPTIONS |
|---|---|---|
| **Property Valuation and Appraisal** | • PropStream by PropStream<br>• HouseCanary by HouseCanary, Inc.<br>• GeoPhy by GeoPhy, a Walker & Dunlop Company<br>• Enodo by Enodo, Inc., a Walker & Dunlop Company<br>• Reonomy by Reonomy, an Altus Group Company<br>• Cherre by Cherre, Inc.<br>• Skyline AI by Skyline AI Ltd.<br>• Valcre by Valcre, LLC<br>• Bowery Valuation by Bowery Valuation, Inc. | • Property Valuation and Appraisal involves using AI to estimate the current or future value of a property based on various factors such as location, size, condition, amenities, market trends, etc.<br>• AI can use computer vision, machine learning, natural language processing, etc., to collect and analyze data from various sources such as public records, listings, images, reports, etc., and generate accurate and consistent property valuations and appraisals. |

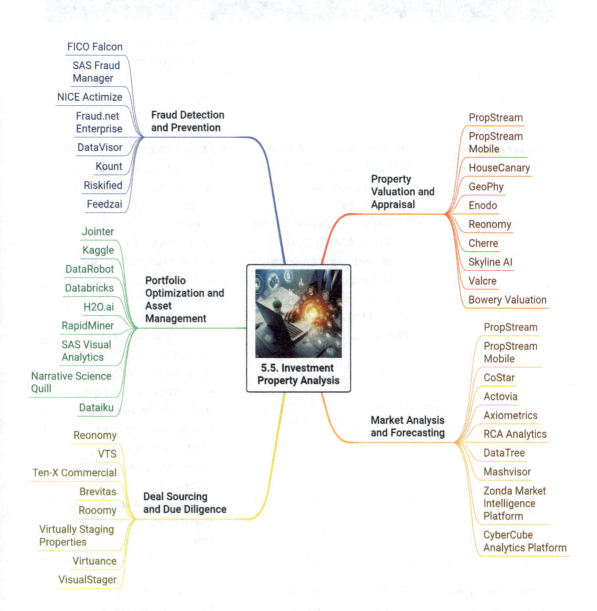

**Fraud Detection and Prevention**
- FICO Falcon
- SAS Fraud Manager
- NICE Actimize
- Fraud.net Enterprise
- DataVisor
- Kount
- Riskified
- Feedzai

**Portfolio Optimization and Asset Management**
- Jointer
- Kaggle
- DataRobot
- Databricks
- H2O.ai
- RapidMiner
- SAS Visual Analytics
- Narrative Science Quill
- Dataiku

**Deal Sourcing and Due Diligence**
- Reonomy
- VTS
- Ten-X Commercial
- Brevitas
- Rooomy
- Virtually Staging Properties
- Virtuance
- VisualStager

**5.5. Investment Property Analysis**

**Property Valuation and Appraisal**
- PropStream
- PropStream Mobile
- HouseCanary
- GeoPhy
- Enodo
- Reonomy
- Cherre
- Skyline AI
- Valcre
- Bowery Valuation

**Market Analysis and Forecasting**
- PropStream
- PropStream Mobile
- CoStar
- Actovia
- Axiometrics
- RCA Analytics
- DataTree
- Mashvisor
- Zonda Market Intelligence Platform
- CyberCube Analytics Platform

| AI APPLICATIONS IN INVESTMENT PROPERTY ANALYSIS | SOLUTIONS PROVIDED BY COMPANIES | SOLUTIONS DESCRIPTIONS |
| --- | --- | --- |
| | | • These solutions help investors evaluate potential deals faster and cheaper than traditional methods. |
| **Market Analysis and Forecasting** | • PropStream by PropStream<br>• CoStar by CoStar Group, Inc.<br>• Actovia by Actovia<br>• RealPage, Inc.<br>• RCA Analytics by Real Capital Analytics, A MSCI Company<br>• DataTree by First American Data Tree LLC<br>• Mashvisor by Mashvisor, Inc.<br>• Zonda Market Intelligence Platform by Zonda, LLC | • Market Analysis and Forecasting involves using AI to understand and predict the dynamics of the real estate market.<br>• AI can use machine learning, natural language processing, geospatial analysis, etc., to collect and analyze data from various sources such as transactions, leases, demographics, economics, etc., and generate insights, trends, projections, etc., that can help investors identify opportunities, assess risks, and optimize strategies.<br>• The solutions help investors gain a competitive edge in the market. |
| **Deal Sourcing and Due Diligence** | • Reonomy by Reonomy, an Altus Group Company<br>• VTS by VTS, Inc. | • Deal Sourcing and Due Diligence involves using AI to find and verify potential deals in the real estate market. |

| AI APPLICATIONS IN INVESTMENT PROPERTY ANALYSIS | SOLUTIONS PROVIDED BY COMPANIES | SOLUTIONS DESCRIPTIONS |
| --- | --- | --- |
| | • Ten-X Commercial by Ten-X, LLC<br>• Brevitas by Brevitas, LLC<br>• PropStream by PropStream<br>• CoStar by CoStar Group, Inc. | • AI can use natural language processing, machine learning, computer vision, etc., to match properties with buyers or sellers based on their preferences, criteria, goals, etc. It can also use natural language processing, machine learning, computer vision, etc., to verify the information, documents, images, etc., related to a property or a deal.<br>• The solutions help investors save time and money in finding and closing deals. |
| **Portfolio Optimization and Asset Management** | • Jointer by Jointer.io<br>• Real Estate Investment by Alpha Realty Capital<br>• Cadre by YieldStreet, Inc.<br>• Asset Investment Management by RealPage, Inc.<br>• Buildium by Buildium, A RealPage Company<br>• Voyager by Yardi Systems, Inc.<br>• Investment Manager by AppFolio, Inc.<br>• Asset Management by RealNex, LLC | • Portfolio Optimization and Asset Management involves using AI to optimize and manage the performance of a portfolio or an asset.<br>• AI can use machine learning, natural language processing, deep learning, etc., to optimize the allocation, diversification, and rebalancing of a portfolio or an asset based on various factors such as risk, return, liquidity, etc. It can also use machine learning, natural language processing, deep learning, etc., to monitor and manage the operations, maintenance, leasing, etc., of a portfolio or an asset. |

| AI APPLICATIONS IN INVESTMENT PROPERTY ANALYSIS | SOLUTIONS PROVIDED BY COMPANIES | SOLUTIONS DESCRIPTIONS |
|---|---|---|
| | | • The solutions help investors maximize their returns and minimize their costs. |
| **Fraud Detection and Prevention** | • FICO Falcon Fraud Manager by Fair Isaac Corporation<br>• DataVisor Fraud Detection Platform by DataVisor, Inc.<br>• Feedzai Fraud Prevention Platform by Feedzai, Inc.<br>• LoanSafe by CoreLogic, Inc. | • Fraud Detection and Prevention involves using AI to detect and prevent fraud in the real estate industry.<br>• AI can use data analytics, machine learning, natural language processing, etc., to detect and prevent fraud such as identity theft, money laundering, mortgage fraud, appraisal fraud, etc. It can also use natural language generation, machine learning, natural language processing, etc., to generate alerts, reports, and recommendations for fraud prevention.<br>• The solutions help investors protect their assets and reputation. |

*Key Takeaways*

- AI is revolutionizing investment property analysis, offering advanced solutions for decision-making.
- Property Valuation and Appraisal with AI provides accurate and efficient property assessments.
- Market Analysis and Forecasting leverages AI for insights, trends, and strategic optimization.
- Deal Sourcing and Due Diligence with AI enhances efficiency in finding and verifying deals.
- Portfolio Optimization and Asset Management using AI maximizes returns and minimizes costs.
- Fraud Detection and Prevention employs AI to safeguard against identity theft, money laundering, and other fraudulent activities.

## 5.6. RENTAL PROPERTY SEARCH

Rental property search is the process of finding and selecting a suitable property to rent for a specific period of time and budget. Rental property search can be done by individuals, families, or businesses who are looking for a place to live, work, or vacation. Rental property search can be challenging and time-consuming, as it involves various factors, such as location, size, amenities, price, availability, and lease terms. The rental property market is also dynamic and competitive, as supply and demand fluctuate depending on the season, economy, and trends. The rental property search industry has been slow to adopt artificial intelligence (AI) in its daily business practices, compared to other industries. However, in recent years, AI has started to transform the industry, offering new opportunities and convenience for renters, landlords, and agents. AI can take many forms in rental property search, as shown below.

| AI APPLICATIONS IN RENTAL PROPERTY SEARCH | SOLUTIONS PROVIDED BY COMPANIES | SOLUTIONS DESCRIPTIONS |
| --- | --- | --- |
| **Property Discovery and Matching** | • Zillow by Zillow Group, Inc.<br>• Trulia by Zillow Group, Inc.<br>• Apartments.com by CoStar Group, Inc.<br>• Rent.com by RentPath, LLC<br>• HotPads by Zillow Group, Inc.<br>• Zumper by Zumper, Inc.<br>• Apartment List by Apartment List, Inc.<br>• RentHop by RentHop.com | • Property Discovery and Matching helps renters find and compare properties that match their preferences and needs.<br>• Property Discovery and Matching uses AI algorithms to analyze millions of listings and provide personalized recommendations to renters.<br>• These solutions also provide various features, such as filters, maps, photos, videos, reviews, and ratings. |

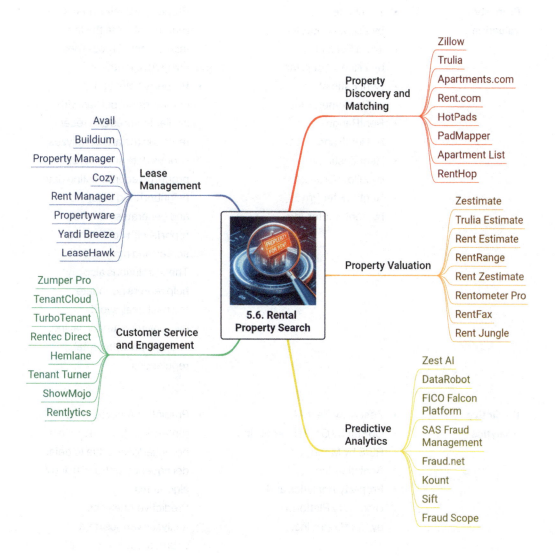

Lease Management
- Avail
- Buildium
- Property Manager
- Cozy
- Rent Manager
- Propertyware
- Yardi Breeze
- LeaseHawk

Customer Service and Engagement
- Zumper Pro
- TenantCloud
- TurboTenant
- Rentec Direct
- Hemlane
- Tenant Turner
- ShowMojo
- Rentlytics

5.6. Rental Property Search

Property Discovery and Matching
- Zillow
- Trulia
- Apartments.com
- Rent.com
- HotPads
- PadMapper
- Apartment List
- RentHop

Property Valuation
- Zestimate
- Trulia Estimate
- Rent Estimate
- RentRange
- Rent Zestimate
- Rentometer Pro
- RentFax
- Rent Jungle

Predictive Analytics
- Zest AI
- DataRobot
- FICO Falcon Platform
- SAS Fraud Management
- Fraud.net
- Kount
- Sift
- Fraud Scope

| AI APPLICATIONS IN RENTAL PROPERTY SEARCH | SOLUTIONS PROVIDED BY COMPANIES | SOLUTIONS DESCRIPTIONS |
|---|---|---|
| **Property Valuation** | • Zestimate by Zillow Group, Inc.<br>• Trulia Estimate by Zillow Group, Inc.<br>• Rent Estimate by Rentometer, Inc.<br>• RentRange by RentRange, LLC<br>• Rent Zestimate by Zillow Group, Inc.<br>• Rentometer Pro by Rentometer, Inc. | • Property Valuation helps renters estimate the fair market rent of properties using AI algorithms.<br>• Property Valuation compares properties with similar features and recent rentals in the area, analyzes various data sources, such as property records, listing data, neighborhood data, etc., and generates valuation reports with confidence scores and ranges.<br>• These solutions also help renters negotiate the best deal, avoid overpaying or underpaying, and comply with rental regulations. |
| **Predictive Analytics** | • Zest AI by Zest AI<br>• CoStar by CoStar Group, Inc.<br>• REIS by Moody's Analytics, Inc.<br>• Property Analytics and Discovery Platform by CoreLogic, Inc. | • Predictive Analytics helps renters identify and prevent potential losses due to default, delinquency, or fraud using AI algorithms.<br>• Predictive Analytics analyzes various data sources, such as credit reports, bank statements, income verification, property appraisal, and social media to detect anomalies and irregularities. |

| AI APPLICATIONS IN RENTAL PROPERTY SEARCH | SOLUTIONS PROVIDED BY COMPANIES | SOLUTIONS DESCRIPTIONS |
|---|---|---|
| | | • These solutions also help renters comply with regulatory requirements and protect their reputation. |
| **Customer Service and Engagement** | • Zumper Pro by Zumper, Inc.<br>• TenantCloud by TenantCloud, LLC<br>• TurboTenant by TurboTenant, Inc.<br>• Rentec Direct by Rentec Direct, LLC<br>• Hemlane by Hemlane, Inc.<br>• Tenant Turner by Tenant Turner, Inc.<br>• Buildium by Buildium, A RealPage Company<br>• Voyager by Yardi Systems, Inc.<br>• Property Manager by AppFolio, Inc. | • Customer Service and Engagement helps renters communicate with landlords and agents using AI chatbots and voice assistants.<br>• Customer Service and Engagement answers renter questions, provides property information, schedules tours, collects feedback, and offers cross-selling and upselling opportunities using natural language processing and generation.<br>• These solutions also help renters improve customer satisfaction, retention, and loyalty. |
| **Lease Management** | • Avail by Avail Software, LLC<br>• Buildium by Buildium, A RealPage Company<br>• Property Manager by AppFolio, Inc.<br>• Cozy by Cozy Services, Ltd.<br>• Rent Manager by London Computer Systems, Inc.<br>• Propertyware by RealPage, Inc. | • Lease Management helps renters manage their lease agreements using AI algorithms.<br>• Lease Management automates the lease creation, signing, renewal, and termination processes, using data-driven insights and personalization. |

| AI APPLICATIONS IN RENTAL PROPERTY SEARCH | SOLUTIONS PROVIDED BY COMPANIES | SOLUTIONS DESCRIPTIONS |
|---|---|---|
| | • Yardi Breeze by Yardi Systems, Inc.<br>• LeaseHawk by LeaseHawk, LLC | • These solutions also help renters comply with lease terms, track payments and expenses, and access legal documents and resources. |

## Key Takeaways

- AI is transforming the rental property search industry, providing convenience and efficiency.
- Property Discovery and Matching with AI offers personalized property recommendations to renters.
- Property Valuation uses AI algorithms to estimate fair market rent, aiding in negotiation and compliance.
- Predictive Analytics helps renters identify and prevent losses due to default, delinquency, or fraud.
- Customer Service and Engagement with AI enhances communication and satisfaction for renters.
- Lease Management using AI automates processes, ensuring compliance and efficient management.

## 5.7. VIRTUAL STAGING

The virtual staging industry is the field of using digital technology to create realistic and appealing interior designs for empty or unfurnished properties. The industry covers various domains, such as real estate, photography, interior design, and architecture. The industry faces many challenges, such as meeting customer expectations, delivering high-quality images, staying updated with design trends, and competing with other service providers. To cope with these challenges, the virtual staging industry has been adopting artificial intelligence (AI) solutions that can enhance creativity, efficiency, quality, and scalability. AI can take many forms in virtual staging, as shown below.

| AI APPLICATIONS IN VIRTUAL STAGING | SOLUTIONS PROVIDED BY COMPANIES | SOLUTIONS DESCRIPTIONS |
|---|---|---|
| **Furniture Removal and Replacement** | • BoxBrownie by BoxBrownie.com Pty Ltd.<br>• Virtual Staging Solutions by Virtual Staging Solutions<br>• VRX Staging by VRX Media Group, LLC<br>• PadStyler by PadStyler, LLC<br>• Virtual Staging Lab by Virtual Staging Lab<br>• Virtual Staging AI by Virtual Staging AI | • Furniture Removal and Replacement involves using AI to remove existing furniture from a property image and replace it with new furniture according to the customer's preferences.<br>• AI can use computer vision and machine learning to detect and erase furniture objects from an image, leaving a clean background. It can also use generative design and image synthesis to create and insert realistic-looking furniture objects that match the room type, style, lighting, and perspective.<br>• These solutions help customers transform empty or unfurnished properties into attractive and furnished ones without physically moving any furniture. |

| AI APPLICATIONS IN VIRTUAL STAGING | SOLUTIONS PROVIDED BY COMPANIES | SOLUTIONS DESCRIPTIONS |
|---|---|---|
| **Room Type and Style Recognition** | • Virtual Staging AI by Virtual Staging AI<br>• VHT Studios by VHT Studios, Inc.<br>• Rooomy by Rooomy, Inc.<br>• Virtually Staging Properties by Virtually Staging Properties<br>• Virtuance by Virtuance, LLC | • Room Type and Style Recognition involves using AI to recognize the room type and style of a property image.<br>• AI can use computer vision and machine learning to classify a property image into one of the predefined room types, such as living room, bedroom, kitchen, etc. It can also use computer vision and machine learning to identify the style of a property image, such as modern, traditional, rustic, etc.<br>• The solutions help customers select the appropriate room type and style for their virtual staging needs. |
| **Image Enhancement and Rendering** | • BoxBrownie by BoxBrownie.com Pty Ltd.<br>• Virtual Staging Solutions by Virtual Staging Solutions<br>• VRX Staging by VRX Media Group, LLC<br>• PadStyler by PadStyler, LLC<br>• Spotless Agency by Spotless Agency, LLC<br>• Virtual Staging Lab by Virtual Staging Lab<br>• Virtual Staging AI by Virtual Staging AI<br>• PhotoUp by PhotoUp, Inc. | • Image Enhancement and Rendering involves using AI to improve the quality and realism of a property image.<br>• AI can use computer vision, machine learning, deep learning, etc., to enhance a property image by adjusting its brightness, contrast, color, sharpness, resolution, etc. It can also use computer vision, machine learning, deep learning, etc., to render a property image with realistic lighting, shadows, reflections, textures, etc. |

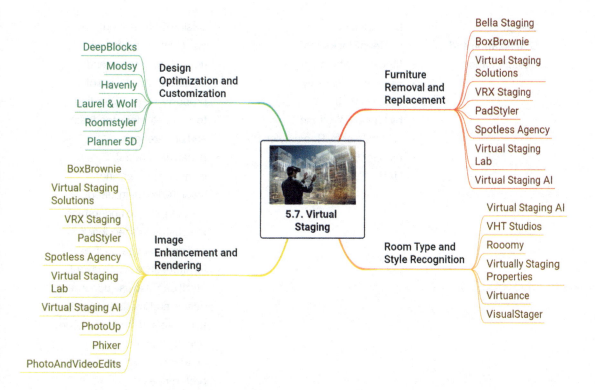

DeepBlocks
Modsy
Havenly
Laurel & Wolf
Roomstyler
Planner 5D

**Design Optimization and Customization**

**Furniture Removal and Replacement**

Bella Staging
BoxBrownie
Virtual Staging Solutions
VRX Staging
PadStyler
Spotless Agency
Virtual Staging Lab
Virtual Staging AI

BoxBrownie
Virtual Staging Solutions
VRX Staging
PadStyler
Spotless Agency
Virtual Staging Lab
Virtual Staging AI
PhotoUp
Phixer
PhotoAndVideoEdits

**Image Enhancement and Rendering**

**5.7. Virtual Staging**

**Room Type and Style Recognition**

Virtual Staging AI
VHT Studios
Rooomy
Virtually Staging Properties
Virtuance
VisualStager

| AI APPLICATIONS IN VIRTUAL STAGING | SOLUTIONS PROVIDED BY COMPANIES | SOLUTIONS DESCRIPTIONS |
| --- | --- | --- |
| | | • The solutions help customers create high-quality and realistic property images that can attract more buyers. |
| Design Optimization and Customization | • DeepBlocks by DeepBlocks, Inc.<br>• Modsy by Modsy, Inc.<br>• Havenly by Havenly, Inc.<br>• Laurel & Wolf by Laurel & Wolf, Inc.<br>• Roomstyler by Roomstyler, BV<br>• Planner 5D by Planner 5D, UAB | • Design Optimization and Customization involves using AI to optimize and customize the design of a property image according to the customer's feedback and preferences.<br>• AI can use natural language processing, machine learning, deep learning, etc., to understand the customer's feedback and preferences, such as furniture style, color, layout, etc. It can also use generative design and image synthesis to create and modify furniture objects that match the customer's feedback and preferences.<br>• The solutions help customers create personalized and optimized property images that can satisfy their needs and expectations. |

## *Key Takeaways*

- AI is transforming the virtual staging industry, providing creativity, efficiency, quality, and scalability.
- Furniture Removal and Replacement with AI transforms empty properties into furnished ones.
- Room Type and Style Recognition helps customers select suitable virtual staging options.
- Image Enhancement and Rendering using AI creates high-quality and realistic property images.
- Design Optimization and Customization with AI tailors property images to customer preferences.

## 5.8. APPRAISAL MANAGEMENT

Appraisal management is the process of coordinating, ordering, tracking, reviewing, and delivering real estate appraisals. Appraisals are valuations of properties based on market data, physical characteristics, and other factors. Appraisal management is essential for lenders, investors, and regulators who need accurate and reliable appraisals for various purposes, such as mortgage origination, refinancing, portfolio management, and risk assessment. Appraisal management is also important for appraisers, who need to comply with industry standards and regulations while delivering high-quality work.

The appraisal management industry has been slow to adopt artificial intelligence (AI) in its operations. However, in recent years, AI has emerged as a powerful tool that can enhance the efficiency, accuracy, and consistency of appraisal management AI can take many forms in appraisal management, as shown below.

| AI APPLICATIONS IN APPRAISAL MANAGEMENT | SOLUTIONS PROVIDED BY COMPANIES | SOLUTIONS DESCRIPTIONS |
|---|---|---|
| **Automated Valuation Models (AVMs)** | • Zillow Zestimate by Zillow Group, Inc. <br> • CoreLogic AVMs by CoreLogic, Inc. <br> • HouseCanary Value Report by HouseCanary, Inc. <br> • VeroVALUE by Veros Real Estate Solutions, LLC. <br> • Quantarium Valuation Model (QVM) by Quantarium, LLC <br> • GeoPhy AVM by GeoPhy, a Walker & Dunlop Company | • AVMs use AI algorithms to estimate the value of a property based on various data sources, such as sales history, tax records, location, features, and market trends. <br> • AVMs provide fast and low-cost valuations for properties that do not require a full appraisal. <br> • AVMs can also supplement human appraisals by providing additional data and insights. |
| **Appraisal Review and Quality Control** | • ACI Sky Review by ACI Worldwide, Inc. <br> • ValueLink QC by ValueLink Software | • Appraisal review and quality control solutions use AI to check the accuracy, completeness, and compliance of appraisal reports. |

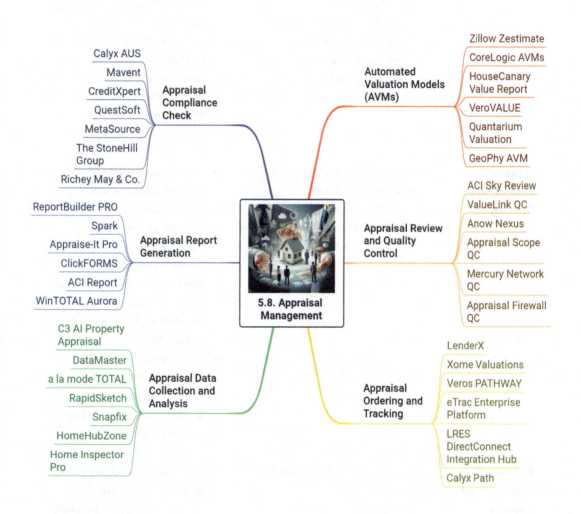

**Appraisal Compliance Check**
- Calyx AUS
- Mavent
- CreditXpert
- QuestSoft
- MetaSource
- The StoneHill Group
- Richey May & Co.

**Automated Valuation Models (AVMs)**
- Zillow Zestimate
- CoreLogic AVMs
- HouseCanary Value Report
- VeroVALUE
- Quantarium Valuation
- GeoPhy AVM

**Appraisal Report Generation**
- ReportBuilder PRO
- Spark
- Appraise-It Pro
- ClickFORMS
- ACI Report
- WinTOTAL Aurora

**Appraisal Review and Quality Control**
- ACI Sky Review
- ValueLink QC
- Anow Nexus
- Appraisal Scope QC
- Mercury Network QC
- Appraisal Firewall QC

**5.8. Appraisal Management**

**Appraisal Data Collection and Analysis**
- C3 AI Property Appraisal
- DataMaster
- a la mode TOTAL
- RapidSketch
- Snapfix
- HomeHubZone
- Home Inspector Pro

**Appraisal Ordering and Tracking**
- LenderX
- Xome Valuations
- Veros PATHWAY
- eTrac Enterprise Platform
- LRES DirectConnect Integration Hub
- Calyx Path

| AI APPLICATIONS IN APPRAISAL MANAGEMENT | SOLUTIONS PROVIDED BY COMPANIES | SOLUTIONS DESCRIPTIONS |
|---|---|---|
| | • Anow Nexus by Anow Software, Inc. <br> • Collateral QC by Mercury Network, LLC <br> • Appraisal Firewall by SharperLending Solutions, LLC | • These solutions can flag errors, inconsistencies, outliers, and potential fraud in appraisals. <br> • These solutions can also provide feedback and recommendations to appraisers and AMCs to improve the quality of their work. |
| Appraisal Ordering and Tracking | • LenderX by LenderX, LLC <br> • Xome Valuations by Xome Holdings, LLC <br> • Veros PATHWAY by Veros Real Estate Solutions, LLC. | • Appraisal ordering and tracking solutions use AI to streamline the workflow of ordering, assigning, scheduling, tracking, and delivering appraisals. <br> • These solutions can automate tasks, optimize schedules, monitor progress, and notify stakeholders. <br> • These solutions can also integrate with various platforms and systems to facilitate data exchange and communication. |
| Appraisal Data Collection and Analysis | • C3 AI Property Appraisal by C3.ai, Inc. <br> • DataMaster by DataMaster, LLC <br> • a la mode by CoreLogic, Inc. <br> • Property Radar by Property Radar <br> • Placer.ai by Placer Labs, Inc. | • Appraisal data collection and analysis solutions use AI to collect, organize, and analyze data relevant to appraisals. <br> • These solutions can capture data from various sources, such as property records, MLS, aerial imagery, and sensors. |

| AI APPLICATIONS IN APPRAISAL MANAGEMENT | SOLUTIONS PROVIDED BY COMPANIES | SOLUTIONS DESCRIPTIONS |
|---|---|---|
| | • Leverton by MRI Software, LLC<br>• ValuTrac by ValuTrac Software, Inc.<br>• Property Valuation Data by ATTOM<br>• Reonomy by Reonomy, an Altus Group Company | • These solutions can also process data using natural language processing, computer vision, and machine learning to extract insights and generate reports. |
| Appraisal Report Generation | • Spark by Appraiser Dashboard, Inc.<br>• Appraise-It Pro by SFREP, Inc.<br>• ClickFORMS by Bradford Technologies, Inc.<br>• WinTOTAL Aurora by CoreLogic, Inc.<br>• Restb.ai Appraisal Suite by Restb.ai | • Appraisal report generation solutions use AI to create appraisal reports that comply with industry standards and regulations.<br>• These solutions can automate the formatting, filling, and filing of appraisal forms and documents.<br>• These solutions can also customize reports according to client specifications and preferences. |
| Appraisal Compliance Check | • Calyx AUS by Calyx Software, Inc.<br>• Mavent Compliance Service by Ellie Mae, Inc.<br>• CreditXpert Compliance Tools by CreditXpert, Inc.<br>• CrossCheck by ValueLink Software | • Appraisal compliance check solutions use AI to verify that appraisals comply with federal, state, and local laws and regulations, as well as industry standards and guidelines.<br>• These solutions can audit appraisals for errors, omissions, inconsistencies, and violations. |

| AI APPLICATIONS IN APPRAISAL MANAGEMENT | SOLUTIONS PROVIDED BY COMPANIES | SOLUTIONS DESCRIPTIONS |
|---|---|---|
| | • Automated Appraisal Review by CoreLogic, Inc. | • These solutions can also provide corrective actions and recommendations to ensure compliance. |

## Key Takeaways

- Appraisal management involves coordinating, ordering, tracking, reviewing, and delivering real estate appraisals.
- The industry is adopting AI to enhance efficiency, accuracy, and consistency in appraisal processes.
- Automated Valuation Models (AVMs) provide fast and low-cost property valuations using AI algorithms.
- Appraisal Review and Quality Control solutions use AI to check the accuracy, completeness, and compliance of appraisal reports.
- Appraisal Ordering and Tracking solutions use AI to streamline workflows and facilitate communication.
- Appraisal Data Collection and Analysis solutions leverage AI to gather and analyze relevant data from various sources.
- Appraisa Report Generation solutions automate the creation of appraisal reports, ensuring compliance with standards.
- Appraisal Compliance Check solutions use AI to verify that appraisals comply with laws, regulations, and industry guidelines.

## 5.9. LEAD GENERATION AND MANAGEMENT

Lead generation and management is the process of attracting, engaging, qualifying, and nurturing potential customers for a business. Leads are prospects who have shown interest in a product or service and have provided their contact information. Lead generation and management is essential for businesses to grow their customer base, increase sales, and improve customer loyalty. Lead generation and management is a complex and challenging task that requires a lot of time, effort, and resources.

The lead generation and management industry has been quick to adopt artificial intelligence (AI) in its operations. AI has transformed the industry, enabling businesses to generate and manage leads more effectively and efficiently. AI can take many forms in lead generation and management, as shown below.

| AI APPLICATIONS IN LEAD GENERATION AND MANAGEMENT | SOLUTIONS PROVIDED BY COMPANIES | SOLUTIONS DESCRIPTIONS |
| --- | --- | --- |
| **Data Collection and Analysis** | • Smart Search by Magicbricks Realty Services Limited<br>• Nestie by NestAway Technologies Private Limited<br>• DataTrace by DataTrace Information Services, LLC<br>• Property Data by ATTOM<br>• HouseCanary Value Report by HouseCanary, Inc.<br>• DataTree by First American Data Tree LLC<br>• BoldLeads by BoldLeads<br>• Zillow Premier Agent by Zillow Group, Inc. | • Data Collection and Analysis involves gathering and processing large amounts of data from various sources, such as websites, social media, email, CRM, etc.<br>• AI can automate data collection and analysis using natural language processing (NLP), computer vision (CV), machine learning (ML), etc.<br>• These solutions provide comprehensive and up-to-date data to support lead generation and management. |

| AI APPLICATIONS IN LEAD GENERATION AND MANAGEMENT | SOLUTIONS PROVIDED BY COMPANIES | SOLUTIONS DESCRIPTIONS |
|---|---|---|
| **Lead Engagement** | • Nestie by NestAway Technologies Private Limited<br>• Airex by Airex, Inc.<br>• VeroVALUE by Veros Real Estate Solutions, LLC.<br>• Casalova by Casalova Realty, Inc.<br>• BoldLeads by BoldLeads<br>• Zillow Premier Agent by Zillow Group, Inc.<br>• Structurely by Reinform, Inc.<br>• Wise Agent by The Wise Agent<br>• Rentlytics by RealPage, Inc. | • Lead Engagement involves interacting with leads through various channels, such as email, phone, chat, social media, etc.<br>• AI can automate lead engagement using ML, NLP, CV, chatbots, virtual assistants, etc.<br>• These solutions provide conversational interfaces that respond to leads' queries, requests, feedbacks, etc. |
| **Lead Scoring and Qualification** | • Pendo.io by Pendo.io, Inc.<br>• Preclose by Preclose, Inc.<br>• Dataminr by Dataminr, Inc.<br>• Beyond Pricing by Beyond Pricing, Inc.<br>• LionDesk CRM by LionDesk, LLC.<br>• Real Geeks by Fidelity National Financial, Inc.<br>• BoldLeads by BoldLeads<br>• Zillow Premier Agent by Zillow Group, Inc. | • Lead Scoring and Qualification involves assigning scores or ratings to leads based on their likelihood to convert or their value to the business.<br>• AI can automate lead scoring and qualification using ML, NLP, CV, predictive analytics, etc.<br>• These solutions provide objective and consistent criteria to prioritize and segment leads. |

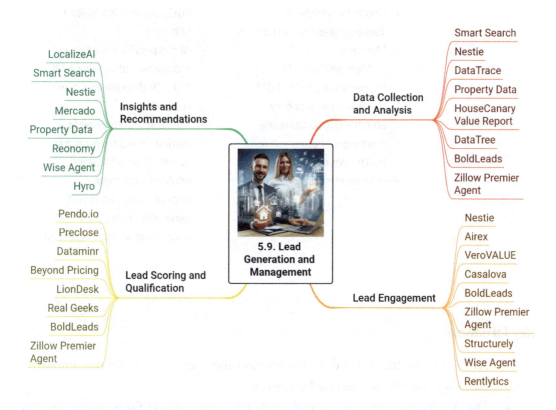

Insights and Recommendations
- LocalizeAI
- Smart Search
- Nestie
- Mercado
- Property Data
- Reonomy
- Wise Agent
- Hyro

Lead Scoring and Qualification
- Pendo.io
- Preclose
- Dataminr
- Beyond Pricing
- LionDesk
- Real Geeks
- BoldLeads
- Zillow Premier Agent

5.9. Lead Generation and Management

Data Collection and Analysis
- Smart Search
- Nestie
- DataTrace
- Property Data
- HouseCanary Value Report
- DataTree
- BoldLeads
- Zillow Premier Agent

Lead Engagement
- Nestie
- Airex
- VeroVALUE
- Casalova
- BoldLeads
- Zillow Premier Agent
- Structurely
- Wise Agent
- Rentlytics

| AI APPLICATIONS IN LEAD GENERATION AND MANAGEMENT | SOLUTIONS PROVIDED BY COMPANIES | SOLUTIONS DESCRIPTIONS |
|---|---|---|
| **Insights and Recommendations** | • LocalizeAI by LocalizeOS<br>• Smart Search by Magicbricks Realty Services Limited<br>• Nestie by NestAway Technologies Private Limited<br>• Mercado by Mercado Labs, Inc.<br>• Property Data by ATTOM<br>• Reonomy by Reonomy, an Altus Group Company<br>• Wise Agent by The Wise Agent<br>• Hyro by Hyro, Inc. | • Insights and Recommendations involves providing actionable insights and recommendations based on data analysis and lead behavior.<br>• AI can provide insights and recommendations using ML, NLP, CV, data visualization, NLG, etc.<br>• These solutions provide market intelligence, pricing optimization, investment analysis, customer engagement, and report generation to support lead generation and management. |

## Key Takeaways

- AI has rapidly transformed lead generation and management, offering improved efficiency and effectiveness for businesses.
- Data Collection and Analysis tools gather and process data from various sources, facilitating comprehensive lead insights.
- Lead Engagement applications, including chatbots and virtual assistants, enhance interactions through various channels.
- Lead Scoring and Qualification benefit from AI automation, providing objective criteria to prioritize and segment leads.
- Insights and Recommendations applications offer actionable suggestions based on data analysis, improving decision-making in lead management.

## 5.10. OPTIMIZED ADVERTISING CAMPAIGNS

Optimized advertising campaigns are those that use artificial intelligence (AI) to improve the performance and efficiency of digital marketing. AI can help advertisers optimize their budgets, target the right audience, personalize their messages, and measure their results. AI can also generate creative content, such as headlines, images, videos, and slogans, that can attract and engage consumers. Optimized advertising campaigns can increase conversions, sales, and brand awareness while reducing costs and waste. The advertising industry has been quick to adopt AI, as it offers a competitive edge in a crowded and dynamic market. AI can help advertisers cope with the challenges of data complexity, consumer behavior, and platform fragmentation. AI can also enhance the creativity and innovation of advertisers, by providing new insights and possibilities. AI is transforming the advertising industry, by enabling smarter, faster, and more effective campaigns.

| AI APPLICATIONS IN LEAD GENERATION AND MANAGEMENT | SOLUTIONS PROVIDED BY COMPANIES | SOLUTIONS DESCRIPTIONS |
|---|---|---|
| Programmatic Advertising | • The Trade Desk by The Trade Desk, Inc.<br>• MediaMath by MediaMath, Inc.<br>• Xandr by AT&T Inc.<br>• Adwerx by Adwerx, Inc.<br>• Zillow Premier Agent by Zillow Group, Inc.<br>• Google Marketing Platform by Google LLC | • Programmatic Advertising automates the process of buying and selling digital ad inventory.<br>• Programmatic Advertising uses AI algorithms to analyze data and optimize bids, placements, and targeting in real-time.<br>• These solutions help advertisers reach the right audience at the right time with the right message across multiple channels and devices. |

| AI APPLICATIONS IN LEAD GENERATION AND MANAGEMENT | SOLUTIONS PROVIDED BY COMPANIES | SOLUTIONS DESCRIPTIONS |
|---|---|---|
| **Ad Personalization** | • Adwerx by Adwerx, Inc.<br>• Magicbricks by Magicbricks Realty Services Limited<br>• Dynamically Creative Optimization (DCO) by Google LLC<br>• Smart Curation Engine by YieldMo | • Ad Personalization helps advertisers create customized ads for each individual consumer based on their profile and context.<br>• Ad Personalization uses AI algorithms to generate, test, and optimize different variations of ad creatives, such as headlines, images, videos, and calls to action.<br>• The solutions help advertisers improve the relevance, engagement, and performance of their ads. |
| **Ad Optimization** | • Ylopo by Ylopo, LLC<br>• CINC Pro by CINC, a Fidelity National Financial, Inc. Company<br>• Smart Curation Engine by YieldMo<br>• Adwerx by Adwerx, Inc.<br>• Kenshoo Ecommerce by Kenshoo Ltd.<br>• Sellozo by Sellozo, Inc.<br>• Real Estate Team OS by Follow Up Boss<br>• Pacvue by Pacvue, LLC<br>• Tinuiti Amazon Marketing Services (AMS) by Tinuiti, Inc. | • Ad Optimization helps advertisers improve the efficiency and effectiveness of their ad campaigns.<br>• Ad Optimization uses AI algorithms to monitor, analyze, and adjust various aspects of ad campaigns, such as keywords, bids, budgets, audiences, and creatives.<br>• The solutions help advertisers maximize their return on ad spend, minimize their cost per acquisition, and achieve their campaign goals. |

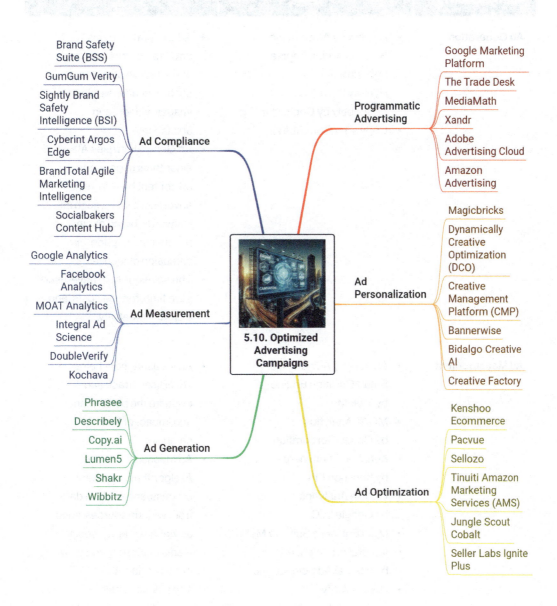

**Ad Compliance**
- Brand Safety Suite (BSS)
- GumGum Verity
- Sightly Brand Safety Intelligence (BSI)
- Cyberint Argos Edge
- BrandTotal Agile Marketing Intelligence
- Socialbakers Content Hub

**Ad Measurement**
- Google Analytics
- Facebook Analytics
- MOAT Analytics
- Integral Ad Science
- DoubleVerify
- Kochava

**Ad Generation**
- Phrasee
- Describely
- Copy.ai
- Lumen5
- Shakr
- Wibbitz

**5.10. Optimized Advertising Campaigns**

**Programmatic Advertising**
- Google Marketing Platform
- The Trade Desk
- MediaMath
- Xandr
- Adobe Advertising Cloud
- Amazon Advertising

**Ad Personalization**
- Magicbricks
- Dynamically Creative Optimization (DCO)
- Creative Management Platform (CMP)
- Bannerwise
- Bidalgo Creative AI
- Creative Factory

**Ad Optimization**
- Kenshoo Ecommerce
- Pacvue
- Sellozo
- Tinuiti Amazon Marketing Services (AMS)
- Jungle Scout Cobalt
- Seller Labs Ignite Plus

| AI APPLICATIONS IN LEAD GENERATION AND MANAGEMENT | SOLUTIONS PROVIDED BY COMPANIES | SOLUTIONS DESCRIPTIONS |
|---|---|---|
| **Ad Generation** | • Adwerx by Adwerx, Inc.<br>• Smart Curation Engine by YieldMo<br>• Hyro by Hyro, Inc.<br>• Describely by Copysmith, Inc.<br>• Copy.ai by CopyAI, Inc. | • Ad Generation helps advertisers create engaging and effective ad content, such as headlines, slogans, images, videos, and animations.<br>• Ad Generation uses AI algorithms to generate ad content based on the advertiser's input, such as keywords, brand name, product description, or campaign objective.<br>• The solutions help advertisers save time, reduce costs, and increase creativity. |
| **Ad Measurement** | • Adwerx by Adwerx, Inc.<br>• Smart Curation Engine by YieldMo<br>• MOAT Analytics by Oracle Corporation<br>• Kenshoo Ecommerce by Kenshoo Ltd.<br>• Google Analytics by Google LLC<br>• Meta Business Suite by Meta<br>• Integral Ad Science by Integral Ad Science, Inc.<br>• DoubleVerify by DoubleVerify, Inc.<br>• Kochava by Kochava, Inc. | • Ad Measurement helps advertisers track and evaluate the performance and impact of their ad campaigns.<br>• Ad Measurement uses AI algorithms to collect, process, and analyze data from various sources, such as websites, apps, social media platforms, and third-party providers.<br>• The solutions help advertisers measure metrics such as impressions, clicks, conversions, sales, revenue, and return on ad spend. |

| AI APPLICATIONS IN LEAD GENERATION AND MANAGEMENT | SOLUTIONS PROVIDED BY COMPANIES | SOLUTIONS DESCRIPTIONS |
|---|---|---|
| Ad Compliance | • Adwerx by Adwerx, Inc.<br>• Smart Curation Engine by YieldMo<br>• Integral Ad Science by Integral Ad Science, Inc.<br>• DoubleVerify by DoubleVerify, Inc.<br>• Brand Safety Suite (BSS) by Zefr, Inc.<br>• GumGum Verity by GumGum, Inc.<br>• Sightly Brand Safety Intelligence (BSI) by Sightly Enterprises, Inc. | • Ad Compliance helps advertisers ensure that their ad campaigns comply with the relevant laws, regulations, policies, and standards in different markets and platforms.<br>• Ad Compliance uses AI algorithms to monitor, audit, and flag any potential issues or violations in ad content, placement, targeting, and disclosure.<br>• The solutions help advertisers avoid fines, penalties, lawsuits, and reputational damage. |

## Key Takeaways

- AI has transformed the advertising industry, enabling smarter, faster, and more effective campaigns.
- Programmatic Advertising automates the buying and selling of digital ad inventory, optimizing bids, placements, and targeting in real-time.
- Ad Personalization creates customized ads for individual consumers, improving relevance and engagement.
- Ad Optimization improves ad campaign efficiency by using AI to monitor, analyze, and adjust keywords, bids, budgets, audiences, and creatives.
- Ad Generation employs AI algorithms to create engaging ad content, saving time and increasing creativity.

- Ad Measurement, utilizing AI, helps advertisers track and evaluate campaign performance, measuring metrics like impressions, clicks, conversions, and return on ad spend.
- Ad Compliance, with AI algorithms, ensures that ad campaigns comply with laws, regulations, and standards, avoiding fines and reputational damage.

## 5.11. 3D MODELING AND AUGMENTED REALITY

3D modeling and augmented reality involve digitally creating and manipulating physical objects and environments using software. Augmented reality overlays digital content onto the real world through devices like smartphones. Artificial intelligence (AI) enhances these technologies by generating realistic 3D models, improving rendering and animation quality, enabling interactive experiences, and recognizing objects and emotions. AI applications personalize and customize content based on user preferences and feedback. In various domains such as entertainment, education, healthcare, engineering, architecture, and art, AI transforms 3D modeling and augmented reality. The table below provides examples of AI applications in these fields, showcasing the diverse and impactful uses of these technologies.

| AI APPLICATIONS IN 3D MODELING AND AUGMENTED REALITY | SOLUTIONS PROVIDED BY COMPANIES | SOLUTIONS DESCRIPTIONS |
|---|---|---|
| 3D Model Generation | • Matterport by Matterport, Inc.<br>• 3D Staging by iStaging Corp.<br>• Archilogic Platform by Archilogic AG<br>• Vuforia Engine by PTC Inc.<br>• Fusion 360 by Autodesk, Inc.<br>• Modern CAD by Onshape<br>• Sketchfab by Sketchfab Inc.<br>• Maya by Autodesk, Inc.<br>• Blender by Blender Foundation | • 3D Model Generation is the process of creating realistic and detailed 3D models from images, videos, or sketches using AI algorithms.<br>• 3D Model Generation uses AI techniques such as generative adversarial networks (GANs), deep convolutional neural networks (DCNNs), and neural style transfer to synthesize 3D models that match the input data.<br>• These solutions help users create 3D models for various purposes, such as design, animation, gaming, or education. |

| AI APPLICATIONS IN 3D MODELING AND AUGMENTED REALITY | SOLUTIONS PROVIDED BY COMPANIES | SOLUTIONS DESCRIPTIONS |
|---|---|---|
| **3D Rendering and Animation** | • Unity by Unity Technologies ApS<br>• Unreal Engine by Epic Games Inc.<br>• Meta Quest by Meta<br>• CryEngine by Crytek GmbH<br>• Arnold by Autodesk, Inc. | • 3D Rendering and Animation is the process of generating realistic and dynamic images or videos from 3D models using AI algorithms.<br>• 3D Rendering and Animation uses AI techniques such as ray tracing, path tracing, global illumination, ambient occlusion, motion capture, facial animation, and physics simulation to enhance the quality and performance of 3D graphics.<br>• The solutions help users create immersive and interactive experiences with 3D models for various applications, such as gaming, filmmaking, or virtual reality. |
| **Augmented Reality Interaction** | • Apple Vision Pro by Apple Inc.<br>• Vuforia Engine by PTC Inc.<br>• Pokémon Go by Niantic, Inc.<br>• Snapchat Lenses by Snap Inc.<br>• Minecraft Earth by Mojang Studios AB<br>• Meta Quest by Meta<br>• Meta Smart Glasses by Meta | • Augmented Reality Interaction is the process of enabling users to interact with digital content overlaid on the real-world using AI algorithms.<br>• Augmented Reality Interaction uses AI techniques such as object recognition, face detection, gesture recognition, emotion analysis, speech recognition, natural |

**Augmented Reality Personalization**
- TerraLook
- Warby Parker Virtual Try-On
- Nike Fit
- Sephora Virtual Artist
- VR/AR Solutions

**3D Model Generation**
- Matterport
- 3D Staging
- Archilogic Platform
- Vuforia Engine
- Fusion 360
- Modern CAD
- Sketchfab
- Maya
- Blender

**5.11. 3D Modeling and Augmented Reality**

**Augmented Reality Interaction**
- Apple Vision Pro
- Vuforia Engine
- Pokémon Go
- Snapchat Lenses
- Minecraft Earth
- Meta Quest
- Meta Smart Glasses

**3D Rendering and Animation**
- Unity
- Unreal Engine
- Meta Quest
- CryEngine
- Arnold

| AI APPLICATIONS IN 3D MODELING AND AUGMENTED REALITY | SOLUTIONS PROVIDED BY COMPANIES | SOLUTIONS DESCRIPTIONS |
|---|---|---|
| | | language processing, and computer vision to mediate the interaction between users and augmented reality content.<br>• The solutions help users engage with augmented reality content in various ways, such as playing games, applying filters, creating art, or learning new skills. |
| **Augmented Reality Personalization** | • TerraLook by Quantarium, LLC<br>• Warby Parker Virtual Try-On by Warby Parker<br>• Nike Fit by Nike, Inc.<br>• Sephora Virtual Artist by Sephora USA, Inc.<br>• VR/AR Solutions by SmartTek, LLC | • Augmented Reality Personalization is the process of customizing augmented reality content based on user preferences and feedback using AI algorithms.<br>• Augmented Reality Personalization uses AI techniques such as recommendation systems, collaborative filtering, content-based filtering, and reinforcement learning to tailor augmented reality content to user needs and interests.<br>• The solutions help users find relevant and useful information, products, or services through augmented reality content. |

*Key Takeaways*

- AI enhances 3D modeling and augmented reality across diverse sectors, such as entertainment, education, healthcare, engineering, architecture, and art.

- 3D Model Generation benefits from AI techniques like GANs and neural style transfer, creating realistic models from images, videos, or sketches.

- 3D Rendering and Animation use AI algorithms, such as ray tracing and motion capture, for high-quality dynamic content in gaming, filmmaking, and virtual reality.

- Augmented Reality Interaction employs AI for user engagement through object and gesture recognition, enhancing experiences in gaming, art, and skill learning.

- Augmented Reality Personalization, using AI like recommendation systems, tailors content based on user preferences, improving experiences in virtual try-on, product visualization, and information retrieval.

## 5.12. MORTGAGES

Mortgages are loans for buying, refinancing, or improving real estate property. They have interest rates, terms, and monthly payments. AI can make mortgages better by automating data collection and verification, enhancing risk assessment and underwriting, optimizing pricing and marketing, providing personalized and real-time customer service, and detecting and preventing fraud and compliance issues. AI applications in mortgages cover different stages and aspects of the process, such as origination, servicing, secondary market, and regulation. Some examples of AI applications in mortgages are listed in the table below.

| AI APPLICATIONS IN MORTGAGES | SOLUTIONS PROVIDED BY COMPANIES | SOLUTIONS DESCRIPTIONS |
|---|---|---|
| **Data Collection and Verification** | • RateSpot by RateSpot<br>• Encompass Data Connect by Ellie Mae, Inc.<br>• Finicity Mortgage Verification Service by Finicity Corporation<br>• PointServ by PointServ Technologies, Inc.<br>• FormFree by FormFree Holdings Corporation<br>• Alesco Data by Alesco Data, LLC<br>• Capacity by Capacity, LLC<br>• DocuSign Agreement Cloud by DocuSign, Inc.<br>• LendingHome Bridge Pro by LendingHome Corporation | • Data Collection and Verification is the process of gathering and validating the data required for mortgage applications, such as income, assets, employment, credit, and identity.<br>• Data Collection and Verification uses AI algorithms to automate the extraction, analysis, and verification of data from various sources, such as bank statements, tax returns, pay stubs, credit reports, and identity documents.<br>• The solutions help lenders reduce manual errors, save time, lower costs, and improve customer experience. |
| **Risk Assessment and Underwriting** | • Zest AI by Zest AI<br>• LendingQB by MeridianLink, Inc.<br>• Blend Intelligence Engine by Blend Labs, Inc. | • Risk Assessment and Underwriting is the process of evaluating the creditworthiness and eligibility of borrowers for mortgage loans. |

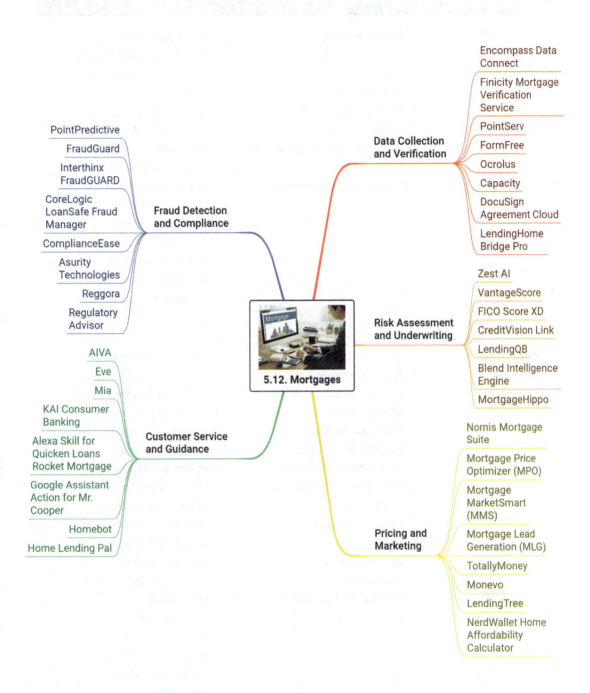

**Fraud Detection and Compliance**
- PointPredictive
- FraudGuard
- Interthinx FraudGUARD
- CoreLogic LoanSafe Fraud Manager
- ComplianceEase
- Asurity Technologies
- Reggora
- Regulatory Advisor

**Customer Service and Guidance**
- AIVA
- Eve
- Mia
- KAI Consumer Banking
- Alexa Skill for Quicken Loans Rocket Mortgage
- Google Assistant Action for Mr. Cooper
- Homebot
- Home Lending Pal

**5.12. Mortgages**

**Data Collection and Verification**
- Encompass Data Connect
- Finicity Mortgage Verification Service
- PointServ
- FormFree
- Ocrolus
- Capacity
- DocuSign Agreement Cloud
- LendingHome Bridge Pro

**Risk Assessment and Underwriting**
- Zest AI
- VantageScore
- FICO Score XD
- CreditVision Link
- LendingQB
- Blend Intelligence Engine
- MortgageHippo

**Pricing and Marketing**
- Nomis Mortgage Suite
- Mortgage Price Optimizer (MPO)
- Mortgage MarketSmart (MMS)
- Mortgage Lead Generation (MLG)
- TotallyMoney
- Monevo
- LendingTree
- NerdWallet Home Affordability Calculator

| AI APPLICATIONS IN MORTGAGES | SOLUTIONS PROVIDED BY COMPANIES | SOLUTIONS DESCRIPTIONS |
|---|---|---|
|  | • MortgageHippo by MortgageHippo, Inc.<br>• Alesco Data by Alesco Data, LLC<br>• RateSpot by RateSpot<br>• VantageScore by VantageScore Solutions, LLC<br>• FICO Score XD by Fair Isaac Corporation | • Risk Assessment and Underwriting uses AI algorithms to analyze data from traditional and alternative sources to assess the borrower's risk profile and find the best rate to charge.<br>• The solutions help lenders make better lending decisions, reduce defaults, increase approvals, and comply with regulations. |
| Pricing and Marketing | • RateSpot by RateSpot<br>• Nomis Mortgage Suite by Nomis Solutions, Inc.<br>• Mortgage Price Optimizer (MPO) by Nomis Solutions, Inc.<br>• Mortgage MarketSmart (MMS) by Black Knight, Inc.<br>• LendingTree by LendingTree, LLC<br>• Alesco Data by Alesco Data, LLC<br>• TotallyMoney by TotallyMoney Limited<br>• Monevo by Monevo Inc. | • Pricing and Marketing is the process of setting and promoting the prices of mortgage products and services to attract and retain customers.<br>• Pricing and Marketing uses AI algorithms to optimize prices based on market conditions, customer segments, demand elasticity, and competitive intelligence.<br>• The solutions help lenders increase revenue, market share, customer loyalty, and profitability. |

| AI APPLICATIONS IN MORTGAGES | SOLUTIONS PROVIDED BY COMPANIES | SOLUTIONS DESCRIPTIONS |
| --- | --- | --- |
| **Customer Service and Guidance** | • AIVA by Black Knight, Inc.<br>• Eve by Roostify, Inc.<br>• Mia by Cloudvirga, Inc.<br>• KAI Consumer Banking by Kasisto, Inc.<br>• Alexa, Pay My Rocket Mortgage<br>• Google Assistant Action for Mr. Cooper by Nationstar Mortgage LLC<br>• Wise Agent by The Wise Agent | • Customer Service and Guidance is the process of providing assistance and advice to customers throughout the mortgage journey.<br>• Customer Service and Guidance uses AI algorithms to deliver personalized and real-time customer service and guidance through various channels, such as chatbots, voice assistants, web portals, and mobile apps.<br>• The solutions help lenders improve customer satisfaction, retention, and referrals. |
| **Fraud Detection and Compliance** | • PointPredictive by PointPredictive, Inc.<br>• FraudGuard by First American Data Tree LLC<br>• CoreLogic LoanSafe Fraud Manager by CoreLogic, Inc.<br>• ComplianceEase by LogicEase Solutions Inc.<br>• Asurity Technologies by Asurity Technologies, LLC<br>• Reggora by Reggora, Inc. | • Fraud Detection and Compliance is the process of preventing and mitigating the losses caused by fraudulent activities and regulatory violations in mortgage transactions.<br>• Fraud Detection and Compliance uses AI algorithms to identify and flag any potential issues or risks in mortgage applications, documents, appraisals, valuations, and audits.<br>• The solutions help lenders protect their reputation, reduce costs, avoid penalties, and ensure compliance. |

## Key Takeaways

- AI is reshaping the mortgage industry, introducing advancements in data processing, risk assessment, pricing, customer service, and compliance.
- Data Collection and Verification benefit from AI automation, improving accuracy and efficiency in gathering and validating essential mortgage application data.
- Risk Assessment and Underwriting leverage AI algorithms to evaluate borrower creditworthiness, enhance lending decisions, and comply with regulations.
- Pricing and Marketing optimize mortgage product pricing using AI to attract customers, increase revenue, and maintain market competitiveness.
- Customer Service and Guidance deploy AI-driven solutions to provide personalized and real-time assistance, enhancing customer satisfaction and loyalty.
- Fraud Detection and Compliance rely on AI algorithms to identify and prevent fraudulent activities and ensure regulatory compliance in mortgage transactions.

## 5.13. COMPETITIVE ANALYSIS

Competitive analysis is the process of identifying, evaluating, and comparing the strengths and weaknesses of your competitors in the market. Competitive analysis helps you understand your competitive position, identify opportunities and threats, and develop effective strategies to gain a competitive edge. Competitive analysis is a vital and challenging aspect of the real estate industry that requires a high level of research, analysis, and innovation. AI has emerged as a powerful tool that can enhance various aspects of the competitive analysis process, such as data collection, market segmentation, competitor profiling, benchmarking, and scenario planning. AI can help competitive analysis professionals reduce costs, increase efficiency, improve accuracy, and optimize performance. AI can also enable competitive analysis professionals to create more comprehensive and insightful reports that meet the needs and preferences of the clients and stakeholders.

| AI APPLICATIONS IN COMPETITIVE ANALYSIS | SOLUTIONS PROVIDED BY COMPANIES | SOLUTIONS DESCRIPTIONS |
| --- | --- | --- |
| **Data Collection** | • Crayon by Crayon, Inc.<br>• Kompyte by Kompyte, Inc.<br>• SimilarWeb by SimilarWeb Ltd.<br>• Propstack by Propstack Services Private Limited<br>• Owler by Meltwater US News Inc.<br>• Contify by Contify, Inc.<br>• Rival IQ by Rival IQ Corporation | • Data Collection is the process of gathering and organizing relevant data for a competitive analysis.<br>• Data Collection uses AI algorithms to collect and analyze various data sources, such as websites, social media, news articles, reviews, and reports.<br>• These solutions help competitive analysis professionals access and integrate high-quality data that can support their market research and competitor intelligence. |

| AI APPLICATIONS IN COMPETITIVE ANALYSIS | SOLUTIONS PROVIDED BY COMPANIES | SOLUTIONS DESCRIPTIONS |
|---|---|---|
| **Market Segmentation** | • Claritas by Claritas, LLC<br>• Nielsen Segmentation & Market Solutions by Nielsen Holdings plc<br>• Propstack by Propstack Services Private Limited<br>• Buxton Analytics Platform by Buxton Company<br>• SAS Customer Intelligence 360 by SAS Institute<br>• SAP Marketing Cloud by SAP SE<br>• Precisely by Precisely Holdings, LLC<br>• Environics Analytics by Environics Analytics Inc. | • Market Segmentation is the process of dividing the market into distinct groups of customers based on their characteristics, needs, preferences, and behaviors.<br>• Market Segmentation uses AI algorithms to leverage data and analytics to identify and profile market segments.<br>• These solutions help competitive analysis professionals understand their target market, measure their market potential, and tailor their marketing strategies. |
| **Competitor Profiling** | • Klue by Klue Labs, Inc.<br>• CBI Insights by CB Insights<br>• Propstack by Propstack Services Private Limited<br>• Owler by Meltwater US News Inc.<br>• Kompyte by Kompyte, Inc.<br>• Datanyze by Datanyze, LLC<br>• BuiltWith by BuiltWith Pty Ltd | • Competitor Profiling is the process of creating detailed profiles of your competitors based on their strengths, weaknesses, opportunities, and threats.<br>• Competitor Profiling uses AI algorithms to leverage data and analytics to evaluate and compare competitors on various dimensions, such as products, services, features, pricing, customers, markets, channels, strategies, and performance. |

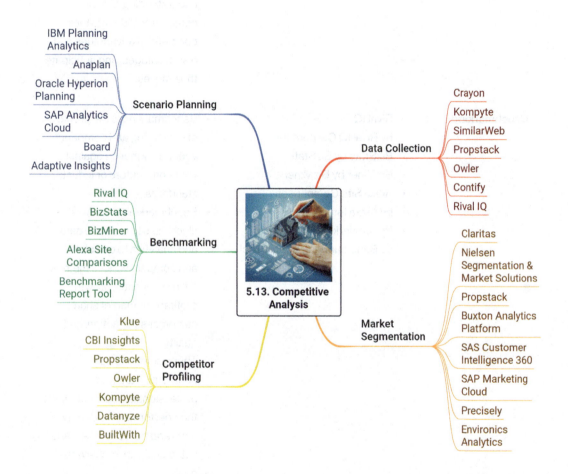

- **Scenario Planning**
  - IBM Planning Analytics
  - Anaplan
  - Oracle Hyperion Planning
  - SAP Analytics Cloud
  - Board
  - Adaptive Insights

- **Benchmarking**
  - Rival IQ
  - BizStats
  - BizMiner
  - Alexa Site Comparisons
  - Benchmarking Report Tool

- **Competitor Profiling**
  - Klue
  - CBI Insights
  - Propstack
  - Owler
  - Kompyte
  - Datanyze
  - BuiltWith

- **5.13. Competitive Analysis**

- **Data Collection**
  - Crayon
  - Kompyte
  - SimilarWeb
  - Propstack
  - Owler
  - Contify
  - Rival IQ

- **Market Segmentation**
  - Claritas
  - Nielsen Segmentation & Market Solutions
  - Propstack
  - Buxton Analytics Platform
  - SAS Customer Intelligence 360
  - SAP Marketing Cloud
  - Precisely
  - Environics Analytics

| AI APPLICATIONS IN COMPETITIVE ANALYSIS | SOLUTIONS PROVIDED BY COMPANIES | SOLUTIONS DESCRIPTIONS |
|---|---|---|
| | | • These solutions help competitive analysis professionals gain a deep understanding of their competitors, identify their competitive advantages and disadvantages, and anticipate their moves. |
| Benchmarking | • Rival IQ by Rival IQ Corporation<br>• BizStats by BizStats<br>• BizMiner by BizMiner<br>• Alexa Site Comparisons by Alexa Internet, Inc.<br>• Benchmarking Report Tool by Benchmarking Report Tool | • Benchmarking is the process of measuring and comparing your performance against your competitors or industry standards.<br>• Benchmarking uses AI algorithms to leverage data and analytics to calculate and compare various metrics, such as revenue, growth, profitability, market share, customer satisfaction, and quality.<br>• These solutions help competitive analysis professionals track and report their performance, identify gaps and best practices, and set realistic and achievable goals. |
| Scenario Planning | • IBM Planning Analytics by IBM Corporation<br>• Anaplan by Anaplan, Inc.<br>• Oracle Hyperion Planning by Oracle Corporation | • Scenario Planning is the process of creating and analyzing alternative scenarios of the future based on various assumptions and uncertainties. |

| AI APPLICATIONS IN COMPETITIVE ANALYSIS | SOLUTIONS PROVIDED BY COMPANIES | SOLUTIONS DESCRIPTIONS |
|---|---|---|
| | • SAP Analytics Cloud by SAP SE<br>• Board by Board International SA<br>• Adaptive Insights by Workday, Inc. | • Scenario Planning uses AI algorithms to leverage data and analytics to model and simulate various scenarios, such as changes in customer demand, competitor behavior, market conditions, economic trends, and technological innovations.<br>• These solutions help competitive analysis professionals explore and evaluate different outcomes, assess their implications and risks, and develop contingency plans. |

*Key Takeaways*

- AI enhances competitive analysis in real estate, improving data collection, market segmentation, competitor profiling, benchmarking, and scenario planning.
- Data Collection tools leverage AI for comprehensive market research.
- AI-driven Market Segmentation solutions facilitate targeted marketing strategies.
- Competitor Profiling, supported by AI, provides a detailed understanding of competitors.
- Benchmarking tools use AI to measure and compare performance metrics.
- AI-powered Scenario Planning assists in effective strategic planning and risk assessment.

## 5.14. REAL ESTATE INVESTMENT

The real estate investment industry involves the acquisition, ownership, management, rental, or sale of properties for the purpose of generating income or capital appreciation. Real estate investors can invest in various types of properties, such as residential, commercial, industrial, or land. Real estate investors can also invest in different ways, such as direct ownership, partnerships, real estate investment trusts (REITs), crowdfunding, or mortgage-backed securities. This industry is complex and risky, requiring thorough research, analysis, and due diligence. AI has emerged as a powerful tool that can enhance the efficiency, effectiveness, and profitability of real estate investment. AI can take many forms in real estate investment, as delineated in the table below. For example, AI-powered platforms can provide data-driven insights and recommendations for property valuation, market analysis, and investment strategy. Overall, the adoption of AI in the real estate investment industry has been gradual but promising.

| AI APPLICATIONS IN REAL ESTATE INVESTMENT | SOLUTIONS PROVIDED BY COMPANIES | SOLUTIONS DESCRIPTIONS |
|---|---|---|
| Property Valuation | • Quantarium Valuation Model (QVM) by Quantarium, LLC<br>• HouseCanary by HouseCanary, Inc.<br>• TerraLook by Quantarium, LLC<br>• Reonomy by Reonomy, an Altus Group Company<br>• CityBldr by CityBldr, Inc.<br>• IBM Watson Discovery by IBM Corporation<br>• Edge by Square Yards Consulting Private Limited<br>• Cherre by Cherre, Inc.<br>• ArcGIS by Environmental Systems Research Institute, Inc. (ESRI)<br>• Precisely by Precisely Holdings, LLC | • Property Valuation is the process of estimating the market value of a property based on various factors, such as location, condition, features, and market trends.<br>• Property Valuation uses AI algorithms to analyze data from multiple sources, such as public records, listings, transactions, and satellite imagery.<br>• These solutions help real estate investors assess the value of properties, compare properties, and identify opportunities. |

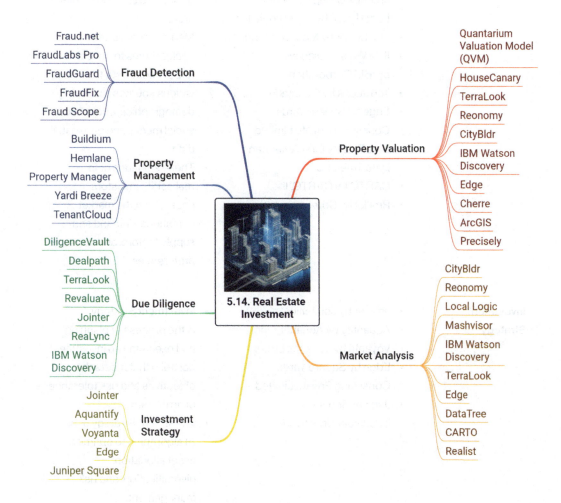

**Fraud Detection**
- Fraud.net
- FraudLabs Pro
- FraudGuard
- FraudFix
- Fraud Scope

**Property Management**
- Buildium
- Hemlane
- Property Manager
- Yardi Breeze
- TenantCloud

**Due Diligence**
- DiligenceVault
- Dealpath
- TerraLook
- Revaluate
- Jointer
- ReaLync
- IBM Watson Discovery

**Investment Strategy**
- Jointer
- Aquantify
- Voyanta
- Edge
- Juniper Square

**5.14. Real Estate Investment**

**Property Valuation**
- Quantarium Valuation Model (QVM)
- HouseCanary
- TerraLook
- Reonomy
- CityBldr
- IBM Watson Discovery
- Edge
- Cherre
- ArcGIS
- Precisely

**Market Analysis**
- CityBldr
- Reonomy
- Local Logic
- Mashvisor
- IBM Watson Discovery
- TerraLook
- Edge
- DataTree
- CARTO
- Realist

| AI APPLICATIONS IN REAL ESTATE INVESTMENT | SOLUTIONS PROVIDED BY COMPANIES | SOLUTIONS DESCRIPTIONS |
|---|---|---|
| Market Analysis | • CityBldr by CityBldr, Inc.<br>• Reonomy by Reonomy, an Altus Group Company<br>• Local Logic by Local Logic Inc.<br>• Mashvisor by Mashvisor, Inc.<br>• IBM Watson Discovery by IBM Corporation<br>• TerraLook by Quantarium, LLC<br>• Edge by Square Yards Consulting Private Limited<br>• DataTree by First American Data Tree LLC<br>• CARTO by CARTO, Inc.<br>• Realist by CoreLogic, Inc. | • Market Analysis is the process of studying the dynamics and trends of a specific market or area.<br>• Market Analysis uses AI algorithms to collect and process data from various sources, such as demographics, economics, social media, and geospatial data.<br>• These solutions help real estate investors understand the market conditions, demand and supply factors, and consumer preferences. |
| Investment Strategy | • Jointer by Jointer.io<br>• Aquantify by Aquantify, Inc.<br>• Voyanta by Voyanta, Ltd.<br>• Edge by Square Yards Consulting Private Limited<br>• Juniper Square by Juniper Square, Inc. | • Investment Strategy is the process of planning and executing an investment portfolio that meets the objectives and risk tolerance of an investor.<br>• Investment Strategy uses AI algorithms to optimize asset allocation, diversification, and risk management.<br>• These solutions help real estate investors create and manage their portfolios, monitor their performance, and adjust their strategy accordingly. |

| AI APPLICATIONS IN REAL ESTATE INVESTMENT | SOLUTIONS PROVIDED BY COMPANIES | SOLUTIONS DESCRIPTIONS |
|---|---|---|
| **Due Diligence** | • DiligenceVault by DiligenceVault, Inc.<br>• Dealpath by Dealpath, Inc.<br>• TerraLook by Quantarium, LLC<br>• Revaluate by Revaluate, Inc.<br>• Jointer by Jointer.io<br>• ReaLync by ReaLync Corporation<br>• IBM Watson Discovery by IBM Corporation | • Due Diligence is the process of verifying and validating the information and documents related to a property or a transaction.<br>• Due Diligence uses AI algorithms to automate tasks, such as data extraction, document analysis, compliance check, and risk assessment.<br>• These solutions help real estate investors conduct due diligence faster, easier, and more accurately. |
| **Property Management** | • Buildium by Buildium, A RealPage Company<br>• Hemlane by Hemlane, Inc.<br>• Property Manager by AppFolio, Inc.<br>• Yardi Breeze by Yardi Systems, Inc.<br>• TenantCloud by TenantCloud, LLC | • Property Management is the process of overseeing the operation, maintenance, and administration of a property or a portfolio of properties.<br>• Property Management uses AI algorithms to automate tasks, such as rent collection, maintenance requests, tenant screening, and lease management.<br>• These solutions help real estate investors manage their properties more efficiently, effectively, and profitably. |
| **Fraud Detection** | • Fraud.net by Fraud.net, Inc.<br>• FraudLabs Pro by FraudLabs Pro, Inc.<br>• FraudGuard by FraudGuard, LLC | • Fraud Detection is the process of identifying and preventing fraudulent activities, such as identity theft, money laundering, and mortgage fraud. |

| AI APPLICATIONS IN REAL ESTATE INVESTMENT | SOLUTIONS PROVIDED BY COMPANIES | SOLUTIONS DESCRIPTIONS |
|---|---|---|
| | • FraudFix by FraudFix, Inc.<br>• Fraud Scope by Codoxo | • Fraud Detection uses AI algorithms to analyze data from various sources, such as credit reports, bank statements, and social media.<br>• These solutions help real estate investors protect their assets, reputation, and legal compliance. |

### Key Takeaways

- AI gradually transforms the real estate investment industry for enhanced efficiency and profitability.
- Property Valuation tools (e.g., CityBldr, Reonomy) leverage AI to estimate property values, aiding investors in assessment and opportunity identification.
- Market Analysis platforms (e.g., IBM Watson Discovery, Mashvisor) use AI for comprehensive market study, understanding conditions, and consumer preferences.
- Investment Strategy applications (e.g., Jointer, Voyanta) optimize asset allocation, diversification, and risk management for investors.
- Due Diligence tools (e.g., DiligenceVault, Dealpath) automate tasks, speeding up data extraction, document analysis, and risk assessment.
- Property Management systems (e.g., AppFolio, Yardi Breeze) employ AI for efficient automation of rent collection, maintenance, and lease management.
- Fraud Detection solutions (e.g., Fraud.net, FraudLabs Pro) utilize AI to identify and prevent fraudulent activities, protecting investors' assets and legal compliance.

## 5.15. REAL ESTATE LEASING

Real estate leasing is the process of renting out properties to tenants for a fixed period of time and a predetermined rent. Leasing is a common way for property owners to generate income from their assets and for tenants to access housing or commercial space without buying. Leasing can also be a flexible and cost-effective option for both parties, as it allows them to adjust to changing needs and market conditions. AI has the potential to transform the leasing process, making it more efficient, convenient, and personalized. AI can assist property owners and managers in finding and retaining tenants, optimizing rents, and managing properties. AI can also help tenants in searching for properties, negotiating leases, and communicating with landlords. AI can take various forms in real estate leasing, as shown below.

| AI APPLICATIONS IN REAL ESTATE LEASING | SOLUTIONS PROVIDED BY COMPANIES | SOLUTIONS DESCRIPTIONS |
| --- | --- | --- |
| **Lease Generation and Analysis** | • LeasePilot by LeasePilot, Inc.<br>• LeaseQuery by LeaseQuery, LLC<br>• LeaseAbstraction by LeaseAbstraction, LLC<br>• Leverton by MRI Software, LLC<br>• Leasecake by Leasecake, Inc.<br>• DocuSign Agreement Cloud by DocuSign, Inc. | • Lease Generation and Analysis automates the creation and review of lease contracts using natural language processing (NLP) and machine learning (ML).<br>• These solutions help property owners and tenants to generate leases faster, extract key information from lease documents, and comply with accounting standards and regulations.<br>• These solutions also enable users to compare lease terms, track lease obligations, and manage lease portfolios. |

| AI APPLICATIONS IN REAL ESTATE LEASING | SOLUTIONS PROVIDED BY COMPANIES | SOLUTIONS DESCRIPTIONS |
|---|---|---|
| **Property Search and Recommendation** | • NestAway by NestAway Technologies Private Limited<br>• Apartments.com by CoStar Group, Inc.<br>• Zillow by Zillow Group, Inc.<br>• Trulia by Zillow Group, Inc.<br>• Rent.com by RentPath, LLC<br>• HotPads by Zillow Group, Inc.<br>• Apartment List by Apartment List, Inc.<br>• PadMapper by Zumper, Inc.<br>• Zumper by Zumper, Inc. | • Property Search and Recommendation uses AI algorithms to match tenants with properties that suit their preferences, budget, and location.<br>• These solutions provide users with personalized recommendations, detailed property information, and interactive maps.<br>• These solutions also allow users to filter properties based on various criteria, such as amenities, pet-friendliness, and commute time. |
| **Tenant Screening and Verification** | • Zolo by Zolo Stays Property Solutions Pvt Ltd<br>• Rentberry by Rentberry, Inc.<br>• RentSpree by RentSpree, LLC<br>• TenantCloud by TenantCloud, LLC<br>• TurboTenant by TurboTenant, Inc.<br>• RentPrep by RentPrep, a Roofstock Company<br>• Rentlytics by RealPage, Inc. | • Tenant Screening and Verification uses AI to evaluate the creditworthiness, background, and identity of potential tenants.<br>• These solutions help property owners and managers to reduce the risk of fraud, default, and eviction.<br>• These solutions also streamline the application process, allowing tenants to submit their information online and receive instant feedback. |
| **Rent Optimization** | • NestAway by NestAway Technologies Private Limited<br>• Zolo by Zolo Stays Property Solutions Pvt Ltd<br>• Rentlogic by Rentlogic, Inc. | • Rent Optimization uses AI to analyze market data, supply and demand, and property characteristics to determine the optimal rent for a property. |

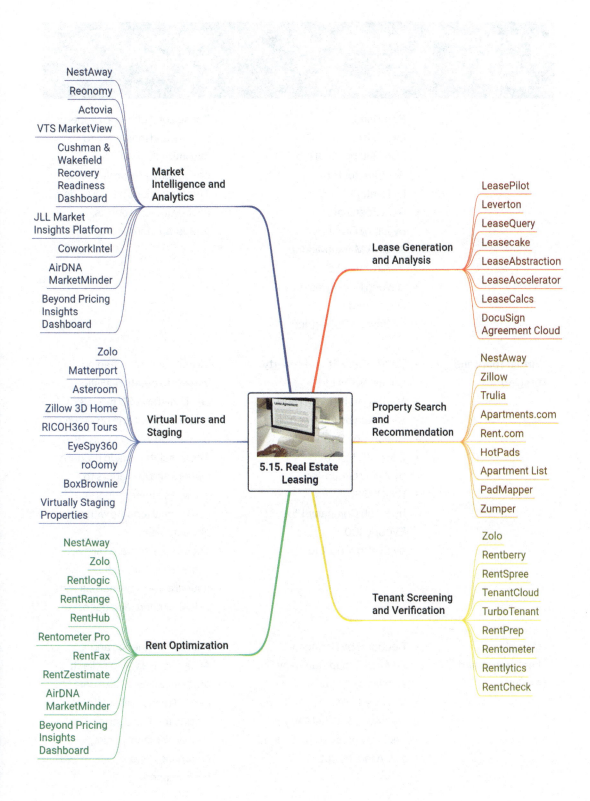

**Market Intelligence and Analytics**
- NestAway
- Reonomy
- Actovia
- VTS MarketView
- Cushman & Wakefield Recovery Readiness Dashboard
- JLL Market Insights Platform
- CoworkIntel
- AirDNA MarketMinder
- Beyond Pricing Insights Dashboard

**Virtual Tours and Staging**
- Zolo
- Matterport
- Asteroom
- Zillow 3D Home
- RICOH360 Tours
- EyeSpy360
- roOomy
- BoxBrownie
- Virtually Staging Properties

**Rent Optimization**
- NestAway
- Zolo
- Rentlogic
- RentRange
- RentHub
- Rentometer Pro
- RentFax
- RentZestimate
- AirDNA MarketMinder
- Beyond Pricing Insights Dashboard

**5.15. Real Estate Leasing**

**Lease Generation and Analysis**
- LeasePilot
- Leverton
- LeaseQuery
- Leasecake
- LeaseAbstraction
- LeaseAccelerator
- LeaseCalcs
- DocuSign Agreement Cloud

**Property Search and Recommendation**
- NestAway
- Zillow
- Trulia
- Apartments.com
- Rent.com
- HotPads
- Apartment List
- PadMapper
- Zumper

**Tenant Screening and Verification**
- Zolo
- Rentberry
- RentSpree
- TenantCloud
- TurboTenant
- RentPrep
- Rentometer
- Rentlytics
- RentCheck

| AI APPLICATIONS IN REAL ESTATE LEASING | SOLUTIONS PROVIDED BY COMPANIES | SOLUTIONS DESCRIPTIONS |
|---|---|---|
| | • RentRange by RentRange, LLC<br>• RentHub by RentHub<br>• Rentometer Pro by Rentometer, Inc.<br>• Rent Zestimate by Zillow Group, Inc.<br>• AirDNA MarketMinder by AirDNA, LLC<br>• Beyond Pricing Insights Dashboard by Beyond Pricing, Inc. | • These solutions help property owners and managers to maximize their revenue, occupancy, and profitability.<br>• These solutions also provide users with rent reports, trends, and forecasts. |
| **Virtual Tours and Staging** | • Zolo by Zolo Stays Property Solutions Pvt Ltd<br>• Matterport by Matterport, Inc.<br>• Asteroom by Asteroom, Inc.<br>• Rooomy by Rooomy, Inc.<br>• Zillow 3D Home by Zillow Group, Inc.<br>• RICOH360 Tours by Ricoh Company, Ltd.<br>• EyeSpy360 by EyeSpy360, Ltd. | • Virtual Tours and Staging uses AI to create realistic and immersive 3D models of properties that can be viewed online or in virtual reality (VR).<br>• These solutions help property owners and managers to showcase their properties to potential tenants without physical visits.<br>• These solutions also allow users to customize the appearance of properties with virtual furniture and decor. |
| **Market Intelligence and Analytics** | • Reonomy by Reonomy, an Altus Group Company<br>• Actovia by Actovia<br>• VTS MarketView by VTS, Inc.<br>• NestAway by NestAway Technologies Private Limited<br>• JLL Azara by JLL, Inc. | • Market Intelligence and Analytics uses AI to collect, process, and visualize data related to the real estate leasing market, such as supply, demand, pricing, occupancy, and performance. |

| AI APPLICATIONS IN REAL ESTATE LEASING | SOLUTIONS PROVIDED BY COMPANIES | SOLUTIONS DESCRIPTIONS |
|---|---|---|
| | • Cushman & Wakefield Recovery Readiness Dashboard by Cushman & Wakefield plc<br>• CoworkIntel by CoworkIntel, LLC<br>• AirDNA MarketMinder by AirDNA, LLC<br>• Beyond Pricing Insights Dashboard by Beyond Pricing, Inc. | • These solutions help property owners and managers to gain insights into the market dynamics, identify opportunities and threats, and benchmark their performance against competitors.<br>• These solutions also provide users with actionable recommendations and alerts. |

## Key Takeaways

- AI is transforming the real estate leasing industry for enhanced efficiency and personalization.
- Lease Generation tools automate lease creation and compliance, streamlining processes.
- Property Search platforms leverage AI for personalized property suggestions.
- Tenant Screening solutions use AI to assess creditworthiness, reducing the risk of fraud and eviction.
- Rent Optimization apps utilize AI to determine optimal rents for property owners and managers.
- Virtual Tours and Staging technologies create immersive 3D models using AI.
- Market Intelligence platforms provide property owners with AI-driven insights into market dynamics.

## 5.16. PROPERTY FINANCING AND MORTGAGE

Property financing and mortgage is the process of obtaining funds to purchase or refinance real estate properties. This process involves various parties, such as borrowers, lenders, brokers, appraisers, and underwriters. Property financing and mortgage is a complex and dynamic industry that requires careful analysis and risk management. AI has the potential to transform the industry, offering benefits such as improved efficiency, accuracy, customer experience, and profitability. AI can be applied to various aspects of property financing and mortgage, as shown below.

| AI APPLICATIONS IN PROPERTY FINANCING AND MORTGAGE | SOLUTIONS PROVIDED BY COMPANIES | SOLUTIONS DESCRIPTIONS |
|---|---|---|
| Credit Scoring | • Zest AI by Zest AI<br>• Upstart by Upstart Network, Inc.<br>• Blend by Blend Labs, Inc.<br>• LenddoEFL by LenddoEFL<br>• CreditVidya by CreditVidya Technologies Pvt Ltd<br>• TurnKey Lender by TurnKey Lender Pte Ltd<br>• Scienaptic by Scienaptic Systems, Inc. | • Credit Scoring is the process of assessing the creditworthiness of borrowers based on their financial history and behavior.<br>• Credit Scoring uses AI algorithms to analyze alternative data sources, such as social media, online transactions, psychometric tests, and biometrics.<br>• These solutions help lenders make better lending decisions, reduce defaults, and expand financial inclusion. |
| Property Valuation | • Quantarium Valuation Model (QVM) by Quantarium, LLC<br>• HouseCanary by HouseCanary, Inc.<br>• GeoPhy by GeoPhy, a Walker & Dunlop Company | • Property Valuation is the process of estimating the market value of real estate properties based on various factors, such as location, size, condition, and amenities. |

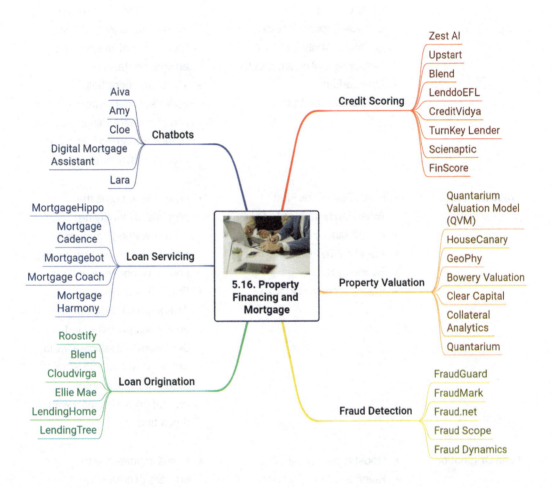

**Chatbots**
- Aiva
- Amy
- Cloe
- Digital Mortgage Assistant
- Lara

**Loan Servicing**
- MortgageHippo
- Mortgage Cadence
- Mortgagebot
- Mortgage Coach
- Mortgage Harmony

**Loan Origination**
- Roostify
- Blend
- Cloudvirga
- Ellie Mae
- LendingHome
- LendingTree

**5.16. Property Financing and Mortgage**

**Credit Scoring**
- Zest AI
- Upstart
- Blend
- LenddoEFL
- CreditVidya
- TurnKey Lender
- Scienaptic
- FinScore

**Property Valuation**
- Quantarium Valuation Model (QVM)
- HouseCanary
- GeoPhy
- Bowery Valuation
- Clear Capital
- Collateral Analytics
- Quantarium

**Fraud Detection**
- FraudGuard
- FraudMark
- Fraud.net
- Fraud Scope
- Fraud Dynamics

| AI APPLICATIONS IN PROPERTY FINANCING AND MORTGAGE | SOLUTIONS PROVIDED BY COMPANIES | SOLUTIONS DESCRIPTIONS |
|---|---|---|
|  | • Bowery Valuation by Bowery Valuation, Inc.<br>• Clear Capital by ClearCapital.com, Inc.<br>• Collateral Analytics by Collateral Analytics, LLC<br>• Quantarium by Quantarium, LLC | • Property Valuation uses AI algorithms to analyze large and diverse data sets, such as sales transactions, listings, aerial imagery, and environmental data.<br>• These solutions help appraisers generate accurate and consistent valuations, reduce turnaround time, and comply with regulations. |
| Fraud Detection | • FraudGUARD by First American Data Tree LLC<br>• FraudMark by CoreLogic, Inc.<br>• Fraud.net by Fraud.net, Inc.<br>• Sygno by Sygno<br>• Fraud Scope by Codoxo | • Fraud Detection is the process of identifying and preventing fraudulent activities in property financing and mortgage transactions.<br>• Fraud Detection uses AI algorithms to detect anomalies, patterns, and behaviors that indicate fraud.<br>• These solutions help lenders reduce losses, protect reputation, and comply with regulations. |
| Loan Origination | • Roostify by Roostify, Inc.<br>• Blend by Blend Labs, Inc.<br>• Cloudvirga by Cloudvirga, Inc.<br>• Ellie Mae by Ellie Mae, Inc.<br>• LendingHome by LendingHome Corporation<br>• LendingTree by LendingTree, LLC | • Loan Origination is the process of creating and processing loan applications from borrowers.<br>• Loan Origination uses AI algorithms to automate tasks, such as data collection, verification, underwriting, and approval. |

| AI APPLICATIONS IN PROPERTY FINANCING AND MORTGAGE | SOLUTIONS PROVIDED BY COMPANIES | SOLUTIONS DESCRIPTIONS |
|---|---|---|
| | | • These solutions help lenders improve efficiency, reduce costs, enhance customer experience, and comply with regulations. |
| **Loan Servicing** | • MortgageHippo by MortgageHippo, Inc.<br>• Mortgage Cadence by Mortgage Cadence, an Accenture Company<br>• Mortgagebot by Finastra<br>• Mortgage Coach by Mortgage Coach, Inc.<br>• Mortgage Harmony by Mortgage Harmony Corp. | • Loan Servicing is the process of managing the ongoing relationship with borrowers after the loan is originated.<br>• Loan Servicing uses AI algorithms to provide services, such as payment processing, escrow management, customer support, and collections.<br>• These solutions help lenders retain customers, increase revenue, reduce risks, and comply with regulations. |
| **Chatbots** | • AIVA by Black Knight, Inc.<br>• Amy by Loanpal, LLC<br>• Cloe by Cloe, Inc.<br>• Digital Mortgage Assistant by Kasisto, Inc.<br>• Lara by Lendesk Technologies, Inc. | • Chatbots are conversational agents that interact with customers via text or voice.<br>• Chatbots use AI algorithms to understand natural language, provide relevant information, answer queries, and guide customers through the loan process.<br>• These solutions help lenders improve customer satisfaction, engagement, and loyalty. |

### *Key Takeaways*

- AI is transforming the property financing and mortgage industry for enhanced efficiency, accuracy, and customer experience.
- Credit Scoring applications leverage AI to analyze alternative data sources, aiding lenders in better decision-making.
- Property Valuation tools use AI algorithms for accurate valuations, reducing turn-around time for appraisers.
- Fraud Detection solutions employ AI to identify anomalies and patterns, helping lenders reduce losses and comply with regulations.
- Loan Origination platforms automate tasks such as data collection and verification, improving efficiency and customer experience.
- Loan Servicing applications use AI for payment processing, customer support, and risk reduction after loan origination.
- Chatbots enhance customer satisfaction and engagement by providing information and guiding customers through the loan process.

# CHAPTER 6
# MODIFY THE PROPERTY AS NEEDED FOR OCCUPANCY

Preparing a property for occupancy is a significant phase in the real estate lifecycle, blending the practicality of construction and design with the anticipation of creating a comfortable, functional space. Traditionally, this process has been fraught with challenges, from coordinating construction tasks to selecting the right home technologies.

AI, as a transformative force, redefines how properties are modified for occupancy. It introduces efficiency, innovation, and sustainability into the mix. This chapter explores how AI is enhancing the modification process, ensuring that properties meet the expectations of modern occupants.

AI-driven construction management streamlines project planning and execution. It optimizes resource allocation, enhancing timelines and cost efficiency. The integration of smart home technologies has been made more accessible by AI, enabling residents to enjoy enhanced connectivity, security, and energy management.

Design and architecture, powered by AI, offer creative insights and efficiency. Property developers and architects use generative design and AI-powered tools to optimize layouts, materials, and sustainability features.

Additionally, AI contributes to sustainability through better resource management and energy efficiency. It brings a new level of intelligence to property development, focusing on reducing environmental impact.

In this chapter, we will delve into the AI-powered transformation of the property modification phase. It introduces a new era of efficiency, innovation, and sustainability, ultimately reshaping properties to meet the expectations of today's occupants.

## 6.1. CONSTRUCTION MANAGEMENT

The construction management industry involves the planning, coordination, and control of a project from inception to completion. Construction managers are responsible for ensuring that the project meets the client's objectives, budget, and schedule, as well as complying with quality standards, safety regulations, and environmental requirements. Construction managers oversee all aspects of the project, such as design, procurement, construction, commissioning, and handover. This industry is complex and challenging, requiring effective communication, collaboration, and problem-solving skills. Artificial intelligence (AI) is a powerful tool that can enhance the efficiency, effectiveness, and profitability of construction management. AI can take many forms in construction management, as delineated in the table below. For example, AI-powered platforms can provide data-driven insights and recommendations for construction execution planning, updating of construction sequences and task management, while keeping all stakeholders always informed. The adoption of AI in the construction management industry has been gradual but promising.

| AI APPLICATIONS IN CONSTRUCTION MANAGEMENT | SOLUTIONS PROVIDED BY COMPANIES | SOLUTIONS DESCRIPTIONS |
| --- | --- | --- |
| Schedule Optimization | • ALICE by ALICE Technologies, Inc.<br>• InEight Schedule by InEight Inc.<br>• PlanRadar by PlanRadar<br>• Bridgit Bench by Bridgit<br>• SmartPM by SmartPM Technologies, Inc.<br>• nPlan by nPlan Ltd.<br>• Buildots by Buildots Ltd.<br>• SiteAware by SiteAware, Inc. | • Schedule Optimization is the process of creating and updating the optimal sequence and duration of tasks for a construction project.<br>• Schedule Optimization uses AI algorithms to analyze historical data, project constraints, resource availability, and external factors.<br>• These solutions help construction managers generate realistic and feasible schedules, reduce delays and costs, and improve performance. |

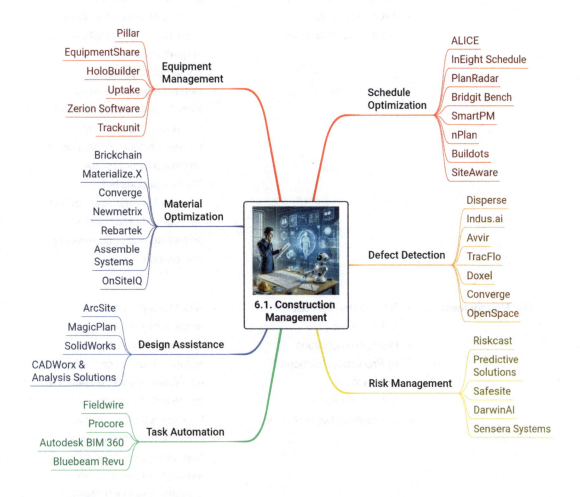

**Equipment Management**
- Pillar
- EquipmentShare
- HoloBuilder
- Uptake
- Zerion Software
- Trackunit

**Schedule Optimization**
- ALICE
- InEight Schedule
- PlanRadar
- Bridgit Bench
- SmartPM
- nPlan
- Buildots
- SiteAware

**Material Optimization**
- Brickchain
- Materialize.X
- Converge
- Newmetrix
- Rebartek
- Assemble Systems
- OnSiteIQ

**Defect Detection**
- Disperse
- Indus.ai
- Avvir
- TracFlo
- Doxel
- Converge
- OpenSpace

**Design Assistance**
- ArcSite
- MagicPlan
- SolidWorks
- CADWorx & Analysis Solutions

**Risk Management**
- Riskcast
- Predictive Solutions
- Safesite
- DarwinAI
- Sensera Systems

**Task Automation**
- Fieldwire
- Procore
- Autodesk BIM 360
- Bluebeam Revu

**6.1. Construction Management**

| AI APPLICATIONS IN CONSTRUCTION MANAGEMENT | SOLUTIONS PROVIDED BY COMPANIES | SOLUTIONS DESCRIPTIONS |
| --- | --- | --- |
| Defect Detection | • Disperse by Disperse<br>• Indus.ai by Indus.ai, Inc.<br>• Avvir by Avvir, Inc.<br>• TracFlo by TracFlo Inc. | • Defect Detection is the process of identifying and locating errors or deviations from the design specifications or quality standards in a construction project.<br>• Defect Detection uses AI algorithms to process images and videos captured by drones, cameras, or sensors on the construction site.<br>• These solutions help construction managers detect defects early, reduce rework and waste, and ensure quality compliance. |
| Risk Management | • Riskcast by Riskcast Solutions Inc.<br>• Predictive Solutions by Predictive Solutions Corporation<br>• Safesite by Safesite<br>• DarwinAI by DarwinAI Corp. | • Risk Management is the process of identifying, assessing, and mitigating potential hazards or uncertainties that may affect a construction project.<br>• Risk Management uses AI algorithms to analyze data from various sources, such as weather forecasts, site conditions, worker behavior, and equipment performance.<br>• These solutions help construction managers monitor risks, prevent accidents and injuries, and optimize resources. |

| AI APPLICATIONS IN CONSTRUCTION MANAGEMENT | SOLUTIONS PROVIDED BY COMPANIES | SOLUTIONS DESCRIPTIONS |
|---|---|---|
| **Task Automation** | • Fieldwire by Fieldwire<br>• Procore by Procore Technologies, Inc.<br>• Autodesk BIM 360 by Autodesk, Inc.<br>• Bluebeam Revu by Bluebeam Software Inc. | • Task Automation is the process of using software or hardware to perform repetitive or routine tasks that would otherwise require human intervention.<br>• Task Automation uses AI algorithms to streamline workflows, reduce errors, and increase efficiency. |
| **Design Assistance** | • ArcSite by ArcSite<br>• MagicPlan by Sensopia Inc.<br>• SolidWorks by SolidWorks Corporation, a Dassault Systèmes SE Company<br>• Fusion 360 by Autodesk, Inc.<br>• Trimble Connect by Trimble Inc. | • Design Assistance is the process of using software or hardware to assist in the creation, modification, or evaluation of design solutions for a construction project.<br>• Design Assistance uses AI algorithms to enhance creativity, decision-making, and collaboration. |
| **Material Optimization** | • Brickchain by Brickchain Ltd.<br>• Materialize.X by Materialize.X Ltd.<br>• Mix AI by Converge<br>• Newmetrix by Newmetrix<br>• Assemble Systems by Assemble Systems Inc.<br>• OnSiteIQ by OnSiteIQ Inc. | • Material Optimization is the process of using software or hardware to optimize the selection, procurement, delivery, and utilization of materials for a construction project.<br>• Material Optimization uses AI algorithms to analyze data from various sources, such as design specifications, inventory, suppliers, and site conditions. |

| AI APPLICATIONS IN CONSTRUCTION MANAGEMENT | SOLUTIONS PROVIDED BY COMPANIES | SOLUTIONS DESCRIPTIONS |
|---|---|---|
| | | • These solutions help construction managers reduce material waste, lower costs, and improve quality. |
| Equipment Management | • Pillar by RECON Dynamics<br>• EquipmentShare by EquipmentShare.com Inc.<br>• Trackunit by Trackunit A/S<br>• HoloBuilder by FARO Technologies, Inc.<br>• Uptake by Uptake Technologies, Inc. | • Equipment Management is the process of using software or hardware to manage the performance, maintenance, and utilization of equipment for a construction project.<br>• Equipment Management uses AI algorithms to monitor equipment data, such as location, status, usage, and condition.<br>• These solutions help construction managers optimize equipment efficiency, prevent breakdowns, and reduce downtime. |

## Key Takeaways

- AI can enhance various aspects of construction management, such as scheduling, defect detection, risk management, task automation, design assistance, material optimization, and equipment management.
- AI can provide data-driven insights and recommendations for construction execution planning, updating of construction sequences and task management, while keeping all stakeholders always informed.
- AI can help construction managers reduce delays, costs, rework, waste, accidents, injuries, errors, and downtime, while improving performance, quality, efficiency, creativity, decision-making, and collaboration.

## 6.2. SMART HOMES

Smart homes are residences that use internet-connected devices to enable the remote monitoring and management of appliances and systems, such as lighting, heating, security, and entertainment. Smart homes aim to provide enhanced comfort, convenience, security, and energy efficiency for the occupants. Smart homes are part of the broader concept of smart cities, which use information and communication technologies to improve the quality of life and sustainability of urban areas. The smart home industry has been slow to adopt artificial intelligence (AI) compared to other sectors, mainly due to the high cost, privacy concerns, and lack of standardization of smart home devices. However, with the advancement of AI technologies and the increasing demand for smart home solutions, the industry is expected to witness significant growth and innovation in the near future.

| AI APPLICATIONS IN SMART HOMES | SOLUTIONS PROVIDED BY COMPANIES | SOLUTIONS DESCRIPTIONS |
|---|---|---|
| **Voice and Facial Recognition** | • Amazon Alexa by Amazon.com, Inc. <br> • Google Assistant by Google LLC <br> • Siri by Apple Inc. <br> • Nest Doorbell by Google LLC <br> • Ring Video Doorbell by Amazon.com, Inc. <br> • Netatmo SmarATTOMt Video Doorbell by Netatmo SA <br> • Bixby by Samsung Electronics Co., Ltd. | • Voice and Facial Recognition enable smart home devices to identify and authenticate users based on their voice or face. <br> • Voice and Facial Recognition allow users to control smart home devices with natural language commands or gestures. <br> • These solutions enhance the user experience, security, and personalization of smart home devices. |
| **Smart Lighting** | • Philips Hue by Signify Holding <br> • LIFX by Lifi Labs, Inc. <br> • Nanoleaf by Nanoleaf BV <br> • Yeelight by Yeelight Technology Co., Ltd. | • Smart Lighting uses AI to adjust the brightness, color, and temperature of the lights according to the user's preferences, mood, and environment. |

| AI APPLICATIONS IN SMART HOMES | SOLUTIONS PROVIDED BY COMPANIES | SOLUTIONS DESCRIPTIONS |
|---|---|---|
|  | • Sengled by Sengled Optoelectronics Co., Ltd.<br>• Wiz by Wiz Connected Lighting Company Limited<br>• Ikea Tradfri by Inter IKEA Systems B.V.<br>• TP-Link Kasa by TP-Link Technologies Co., Ltd. | • Smart Lighting can be controlled remotely via smartphone apps or voice assistants.<br>• These solutions improve the energy efficiency, ambiance, and security of smart homes. |
| **Smart Thermostats** | • Nest Learning Thermostat by Google LLC<br>• Ecobee Smart Thermostat by Ecobee Inc.<br>• Honeywell Home by Resideo Technologies, Inc.<br>• Tado Smart Thermostat by Tado GmbH<br>• Netatmo Smart Thermostat by Netatmo SA<br>• Mysa Smart Thermostat by Empowered Homes Inc.<br>• Sensi Smart Thermostat by Emerson Electric Co.<br>• Bosch Connected Control by Robert Bosch GmbH | • Smart Thermostats use AI to learn the user's habits and preferences and automatically adjust the temperature and humidity of the home.<br>• Smart Thermostats can be controlled remotely via smartphone apps or voice assistants.<br>• These solutions optimize the comfort, health, and energy efficiency of smart homes. |
| **Smart Security** | • Arlo Smart by Arlo Technologies, Inc.<br>• Nest Cam by Google LLC<br>• Ring Alarm by Amazon.com, Inc.<br>• SimpliSafe by SimpliSafe, Inc.<br>• Abode by Abode Systems, Inc.<br>• Wyze Cam by Wyze Labs, Inc. | • Smart Security uses AI to monitor and protect the home from intruders, fire, smoke, water leaks, and other hazards.<br>• Smart Security can send alerts, notifications, and live video feeds to the user's smartphone or smart display. |

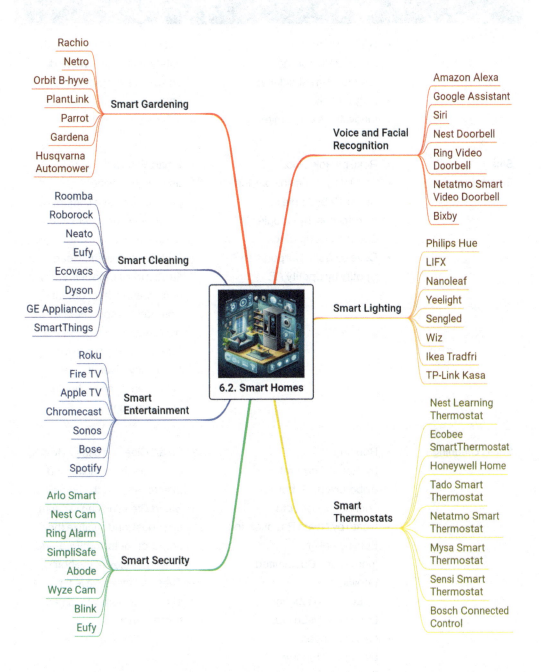

**Smart Gardening**
- Rachio
- Netro
- Orbit B-hyve
- PlantLink
- Parrot
- Gardena
- Husqvarna Automower

**Smart Cleaning**
- Roomba
- Roborock
- Neato
- Eufy
- Ecovacs
- Dyson
- GE Appliances
- SmartThings

**Smart Entertainment**
- Roku
- Fire TV
- Apple TV
- Chromecast
- Sonos
- Bose
- Spotify

**Smart Security**
- Arlo Smart
- Nest Cam
- Ring Alarm
- SimpliSafe
- Abode
- Wyze Cam
- Blink
- Eufy

**6.2. Smart Homes**

**Voice and Facial Recognition**
- Amazon Alexa
- Google Assistant
- Siri
- Nest Doorbell
- Ring Video Doorbell
- Netatmo Smart Video Doorbell
- Bixby

**Smart Lighting**
- Philips Hue
- LIFX
- Nanoleaf
- Yeelight
- Sengled
- Wiz
- Ikea Tradfri
- TP-Link Kasa

**Smart Thermostats**
- Nest Learning Thermostat
- Ecobee SmartThermostat
- Honeywell Home
- Tado Smart Thermostat
- Netatmo Smart Thermostat
- Mysa Smart Thermostat
- Sensi Smart Thermostat
- Bosch Connected Control

| AI APPLICATIONS IN SMART HOMES | SOLUTIONS PROVIDED BY COMPANIES | SOLUTIONS DESCRIPTIONS |
|---|---|---|
| | • Blink by Immedia Semiconductor, Inc. (an Amazon subsidiary)<br>• Eufy by Anker Innovations Co., Limited | • These solutions enhance the safety, peace of mind, and convenience of smart home owners. |
| **Smart Entertainment** | • Roku by Roku, Inc.<br>• Fire TV by Amazon.com, Inc.<br>• Apple TV by Apple Inc.<br>• Chromecast by Google LLC<br>• Sonos by Sonos, Inc.<br>• Bose by Bose Corporation<br>• Spotify by Spotify AB | • Smart Entertainment uses AI to provide personalized and immersive entertainment experiences for the user.<br>• Smart Entertainment can stream music, movies, shows, games, and other content from various sources and platforms.<br>• These solutions improve the quality, diversity, and enjoyment of smart home entertainment. |
| **Smart Cleaning** | • Roomba by iRobot Corporation<br>• Roborock by Roborock Technology Co., Ltd.<br>• Neato by Neato Robotics, Inc.<br>• Eufy by Anker Innovations Co., Limited<br>• Ecovacs by Ecovacs Robotics<br>• Dyson by Dyson Ltd.<br>• GE Appliances by General Electric<br>• SmartThings by Samsung Electronics Co., Ltd. | • Smart Cleaning uses AI to automate the cleaning and maintenance of the home.<br>• Smart Cleaning can vacuum, mop, dust, and sanitize the floors, carpets, furniture, and other surfaces of the home.<br>• These solutions save time, effort, and money for smart home owners. |

| AI APPLICATIONS IN SMART HOMES | SOLUTIONS PROVIDED BY COMPANIES | SOLUTIONS DESCRIPTIONS |
|---|---|---|
| Smart Gardening | • Rachio by Rachio, Inc.<br>• Netro by Netro Inc.<br>• Orbit B-hyve by Orbit Irrigation Products, LLC<br>• PlantLink by Oso Technologies, Inc.<br>• Parrot by Parrot SA<br>• Gardena by Husqvarna AB<br>• Husqvarna Automower by Husqvarna AB | • Smart Gardening uses AI to monitor and manage the watering, fertilizing, and mowing of the lawn and plants.<br>• Smart Gardening can adjust the irrigation and nutrition levels based on the weather, soil, and plant conditions.<br>• These solutions improve the beauty, health, and sustainability of smart home gardens. |

## Key Takeaways

- AI integration in smart homes enhances efficiency, making buildings more intelligent and adaptive.
- Energy Management in smart homes reduces costs and carbon footprint while improving energy efficiency and reliability.
- Predictive Maintenance prevents failures, extending asset lifespan and maintaining efficiency.
- Occupant Comfort and Well-being create personalized, healthy spaces, enhancing satisfaction and productivity.
- Security and Access Control protect against threats, enforcing policies, and ensuring compliance.
- Space Optimization maximizes efficiency, supporting flexible and agile work environments.
- Sustainability and Resilience reduce waste, pollution, and resource consumption, improving health and safety.
- AI's integration with IoT, cloud, and blockchain creates new opportunities and challenges, demanding continuous innovation and collaboration in smart home technology.

## 6.3. SMART BUILDINGS

Smart buildings are structures that use advanced technologies and data analytics to optimize various aspects of building performance, such as energy efficiency, comfort, security, and sustainability. Smart buildings leverage sensors, actuators, controllers, and communication networks to collect, process, and act on data from the building and its environment. Smart buildings can also interact with other smart systems, such as smart grids, smart cities, and smart transportation, to create a more integrated and intelligent urban ecosystem. The smart building industry has been slow to adopt artificial intelligence (AI) compared to other sectors, such as manufacturing, healthcare, and retail. However, in recent years, the industry has witnessed a surge of interest and investment in AI solutions, driven by the growing demand for green buildings, cost savings, and enhanced occupant experience. AI can enable smart buildings to become more adaptive, autonomous, and responsive, as well as to generate insights and recommendations for improvement.

| AI APPLICATIONS IN SMART BUILDINGS | SOLUTIONS PROVIDED BY COMPANIES | SOLUTIONS DESCRIPTIONS |
|---|---|---|
| **Energy Management** | • Verdigris by Verdigris Technologies, Inc.<br>• Carbon Lighthouse by Carbon Lighthouse, Inc.<br>• BrainBox AI by BrainBox AI, Inc.<br>• Self Supervised AI by Pametan AI<br>• Gridium by Gridium, Inc.<br>• Enertiv by Enertiv, Inc.<br>• Switch Automation by Switch Automation Pty Ltd<br>• BuildingIQ by CIM Enviro Pty Ltd | • Energy Management optimizes energy consumption and generation in smart buildings.<br>• Energy Management uses AI algorithms to analyze data from sensors, meters, weather, and other sources, and to control HVAC, lighting, and other systems.<br>• These solutions help smart buildings reduce energy costs, carbon emissions, and peak demand, as well as to increase energy efficiency, reliability, and resilience. |

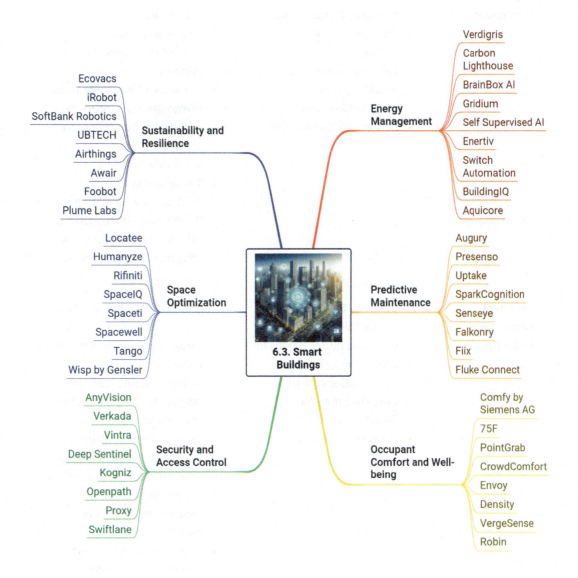

Sustainability and Resilience
- Ecovacs
- iRobot
- SoftBank Robotics
- UBTECH
- Airthings
- Awair
- Foobot
- Plume Labs

Energy Management
- Verdigris
- Carbon Lighthouse
- BrainBox AI
- Gridium
- Self Supervised AI
- Enertiv
- Switch Automation
- BuildingIQ
- Aquicore

Space Optimization
- Locatee
- Humanyze
- Rifiniti
- SpaceIQ
- Spaceti
- Spacewell
- Tango
- Wisp by Gensler

6.3. Smart Buildings

Predictive Maintenance
- Augury
- Presenso
- Uptake
- SparkCognition
- Senseye
- Falkonry
- Fiix
- Fluke Connect

Security and Access Control
- AnyVision
- Verkada
- Vintra
- Deep Sentinel
- Kogniz
- Openpath
- Proxy
- Swiftlane

Occupant Comfort and Well-being
- Comfy by Siemens AG
- 75F
- PointGrab
- CrowdComfort
- Envoy
- Density
- VergeSense
- Robin

| AI APPLICATIONS IN SMART BUILDINGS | SOLUTIONS PROVIDED BY COMPANIES | SOLUTIONS DESCRIPTIONS |
| --- | --- | --- |
| **Predictive Maintenance** | • Augury by Augury Systems, Inc.<br>• Presenso by Presenso<br>• Uptake by Uptake Technologies, Inc.<br>• SparkCognition by SparkCognition, Inc.<br>• Senseye by Senseye Ltd | • Predictive Maintenance anticipates and prevents failures and breakdowns of building equipment and systems.<br>• Predictive Maintenance uses AI algorithms to monitor the condition and performance of assets, and to detect anomalies and faults.<br>• These solutions help smart buildings avoid costly repairs, downtime, and safety risks, as well as to extend the lifespan and efficiency of assets. |
| **Occupant Comfort and Well-being** | • Comfy by Siemens AG<br>• 75F by 75F, LLC<br>• PointGrab by PointGrab Ltd<br>• CrowdComfort by CrowdComfort, Inc.<br>• Envoy by Envoy, Inc.<br>• Density by Density, Inc.<br>• VergeSense by VergeSense | • Occupant Comfort and Well-being enhances the quality of life and productivity of building occupants.<br>• Occupant Comfort and Well-being uses AI algorithms to understand and respond to occupant preferences, behaviors, and feedback, and to adjust indoor environmental conditions, such as temperature, lighting, and air quality.<br>• These solutions help smart buildings create personalized, comfortable, and healthy spaces, as well as to improve occupant satisfaction, engagement, and loyalty. |

| AI APPLICATIONS IN SMART BUILDINGS | SOLUTIONS PROVIDED BY COMPANIES | SOLUTIONS DESCRIPTIONS |
| --- | --- | --- |
| **Security and Access Control** | • OnWatch by Oosto<br>• Verkada by Verkada, Inc.<br>• Vintra by Vintra, Inc.<br>• Deep Sentinel by Deep Sentinel Corp.<br>• Kogniz by Kogniz, Inc.<br>• Openpath by Openpath Security, Inc.<br>• Proxy by Proxy, Inc. | • Security and Access Control protects smart buildings from unauthorized access, theft, vandalism, and other threats.<br>• Security and Access Control uses AI algorithms to analyze data from cameras, sensors, and other devices, and to recognize faces, objects, and activities.<br>• These solutions help smart buildings monitor and control entry and exit points, alert and respond to incidents, and enforce security policies and compliance. |
| **Space Optimization** | • Locatee by Locatee AG<br>• Humanyze by Humanyze Analytics, Inc.<br>• Rifiniti by Rifiniti, Inc.<br>• SpaceIQ by SpaceIQ, Inc.<br>• Spaceti by Spaceti s.r.o.<br>• Spacewell by Spacewell NV<br>• Tango by Tango<br>• Wisp by Gensler | • Space Optimization maximizes the utilization and efficiency of building space.<br>• Space Optimization uses AI algorithms to collect and analyze data from sensors, badges, and other sources, and to measure and visualize space occupancy, availability, and demand.<br>• These solutions help smart buildings optimize space allocation, layout, and design, as well as to support flexible and agile work environments. |

| AI APPLICATIONS IN SMART BUILDINGS | SOLUTIONS PROVIDED BY COMPANIES | SOLUTIONS DESCRIPTIONS |
|---|---|---|
| **Sustainability and Resilience** | • Airthings by Airthings AS<br>• Awair by Awair Inc.<br>• Ecovacs by Ecovacs Robotics<br>• iRobot by iRobot Corporation | • Sustainability and Resilience improves the environmental and social impact of smart buildings.<br>• Sustainability and Resilience uses AI algorithms to automate and enhance various tasks and functions, such as cleaning, waste management, air quality monitoring, and disaster response.<br>• These solutions help smart buildings reduce waste, pollution, and resource consumption, as well as to improve health, safety, and well-being of occupants and communities. |

## Key Takeaways

- AI has enabled smart buildings to become more intelligent, adaptive, and autonomous, improving various aspects of building performance and occupant experience.
- Energy Management reduces energy costs and carbon footprint, while increasing energy efficiency and reliability.
- Predictive Maintenance prevents failures and breakdowns, while extending asset lifespan and efficiency.
- Occupant Comfort and Well-being creates personalized, comfortable, and healthy spaces, while improving occupant satisfaction and productivity.
- Security and Access Control protects buildings from threats and incidents, while enforcing security policies and compliance.

- Space Optimization maximizes space utilization and efficiency, while supporting flexible and agile work environments.
- Sustainability and Resilience reduces waste, pollution, and resource consumption, while improving health, safety, and well-being of occupants and communities.
- The integration of AI with other technologies, such as IoT, cloud, and blockchain, creates new opportunities and challenges for smart buildings, requiring continuous innovation and collaboration.

## 6.4. ARCHITECTURE AND DESIGN

Architecture and design are creative fields that involve planning, designing, and constructing buildings and spaces. Architects and designers use their artistic vision, technical skills, and knowledge of materials, structures, and environments to create functional and aesthetic solutions for various purposes and contexts. Architecture and design have a significant impact on the quality of life, culture, and economy of societies. Artificial intelligence (AI) is a powerful tool that can enhance the efficiency, effectiveness, and innovation of architecture and design. AI can assist architects and designers in various stages of their work, from conceptualization to execution, as well as in various aspects, such as creativity, efficiency, collaboration, and sustainability. AI can also challenge and inspire architects and designers to explore new forms, functions, and meanings in their projects.

| AI APPLICATIONS IN ARCHITECTURE AND DESIGN | SOLUTIONS PROVIDED BY COMPANIES | SOLUTIONS DESCRIPTIONS |
|---|---|---|
| Generative Design | • Dreamcatcher by Autodesk, Inc. <br> • Project Refinery by Autodesk, Inc. <br> • GenerativeComponents by Bentley Systems, Incorporated <br> • Grasshopper by Robert McNeel & Associates <br> • Wallacei by Wallacei <br> • SolidWorks by SolidWorks Corporation, a Dassault Systèmes SE Company <br> • CATIA by SolidWorks Corporation, a Dassault Systèmes SE Company <br> • ArchiCAD by Graphisoft | • Generative Design is the process of using AI algorithms to generate multiple design options based on predefined goals and constraints. <br> • Generative Design can help architects and designers explore a wide range of possible solutions, optimize performance and efficiency, and discover new forms and functions. <br> • The solutions can be used for various types of design problems, such as spatial layout, structural optimization, material selection, and environmental adaptation. |

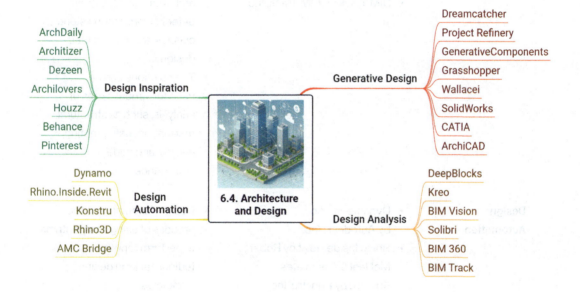

ArchDaily
Architizer
Dezeen
Archilovers
Houzz
Behance
Pinterest

**Design Inspiration**

Dynamo
Rhino.Inside.Revit
Konstru
Rhino3D
AMC Bridge

**Design Automation**

**6.4. Architecture and Design**

**Generative Design**

Dreamcatcher
Project Refinery
GenerativeComponents
Grasshopper
Wallacei
SolidWorks
CATIA
ArchiCAD

**Design Analysis**

DeepBlocks
Kreo
BIM Vision
Solibri
BIM 360
BIM Track

| AI APPLICATIONS IN ARCHITECTURE AND DESIGN | SOLUTIONS PROVIDED BY COMPANIES | SOLUTIONS DESCRIPTIONS |
| --- | --- | --- |
| **Design Analysis** | • DeepBlocks by DeepBlocks, Inc.<br>• Kreo by Kreo Software Ltd.<br>• BIM Vision by Datacomp Sp. z o.o.<br>• Solibri by Solibri, Inc.<br>• BIM 360 by Autodesk, Inc.<br>• BIM Track by BIM Track, Inc. | • Design Analysis is the process of using AI algorithms to evaluate and validate the quality, feasibility, and compliance of design models.<br>• Design Analysis can help architects and designers detect errors, inconsistencies, clashes, and risks in their designs.<br>• The solutions can be used for various types of analysis, such as structural, thermal, acoustic, lighting, energy, and code compliance. |
| **Design Automation** | • Dynamo Studio by Autodesk, Inc.<br>• Rhino.Inside.Revit by Robert McNeel & Associates<br>• Konstru by Konstru, Inc.<br>• Rhino3D by Robert McNeel & Associates<br>• AMC Bridge by AMC Bridge, Inc. | • Design Automation is the process of using AI algorithms to perform repetitive or tedious tasks in design workflows.<br>• Design Automation can help architects and designers save time, improve accuracy, and increase productivity.<br>• The solutions can be used for various types of tasks, such as data extraction, geometry creation, model conversion, parameterization, documentation, and visualization. |

| AI APPLICATIONS IN ARCHITECTURE AND DESIGN | SOLUTIONS PROVIDED BY COMPANIES | SOLUTIONS DESCRIPTIONS |
| --- | --- | --- |
| Design Inspiration | • ArchDaily by ArchDaily, Inc.<br>• Architizer by Architizer, Inc.<br>• Dezeen by Dezeen Limited<br>• Archilovers by Archilovers S.r.l.<br>• Houzz by Houzz, Inc.<br>• Behance by Adobe Inc.<br>• Pinterest by Pinterest, Inc. | • Design Inspiration is the process of using AI algorithms to discover and explore new ideas and trends in design.<br>• Design Inspiration can help architects and designers find inspiration, learn from best practices, and stay updated on the latest developments in the field.<br>• The solutions can be used for various types of inspiration, such as images, videos, articles, projects, products, and styles. |

## Key Takeaways

- AI is gradually transforming architecture and design, offering new creative possibilities and efficiencies.
- Generative Design tools use AI algorithms to generate multiple design options based on predefined goals and constraints.
- Design Analysis solutions use AI algorithms to evaluate and validate the quality, feasibility, and compliance of design models.
- Design Automation applications use AI algorithms to perform repetitive or tedious tasks in design workflows.
- Design Collaboration platforms use AI algorithms to facilitate and enhance communication and cooperation among design team members and stakeholders.
- Design Inspiration services use AI algorithms to discover and explore new ideas and trends in design.

## 6.5. CONSTRUCTION

The construction industry is one of the largest and most important sectors in the global economy, generating about 13% of the world's GDP and employing over 7% of the global workforce. The industry is responsible for creating, maintaining, and improving the built environment, which includes buildings, infrastructure, and public spaces. The industry faces many challenges, such as rising costs, labor shortages, safety risks, environmental impacts, and customer demands. To overcome these challenges, the construction industry has been increasingly adopting artificial intelligence (AI) solutions that can enhance productivity, quality, efficiency, and sustainability. AI can take many forms in construction, as shown below. For example, AI can help with planning and design, site management, safety monitoring, quality control, and predictive maintenance. AI can also enable new business models and opportunities for the construction industry, such as modular construction, digital twins, and smart buildings. AI is transforming the construction industry, creating value for stakeholders and society.

| AI APPLICATIONS IN CONSTRUCTION | SOLUTIONS PROVIDED BY COMPANIES | SOLUTIONS DESCRIPTIONS |
|---|---|---|
| Planning and Design | • ALICE by ALICE Technologies, Inc.<br>• InEight Schedule by InEight Inc.<br>• SmartBid by ConstructConnect<br>• BIM 360 by Autodesk, Inc.<br>• Bidtracer by Bidtracer<br>• PlanRadar by PlanRadar<br>• Revit by Autodesk, Inc.<br>• SketchUp by Trimble Inc. | • Planning and Design involves using AI to optimize project schedules, budgets, resources, and designs.<br>• AI can generate multiple scenarios and trade-offs based on project constraints and objectives.<br>• These solutions help construction managers and engineers plan and execute projects more efficiently and effectively. |

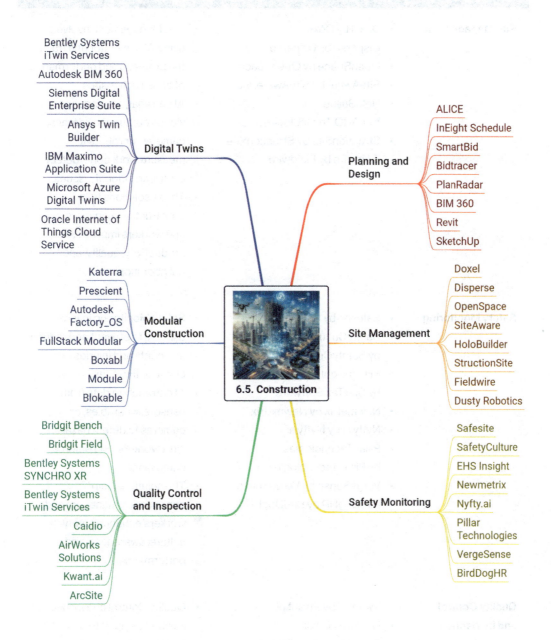

**Digital Twins**
- Bentley Systems iTwin Services
- Autodesk BIM 360
- Siemens Digital Enterprise Suite
- Ansys Twin Builder
- IBM Maximo Application Suite
- Microsoft Azure Digital Twins
- Oracle Internet of Things Cloud Service

**Modular Construction**
- Katerra
- Prescient
- Autodesk Factory_OS
- FullStack Modular
- Boxabl
- Module
- Blokable

**Quality Control and Inspection**
- Bridgit Bench
- Bridgit Field
- Bentley Systems SYNCHRO XR
- Bentley Systems iTwin Services
- Caidio
- AirWorks Solutions
- Kwant.ai
- ArcSite

**6.5. Construction**

**Planning and Design**
- ALICE
- InEight Schedule
- SmartBid
- Bidtracer
- PlanRadar
- BIM 360
- Revit
- SketchUp

**Site Management**
- Doxel
- Disperse
- OpenSpace
- SiteAware
- HoloBuilder
- StructionSite
- Fieldwire
- Dusty Robotics

**Safety Monitoring**
- Safesite
- SafetyCulture
- EHS Insight
- Newmetrix
- Nyfty.ai
- Pillar Technologies
- VergeSense
- BirdDogHR

| AI APPLICATIONS IN CONSTRUCTION | SOLUTIONS PROVIDED BY COMPANIES | SOLUTIONS DESCRIPTIONS |
|---|---|---|
| **Site Management** | • Doxel by Doxel<br>• Disperse by Disperse<br>• OpenSpace by OpenSpace<br>• SiteAware by SiteAware, Inc.<br>• HoloBuilder by FARO Technologies, Inc.<br>• StructionSite by StructionSite<br>• Fieldwire by Fieldwire | • Site Management involves using AI to monitor and track the progress and performance of constructionsites.<br>• AI can analyze images and videos captured by drones, cameras, or robots to measure work done, detect errors, and identify issues.<br>• These solutions help construction managers and workers improve site productivity, quality, and collaboration. |
| **Safety Monitoring** | • Safesite by Safesite<br>• SafetyCulture by SafetyCulture<br>• EHS Insight by StarTex Software<br>• Newmetrix by Newmetrix<br>• Nyfty.ai by Nyfty.ai<br>• Pillar Technologies by Pillar Technologies Inc.<br>• VergeSense by VergeSense<br>• BirdDogHR by BirdDogHR | • Safety Monitoring involves using AI to prevent and reduce accidents and injuries on construction sites.<br>• AI can analyze data from sensors, wearables, or cameras to detect hazards, alert workers, and enforce compliance.<br>• The solutions help construction managers and workers enhance safety culture, awareness, and performance. |
| **Quality Control and Inspection** | • Kwant.ai by Kwant.ai<br>• Caidio by Caidio<br>• Bridgit Bench by Bridgit<br>• Bridgit Field by Bridgit | • Quality Control and Inspection involves using AI to ensure that the construction work meets the required standards and specifications. |

| AI APPLICATIONS IN CONSTRUCTION | SOLUTIONS PROVIDED BY COMPANIES | SOLUTIONS DESCRIPTIONS |
|---|---|---|
| | • Bentley Systems SYNCHRO XR by Bentley Systems <br> • Bentley Systems iTwin Services by Bentley Systems <br> • AirWorks Solutions by AirWorks Solutions <br> • ArcSite by ArcSite | • AI can compare the actual work with the design models or drawings to identify defects, deviations, or errors. <br> • The solutions help construction managers and workers improve quality assurance, compliance, and customer satisfaction. |
| Modular Construction | • Prescient by Prescient Co Inc. <br> • Factory_OS by Factory_OS <br> • FullStack Modular by FullStack Modular LLC <br> • Boxabl by Boxabl Inc. <br> • Module by Module Housing Inc. | • Modular Construction involves using AI to design and manufacture standardized and prefabricated modules that can be assembled on-site. <br> • AI can optimize the module configuration, layout, and fabrication process to meet the project requirements and specifications. <br> • The solutions help construction managers and workers save time, money, and materials, as well as improve quality and sustainability. |
| Digital Twins | • Bentley Systems iTwin Services by Bentley Systems, Incorporated <br> • Autodesk BIM 360 by Autodesk, Inc. <br> • Siemens Digital Enterprise Suite by Siemens AG <br> • Ansys Twin Builder by Ansys Inc. | • Digital Twins involve using AI to create and maintain virtual replicas of physical assets, systems, or processes. <br> • AI can simulate the behavior and performance of the real-world counterparts under various scenarios and conditions. |

| AI APPLICATIONS IN CONSTRUCTION | SOLUTIONS PROVIDED BY COMPANIES | SOLUTIONS DESCRIPTIONS |
|---|---|---|
| | • Microsoft Azure Digital Twins by Microsoft Corporation<br>• Oracle Internet of Things Cloud Service by Oracle Corporation<br>• IBM Maximo Application Suite by IBM Corporation | • The solutions help construction managers and workers optimize design, operation, maintenance, and management of the built environment. |

## Key Takeaways

- The construction industry, a major global economic contributor, is leveraging AI to enhance productivity, quality, and sustainability.
- Planning and Design solutions optimize project schedules, budgets, and resources through AI-generated scenarios.
- Site Management tools use AI to monitor and track construction site progress, enhancing productivity and collaboration.
- Safety Monitoring applications employ AI to prevent accidents, analyzing data from sensors and cameras.
- Quality Control and Inspection solutions use AI to ensure construction work meets standards and specifications.
- Modular Construction platforms optimize design and fabrication, saving time, money, and materials.
- Digital Twins technology creates virtual replicas to simulate real-world assets and optimize their performance.

## 6.6. REAL ESTATE DEVELOPMENT

The real estate development industry involves the purchase of raw land, rezoning, construction and renovation of buildings, and sale or lease of the finished product to end users. Developers earn a profit by adding value to the land and taking the risk of financing a project. This industry is constantly evolving and adapting to changes in the market, such as shifts in demand for different types of properties and changes in economic conditions. Despite the challenges, real estate continues to attract capital and demonstrate its stability and appeal over other asset classes. Artificial intelligence (AI) is a powerful tool that can enhance the efficiency, effectiveness, and innovation of real estate development. AI can assist developers in various aspects of their work, such as site selection, market analysis, pricing optimization, and legal automation. AI can also enable new business models and opportunities for the real estate development industry, such as crowdfunding, tokenization, and smart contracts. AI is reshaping the industry, creating value for developers and customers.

| AI APPLICATIONS IN REAL ESTATE DEVELOPMENT | SOLUTIONS PROVIDED BY COMPANIES | SOLUTIONS DESCRIPTIONS |
|---|---|---|
| Site Selection | • CityBldr by CityBldr, Inc.<br>• Land Intelligence by Land Intelligence, Inc.<br>• LandVision by Lightbox Holdings LP<br>• Sitely by Sitely, LLC<br>• SiteSeer Pro by SiteSeer<br>• Regrid by Regrid<br>• Reonomy by Reonomy, an Altus Group Company<br>• Cherre by Cherre, Inc.<br>• CoreLogic Growth Solutions by CoreLogic, Inc.<br>• Tango Predictive Analytics by Tango<br>• Location Intelligence by Kalibrate Technologies Ltd | • Site Selection involves using AI to identify and evaluate potential sites for development projects.<br>• AI can analyze data from various sources, such as zoning regulations, environmental factors, market demand, and property characteristics.<br>• These solutions help developers find the best locations, assess feasibility, and reduce risk. |

| AI APPLICATIONS IN REAL ESTATE DEVELOPMENT | SOLUTIONS PROVIDED BY COMPANIES | SOLUTIONS DESCRIPTIONS |
| --- | --- | --- |
| **Market Analysis** | • HouseCanary by HouseCanary, Inc.<br>• Mashvisor by Mashvisor, Inc.<br>• Reonomy by Reonomy, an Altus Group Company<br>• Cherre by Cherre, Inc.<br>• Zillow Zestimate by Zillow Group, Inc.<br>• AirDNA by AirDNA, LLC<br>• Rentometer by Rentometer, Inc. | • Market Analysis involves using AI to understand and predict the trends and dynamics of the real estate market.<br>• AI can provide data and insights on property values, rental rates, occupancy rates, supply and demand, and customer preferences.<br>• The solutions help developers make informed decisions, optimize strategies, and increase profitability. |
| **Pricing Optimization** | • Livly Pricing Engine by Livly, Inc.<br>• Rentlytics by RealPage, Inc.<br>• Opendoor by Opendoor Labs, Inc.<br>• Kelvin Home Value Estimator by Kelvin, Inc. | • Pricing Optimization involves using AI to determine the optimal price for selling or rentjuroing properties.<br>• AI can use data-driven models to estimate the fair market value of properties, taking into account various factors such as location, size, condition, amenities, and competition.<br>• The solutions help developers maximize revenue, minimize vacancy, and attract customers. |
| **Legal Automation** | • Leverton by MRI Software, LLC<br>• Kira Systems by Kira Systems, Inc.<br>• Luminance by Luminance Technologies, Ltd. | • Legal Automation involves using AI to automate and streamline various legal processes related to real estate development. |

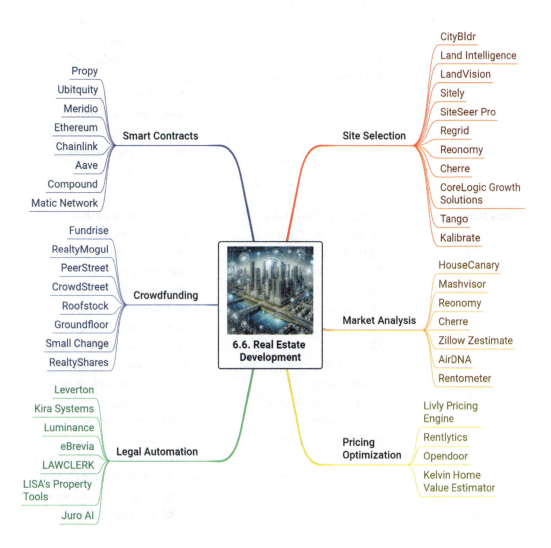

Smart Contracts
- Propy
- Ubitquity
- Meridio
- Ethereum
- Chainlink
- Aave
- Compound
- Matic Network

Crowdfunding
- Fundrise
- RealtyMogul
- PeerStreet
- CrowdStreet
- Roofstock
- Groundfloor
- Small Change
- RealtyShares

Legal Automation
- Leverton
- Kira Systems
- Luminance
- eBrevia
- LAWCLERK
- LISA's Property Tools
- Juro AI

**6.6. Real Estate Development**

Site Selection
- CityBldr
- Land Intelligence
- LandVision
- Sitely
- SiteSeer Pro
- Regrid
- Reonomy
- Cherre
- CoreLogic Growth Solutions
- Tango
- Kalibrate

Market Analysis
- HouseCanary
- Mashvisor
- Reonomy
- Cherre
- Zillow Zestimate
- AirDNA
- Rentometer

Pricing Optimization
- Livly Pricing Engine
- Rentlytics
- Opendoor
- Kelvin Home Value Estimator

| AI APPLICATIONS IN REAL ESTATE DEVELOPMENT | SOLUTIONS PROVIDED BY COMPANIES | SOLUTIONS DESCRIPTIONS |
|---|---|---|
| | • eBrevia by Donnelley Financial Solutions, Inc.<br>• LAWCLERK by LAWCLERK.Legal<br>• LISA's Property Tools by Robot Lawyer LISA<br>• Juro AI by Juro | • AI can extract and analyze information from contracts, leases, deeds, and other documents; generate legal documents; and provide legal advice.<br>• The solutions help developers save time, money, and resources; reduce errors; and ensure compliance. |
| Crowdfunding | • Fundrise by Fundrise, LLC<br>• RealtyMogul by RealtyMogul.com, LLC<br>• PeerStreet by PeerStreet, Inc.<br>• CrowdStreet by CrowdStreet, Inc.<br>• Roofstock by Roofstock, Inc.<br>• Groundfloor by Groundfloor Finance, Inc.<br>• Small Change by Small Change, LLC<br>• RealtyShares by RealtyShares, Inc. | • Crowdfunding involves using AI to connect real estate developers with investors who can fund their projects.<br>• AI can match developers with suitable investors based on their preferences, risk profiles, and goals; provide data and analytics on the projects; and facilitate transactions and communication.<br>• The solutions help developers raise capital, diversify funding sources, and access a wider pool of investors. |
| Smart Contracts | • Propy by Propy, Inc.<br>• Ubitquity by Ubitquity, LLC<br>• Meridio by Meridio<br>• Ethereum by Ethereum Foundation | • Smart Contracts involve using AI to execute and enforce agreements between parties in real estate transactions. |

| AI APPLICATIONS IN REAL ESTATE DEVELOPMENT | SOLUTIONS PROVIDED BY COMPANIES | SOLUTIONS DESCRIPTIONS |
| --- | --- | --- |
| | • Chainlink by Chainlink Labs<br>• Aave by Aave, Ltd.<br>• Compound by Compound Labs, Inc.<br>• Matic Network by Matic Network | • AI can use blockchain technology to create self-executing contracts that are triggered by predefined conditions and events; provide trust and verification; and reduce intermediaries and fees.<br>• The solutions help developers simplify processes, increase efficiency, and ensure compliance. |

*Key Takeaways*

- The real estate development industry is leveraging AI for site selection, market analysis, pricing optimization, legal automation, crowdfunding, and smart contracts.
- Site Selection tools use AI to analyze zoning, environmental factors, and market demand, aiding in finding optimal locations.
- Market Analysis solutions leverage AI for insights on property values, rental rates, and market trends, guiding informed decisions.
- Pricing Optimization platforms utilize AI-driven models for optimal selling or rental prices, maximizing revenue and minimizing vacancy.
- Legal Automation applications streamline legal processes, extracting information from contracts, saving time and resources.
- Crowdfunding platforms use AI to connect developers with investors, facilitating transactions and providing project data, diversifying funding sources.
- Smart Contracts technology uses AI to execute and enforce agreements, ensuring efficiency, transparency, and compliance.

# CHAPTER 7
# MANAGE THE PROPERTY

Property management, an essential aspect of real estate, involves overseeing and maintaining properties to ensure they function efficiently and retain their value. Traditionally, it has been a labor-intensive and sometimes complex process, involving numerous tasks, from tenant relations to facility maintenance.

Artificial Intelligence (AI) is revolutionizing property management, making it more efficient, cost-effective, and tenant-friendly. This chapter explores the ways in which AI is transforming property management and enhancing the experience for both property owners and tenants.

AI-powered property management systems optimize tasks such as rent collection, maintenance scheduling, and communication with tenants. AI chatbots and virtual assistants handle routine inquiries, freeing up property managers to focus on more complex issues. These technologies ensure a more streamlined and responsive property management process.

Real estate portfolio management benefits from AI's predictive analytics and data-driven insights. Property managers can make informed decisions about property acquisitions, divestitures, and ongoing operations based on AI-generated recommendations.

AI also plays a crucial role in security and safety. Smart surveillance systems with AI capabilities can detect security threats and emergencies, enhancing property safety. Furthermore, AI-driven asset management solutions offer insights into property performance, helping property owners optimize their portfolios.

This chapter explores the myriad ways in which AI is enhancing property management, from streamlining administrative tasks to improving tenant satisfaction. By delving into these transformations, we gain a deeper understanding of how AI is reshaping the real estate industry.

## 7.1.   PROPERTY MANAGEMENT

Property management is the process of overseeing the operation, maintenance, and leasing of real estate properties. Property managers are responsible for ensuring that the properties under their care are safe, functional, and profitable. They can work with various types of properties, such as residential, commercial, industrial, or mixed-use. Property management is a challenging and dynamic industry that requires a high level of expertise, communication, and problem-solving skills. Artificial intelligence (AI) is a powerful tool that can enhance the efficiency, effectiveness, and innovation of property management. AI can assist property managers in various aspects of their work, such as tenant screening, rent collection, maintenance requests, energy efficiency, and market analysis. AI can help property managers reduce costs, increase revenue, improve customer satisfaction, and optimize performance. AI can also enable property managers to create more sustainable and livable environments that meet the needs and preferences of the tenants.

| AI APPLICATIONS IN PROPERTY MANAGEMENT | SOLUTIONS PROVIDED BY COMPANIES | SOLUTIONS DESCRIPTIONS |
|---|---|---|
| **Tenant Screening** | • Rentberry by Rentberry, Inc.<br>• TurboTenant by TurboTenant, Inc.<br>• LeaseRunner by LeaseRunner, Inc.<br>• Cozy by Cozy Services, Ltd.<br>• Zumper by Zumper, Inc.<br>• Avail by Avail Software, LLC<br>• TenantCloud by TenantCloud, LLC<br>• RentPrep by RentPrep, a Roofstock Company | • Tenant Screening is the process of evaluating potential tenants for a rental property.<br>• Tenant Screening uses AI algorithms to analyze various data sources, such as credit reports, background checks, income verification, and references.<br>• These solutions help property managers find qualified and reliable tenants that match their property criteria and expectations. |
| **Rent Collection** | • PayRent by PayRent, LLC<br>• RentRedi by RentRedi, Inc.<br>• Hemlane by Hemlane, Inc. | • Rent Collection is the process of collecting rent payments from tenants on a regular basis. |

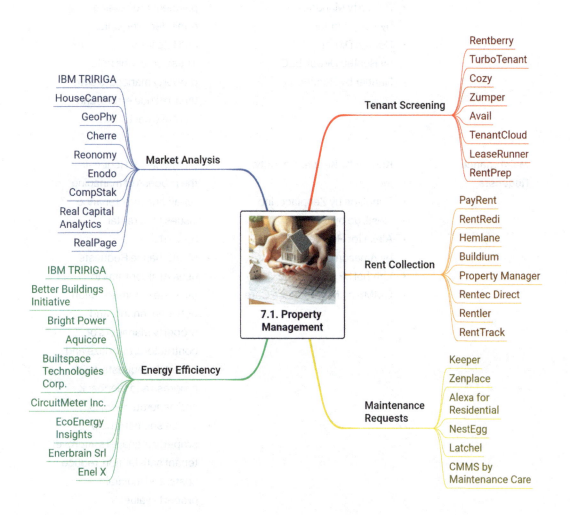

**Market Analysis**
- IBM TRIRIGA
- HouseCanary
- GeoPhy
- Cherre
- Reonomy
- Enodo
- CompStak
- Real Capital Analytics
- RealPage

**Energy Efficiency**
- IBM TRIRIGA
- Better Buildings Initiative
- Bright Power
- Aquicore
- Builtspace Technologies Corp.
- CircuitMeter Inc.
- EcoEnergy Insights
- Enerbrain Srl
- Enel X

**7.1. Property Management**

**Tenant Screening**
- Rentberry
- TurboTenant
- Cozy
- Zumper
- Avail
- TenantCloud
- LeaseRunner
- RentPrep

**Rent Collection**
- PayRent
- RentRedi
- Hemlane
- Buildium
- Property Manager
- Rentec Direct
- Rentler
- RentTrack

**Maintenance Requests**
- Keeper
- Zenplace
- Alexa for Residential
- NestEgg
- Latchel
- CMMS by Maintenance Care

| AI APPLICATIONS IN PROPERTY MANAGEMENT | SOLUTIONS PROVIDED BY COMPANIES | SOLUTIONS DESCRIPTIONS |
|---|---|---|
| | • Buildium by Buildium, A RealPage Company<br>• Property Manager by AppFolio, Inc.<br>• Rentec Direct by Rentec Direct, LLC<br>• Rentler by Rentler, Inc. | • Rent Collection uses AI algorithms to automate payment processing, reminders, receipts, and late fees.<br>• These solutions help property managers save time, reduce errors, and increase cash flow. |
| **Maintenance Requests** | • Keeper by Keeper Security, Inc.<br>• Zenplace by Zenplace, Inc.<br>• NestEgg by NestEgg<br>• Alexa for Residential by Amazon.com, Inc.<br>• Latchel by Latchel, Inc.<br>• CMMS by Maintenance Care | • Maintenance Requests is the process of managing repair and maintenance issues for a rental property.<br>• Maintenance Requests uses AI algorithms to facilitate communication between tenants and property managers or contractors, prioritize and schedule requests, track progress and feedback, and generate reports.<br>• These solutions help property managers improve tenant satisfaction, reduce costs, and maintain property value. |
| **Energy Efficiency** | • Bright Power by Bright Power, Inc.<br>• Builtspace Technologies Corp. by Builtspace Technologies Corp. | • Energy Efficiency is the process of reducing energy consumption and greenhouse gas emissions for a rental property. |

| AI APPLICATIONS IN PROPERTY MANAGEMENT | SOLUTIONS PROVIDED BY COMPANIES | SOLUTIONS DESCRIPTIONS |
| --- | --- | --- |
| | • Aquicore by Aquicore, Inc.<br>• CircuitMeter Inc. by CircuitMeter Inc.<br>• EcoEnergy Insights by EcoEnergy Insights, a part of Carrier Global Corporation<br>• Enerbrain Srl by Enerbrain Srl<br>• IBM TRIRIGA by IBM Corporation<br>• Better Buildings Initiative by U.S. Department of Energy<br>• Enel X by Enel X North America, Inc. | • Energy Efficiency uses AI algorithms to monitor and optimize energy usage, identify and correct inefficiencies, provide recommendations and incentives, and integrate with smart devices.<br>• These solutions help property managers save money, enhance tenant comfort, and comply with environmental regulations. |
| **Market Analysis** | • HouseCanary by HouseCanary, Inc.<br>• GeoPhy by GeoPhy, a Walker & Dunlop Company<br>• Cherre by Cherre, Inc.<br>• Reonomy by Reonomy, an Altus Group Company<br>• Enodo by Enodo, Inc., a Walker & Dunlop Company<br>• CompStak by CompStak, Inc.<br>• IBM TRIRIGA by IBM Corporation | • Market Analysis is the process of researching and evaluating the current and future trends and opportunities in the real estate market.<br>• Market Analysis uses AI algorithms to collect and analyze various data sources, such as property listings, sales transactions, rental rates, occupancy rates, demographics, and economic indicators.<br>• These solutions help property managers make informed decisions, identify risks and opportunities, and optimize pricing and marketing strategies. |

## Key Takeaways

- Property management is evolving through AI applications like tenant screening, rent collection, maintenance requests, energy efficiency, and market analysis.

- Tenant Screening tools use AI to assess credit reports, background checks, and references, aiding property managers in finding reliable tenants.

- Rent Collection solutions employ AI for automated payment processing, reminders, and late fees, streamlining collections and enhancing cash flow.

- Maintenance Requests platforms leverage AI algorithms to manage repairs, improving communication, prioritizing requests, and reducing costs.

- Energy Efficiency applications use AI to optimize energy usage, identify inefficiencies, and provide recommendations, helping property managers save costs and meet environmental standards.

- Market Analysis tools use AI to analyze property data, aiding property managers in making informed decisions and optimizing pricing strategies.

## 7.2. TENANT MANAGEMENT

Tenant management is the process of managing the relationship between landlords and tenants. Tenant management involves various tasks, such as marketing vacancies, screening applicants, signing leases, collecting rent, handling complaints, resolving disputes, and conducting inspections. Tenant management is a crucial and challenging aspect of the real estate industry that requires a high level of customer service, communication, and problem-solving skills. Artificial intelligence (AI) is a powerful tool that can enhance the efficiency, effectiveness, and innovation of tenant management. AI can assist landlords and property managers in various aspects of their work, such as tenant screening, rent collection, maintenance requests, tenant retention, and tenant satisfaction. AI can help landlords and property managers reduce costs, increase revenue, improve efficiency, and optimize performance. AI can also enable landlords and property managers to create more personalized and engaging experiences for their tenants.

| AI APPLICATIONS IN TENANT MANAGEMENT | SOLUTIONS PROVIDED BY COMPANIES | SOLUTIONS DESCRIPTIONS |
|---|---|---|
| Tenant Screening | • Rentberry by Rentberry, Inc.<br>• TurboTenant by TurboTenant, Inc.<br>• LeaseRunner by LeaseRunner, Inc.<br>• Cozy by Cozy Services, Ltd.<br>• Zumper by Zumper, Inc.<br>• Avail by Avail Software, LLC<br>• TenantCloud by TenantCloud, LLC<br>• RentPrep by RentPrep, a Roofstock Company | • Tenant Screening is the process of evaluating potential tenants for a rental property.<br>• Tenant Screening uses AI algorithms to analyze various data sources, such as credit reports, background checks, income verification, and references.<br>• These solutions help landlords and property managers find qualified and reliable tenants that match their property criteria and expectations. |

| AI APPLICATIONS IN TENANT MANAGEMENT | SOLUTIONS PROVIDED BY COMPANIES | SOLUTIONS DESCRIPTIONS |
|---|---|---|
| **Rent Collection** | • PayRent by PayRent, LLC<br>• RentRedi by RentRedi, Inc.<br>• Hemlane by Hemlane, Inc.<br>• Buildium by Buildium, A RealPage Company<br>• Property Manager by AppFolio, Inc.<br>• Rentec Direct by Rentec Direct, LLC<br>• Rentler by Rentler, Inc. | • Rent Collection is the process of collecting rent payments from tenants on a regular basis.<br>• Rent Collection uses AI algorithms to automate payment processing, reminders, receipts, and late fees.<br>• These solutions help landlords and property managers save time, reduce errors, and increase cash flow. |
| **Maintenance Requests** | • Keeper by Keeper Security, Inc.<br>• Zenplace by Zenplace, Inc.<br>• NestEgg by NestEgg<br>• Alexa for Residential by Amazon.com, Inc.<br>• Latchel by Latchel, Inc.<br>• CMMS by Maintenance Care | • Maintenance Requests is the process of managing repair and maintenance issues for a rental property.<br>• Maintenance Requests uses AI algorithms to facilitate communication between tenants and landlords or property managers or contractors, prioritize and schedule requests, track progress and feedback, and generate reports.<br>• These solutions help landlords and property managers improve tenant satisfaction, reduce costs, and maintain property value. |

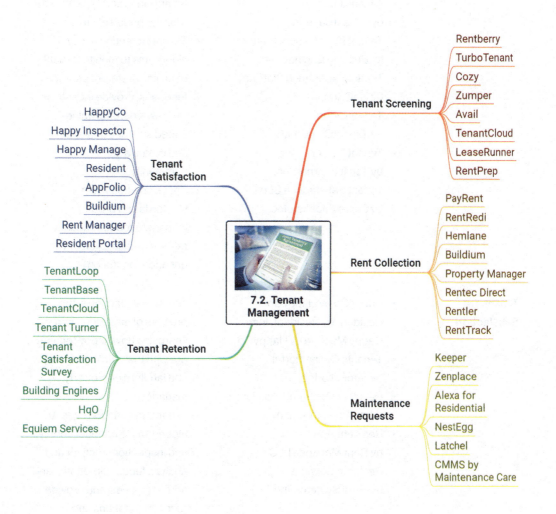

**Tenant Satisfaction**
- HappyCo
- Happy Inspector
- Happy Manage
- Resident
- AppFolio
- Buildium
- Rent Manager
- Resident Portal

**Tenant Retention**
- TenantLoop
- TenantBase
- TenantCloud
- Tenant Turner
- Tenant Satisfaction Survey
- Building Engines
- HqO
- Equiem Services

**7.2. Tenant Management**

**Tenant Screening**
- Rentberry
- TurboTenant
- Cozy
- Zumper
- Avail
- TenantCloud
- LeaseRunner
- RentPrep

**Rent Collection**
- PayRent
- RentRedi
- Hemlane
- Buildium
- Property Manager
- Rentec Direct
- Rentler
- RentTrack

**Maintenance Requests**
- Keeper
- Zenplace
- Alexa for Residential
- NestEgg
- Latchel
- CMMS by Maintenance Care

| AI APPLICATIONS IN TENANT MANAGEMENT | SOLUTIONS PROVIDED BY COMPANIES | SOLUTIONS DESCRIPTIONS |
|---|---|---|
| **Tenant Retention** | • TenantLoop by TenantLoop, LLC<br>• TenantBase by TenantBase, Inc.<br>• Tenant Engagement Platform by Building Engines, Inc.<br>• Tenant Experience Platform by HqO, Inc.<br>• TenantCloud by TenantCloud, LLC<br>• Tenant Turner by Tenant Turner, Inc.<br>• Tenant Satisfaction Survey by SurveyMonkey, Inc. | • Tenant Retention is the process of keeping existing tenants in a rental property for a longer period of time.<br>• Tenant Retention uses AI algorithms to monitor tenant behavior, preferences, and feedback, provide incentives and rewards, offer value-added services and amenities, and create a sense of community.<br>• These solutions help landlords and property managers reduce vacancy rates, increase loyalty, and enhance reputation. |
| **Tenant Satisfaction** | • HappyCo by HappyCo<br>• Resident by Resident, Inc.<br>• Happy Manage by HappyCo<br>• Tenants Online Portal by AppFolio, Inc.<br>• Resident Center by Buildium, A RealPage Company<br>• Resident App by Rent Manager, LLC<br>• Resident Services by Yardi Systems, Inc. | • Tenant Satisfaction is the process of measuring and improving how happy tenants are with their rental property and landlord or property manager.<br>• Tenant Satisfaction uses AI algorithms to conduct surveys and inspections, collect and analyze feedback, identify and address issues, and provide recommendations and solutions.<br>• These solutions help landlords and property managers increase tenant satisfaction, retention, and referrals. |

*Key Takeaways*

- Tenant Management, essential for landlords and property managers, is evolving with AI applications such as tenant screening, rent collection, maintenance requests, tenant retention, and tenant satisfaction.

- Tenant Screening tools use AI to assess credit reports, background checks, and references, aiding landlords and property managers in selecting reliable tenants.

- Rent Collection solutions employ AI for automated payment processing, reminders, and late fees, streamlining collections and enhancing cash flow.

- Maintenance Requests platforms leverage AI algorithms to manage repairs, improving communication, prioritizing requests, and reducing costs for landlords and property managers.

- Tenant Retention applications use AI to monitor tenant behavior, preferences, and feedback, reducing vacancy rates and increasing loyalty.

- Tenant Satisfaction tools leverage AI for conducting surveys and inspections, analyzing feedback, addressing issues, and improving overall tenant satisfaction, retention, and referrals.

## 7.3.   REAL ESTATE PORTFOLIO MANAGEMENT

Real estate portfolio management is the process of managing a collection of real estate assets to achieve specific investment objectives. Real estate portfolio managers are responsible for selecting, acquiring, disposing, and optimizing real estate properties that match the risk-return profile and diversification strategy of their investors. Real estate portfolio management is a complex and dynamic industry that requires a high level of expertise, capital, and creativity. Artificial intelligence (AI) is a powerful tool that can enhance various aspects of the real estate portfolio management process, such as market analysis, property valuation, portfolio optimization, risk management, and performance measurement. AI can help real estate portfolio managers reduce costs, increase returns, improve efficiency, and optimize performance. AI can also enable real estate portfolio managers to create more sustainable and resilient portfolios that meet the needs and preferences of their investors.

| AI APPLICATIONS IN REAL ESTATE PORTFOLIO MANAGEMENT | SOLUTIONS PROVIDED BY COMPANIES | SOLUTIONS DESCRIPTIONS |
|---|---|---|
| Market Analysis | • HouseCanary by HouseCanary, Inc.<br>• GeoPhy by GeoPhy, a Walker & Dunlop Company<br>• Cherre by Cherre, Inc.<br>• Reonomy by Reonomy, an Altus Group Company<br>• Enodo by Enodo, Inc., a Walker & Dunlop Company<br>• CompStak by CompStak, Inc. | • Market Analysis is the process of researching and evaluating the current and future trends and opportunities in the real estate market.<br>• Market Analysis uses AI algorithms to collect and analyze various data sources, such as property listings, sales transactions, rental rates, occupancy rates, demographics, and economic indicators.<br>• These solutions help real estate portfolio managers make informed decisions, identify risks and opportunities, and optimize pricing and marketing strategies. |

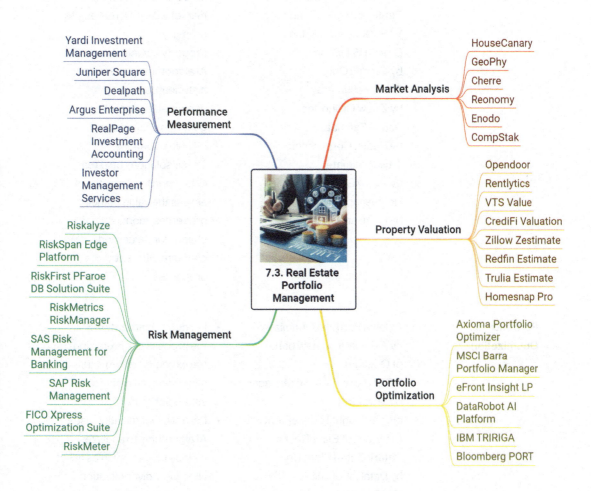

**Performance Measurement**
- Yardi Investment Management
- Juniper Square
- Dealpath
- Argus Enterprise
- RealPage Investment Accounting
- Investor Management Services

**Risk Management**
- Riskalyze
- RiskSpan Edge Platform
- RiskFirst PFaroe DB Solution Suite
- RiskMetrics RiskManager
- SAS Risk Management for Banking
- SAP Risk Management
- FICO Xpress Optimization Suite
- RiskMeter

**7.3. Real Estate Portfolio Management**

**Market Analysis**
- HouseCanary
- GeoPhy
- Cherre
- Reonomy
- Enodo
- CompStak

**Property Valuation**
- Opendoor
- Rentlytics
- VTS Value
- CrediFi Valuation
- Zillow Zestimate
- Redfin Estimate
- Trulia Estimate
- Homesnap Pro

**Portfolio Optimization**
- Axioma Portfolio Optimizer
- MSCI Barra Portfolio Manager
- eFront Insight LP
- DataRobot AI Platform
- IBM TRIRIGA
- Bloomberg PORT

| AI APPLICATIONS IN REAL ESTATE PORTFOLIO MANAGEMENT | SOLUTIONS PROVIDED BY COMPANIES | SOLUTIONS DESCRIPTIONS |
|---|---|---|
| **Property Valuation** | • Opendoor by Opendoor Labs, Inc.<br>• Rentlytics by RealPage, Inc.<br>• VTS Value by VTS, Inc.<br>• CrediFi Valuation by CrediFi Corp.<br>• Zillow Zestimate by Zillow Group, Inc.<br>• Redfin Estimate by Redfin Corporation<br>• Trulia Estimate by Zillow Group, Inc.<br>• Homesnap Pro by Homesnap, Inc. | • Property Valuation is the process of estimating the market value of a real estate property.<br>• Property Valuation uses AI algorithms to leverage historical data and comparable properties to generate accurate and reliable valuations.<br>• These solutions help real estate portfolio managers assess the value of their properties, monitor changes in value, and compare different properties. |
| **Portfolio Optimization** | • Axioma Portfolio Optimizer by Axioma, Inc. (now part of Qontigo)<br>• MSCI Barra Portfolio Manager by MSCI, Inc.<br>• eFront Insight LP by eFront SA (now part of BlackRock)<br>• DataRobot AI Platform by DataRobot, Inc.<br>• IBM TRIRIGA by IBM Corporation<br>• Bloomberg PORT by Bloomberg L.P. | • Portfolio Optimization is the process of maximizing the expected return and minimizing the risk of a real estate portfolio.<br>• Portfolio Optimization uses AI algorithms to analyze various factors, such as asset allocation, diversification, correlation, volatility, and liquidity.<br>• These solutions help real estate portfolio managers optimize their portfolio composition, performance, and risk-adjusted returns. |

| AI APPLICATIONS IN REAL ESTATE PORTFOLIO MANAGEMENT | SOLUTIONS PROVIDED BY COMPANIES | SOLUTIONS DESCRIPTIONS |
| --- | --- | --- |
| Risk Management | • Riskalyze by Riskalyze, Inc.<br>• RiskSpan Edge Platform by RiskSpan, Inc.<br>• RiskFirst PFaroe DB Solution Suite by RiskFirst Group Limited<br>• RiskMetrics RiskManager by MSCI, Inc.<br>• SAS Risk Management for Banking by SAS Institute<br>• SAP Risk Management by SAP SE<br>• FICO Xpress Optimization Suite by Fair Isaac Corporation<br>• RiskMeter by CoreLogic, Inc. | • Risk Management is the process of identifying, measuring, and mitigating the potential losses or uncertainties associated with a real estate portfolio.<br>• Risk Management uses AI algorithms to model various scenarios, such as market fluctuations, interest rate changes, regulatory changes, and natural disasters.<br>• These solutions help real estate portfolio managers manage their exposure, hedge their risks, and comply with regulations. |
| Performance Measurement | • Yardi Investment Management by Yardi Systems, Inc.<br>• Juniper Square by Juniper Square, Inc.<br>• Dealpath by Dealpath, Inc.<br>• Argus Enterprise by Altus Group Limited<br>• RealPage Investment Accounting by RealPage, Inc.<br>• Investor Management Services by Investor Management Services, LLC | • Performance Measurement is the process of evaluating the financial performance and return on investment of a real estate portfolio.<br>• Performance Measurement uses AI algorithms to calculate various metrics, such as net operating income, cash flow, internal rate of return, net present value, and capitalization rate.<br>• These solutions help real estate portfolio managers track and report their portfolio performance, benchmark against peers or indices, and communicate with investors. |

*Key Takeaways*

- AI is transforming Real Estate Portfolio Management, impacting key areas such as Market Analysis, Property Valuation, Portfolio Optimization, Risk Management, and Performance Measurement.
- Market Analysis tools use AI to collect and analyze data, aiding in decision-making, risk assessment, and optimization of pricing and marketing strategies.
- Property Valuation platforms utilize AI to leverage historical data and comparable properties, generating accurate and reliable property value estimations, supporting portfolio managers in assessment and decision-making.
- Portfolio Optimization solutions leverage AI to analyze factors like asset allocation and diversification, optimizing portfolio composition and performance.
- Risk Management tools use AI to model scenarios, helping portfolio managers identify, measure, and mitigate potential losses or uncertainties.
- Performance Measurement platforms use AI algorithms to calculate financial metrics, aiding in evaluating and communicating portfolio performance.

## 7.4. ASSET MANAGEMENT

Asset management is the process of managing the investments of individuals, institutions, or governments to achieve specific financial goals. Asset managers are responsible for selecting, allocating, and monitoring various types of assets, such as stocks, bonds, commodities, real estate, and alternative investments. Asset management is a competitive and dynamic industry that requires a high level of expertise, analysis, and innovation. Artificial intelligence (AI) is a powerful tool that can enhance various aspects of the asset management process, such as market analysis, portfolio optimization, risk management, performance measurement, and client service. AI can help asset managers reduce costs, increase returns, improve efficiency, and optimize performance. AI can also enable asset managers to create more customized and diversified portfolios that meet the needs and preferences of their clients.

| AI APPLICATIONS IN ASSET MANAGEMENT | SOLUTIONS PROVIDED BY COMPANIES | SOLUTIONS DESCRIPTIONS |
| --- | --- | --- |
| Market Analysis | • DataRobot AI Platform by DataRobot, Inc.<br>• Axioma Portfolio Optimizer by Axioma, Inc. (now part of Qontigo)<br>• MSCI Barra Portfolio Manager by MSCI, Inc.<br>• Bloomberg PORT by Bloomberg L.P.<br>• Morningstar Direct by Morningstar, Inc.<br>• eFront Insight LP by eFront SA (now part of BlackRock) | • Market Analysis is the process of researching and evaluating the current and future trends and opportunities in the financial market.<br>• Market Analysis uses AI algorithms to collect and analyze various data sources, such as market prices, news articles, social media posts, and economic indicators.<br>• These solutions help asset managers make informed decisions, identify risks and opportunities, and optimize pricing and trading strategies. |

| AI APPLICATIONS IN ASSET MANAGEMENT | SOLUTIONS PROVIDED BY COMPANIES | SOLUTIONS DESCRIPTIONS |
|---|---|---|
| Portfolio Optimization | • DataRobot AI Platform by DataRobot, Inc.<br>• Axioma Portfolio Optimizer by Axioma, Inc. (now part of Qontigo)<br>• RiskFirst PFaroe DB Solution Suite by RiskFirst Group Limited<br>• Riskalyze by Riskalyze, Inc.<br>• RiskSpan Edge Platform by RiskSpan, Inc.<br>• RiskMetrics RiskManager by MSCI, Inc.<br>• SAS Risk Management Software by SAS Institute<br>• SAP Risk Management by SAP SE<br>• FICO Xpress Optimization Suite by Fair Isaac Corporation | • Portfolio Optimization is the process of maximizing the expected return and minimizing the risk of an investment portfolio.<br>• Portfolio Optimization uses AI algorithms to analyze various factors, such as asset allocation, diversification, correlation, volatility, and liquidity.<br>• These solutions help asset managers optimize their portfolio composition, performance, and risk-adjusted returns. |
| Risk Management | • Riskalyze by Riskalyze, Inc.<br>• RiskSpan Edge Platform by RiskSpan, Inc.<br>• RiskFirst PFaroe DB Solution Suite by RiskFirst Group Limited<br>• RiskMetrics RiskManager by MSCI, Inc.<br>• SAS Risk Management Software by SAS Institute<br>• SAP Risk Management by SAP SE<br>• FICO Xpress Optimization Suite by Fair Isaac Corporation | • Risk Management is the process of identifying, measuring, and mitigating the potential losses or uncertainties associated with an investment portfolio.<br>• Risk Management uses AI algorithms to model various scenarios, such as market fluctuations, interest rate changes, regulatory changes, and natural disasters.<br>• These solutions help asset managers manage their exposure, hedge their risks, and comply with regulations. |

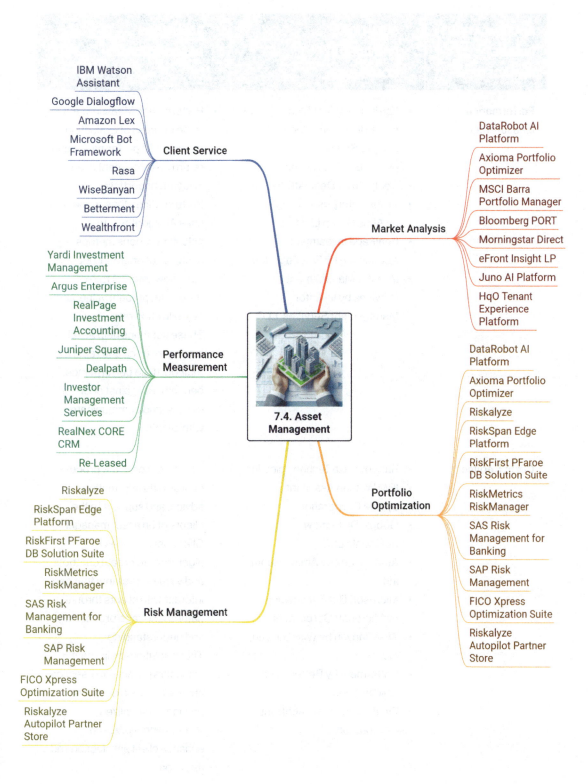

**Client Service**
- IBM Watson Assistant
- Google Dialogflow
- Amazon Lex
- Microsoft Bot Framework
- Rasa
- WiseBanyan
- Betterment
- Wealthfront

**Market Analysis**
- DataRobot AI Platform
- Axioma Portfolio Optimizer
- MSCI Barra Portfolio Manager
- Bloomberg PORT
- Morningstar Direct
- eFront Insight LP
- Juno AI Platform
- HqO Tenant Experience Platform

**Performance Measurement**
- Yardi Investment Management
- Argus Enterprise
- RealPage Investment Accounting
- Juniper Square
- Dealpath
- Investor Management Services
- RealNex CORE CRM
- Re-Leased

**7.4. Asset Management**

**Portfolio Optimization**
- DataRobot AI Platform
- Axioma Portfolio Optimizer
- Riskalyze
- RiskSpan Edge Platform
- RiskFirst PFaroe DB Solution Suite
- RiskMetrics RiskManager
- SAS Risk Management for Banking
- SAP Risk Management
- FICO Xpress Optimization Suite
- Riskalyze Autopilot Partner Store

**Risk Management**
- Riskalyze
- RiskSpan Edge Platform
- RiskFirst PFaroe DB Solution Suite
- RiskMetrics RiskManager
- SAS Risk Management for Banking
- SAP Risk Management
- FICO Xpress Optimization Suite
- Riskalyze Autopilot Partner Store

| AI APPLICATIONS IN ASSET MANAGEMENT | SOLUTIONS PROVIDED BY COMPANIES | SOLUTIONS DESCRIPTIONS |
|---|---|---|
| Performance Measurement | • Yardi Investment Management by Yardi Systems, Inc.<br>• Juniper Square by Juniper Square, Inc.<br>• Dealpath by Dealpath, Inc.<br>• Argus Enterprise by Altus Group Limited<br>• RealPage Investment Accounting by RealPage, Inc.<br>• Investor Management Services by Investor Management Services, LLC | • Performance Measurement is the process of evaluating the financial performance and return on investment of an investment portfolio.<br>• Performance Measurement uses AI algorithms to calculate various metrics, such as net operating income, cash flow, internal rate of return, net present value, and capitalization rate.<br>• These solutions help asset managers track and report their portfolio performance, benchmark against peers or indices, and communicate with clients. |
| Client Service | • Rasa by Rasa Technologies, Inc.<br>• IBM Watson Assistant by IBM Corporation<br>• Google Dialogflow by Google LLC<br>• Amazon Lex by Amazon.com, Inc.<br>• Microsoft Bot Framework by Microsoft Corporation<br>• WiseBanyan by WiseBanyan, Inc.<br>• Betterment by Betterment Holdings, Inc.<br>• Wealthfront by Wealthfront Corporation | • Client Service is the process of providing information, advice, and support to the clients of an asset manager.<br>• Client Service uses AI algorithms to create chatbots and virtual assistants that can interact with clients through natural language processing and understanding.<br>• These solutions help asset managers provide 24/7 service, answer common questions, provide personalized recommendations, and enhance client satisfaction and retention. |

## *Key Takeaways*

- AI is reshaping Asset Management across key areas such as Market Analysis, Portfolio Optimization, Risk Management, Performance Measurement, and Client Service.
- Market Analysis tools use AI to collect and analyze diverse data sources, enabling informed decisions, risk identification, and optimization of pricing and trading strategies.
- Portfolio Optimization solutions leverage AI for analyzing factors like asset allocation and diversification, optimizing portfolio composition and enhancing risk-adjusted returns.
- Risk Management tools use AI to model scenarios, assisting asset managers in identifying, measuring, and mitigating potential losses or uncertainties.
- Performance Measurement platforms use AI algorithms to calculate various financial metrics, aiding asset managers in evaluating and communicating portfolio performance.
- Client Service applications leverage AI to create chatbots and virtual assistants for 24/7 client interaction, answering queries, providing recommendations, and enhancing client satisfaction and retention.

## 7.5. REAL ESTATE SECURITY AND SAFETY

Real estate security and safety are essential aspects of the real estate industry, as they involve protecting properties, assets, and people from various threats and hazards. Real estate security and safety can cover a wide range of topics, such as crime prevention, fire protection, emergency response, environmental health, and building codes. Real estate professionals need to be aware of the potential risks and liabilities associated with their properties, and take appropriate measures to ensure the security and safety of their clients, tenants, and employees. Artificial intelligence (AI) is a valuable tool that can enhance and improve the security and safety of real estate properties and operations. AI can assist real estate professionals in various ways, such as monitoring, detecting, alerting, and responding to various security and safety issues. AI can also help real estate professionals optimize their security and safety strategies, reduce costs, and increase efficiency.

| AI APPLICATIONS IN REAL ESTATE SECURITY AND SAFETY | SOLUTIONS PROVIDED BY COMPANIES | SOLUTIONS DESCRIPTIONS |
| --- | --- | --- |
| Security Monitoring | • Verkada by Verkada, Inc.<br>• Deep Sentinel by Deep Sentinel Corp.<br>• Rhombus Systems by Rhombus Systems, Inc.<br>• Eagle Eye Networks by Eagle Eye Networks, Inc.<br>• Camio by Camio, Inc.<br>• OnWatch by Oosto<br>• Vintra by Vintra, Inc.<br>• Umbo AiCameras by Umbo Computer Vision, Inc. | • Security Monitoring is the process of using AI algorithms to observe and record the activities and events that occur in real estate properties.<br>• Security Monitoring uses cameras, sensors, and cloud computing to analyze video feeds, audio signals, and other data sources.<br>• These solutions help real estate professionals prevent unauthorized access, deter theft and vandalism, and ensure compliance with regulations. |

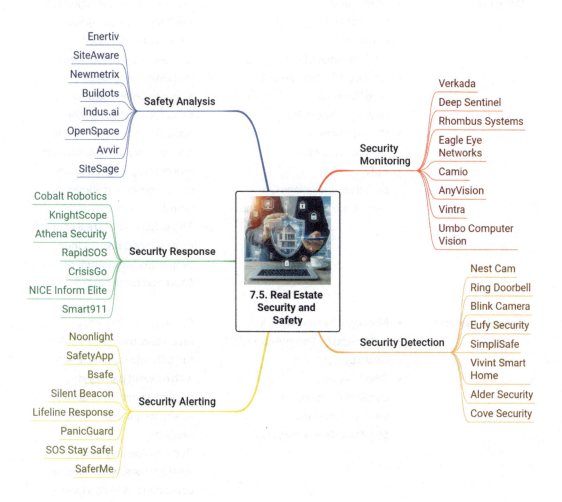

Enertiv
SiteAware
Newmetrix
Buildots
Indus.ai
OpenSpace
Avvir
SiteSage

**Safety Analysis**

Verkada
Deep Sentinel
Rhombus Systems
Eagle Eye Networks
Camio
AnyVision
Vintra
Umbo Computer Vision

**Security Monitoring**

Cobalt Robotics
KnightScope
Athena Security
RapidSOS
CrisisGo
NICE Inform Elite
Smart911

**Security Response**

**7.5. Real Estate Security and Safety**

Nest Cam
Ring Doorbell
Blink Camera
Eufy Security
SimpliSafe
Vivint Smart Home
Alder Security
Cove Security

**Security Detection**

Noonlight
SafetyApp
Bsafe
Silent Beacon
Lifeline Response
PanicGuard
SOS Stay Safe!
SaferMe

**Security Alerting**

223

| AI APPLICATIONS IN REAL ESTATE SECURITY AND SAFETY | SOLUTIONS PROVIDED BY COMPANIES | SOLUTIONS DESCRIPTIONS |
|---|---|---|
| **Security Detection** | • Vivint Smart Home by Vivint<br>• Alder Security by Alder Holdings, LLC<br>• Cove Security by Cove Smart, LLC<br>• Nest Cam by Google LLC<br>• Ring Doorbell by Amazon.com, Inc.<br>• Blink Camera by Amazon.com, Inc.<br>• Eufy Security by Anker Innovations Co.<br>• SimpliSafe by SimpliSafe, Inc. | • Security Detection is the process of using AI algorithms to identify and recognize various objects, faces, behaviors, and anomalies in real estate properties.<br>• Security Detection uses facial recognition, motion detection, object detection, and anomaly detection to alert real estate professionals of any suspicious or abnormal activity.<br>• The solutions help real estate professionals protect their properties from intruders, fire, flood, and other hazards. |
| **Security Alerting** | • Noonlight by Noonlight, Inc.<br>• SafetyApp by SafetyApp, LLC<br>• Bsafe by Bsafe AS<br>• Silent Beacon by Silent Beacon, LLC<br>• Lifeline Response by Lifeline Response, LLC | • Security Alerting is the process of using AI algorithms to notify and communicate with relevant parties in case of a security or safety emergency in real estate properties.<br>• Security Alerting uses smartphones, wearables, or panic buttons to send alerts to emergency services, property managers, or trusted contacts.<br>• The solutions help real estate professionals get immediate assistance, share their location, or record evidence. |

| AI APPLICATIONS IN REAL ESTATE SECURITY AND SAFETY | SOLUTIONS PROVIDED BY COMPANIES | SOLUTIONS DESCRIPTIONS |
| --- | --- | --- |
| **Security Response** | • Cobalt Robotics by Cobalt Robotics, Inc. <br> • KnightScope by KnightScope, Inc. <br> • Athena Security by Athena Security, Inc. <br> • RapidSOS by RapidSOS, Inc. <br> • CrisisGo by CrisisGo, Inc. | • Security Response is the process of using AI algorithms to provide or coordinate appropriate actions or interventions in case of a security or safety emergency in real estate properties. <br> • Security Response uses robots, drones, or software to patrol, intervene, or assist in emergency situations. <br> • The solutions help real estate professionals reduce response time, mitigate risks, and save lives. |
| **Safety Analysis** | • Enertiv by Enertiv, Inc. <br> • SiteAware by SiteAware, Inc. <br> • Buildots by Buildots Ltd. <br> • Newmetrix by Newmetrix <br> • Indus.ai by Indus.ai, Inc. <br> • Avvir by Avvir, Inc. | • Safety Analysis is the process of using AI algorithms to evaluate and improve the safety and health conditions of real estate properties. <br> • Safety Analysis uses sensors, cameras, and cloud computing to collect and analyze data on various safety and health factors, such as fire hazards, air quality, water quality, noise levels, and structural integrity. <br> • The solutions help real estate professionals prevent accidents, injuries, illnesses, and damages. |

## Key Takeaways

- AI is reshaping Real Estate Security and Safety in areas like Security Monitoring, Detection, Alerting, Response, and Safety Analysis.

- Security Monitoring tools use AI to observe and record the activities and events that occur in real estate properties, preventing unauthorized access, deterring theft, and ensuring compliance.

- Security Detection tools use AI to identify and recognize objects and behaviors, alerting real estate professionals of any suspicious or abnormal activity, and protecting properties from various threats.

- Security Alerting tools use AI to notify and communicate with relevant parties in case of a security or safety emergency, providing immediate assistance, location sharing, or evidence recording.

- Security Response tools use AI to provide or coordinate appropriate actions or interventions in case of a security or safety emergency, reducing response time, mitigating risks, and saving lives.

- Safety Analysis tools use AI to evaluate and improve the safety and health conditions of real estate properties, preventing accidents, injuries, illnesses, and damages.

# CHAPTER 8
# DISPOSE OF THE OWNED OR LEASED PROPERTY

The disposition of owned or leased properties is a significant milestone in the real estate industry. Whether selling a residential home, a commercial building, or deciding not to renew a lease, this process involves multifaceted decisions influenced by market dynamics, legal requirements, and property valuation.

Artificial Intelligence (AI) is making its mark on this critical aspect of real estate, providing valuable insights and tools to streamline the property disposal process. In this chapter, we explore how AI is transforming property disposition and bringing efficiency, accuracy, and strategic decision-making to the forefront.

AI-driven property appraisal management tools are providing more precise valuations, helping property owners and sellers set competitive prices. These tools analyze a multitude of data points, from recent property sales to market trends, ensuring a well-informed approach to property valuation.

Title and closing services also benefit from AI, simplifying the closing process by automating tasks and reducing human errors. Competitive analysis tools powered by AI offer sellers valuable market insights, helping them position their properties effectively.

Sales and marketing have witnessed a transformation with AI, as predictive analytics guide property sellers in identifying the right target audience. AI-powered brokerage platforms facilitate the transaction process, making it faster and more transparent.

Property valuation and appraisal, driven by AI, offer a competitive edge in the market. As a result, sellers and owners can make informed decisions and optimize their property's financial outcome.

This chapter delves into the exciting ways AI is reshaping the disposal of owned or leased properties. By providing an overview of these innovations, we gain insight into the evolving landscape of real estate transactions.

## 8.1. TITLE AND CLOSING SERVICES

Title and closing services are the processes of verifying the ownership, validity, and transferability of a property title, and facilitating the closing of a real estate transaction. They are essential for buyers, sellers, lenders, and agents who need to ensure that the property title is clear, accurate, and free of any liens, encumbrances, or defects, and that the closing is conducted smoothly, securely, and legally. Title and closing services are also important for title companies, escrow agents, and closing attorneys, who need to comply with industry standards and regulations while delivering high-quality work. Artificial intelligence (AI) is a powerful tool that can enhance the efficiency, accuracy, and security of title and closing services. AI can take many forms in title and closing services, as outlined in the table below. For example, AI can automate title search and examination, generate title reports and commitments, detect errors and fraud, and provide quality control and compliance checks. These solutions can help title and closing service providers and professionals reduce costs, save time, improve customer satisfaction, and mitigate risks.

| AI APPLICATIONS IN TITLE AND CLOSING SERVICES | SOLUTIONS PROVIDED BY COMPANIES | SOLUTIONS DESCRIPTIONS |
|---|---|---|
| Automated Title Search and Examination | • Qualia Data by Qualia Labs, Inc.<br>• TitleWave by TitleWave Real Estate Solutions<br>• Title Search by TitleCapture, LLC<br>• TitleFlex by DataTrace Information Services LLC.<br>• Title Search by DataTrace Information Services, LLC | • Automated title search and examination solutions use AI to search and analyze public records, such as deeds, mortgages, judgments, liens, taxes, and maps, to determine the ownership and status of a property title.<br>• These solutions provide fast and low-cost title searches and examinations for properties that do not require a full title abstract.<br>• These solutions can also supplement human title searches and examinations by providing additional data and insights. |

Qualia Shield
WireSafe
SafeChain
FundingShield
Secure Insight
PropLogix

**Title and Closing Fraud Detection and Prevention**

Qualia Data
TitleCapture
TitleFlex
TitleWave
DataTrace Information Services
PropertyInfo Corporation

**Automated Title Search and Examination**

**8.1. Title and Closing Services**

Qualia
CloseSimple
Close Happy
Federal Title & Escrow
Snapdocs
Notarize

**Title and Closing Quality Control and Compliance Check**

TitleGenius
Title Forward
Spruce Holdings
States Title Holding
Endpoint Closing
JetClosing

**Title Report and Commitment Generation**

| AI APPLICATIONS IN TITLE AND CLOSING SERVICES | SOLUTIONS PROVIDED BY COMPANIES | SOLUTIONS DESCRIPTIONS |
|---|---|---|
| **Title Report and Commitment Generation** | • TitleGenius by REX - Real Estate Exchange, Inc. <br> • Title Report by Title Forward, LLC <br> • Title Report by Spruce Holdings, Inc. <br> • Title Report by States Title Holding, Inc. | • Title report and commitment generation solutions use AI to create title reports and commitments that comply with industry standards and regulations. <br> • These solutions can automate the formatting, filling, and filing of title forms and documents. <br> • These solutions can also customize reports and commitments according to client specifications and preferences. |
| **Title and Closing Quality Control and Compliance Check** | • Alanna by Alanna.ai <br> • Qualia Assurance by Qualia Labs, Inc. <br> • CloseSimple by CloseSimple, LLC <br> • States Title by States Title <br> • Pioneer Title by Pioneer Holding Inc. <br> • eClosing by Snapdocs, Inc. | • Title and closing quality control and compliance check solutions use AI to verify that title and closing processes and documents comply with federal, state, and local laws and regulations, as well as industry standards and guidelines. <br> • These solutions can audit title and closing files for errors, omissions, inconsistencies, and violations. <br> • These solutions can also provide corrective actions and recommendations to ensure quality and compliance. |

| AI APPLICATIONS IN TITLE AND CLOSING SERVICES | SOLUTIONS PROVIDED BY COMPANIES | SOLUTIONS DESCRIPTIONS |
|---|---|---|
| **Title and Closing Fraud Detection and Prevention** | • Qualia Shield by Qualia Labs, Inc.<br>• WireSafe by CertifID, LLC<br>• SafeChain by CyStack.,JSC<br>• Blockchain Platform by Clear Blockchain Technologies LTD<br>• Closinglock by Closinglock, Inc. | • Title and closing fraud detection and prevention solutions use AI to identify and prevent fraudulent activities, such as identity theft, wire fraud, forgery, and phishing, in title and closing transactions.<br>• These solutions can verify the identity, credentials, and reputation of parties involved in title and closing transactions.<br>• These solutions can also protect the transfer of funds and documents using encryption, authentication, and verification. |

## Key Takeaways

- AI is transforming Title and Closing Services, improving efficiency, accuracy, and security.
- Automated Title Search and Examination tools leverage AI for quick, low-cost title searches and examinations based on public records.
- Title Report and Commitment Generation use AI to create title reports and commitments that comply with industry standards and regulations.
- Title and Closing Quality Control and Compliance Check tools use AI to verify that title and closing processes and documents adhere to legal and industry regulations, providing audits and corrective actions when needed.
- Title and Closing Fraud Detection and Prevention solutions use AI to identify and prevent fraudulent activities, such as identity theft, wire fraud, and phishing, in title and closing transactions.

## 8.2.   SALES AND MARKETING

Sales and marketing are the processes of promoting and selling products or services to potential and existing customers. Sales and marketing involve various activities, such as identifying target markets, generating leads, qualifying prospects, presenting solutions, negotiating prices, closing deals, and retaining customers. Sales and marketing are vital and challenging aspects of the real estate industry that require a high level of skills, creativity, and communication. Artificial intelligence (AI) is a powerful tool that can enhance various aspects of the sales and marketing process, such as data analysis, lead generation, content creation, personalization, optimization, and automation. AI can help sales and marketing professionals reduce costs, increase efficiency, improve quality, and optimize performance. AI can also enable sales and marketing professionals to create more effective and engaging campaigns that meet the needs and preferences of the customers and stakeholders.

| AI APPLICATIONS IN SALES AND MARKETING | SOLUTIONS PROVIDED BY COMPANIES | SOLUTIONS DESCRIPTIONS |
| --- | --- | --- |
| Data Analysis | • Placer.ai by Placer Labs, Inc.<br>• LionDesk CRM by LionDesk, LLC.<br>• Property Base by Property Base, Inc.<br>• NAR's AI for REALTORS by National Association of REALTORS®<br>• CINC Pro by CINC, a Fidelity National Financial, Inc. Company<br>• Dippidi by Dippidi, LLC. | • Data Analysis is the process of collecting, processing, and interpreting data related to sales and marketing activities.<br>• Data Analysis uses AI algorithms to leverage data and analytics to provide insights and recommendations for sales and marketing strategies.<br>• These solutions help sales and marketing professionals measure and report their performance, identify trends and patterns, segment customers and markets, forecast results, and optimize campaigns. |

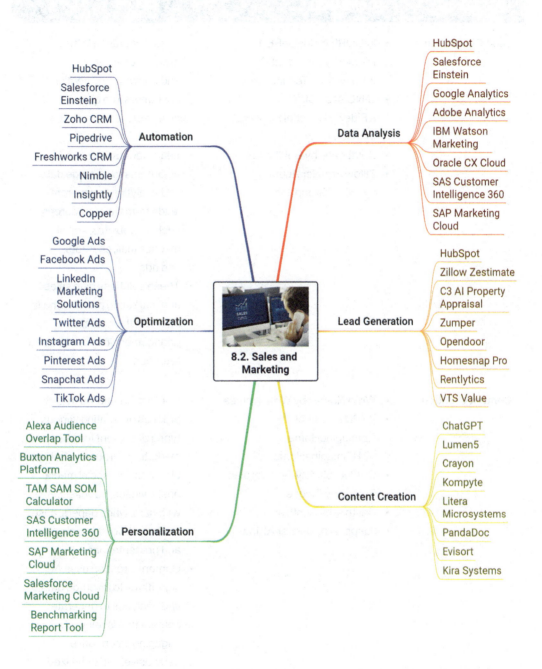

Automation
- HubSpot
- Salesforce Einstein
- Zoho CRM
- Pipedrive
- Freshworks CRM
- Nimble
- Insightly
- Copper

Data Analysis
- HubSpot
- Salesforce Einstein
- Google Analytics
- Adobe Analytics
- IBM Watson Marketing
- Oracle CX Cloud
- SAS Customer Intelligence 360
- SAP Marketing Cloud

Optimization
- Google Ads
- Facebook Ads
- LinkedIn Marketing Solutions
- Twitter Ads
- Instagram Ads
- Pinterest Ads
- Snapchat Ads
- TikTok Ads

Lead Generation
- HubSpot
- Zillow Zestimate
- C3 AI Property Appraisal
- Zumper
- Opendoor
- Homesnap Pro
- Rentlytics
- VTS Value

8.2. Sales and Marketing

Personalization
- Alexa Audience Overlap Tool
- Buxton Analytics Platform
- TAM SAM SOM Calculator
- SAS Customer Intelligence 360
- SAP Marketing Cloud
- Salesforce Marketing Cloud
- Benchmarking Report Tool

Content Creation
- ChatGPT
- Lumen5
- Crayon
- Kompyte
- Litera Microsystems
- PandaDoc
- Evisort
- Kira Systems

| AI APPLICATIONS IN SALES AND MARKETING | SOLUTIONS PROVIDED BY COMPANIES | SOLUTIONS DESCRIPTIONS |
|---|---|---|
| **Lead Generation** | • kvCORE by InsideRE, LLC<br>• Dippidi by Dippidi, LLC.<br>• Xara by Xara Technologies<br>• CINC AI by CINC, a Fidelity National Financial, Inc. Company<br>• BoldLeads by BoldLeads<br>• Zillow Premier Agent by Zillow Group, Inc. | • Lead Generation is the process of attracting and converting potential customers into qualified prospects for a product or service.<br>• Lead Generation uses AI algorithms to leverage data and analytics to generate leads from various sources, such as websites, social media, email, chatbots, and ads.<br>• These solutions help sales and marketing professionals increase their reach, engagement, conversion, and retention. |
| **Content Creation** | • Write.Homes by Write.Homes<br>• ValPal by ValPal<br>• REimagineHome by REimagineHome<br>• Getfloorplan by Getfloorplan<br>• Epique by Epique<br>• Restb.ai by Restb.ai<br>• Jasper.ai by Jasper AI, Inc. | • Content Creation is the process of creating various types of content for sales and marketing purposes, such as blogs, emails, social media posts, videos, podcasts, webinars, white papers, case studies, ebooks, infographics, and presentations.<br>• Content Creation uses AI algorithms to leverage data and analytics to generate content that is relevant, engaging, informative, persuasive, and optimized for search engines and social media platforms. |

| AI APPLICATIONS IN SALES AND MARKETING | SOLUTIONS PROVIDED BY COMPANIES | SOLUTIONS DESCRIPTIONS |
|---|---|---|
| | | • These solutions help sales and marketing professionals save time, reduce costs, improve quality, and increase conversions. |
| **Personalization** | • SmartZip by SmartZip Analytics, Inc.<br>• BoomTown by BoomTown ROI<br>• Lofty by Lofty, Inc.<br>• Real Geeks by Fidelity National Financial, Inc.<br>• Ylopo by Ylopo, LLC<br>• Placester by Placester, Inc.<br>• IXACT Contact by IXACT Contact Solutions, Inc. | • Personalization is the process of tailoring sales and marketing messages and offers to the individual needs, preferences, and behaviors of each customer or prospect.<br>• Personalization uses AI algorithms to leverage data and analytics to create personalized content, recommendations, pricing, and actions.<br>• These solutions help sales and marketing professionals increase customer satisfaction, loyalty, and retention. |
| **Optimization** | • Optimizely by Optimizely, Inc.<br>• Unbounce by Unbounce Marketing Solutions, Inc.<br>• HubSpot by HubSpot, Inc.<br>• BoomTown by BoomTown ROI<br>• Adwerx by Adwerx, Inc.<br>• Curaytor by Curaytor, LLC<br>• Realvolve by Realvolve, LLC<br>• Follow Up Boss by Follow Up Boss | • Optimization is the process of improving the effectiveness and efficiency of sales and marketing campaigns.<br>• Optimization uses AI algorithms to leverage data and analytics to test and optimize various elements of a campaign, such as keywords, headlines, images, videos, copy, landing pages, calls to action, and channels. |

| AI APPLICATIONS IN SALES AND MARKETING | SOLUTIONS PROVIDED BY COMPANIES | SOLUTIONS DESCRIPTIONS |
|---|---|---|
| | | • These solutions help sales and marketing professionals increase their reach, engagement, conversion, and return on investment. |
| **Automation** | • Realvolve by Realvolve, LLC<br>• Follow Up Boss by Follow Up Boss<br>• Verse by Verse.io<br>• Rechat by Rechat, Inc.<br>• Structurely by Reinform, Inc.<br>• Revaluate by Revaluate, Inc.<br>• Reonomy by Reonomy, an Altus Group Company | • Automation is the process of automating repetitive and manual tasks in sales and marketing.<br>• Automation uses AI algorithms to leverage data and analytics to automate tasks such as lead scoring, lead nurturing, email marketing, social media marketing, chatbot marketing, appointment scheduling, follow-up reminders, contract management, and invoice management.<br>• These solutions help sales and marketing professionals save time, reduce errors, and improve productivity. |

## Key Takeaways

- AI is transforming Sales and Marketing, optimizing processes such as data analysis, lead generation, content creation, personalization, optimization, and automation.
- Data Analysis tools use AI to interpret sales and marketing data, offering insights for strategy improvement.
- Lead Generation solutions use AI to generate leads from diverse sources, increasing reach, engagement, conversion, and retention.

- Content Creation tools use AI to generate diverse and engaging content, saving time and improving quality.
- Personalization tools use AI to tailor messages and offers to individual customer needs, enhancing satisfaction and loyalty.
- Optimization tools use AI to test and improve various campaign elements, boosting reach, engagement, and return on investment.
- Automation tools use AI to automate repetitive tasks, improving efficiency and reducing errors in sales and marketing processes.

## 8.3. VALUATION AND APPRAISAL

Valuation and appraisal are the processes of estimating the market value of a real estate property based on various factors, such as location, condition, features, amenities, and market trends. Valuation and appraisal are essential and complex aspects of the real estate industry that require a high level of expertise, accuracy, and compliance. Valuation and appraisal are used for various purposes, such as buying, selling, renting, financing, investing, insuring, and taxing real estate properties. Artificial intelligence (AI) is a powerful tool that can enhance various aspects of the valuation and appraisal process, such as data collection, data analysis, valuation methods, quality control, and reporting. AI can help valuation and appraisal professionals reduce costs, increase efficiency, improve quality, and optimize performance. AI can also enable valuation and appraisal professionals to create more consistent and reliable valuations that meet the needs and preferences of the clients and stakeholders.

| AI APPLICATIONS IN VALUATION AND APPRAISAL | SOLUTIONS PROVIDED BY COMPANIES | SOLUTIONS DESCRIPTIONS |
|---|---|---|
| Data Collection | • Zillow by Zillow Group, Inc.<br>• Redfin by Redfin Corporation<br>• HomeLight by HomeLight, Inc.<br>• Trulia by Zillow Group, Inc.<br>• Realtor.com by Move, Inc. | • Data Collection is the process of gathering and organizing relevant data for a real estate property valuation.<br>• Data Collection uses AI algorithms to collect and analyze various data sources, such as property listings, sales transactions, rental rates, occupancy rates, demographics, and economic indicators.<br>• These solutions help valuation and appraisal professionals access and integrate high-quality data that can support their valuation models and assumptions. |

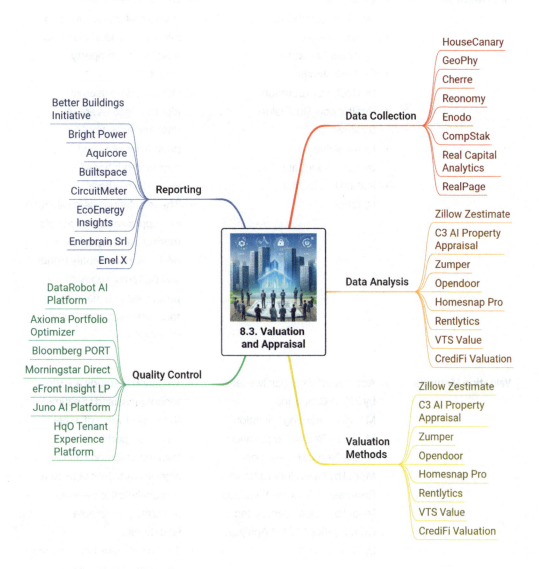

**Data Collection**
- HouseCanary
- GeoPhy
- Cherre
- Reonomy
- Enodo
- CompStak
- Real Capital Analytics
- RealPage

**Reporting**
- Better Buildings Initiative
- Bright Power
- Aquicore
- Builtspace
- CircuitMeter
- EcoEnergy Insights
- Enerbrain Srl
- Enel X

**Data Analysis**
- Zillow Zestimate
- C3 AI Property Appraisal
- Zumper
- Opendoor
- Homesnap Pro
- Rentlytics
- VTS Value
- CrediFi Valuation

**8.3. Valuation and Appraisal**

**Quality Control**
- DataRobot AI Platform
- Axioma Portfolio Optimizer
- Bloomberg PORT
- Morningstar Direct
- eFront Insight LP
- Juno AI Platform
- HqO Tenant Experience Platform

**Valuation Methods**
- Zillow Zestimate
- C3 AI Property Appraisal
- Zumper
- Opendoor
- Homesnap Pro
- Rentlytics
- VTS Value
- CrediFi Valuation

| AI APPLICATIONS IN VALUATION AND APPRAISAL | SOLUTIONS PROVIDED BY COMPANIES | SOLUTIONS DESCRIPTIONS |
|---|---|---|
| **Data Analysis** | • Zestimate by Zillow Group, Inc.<br>• Trulia Estimate by Zillow Group, Inc.<br>• Redfin Estimate by Redfin Corporation<br>• Realtor.com RealValue by Move, Inc.<br>• Home Value by Opendoor Labs, Inc.<br>• Instant Cash Offer by Offerpad | • Data Analysis is the process of processing and interpreting data related to a real estate property valuation.<br>• Data Analysis uses AI algorithms to leverage data and analytics to provide insights and recommendations for valuation methods.<br>• These solutions help valuation and appraisal professionals measure and report their performance, identify trends and patterns, segment properties and markets, forecast results, and optimize valuations. |
| **Valuation Methods** | • Automated Valuation Model by Zillow Group, Inc.<br>• Machine Learning Valuation Model by Redfin Corporation<br>• Neural Network Valuation Model by Opendoor Labs, Inc.<br>• Regression Analysis Valuation Model by HouseCanary, Inc.<br>• Comparative Market Analysis by Realtor.com | • Valuation Methods are the techniques used to estimate the market value of a real estate property.<br>• Valuation Methods use AI algorithms to leverage data and analytics to generate accurate and reliable valuations.<br>• These solutions help valuation and appraisal professionals assess the value of their properties, monitor changes in value, and compare different properties. |

| AI APPLICATIONS IN VALUATION AND APPRAISAL | SOLUTIONS PROVIDED BY COMPANIES | SOLUTIONS DESCRIPTIONS |
| --- | --- | --- |
| **Quality Control** | • Clear Capital by ClearCapital.com, Inc.<br>• CoreLogic by CoreLogic, Inc.<br>• Appraisal Firewall by SharperLending Solutions, LLC<br>• Appraisal Scope by Appraisal Scope<br>• Appraisal Review by Bradford Technologies, Inc. | • Quality Control is the process of ensuring that the valuations are consistent, accurate, and compliant with the standards and regulations of the industry.<br>• Quality Control uses AI algorithms to review and validate the valuations, identify and correct errors or inconsistencies, provide feedback and recommendations, and generate reports.<br>• These solutions help valuation and appraisal professionals improve the quality and credibility of their valuations, reduce errors and disputes, and comply with regulations. |
| **Reporting** | • Appraisal Report by ClearCapital.com, Inc.<br>• Valuation Report by CoreLogic, Inc.<br>• Property Report by Zillow Group, Inc.<br>• Home Report by Redfin Corporation<br>• Market Report by Realtor.com<br>• Insight Report by HouseCanary | • Reporting is the process of communicating the results and findings of the valuations to the clients and stakeholders.<br>• Reporting uses AI algorithms to create and customize reports that present the valuations in a clear, concise, and informative manner. |

| AI APPLICATIONS IN VALUATION AND APPRAISAL | SOLUTIONS PROVIDED BY COMPANIES | SOLUTIONS DESCRIPTIONS |
|---|---|---|
| | • Property Analytics Report by CoStar Group, Inc. | • These solutions help valuation and appraisal professionals deliver reports that meet the expectations and requirements of the clients and stakeholders, and provide insights and evidence to support their valuations. |

## Key Takeaways

- AI is revolutionizing Valuation and Appraisal, enhancing processes such as data collection, data analysis, valuation methods, quality control, and reporting.
- Data Collection tools utilize AI to gather and analyze diverse data sources, including property listings, sales transactions, rental rates, demographics, and economic indicators.
- Data Analysis solutions, leverage AI to interpret valuation-related data, providing insights and recommendations for improved methods.
- ValuationMethods tools AI Property Appraisal use AI algorithms to generate accurate and reliable property valuations, aiding professionals in assessment and comparison.
- Quality Control solutions, employ AI to ensure consistent, accurate, and compliant valuations, reducing errors, disputes, and enhancing credibility.
- Reporting tools like Better Buildings Initiative and Bright Power leverage AI algorithms to create customized reports, presenting valuations in a clear, concise, and informative manner to meet client and stakeholder expectations.

## 8.4.  REAL ESTATE BROKERAGE

The real estate brokerage industry involves the representation of buyers and sellers of properties in the process of purchase, sale, or lease. Real estate brokers act as intermediaries between the parties, providing services such as market analysis, negotiation, contract preparation, and closing. Real estate brokers earn commissions from the transactions they facilitate, usually a percentage of the sale price or the rent. This industry is highly regulated and competitive, requiring compliance with laws and ethics, as well as differentiation and value proposition. AI has emerged as a powerful tool that can enhance the efficiency, effectiveness, and profitability of real estate brokerage. AI can take many forms in real estate brokerage, as delineated in the table below. For example, AI-powered chatbots can provide instant and personalized responses to customer inquiries, increasing engagement and conversion rates. Overall, the adoption of AI in the real estate brokerage industry has been gradual but promising.

| AI APPLICATIONS IN REAL ESTATE BROKERAGE | SOLUTIONS PROVIDED BY COMPANIES | SOLUTIONS DESCRIPTIONS |
| --- | --- | --- |
| Lead Generation | • BoldLeads by BoldLeads<br>• Zillow Premier Agent by Zillow Group, Inc.<br>• kvCORE by InsideRE, LLC<br>• Dippidi by Dippidi, LLC.<br>• Xara by Xara Technologies | • Lead Generation is the process of identifying and attracting potential customers for a product or service.<br>• Lead Generation uses AI algorithms to analyze data from various sources, such as social media, online behavior, demographics, and property records.<br>• These solutions help real estate brokers find and target high-quality leads, optimize their marketing campaigns, and increase their conversion rates. |

| AI APPLICATIONS IN REAL ESTATE BROKERAGE | SOLUTIONS PROVIDED BY COMPANIES | SOLUTIONS DESCRIPTIONS |
|---|---|---|
| Chatbots | • AlphaChat by AlphaChat<br>• Rulai by Rulai<br>• Meya by Meya<br>• SnapEngage by SnapEngage<br>• Mobile Monkey by Mobile Monkey<br>• Ebi by Ebi<br>• Outgrow by Outgrow<br>• Botsify by Botsify<br>• Hyro by Hyro<br>• FloatChat by FloatChat | • Chatbots are software applications that simulate human conversations with users via text or voice.<br>• Chatbots use natural language processing (NLP) and machine learning (ML) to understand user queries and provide relevant responses.<br>• These solutions help real estate brokers automate customer service, lead qualification, appointment scheduling, and follow-up tasks. |
| Image Recognition | • Restb.ai by Restb.ai<br>• Realtor.com by Move, Inc.<br>• Reali by Reali, Inc.<br>• Trulia by Trulia, LLC<br>• Zillow by Zillow Group, Inc.<br>• Roofstock by Roofstock, Inc.<br>• Homesnap by Homesnap, Inc. | • Image Recognition is the ability of a computer system to identify and process images.<br>• Image Recognition uses computer vision and deep learning to analyze images and extract valuable information.<br>• These solutions help real estate brokers create immersive 3D tours, floor plans, virtual staging, and property valuation. |
| Predictive Analytics | • Livv.ai by Livv.ai<br>• Likely.AI by Likely.AI<br>• SmartZip by SmartZip Analytics, Inc.<br>• TopHap by TopHap, Inc.<br>• Revaluate by Revaluate, Inc. | • Predictive Analytics is the use of statistical techniques and machine learning models to analyze historical data and make predictions about future outcomes. |

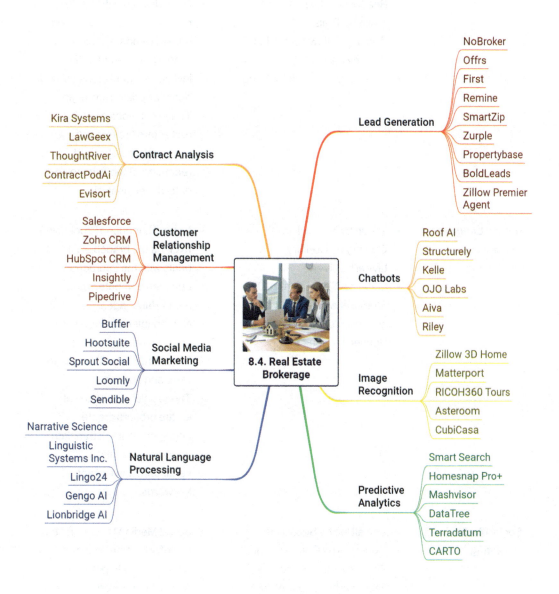

**Contract Analysis**
- Kira Systems
- LawGeex
- ThoughtRiver
- ContractPodAi
- Evisort

**Customer Relationship Management**
- Salesforce
- Zoho CRM
- HubSpot CRM
- Insightly
- Pipedrive

**Social Media Marketing**
- Buffer
- Hootsuite
- Sprout Social
- Loomly
- Sendible

**Natural Language Processing**
- Narrative Science
- Linguistic Systems Inc.
- Lingo24
- Gengo AI
- Lionbridge AI

**8.4. Real Estate Brokerage**

**Lead Generation**
- NoBroker
- Offrs
- First
- Remine
- SmartZip
- Zurple
- Propertybase
- BoldLeads
- Zillow Premier Agent

**Chatbots**
- Roof AI
- Structurely
- Kelle
- OJO Labs
- Aiva
- Riley

**Image Recognition**
- Zillow 3D Home
- Matterport
- RICOH360 Tours
- Asteroom
- CubiCasa

**Predictive Analytics**
- Smart Search
- Homesnap Pro+
- Mashvisor
- DataTree
- Terradatum
- CARTO

| AI APPLICATIONS IN REAL ESTATE BROKERAGE | SOLUTIONS PROVIDED BY COMPANIES | SOLUTIONS DESCRIPTIONS |
|---|---|---|
| | • Realtor.com by Move, Inc.<br>• Trulia by Trulia, LLC<br>• Zillow by Zillow Group, Inc.<br>• Reali by Reali, Inc.<br>• Roofstock by Roofstock, Inc. | • Predictive Analytics helps real estate brokers forecast market trends, evaluate property values, identify investment opportunities, and optimize pricing strategies.<br>• These solutions provide real estate brokers with actionable insights and recommendations based on data-driven analysis. |
| Natural Language Processing | • Yseop by Yseop, Inc.<br>• Co-libry by Co-libry<br>• Livv.ai by Livv.ai<br>• LocalizeOS by LocalizeOS<br>• AlphaSense by AlphaSense, Inc.<br>• Sentieo by Sentieo, Inc. | • Natural Language Processing (NLP) is the branch of AI that deals with the interaction between computers and human languages.<br>• NLP enables computers to understand, generate, and manipulate natural language texts and speech.<br>• These solutions help real estate brokers create engaging content, translate documents, analyze sentiment, and extract keywords. |
| Social Media Marketing | • SocialBee by SocialBee<br>• Compass by Compass, Inc.<br>• Zillow by Zillow Group, Inc.<br>• Jasper.ai by Jasper AI, Inc.<br>• Hyro by Hyro, Inc. | • Social Media Marketing is the use of social media platforms and websites to promote a product or service.<br>• Social Media Marketing uses AI to optimize content creation, distribution, and analysis. |

| AI APPLICATIONS IN REAL ESTATE BROKERAGE | SOLUTIONS PROVIDED BY COMPANIES | SOLUTIONS DESCRIPTIONS |
|---|---|---|
| | | • These solutions help real estate brokers manage their social media presence, reach their target audience, and measure their performance. |
| **Customer Relationship Management** | • Follow Up Boss by Follow Up Boss<br>• LionDesk CRM by LionDesk, LLC.<br>• Propertybase by Propertybase<br>• BoomTown by BoomTown ROI<br>• Lofty by Lofty, Inc.<br>• kvCORE by InsideRE, LLC<br>• IXACT Contact by IXACT Contact Solutions, Inc. | • Customer Relationship Management (CRM) is the process of managing interactions with current and potential customers.<br>• CRM uses AI to automate tasks, personalize communication, and provide insights.<br>• These solutions help real estate brokers organize their contacts, track their activities, and nurture their relationships. |
| **Contract Analysis** | • Analyse Documents by Elevate<br>• ThoughtTrace by ThoughtTrace<br>• ContractPodAi by ContractPod Technologies Ltd.<br>• Google Contract DocAI by Google LLC<br>• Zuva DocAI by Zuva | • Contract Analysis is the process of reviewing and extracting information from contracts and other legal documents.<br>• Contract Analysis uses AI to automate tasks, identify risks, and provide recommendations.<br>• These solutions help real estate brokers streamline their contract management, ensure compliance, and reduce costs. |

## *Key Takeaways*

- Real estate brokerage adopts AI" for increased efficiency and profitability.
- AI-driven Lead Generation tools optimize marketing campaigns and boost conversion rates.
- Chatbots automate customer service and lead qualification, enhancing engagement.
- Image Recognition solutions offer immersive property experiences through 3D tours and virtual staging.
- Predictive Analytics tools aid brokers in forecasting market trends, evaluating property values, and optimizing pricing strategies.
- Natural Language Processing (NLP) tools help create engaging content and analyze sentiment.
- Social Media Marketing platforms leverage AI for effective online presence.
- AI-powered Customer Relationship Management (CRM) systems enhance customer interactions.
- Contract Analysis tools automate contract management, ensuring compliance and reducing costs for real estate brokers.

# CHAPTER 9
# PUBLIC SECTOR
## (INDUSTRY REGULATORS, COURTROOM OFFICIALS, ETC.)

The public sector plays a crucial role in regulating, overseeing, and facilitating real estate operations. Industry regulators, courtroom officials, and government bodies are responsible for ensuring compliance, fairness, and the rule of law in the real estate domain.

In recent years, artificial intelligence (AI) has begun to reshape the public sector's involvement in real estate, introducing innovative solutions that enhance efficiency, transparency, and ethical standards.

AI-powered dispute resolution tools offer a streamlined approach to settling real estate conflicts. These technologies enable timely and impartial resolutions, reducing the burden on legal systems.

Ethics and regulation in the real estate industry have received a boost from AI, with tools that monitor and enforce adherence to ethical and legal standards. This ensures that industry professionals conduct their business ethically, maintaining the integrity of the sector.

Law and compliance are vital in real estate, with numerous laws, regulations, and contracts governing property transactions. AI assists in parsing, analyzing, and ensuring compliance with these intricate legal documents, reducing the chances of errors and disputes.

This chapter delves into the AI-driven advancements in the public sector's role in real estate, shedding light on how technology is transforming the regulation and ethical standards within the industry. By exploring these developments, we gain insight into the evolving landscape of real estate governance and its impact on professionals and consumers.

## 9.1.  DISPUTE RESOLUTION

The dispute resolution industry is the field of law that deals with resolving conflicts and disputes between parties, such as individuals, businesses, or governments. Dispute resolution can take various forms, such as litigation, arbitration, mediation, negotiation, or online dispute resolution (ODR). The industry faces many challenges, such as high costs, long delays, complex procedures, and limited access to justice. To overcome these challenges, the dispute resolution industry has been adopting artificial intelligence (AI) solutions that can enhance efficiency, accuracy, fairness, and satisfaction. AI can take many forms in dispute resolution, as shown below. For example, AI can help disputants with case assessment, document analysis, evidence discovery, and settlement prediction. AI can also enable new modes and platforms for dispute resolution, such as smart contracts, blockchain arbitration, and AI mediators. AI is transforming the dispute resolution industry, creating value for disputants and practitioners.

| AI APPLICATIONS IN DISPUTE RESOLUTION | SOLUTIONS PROVIDED BY COMPANIES | SOLUTIONS DESCRIPTIONS |
|---|---|---|
| **Case Assessment** | • Lex Machina Legal Analytics by LexisNexis, a RELX Company<br>• Logikcull by Logikcull<br>• CaseMetrix by CaseMetrix<br>• BrightSight by BrightSight<br>• Epiq Legal Solutions by Epiq Legal Solutions<br>• eBrevia Case Analysis by eBrevia<br>• Concord Legal AI for Real Estate Disputes by Concord Legal | • Ethical Analysis involves using AI to assess the ethical implications of AI systems and applications.<br>• AI can use data analytics and machine learning to identify ethical issues, risks, and trade-offs.<br>• These solutions help developers, users, and regulators evaluate and improve the ethical quality of AI systems and applications. |
| **Document Analysis** | • Lex Machina Legal Analytics by LexisNexis, a RELX Company<br>• Westlaw by Thomson Reuters<br>• Everlaw by Everlaw | • Document Analysis involves using AI to extract and analyze information from contracts, agreements, and other legal documents. |

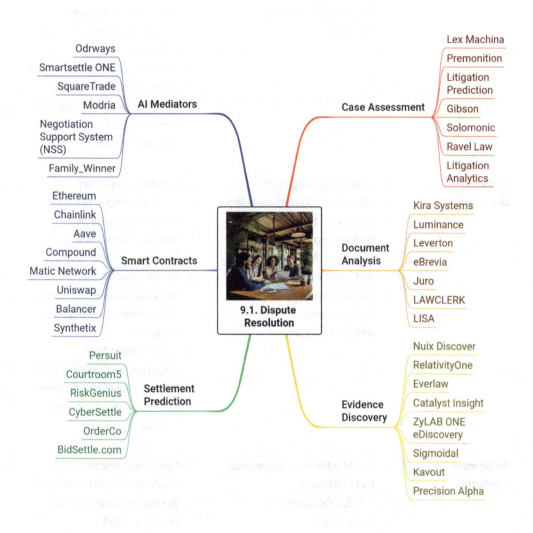

**AI Mediators**
- Odrways
- Smartsettle ONE
- SquareTrade
- Modria
- Negotiation Support System (NSS)
- Family_Winner

**Smart Contracts**
- Ethereum
- Chainlink
- Aave
- Compound
- Matic Network
- Uniswap
- Balancer
- Synthetix

**Settlement Prediction**
- Persuit
- Courtroom5
- RiskGenius
- CyberSettle
- OrderCo
- BidSettle.com

**9.1. Dispute Resolution**

**Case Assessment**
- Lex Machina
- Premonition
- Litigation Prediction
- Gibson
- Solomonic
- Ravel Law
- Litigation Analytics

**Document Analysis**
- Kira Systems
- Luminance
- Leverton
- eBrevia
- Juro
- LAWCLERK
- LISA

**Evidence Discovery**
- Nuix Discover
- RelativityOne
- Everlaw
- Catalyst Insight
- ZyLAB ONE eDiscovery
- Sigmoidal
- Kavout
- Precision Alpha

| AI APPLICATIONS IN DISPUTE RESOLUTION | SOLUTIONS PROVIDED BY COMPANIES | SOLUTIONS DESCRIPTIONS |
|---|---|---|
| | • DISCO by CS Disco, Inc.<br>• Logikcull by Logikcull<br>• eBrevia Case Analysis by eBrevia | • AI can use natural language processing and machine learning to identify key terms, clauses, and risks.<br>• The solutions help disputants and practitioners review documents faster, more accurately, and more comprehensively. |
| Evidence Discovery | • Logikcull by Logikcull<br>• eBrevia eDiscovery by eBrevia<br>• Epiq Legal Solutions by Epiq Legal Solutions<br>• CloudLex Real Estate Suite by CloudLex<br>• Lex Machina Legal Analytics by LexisNexis, a RELX Company | • Evidence Discovery involves using AI to collect and analyze evidence from various sources and formats.<br>• AI can use data analytics and machine learning to search, filter, classify, and organize evidence.<br>• The solutions help disputants and practitioners find relevant evidence faster, more efficiently, and more reliably. |
| Settlement Prediction | • Lex Machina Legal Analytics by LexisNexis, a RELX Company<br>• Clausehound by Clausehound Inc.<br>• Litigation Analytics by Litigation Analytics<br>• Logikcull by Logikcull<br>• Epiq Legal Solutions by Epiq Legal Solutions | • Settlement Prediction involves using AI to estimate the likelihood and amount of a settlement.<br>• AI can use data-driven models to calculate settlement ranges based on various factors such as case type, jurisdiction, parties involved, and damages claimed. |

| AI APPLICATIONS IN DISPUTE RESOLUTION | SOLUTIONS PROVIDED BY COMPANIES | SOLUTIONS DESCRIPTIONS |
|---|---|---|
| | | • The solutions help disputants and practitioners negotiate settlements more effectively and efficiently. |
| **Smart Contracts** | • Logikcull by Logikcull<br>• Epiq Legal Solutions by Epiq Legal Solutions<br>• Lex Machina Legal Analytics by LexisNexis, a RELX Company<br>• Litigation Analytics by Litigation Analytics | • Smart Contracts involve using AI to create and execute agreements between parties in a digital and decentralized manner.<br>• AI can use blockchain technology to encode the terms and conditions of the agreement, verify the performance of the obligations, and enforce the outcomes.<br>• The solutions help disputants and practitioners simplify processes, reduce costs, and ensure compliance. |
| **AI Mediators** | • Logikcull by Logikcull<br>• Epiq Legal Solutions by Epiq Legal Solutions<br>• Clausehound by Clausehound Inc. | • AI Mediators involve using AI to facilitate the communication and negotiation between disputing parties.<br>• AI can use natural language processing and machine learning to provide information, suggestions, feedback, and proposals to the parties.<br>• The solutions help disputants and practitioners reach mutually acceptable resolutions. |

## *Key Takeaways*

- AI is transforming the Dispute Resolution industry, addressing challenges like high costs, long delays, and limited access to justice.

- Case Assessment, uses AI to evaluate case merits by analyzing data from previous cases, aiding informed decisions and strategy development.

- Document Analysis, leverages AI for extracting and analyzing information from legal documents, enhancing document review efficiency and accuracy.

- Evidence Discovery, involves AI in collecting and analyzing evidence from various sources, improving the efficiency and reliability of evidence retrieval.

- Settlement Prediction, utilizes AI to estimate settlement likelihood and amount, enhancing negotiation effectiveness and efficiency.

- Smart Contracts, use AI to create and execute digital and decentralized agreements, simplifying processes, reducing costs, and ensuring compliance.

- AI Mediators, employ AI to facilitate communication and negotiation between disputing parties, helping reach mutually acceptable resolutions.

## 9.2. ETHICS AND REGULATIONS

The ethics and regulations industry is the field of law and philosophy that deals with the moral and legal implications of artificial intelligence (AI) and its applications. Ethics and regulations aim to ensure that AI is developed and used in a way that respects human dignity, rights, values, and interests. The industry faces many challenges, such as defining ethical principles and frameworks, establishing governance and oversight mechanisms, addressing social and economic impacts, and ensuring accountability and transparency. To cope with these challenges, the ethics and regulations industry has been engaging with various stakeholders, such as policymakers, researchers, developers, users, and civil society. AI can take many forms in ethics and regulations, as shown below. For example, AI can help with ethical analysis, legal compliance, policy formulation, and public consultation. AI can also pose new ethical and regulatory dilemmas, such as bias, privacy, autonomy, and responsibility. AI is transforming the ethics and regulations industry, creating opportunities and risks for society.

| AI APPLICATIONS IN ETHICS AND REGULATIONS | SOLUTIONS PROVIDED BY COMPANIES | SOLUTIONS DESCRIPTIONS |
|---|---|---|
| Ethical Analysis | • Ethica by Ethica Data Services, Inc.<br>• Ethical OS by Institute for the Future<br>• Ethics Canvas by Ethics Canvas<br>• Ethical Explorer by Salesforce.com, Inc.<br>• Ethics Litmus Test by Ethics Litmus Test<br>• Ethical Intelligence by Ethical Intelligence Associates Ltd.<br>• EthicsAI by EthicsAI Ltd.<br>• Ethixbase by Ethixbase Pte. Ltd. | • Ethical Analysis involves using AI to assess the ethical implications of AI systems and applications.<br>• AI can use data analytics and machine learning to identify ethical issues, risks, and trade-offs.<br>• These solutions help developers, users, and regulators evaluate and improve the ethical quality of AI systems and applications. |

| AI APPLICATIONS IN ETHICS AND REGULATIONS | SOLUTIONS PROVIDED BY COMPANIES | SOLUTIONS DESCRIPTIONS |
| --- | --- | --- |
| **Legal Compliance** | • Luminance by Luminance Technologies, Ltd.<br>• Kira Systems by Kira Systems, Inc.<br>• Leverton by MRI Software, LLC<br>• eBrevia by Donnelley Financial Solutions, Inc.<br>• Juro AI by Juro<br>• LAWCLERK by LAWCLERK. Legal<br>• LISA by Robot Lawyer LISA | • Legal Compliance involves using AI to ensure that AI systems and applications comply with relevant laws and regulations.<br>• AI can use natural language processing and machine learning to extract and analyze information from legal documents, such as contracts, agreements, policies, and standards.<br>• The solutions help developers, users, and regulators review documents faster, more accurately, and more comprehensively. |
| **Policy Formulation** | • Nesta by Nesta<br>• The GovLab by The GovLab<br>• Carnegie Endowment for International Peace by Carnegie Endowment for International Peace<br>• Berkman Klein Center for Internet & Society by Harvard University<br>• Oxford Internet Institute by University of Oxford<br>• The Alan Turing Institute by The Alan Turing Institute<br>• The Partnership on AI by The Partnership on AI | • Policy Formulation involves using AI to develop and implement policies and guidelines for the ethical and responsible use of AI.<br>• AI can use data analytics and machine learning to provide insights, recommendations, best practices, and standards for various aspects of AI governance.<br>• The solutions help policymakers, researchers, developers, users, and civil society collaborate and coordinate on shaping the future of AI. |

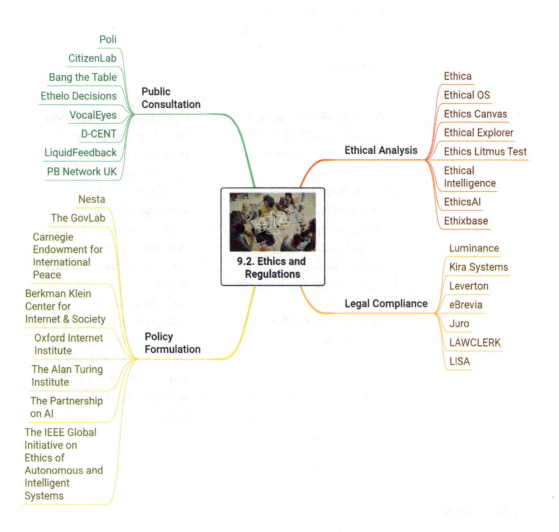

Poli
CitizenLab
Bang the Table
Ethelo Decisions
VocalEyes
D-CENT
LiquidFeedback
PB Network UK

**Public Consultation**

Nesta
The GovLab
Carnegie Endowment for International Peace
Berkman Klein Center for Internet & Society
Oxford Internet Institute
The Alan Turing Institute
The Partnership on AI
The IEEE Global Initiative on Ethics of Autonomous and Intelligent Systems

**Policy Formulation**

**9.2. Ethics and Regulations**

**Ethical Analysis**

Ethica
Ethical OS
Ethics Canvas
Ethical Explorer
Ethics Litmus Test
Ethical Intelligence
EthicsAI
Ethixbase

**Legal Compliance**

Luminance
Kira Systems
Leverton
eBrevia
Juro
LAWCLERK
LISA

| AI APPLICATIONS IN ETHICS AND REGULATIONS | SOLUTIONS PROVIDED BY COMPANIES | SOLUTIONS DESCRIPTIONS |
|---|---|---|
| | • The IEEE Global Initiative on Ethics of Autonomous and Intelligent Systems by The IEEE Global Initiative on Ethics of Autonomous and Intelligent Systems | |
| Public Consultation | • Poli by Poli Technologies, Inc.<br>• CitizenLab by CitizenLab NV<br>• Bang the Table by Bang the Table Pty Ltd.<br>• Ethelo Decisions by Ethelo Decisions Inc.<br>• VocalEyes by VocalEyes Digital Democracy Ltd.<br>• D-CENT by D-CENT<br>• LiquidFeedback by Interaktive Demokratie e.V.<br>• PB Network UK by PB Network UK | • Public Consultation involves using AI to engage with the public on the ethical and social issues of AI.<br>• AI can use natural language processing and machine learning to facilitate dialogue, feedback, and participation among various stakeholders.<br>• The solutions help policymakers, researchers, developers, users, and civil society understand and address the public's views, concerns, and expectations on AI. |

## Key Takeaways

- AI is reshaping the Ethics and Regulations industry, addressing challenges in defining ethical principles, establishing governance, and ensuring accountability in AI development and use.
- Ethical Analysis, uses AI to assess the ethical implications of AI systems, helping developers, users, and regulators evaluate and improve ethical quality.

- Legal Compliance, involves AI ensuring that AI systems comply with relevant laws and regulations, enhancing document review efficiency and accuracy.
- Policy Formulation, uses AI to develop policies and guidelines for the ethical and responsible use of AI, aiding collaboration among stakeholders.
- Public Consultation, engages the public on AI's ethical and social issues using AI to facilitate dialogue, feedback, and participation among various stakeholders.
- AI plays a crucial role in defining and ensuring ethical standards, legal compliance, policy development, and public engagement in the Ethics and Regulations industry.

## 9.3. LAW AND COMPLIANCE

The law and compliance industry is the field of law that deals with ensuring that organizations and individuals adhere to the relevant laws, regulations, standards, and ethical practices in their operations and activities. Law and compliance covers various domains, such as corporate governance, risk management, anti-corruption, data protection, environmental protection, human rights, and social responsibility. The industry faces many challenges, such as increasing complexity and diversity of regulations, growing expectations from stakeholders, and rising costs and penalties for non-compliance. To cope with these challenges, the law and compliance industry has been adopting artificial intelligence (AI) solutions that can enhance efficiency, accuracy, quality, and profitability. AI can take many forms in law and compliance, as shown below. For example, AI can help with contract analysis, document review, litigation support, legal research, compliance management, and dispute resolution. AI can also create new challenges and opportunities for the law and compliance industry, such as ethical and regulatory issues, new business models, and new forms of legal services. AI is transforming the law and compliance industry, creating value for organizations and individuals.

| AI APPLICATIONS IN LAW AND COMPLIANCE | SOLUTIONS PROVIDED BY COMPANIES | SOLUTIONS DESCRIPTIONS |
|---|---|---|
| Contract Analysis | • Kira by Kira Systems<br>• LawGeex by LawGeex<br>• Analyse Documents by Elevate<br>• ContractPodAi by ContractPod Technologies Ltd. | • Contract Analysis involves using AI to extract and analyze information from contracts, agreements, and other legal documents.<br>• AI can use natural language processing and machine learning to identify key terms, clauses, and risks.<br>• These solutions help lawyers and compliance professionals review documents faster, more accurately, and more comprehensively. |

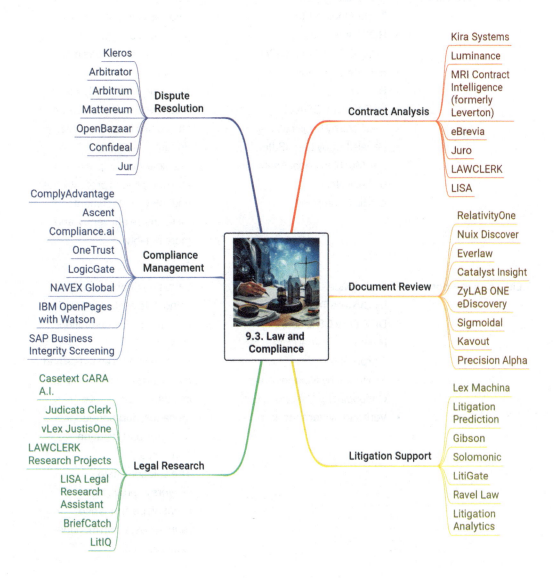

**Dispute Resolution**
- Kleros
- Arbitrator
- Arbitrum
- Mattereum
- OpenBazaar
- Confideal
- Jur

**Contract Analysis**
- Kira Systems
- Luminance
- MRI Contract Intelligence (formerly Leverton)
- eBrevia
- Juro
- LAWCLERK
- LISA

**Compliance Management**
- ComplyAdvantage
- Ascent
- Compliance.ai
- OneTrust
- LogicGate
- NAVEX Global
- IBM OpenPages with Watson
- SAP Business Integrity Screening

**Document Review**
- RelativityOne
- Nuix Discover
- Everlaw
- Catalyst Insight
- ZyLAB ONE eDiscovery
- Sigmoidal
- Kavout
- Precision Alpha

**9.3. Law and Compliance**

**Legal Research**
- Casetext CARA A.I.
- Judicata Clerk
- vLex JustisOne
- LAWCLERK Research Projects
- LISA Legal Research Assistant
- BriefCatch
- LitIQ

**Litigation Support**
- Lex Machina
- Litigation Prediction
- Gibson
- Solomonic
- LitiGate
- Ravel Law
- Litigation Analytics

| AI APPLICATIONS IN LAW AND COMPLIANCE | SOLUTIONS PROVIDED BY COMPANIES | SOLUTIONS DESCRIPTIONS |
|---|---|---|
| Document Review | • Luminance by Luminance Technologies, Ltd.<br>• ROSS Intelligence by ROSS Intelligence, Inc.<br>• Everlaw by Everlaw<br>• Relativity by Relativity ODA LLC<br>• Logikcull by Logikcull<br>• Legalsifter by LegalSifter, Inc.<br>• Lex Machina Legal Analytics by LexisNexis, a RELX Company | • Document Review involves using AI to collect and analyze documents from various sources and formats.<br>• AI can use data analytics and machine learning to search, filter, classify, and organize documents.<br>• The solutions help lawyers and compliance professionals find relevant documents faster, more efficiently, and more reliably. |
| Litigation Support | • Brainspace by Cyxtera Technologies<br>• DISCO by CS Disco, Inc.<br>• Reveal by Reveal Data Corporation<br>• Nextpoint by Nextpoint, Inc.<br>• Casepoint by Casepoint LLC<br>• Veritone by Veritone, Inc. | • Litigation Support involves using AI to assist lawyers in preparing and conducting litigation.<br>• AI can use data analytics and machine learning to provide insights on case outcomes, damages, duration, judge behavior, and litigation strategies.<br>• The solutions help lawyers improve their litigation performance, reduce costs, and manage expectations. |
| Legal Research | • Casetext by Casetext, Inc.<br>• ROSS Intelligence by ROSS Intelligence, Inc.<br>• Westlaw by Thomson Reuters | • Legal Research involves using AI to find and analyze legal information from various sources. |

| AI APPLICATIONS IN LAW AND COMPLIANCE | SOLUTIONS PROVIDED BY COMPANIES | SOLUTIONS DESCRIPTIONS |
|---|---|---|
| | • LexisNexis by LexisNexis, a RELX Company<br>• Fastcase by Fastcase, Inc. | • AI can use natural language processing and machine learning to understand natural language queries, retrieve relevant cases, statutes, regulations, and articles, and provide summaries and citations.<br>• The solutions help lawyers conduct legal research faster, more thoroughly, and more accurately. |
| Compliance Management | • Compliance.ai by Compliance.ai<br>• Ascent by Ascent Technologies, Inc.<br>• ComplyAdvantage by ComplyAdvantage<br>• Onna by Onna Technologies, Inc.<br>• OneTrust by OneTrust LLC<br>• LogicGate by LogicGate, Inc. | • Compliance Management involves using AI to monitor and ensure compliance with relevant laws, regulations, standards, and ethical practices.<br>• AI can use data analytics and machine learning to track and update regulatory changes, identify and assess compliance risks, automate compliance tasks, and generate compliance reports.<br>• The solutions help organizations and individuals reduce compliance costs, avoid penalties, and enhance reputation. |
| Dispute Resolution | • Smartsettle by iCan Systems Inc.<br>• Modria by Tyler Technologies, Inc. | • Dispute Resolution involves using AI to resolve disputes arising from legal transactions or contracts. |

| AI APPLICATIONS IN LAW AND COMPLIANCE | SOLUTIONS PROVIDED BY COMPANIES | SOLUTIONS DESCRIPTIONS |
|---|---|---|
| | • Kleros by Kleros<br>• Clause by Clause, Inc.<br>• Picture It Settled by Picture It Settled, LLC<br>• Lex Machina Legal Analytics by LexisNexis, a RELX Company<br>• ROSS Intelligence by ROSS Intelligence, Inc. | • AI can use blockchain technology to select arbitrators, submit evidence, apply rules, and deliver awards.<br>• The solutions help parties access fast, secure, and transparent dispute resolution. |

### Key Takeaways

- AI is revolutionizing the Law and Compliance industry, addressing challenges in diverse regulations, stakeholder expectations, and compliance costs.
- Contract Analysis, leverages AI to extract and analyze information from legal documents, enhancing review efficiency.
- Document Review, uses AI for efficient collection, analysis, and organization of documents, aiding lawyers and compliance professionals.
- Litigation Support, employs AI to provide insights on case outcomes, judge behavior, and litigation strategies, enhancing overall litigation performance.
- Legal Research, utilizes AI for faster and more accurate retrieval and analysis of legal information from various sources.
- Compliance Management, employs AI to monitor, assess compliance risks, automate tasks, and generate reports, helping organizations reduce costs and enhance reputation.
- Dispute Resolution, uses AI and blockchain technology for transparent, secure, and efficient resolution of legal disputes, providing parties with faster access to resolutions.
- AI creates new challenges and opportunities, shaping a future with enhanced efficiency, accuracy, and quality in legal and compliance operations.

# CHAPTER 10
# EDUCATION

This chapter focuses on the pivotal role of artificial intelligence (AI) in reshaping real estate education. Education in the real estate industry is indispensable, equipping professionals with essential skills, knowledge, and adaptability. AI has emerged as a transformative force in this domain, enhancing the quality and accessibility of real estate education. Here are the key highlights:

### Significance of Real Estate Education:

- Real estate education goes beyond the basics, encompassing skill development, networking, credibility, and adaptability.
- It plays a crucial role in preparing professionals to thrive in the dynamic real estate industry.

### AI's Impact on Real Estate Education:

- AI offers personalized learning experiences, tailoring content and assessments to individual needs.
- Interactive simulations enable hands-on skill development, replicating real-world scenarios.
- Language processing tools provide instant feedback on communication skills.
- Access to extensive real estate data and insights enhances practical learning.

### Online Learning Platforms and Courses:

- AI integration with online education platforms offers flexibility, cost-efficiency, and global reach.
- Learners worldwide access industry-relevant content, certifications, and networking opportunities.
- Real-time updates keep courses aligned with the evolving real estate landscape.
- Online platforms provide recognized certifications and networking opportunities.

### The Future of AI in Real Estate Education:

- AI continues to advance, promising even more personalized, adaptive, and industry-relevant learning experiences.
- It ensures that professionals stay updated in a rapidly changing real estate landscape.

This chapter explores how AI revolutionizes real estate education, making it more accessible, personalized, and industry-relevant. This evolution underscores AI's crucial role in transforming how real estate professionals learn and succeed in their careers.

## 10.1. EDUCATION AND TRAINING

The education and training industry is the field of providing learning opportunities and skills development for individuals and groups. Education and training can take place in formal or informal settings, such as schools, universities, workplaces, or online platforms. The industry faces many challenges, such as meeting the diverse needs and preferences of learners, ensuring the quality and relevance of learning outcomes, and adapting to the changing demands of the labor market and society. To cope with these challenges, the education and training industry has been adopting artificial intelligence (AI) solutions that can enhance efficiency, effectiveness, personalization, and engagement. AI can take many forms in education and training, as shown below. For example, AI can help with learning assistance, personalized education, improved accessibility, AI tutoring, smart content, and intelligent tutoring systems. AI can also create new challenges and opportunities for the education and training industry, such as ethical and regulatory issues, new pedagogical approaches, and new forms of learning and assessment. AI is transforming the education and training industry, creating value for learners and educators.

| AI APPLICATIONS IN EDUCATION AND TRAINING | SOLUTIONS PROVIDED BY COMPANIES | SOLUTIONS DESCRIPTIONS |
|---|---|---|
| Learning Assistance | • Real Estate Technology Institute (RETI) by Real Estate Technology Institute<br>• PropTech School by PropTech School<br>• MIT Center for Real Estate by Massachusetts Institute of Technology<br>• Coursera by Coursera, Inc.<br>• edX by edX, Inc.<br>• Udacity by Udacity, Inc.<br>• Udemy by Udemy, Inc.<br>• Skillshare by Skillshare, Inc. | • Learning Assistance involves using AI to provide learners with access to various learning resources and platforms.<br>• AI can use natural language processing and machine learning to deliver content, feedback, and guidance to learners.<br>• These solutions help learners acquire knowledge and skills at their own pace, place, and preference. |

| AI APPLICATIONS IN EDUCATION AND TRAINING | SOLUTIONS PROVIDED BY COMPANIES | SOLUTIONS DESCRIPTIONS |
|---|---|---|
| **Personalized Education** | • Real Estate Technology Institute (RETI) by Real Estate Technology Institute<br>• PropStream by PropStream<br>• Squirrel AI by Squirrel AI Learning by Yixue Group<br>• CogBooks by CogBooks Ltd.<br>• Knewton by Knewton, Inc.<br>• DreamBox Learning by DreamBox Learning, Inc.<br>• ALEKS by McGraw Hill Education, Inc. | • Personalized Education involves using AI to tailor the learning experience to the individual needs and goals of each learner.<br>• AI can use data analytics and machine learning to track and analyze the learner's progress, preferences, strengths, and weaknesses.<br>• The solutions help learners receive customized content, feedback, recommendations, and support. |
| **Improved Accessibility** | • Real Estate Technology Institute (RETI) by Real Estate Technology Institute<br>• W3C Web Accessibility Initiative (WAI) by World Wide Web Consortium<br>• Tobii Dynavox Snap + Core First by Tobii Dynavox LLC<br>• Kurzweil 3000 by Kurzweil Education, Inc.<br>• Nuance Dragon NaturallySpeaking by Nuance Communications, Inc.<br>• Ghotit Real Writer & Reader by Ghotit Ltd.<br>• MindView AT by MatchWare A/S | • Improved Accessibility involves using AI to enable learners with disabilities or special needs to access learning resources and platforms.<br>• AI can use speech recognition, text-to-speech, image recognition, eye tracking, and other technologies to assist learners with various impairments.<br>• The solutions help learners overcome barriers and participate in learning activities. |

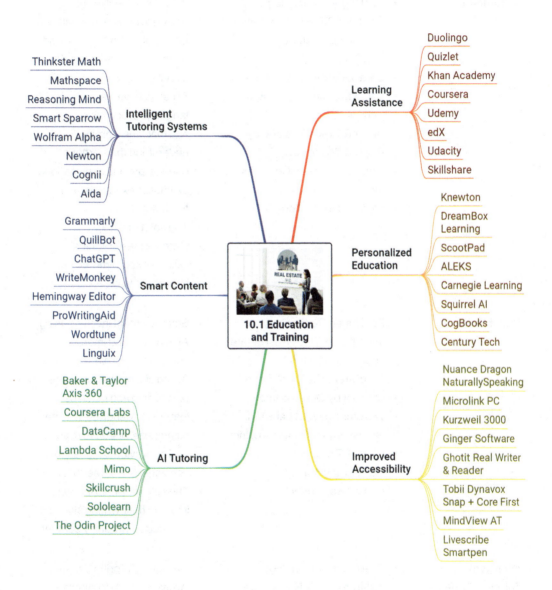

**Intelligent Tutoring Systems**
- Thinkster Math
- Mathspace
- Reasoning Mind
- Smart Sparrow
- Wolfram Alpha
- Newton
- Cognii
- Aida

**Smart Content**
- Grammarly
- QuillBot
- ChatGPT
- WriteMonkey
- Hemingway Editor
- ProWritingAid
- Wordtune
- Linguix

**AI Tutoring**
- Baker & Taylor Axis 360
- Coursera Labs
- DataCamp
- Lambda School
- Mimo
- Skillcrush
- Sololearn
- The Odin Project

**10.1 Education and Training**

**Learning Assistance**
- Duolingo
- Quizlet
- Khan Academy
- Coursera
- Udemy
- edX
- Udacity
- Skillshare

**Personalized Education**
- Knewton
- DreamBox Learning
- ScootPad
- ALEKS
- Carnegie Learning
- Squirrel AI
- CogBooks
- Century Tech

**Improved Accessibility**
- Nuance Dragon NaturallySpeaking
- Microlink PC
- Kurzweil 3000
- Ginger Software
- Ghotit Real Writer & Reader
- Tobii Dynavox Snap + Core First
- MindView AT
- Livescribe Smartpen

| AI APPLICATIONS IN EDUCATION AND TRAINING | SOLUTIONS PROVIDED BY COMPANIES | SOLUTIONS DESCRIPTIONS |
| --- | --- | --- |
| **AI Tutoring** | • Real Estate Technology Institute (RETI) by Real Estate Technology Institute<br>• PropStream by PropStream<br>• DataCamp by DataCamp, Inc.<br>• Lambda School by Lambda School, Inc.<br>• Baker & Taylor Axis 360 by Baker & Taylor, LLC<br>• Coursera Labs by Coursera, Inc.<br>• Skillcrush by Skillcrush, Inc. | • AI Tutoring involves using AI to provide learners with personalized instruction and guidance on specific topics or skills.<br>• AI can use natural language processing and machine learning to understand the learner's queries, provide explanations, examples, exercises, and feedback.<br>• The solutions help learners master topics or skills in a self-directed and interactive way. |
| **Smart Content** | • Real Estate Technology Institute (RETI) by Real Estate Technology Institute<br>• PropStream by PropStream<br>• QuillBot by QuillBot, Inc.<br>• Wordtune by AI21 Labs Ltd.<br>• Grammarly by Grammarly, Inc.<br>• ChatGPT by OpenAI<br>• Hemingway App by Hemingway Editor | • Smart Content involves using AI to create and improve content for learning purposes.<br>• AI can use natural language processing and machine learning to generate, rewrite, summarize, or edit text, as well as provide suggestions, corrections, and feedback.<br>• The solutions help learners improve their writing skills and produce high-quality content. |
| **Intelligent Tutoring Systems** | • Real Estate Technology Institute (RETI): Real Estate Technology Institute<br>• PropStream: PropStream<br>• Cognii by Cognii, Inc. | • Intelligent Tutoring Systems involve using AI to simulate human tutors and provide learners with adaptive and personalized learning experiences. |

| AI APPLICATIONS IN EDUCATION AND TRAINING | SOLUTIONS PROVIDED BY COMPANIES | SOLUTIONS DESCRIPTIONS |
| --- | --- | --- |
| | • Aida by Pearson Education, Inc.<br>• Smart Sparrow by Smart Sparrow Pty Ltd.<br>• Newton by Area9 Lyceum A/S<br>• Wolfram Alpha by Wolfram Alpha LLC<br>• Thinkster Math by Thinkster Math | • AI can use natural language processing, machine learning, and cognitive modeling to diagnose the learner's knowledge, skills, and misconceptions, and provide feedback, hints, scaffolding, and remediation.<br>• The solutions help learners achieve deeper understanding and higher retention of the learning material. |

### Key Takeaways

- AI is transforming the Education and Training sector by addressing challenges related to diverse learner needs, quality of outcomes, and labor market demands.
- Learning Assistance harnesses AI for content delivery, feedback, and guidance, offering learners adaptable access to resources.
- Personalized Education tailors learning experiences based on individual progress, preferences, strengths, and weaknesses, amplifying customization.
- Improved Accessibility employs AI to aid learners with disabilities, utilizing technologies like speech recognition and text-to-speech.
- AI Tutoring provides individualized instruction through natural language processing and machine learning, promoting interactive self-guided learning.
- Smart Content uses AI for content enhancement, aiding learners in refining writing abilities and generating quality content.
- Intelligent Tutoring Systems simulate human tutors, delivering adaptive learning experiences through advanced AI techniques. AI presents both challenges and prospects, molding the future of education with increased efficiency, personalization, and engagement for both learners and educators.

# CHAPTER 11
# AI'S MULTIFACETED INFLUENCE ACROSS REAL ESTATE

Artificial intelligence (AI) in real estate is not merely a tool but a transformative and adaptable force that defies conventional boundaries. Its influence permeates every corner of the industry, redefining traditional categories and delivering innovations that were once unimaginable.

**AI: A Seamless Integration:** AI is the unifying thread that runs through the tapestry of real estate, seamlessly connecting and enhancing various facets of the industry. Its adaptability and transformative power enable it to transcend predefined categories, creating an ecosystem of endless possibilities.

**Versatility Redefined:** In this section, we explore AI applications that blur the lines of traditional categorization. These applications epitomize AI's multifaceted role in shaping and enriching the real estate landscape.

This chapter stands as a testament to AI's boundless potential within real estate. It highlights AI's ability to transcend established categories, offering a transformative impact across various aspects of the industry. By delving into these applications, we gain a deeper understanding of AI's ever-evolving role in real estate, continuously reshaping and redefining industry norms.

## 11.1. PREDICTIVE ANALYTICS AND FORECASTING IN REAL ESTATE

Predictive analytics and forecasting, when applied to the real estate industry, involve leveraging data and AI to make informed predictions about the future of the real estate market. This strategic approach aids real estate businesses and professionals in decision-making, performance optimization, risk reduction, and profit maximization. The scope of predictive analytics and forecasting in real estate encompasses property valuation, market trends, customer behavior, demand and supply dynamics, as well as risk and compliance considerations. However, this field encounters challenges such as managing large and complex datasets, ensuring data quality and reliability, selecting appropriate methods and models, and effectively interpreting and communicating results. AI emerges as a crucial ally, enhancing accuracy, speed, scalability, and automation in addressing these challenges. As AI transforms the landscape, it introduces new challenges and opportunities, including ethical and regulatory considerations, novel business models, and innovative data and insights.

| AI APPLICATIONS IN PREDICTIVE ANALYTICS AND FORECASTING IN REAL ESTATE | SOLUTIONS PROVIDED BY COMPANIES | SOLUTIONS DESCRIPTIONS |
|---|---|---|
| **Property Valuation** | • Zillow Zestimate by Zillow Group, Inc.<br>• Redfin Estimate by Redfin Corporation<br>• Realtor.com RealValue by Move, Inc.<br>• Trulia Estimate by Zillow Group, Inc.<br>• HouseCanary Value Report by HouseCanary, Inc.<br>• CoreLogic Automated Valuation Model by CoreLogic, Inc. | • Property Valuation employs AI to estimate a property's current market value based on historical data and external factors.<br>• AI utilizes data analytics and machine learning to analyze property features, location, condition, comparables, and market trends.<br>• These solutions assist real estate professionals in property appraisal, pricing, and negotiation. |

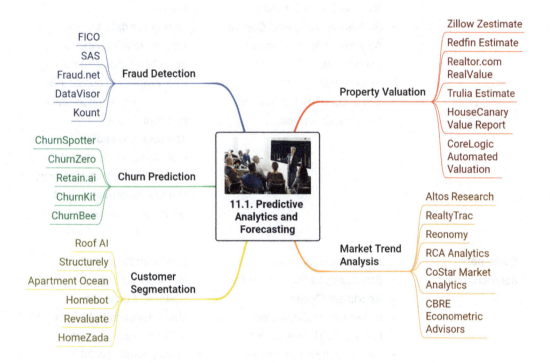

Fraud Detection
- FICO
- SAS
- Fraud.net
- DataVisor
- Kount

Churn Prediction
- ChurnSpotter
- ChurnZero
- Retain.ai
- ChurnKit
- ChurnBee

Customer Segmentation
- Roof AI
- Structurely
- Apartment Ocean
- Homebot
- Revaluate
- HomeZada

**11.1. Predictive Analytics and Forecasting**

Property Valuation
- Zillow Zestimate
- Redfin Estimate
- Realtor.com RealValue
- Trulia Estimate
- HouseCanary Value Report
- CoreLogic Automated Valuation

Market Trend Analysis
- Altos Research
- RealtyTrac
- Reonomy
- RCA Analytics
- CoStar Market Analytics
- CBRE Econometric Advisors

| AI APPLICATIONS IN PREDICTIVE ANALYTICS AND FORECASTING IN REAL ESTATE | SOLUTIONS PROVIDED BY COMPANIES | SOLUTIONS DESCRIPTIONS |
|---|---|---|
| **Market Trend Analysis** | • Altos Research by Altos Research LLC<br>• RealtyTrac by RealtyTrac<br>• Reonomy by Reonomy, an Altus Group Company<br>• RCA Analytics by Real Capital Analytics, A MSCI Company<br>• CoStar Market Analytics by CoStar Group, Inc.<br>• CBRE Econometric Advisors by CBRE Group, Inc. | • Market Trend Analysis uses AI to monitor and forecast changes and patterns in the real estate market.<br>• AI employs data analytics and machine learning to collect and analyze data from property listings, sales transactions, demographics, and economics.<br>• The solutions enable real estate businesses to understand market dynamics, identify opportunities, and devise effective strategies. |
| **Customer Segmentation** | • Roof AI by Roof AI, Inc.<br>• Structurely by Structurely, Inc.<br>• Apartment Ocean by Apartment Ocean, Inc.<br>• Homebot by Homebot, Inc.<br>• Revaluate by Revaluate, Inc.<br>• HomeZada by HomeZada, Inc. | • Customer Segmentation involves AI grouping customers based on characteristics, behaviors, preferences, and needs.<br>• AI utilizes data analytics and machine learning to cluster customers into homogeneous segments using various criteria.<br>• The solutions enhance real estate businesses' understanding of customers, enabling targeted marketing and improved customer loyalty. |

| AI APPLICATIONS IN PREDICTIVE ANALYTICS AND FORECASTING IN REAL ESTATE | SOLUTIONS PROVIDED BY COMPANIES | SOLUTIONS DESCRIPTIONS |
| --- | --- | --- |
| **Churn Prediction** | • ChurnSpotter by ChurnSpotter SAS<br>• ChurnZero by ChurnZero, Inc.<br>• Retain.ai by Retain.ai, Inc.<br>• ChurnKit by ChurnKit, Inc.<br>• ChurnBee by ChurnBee, Inc. | • Churn Prediction uses AI to predict customers likely to stop using a product or service.<br>• AI analyzes customer behavior, feedback, satisfaction, engagement, and loyalty through data analytics and machine learning.<br>• The solutions aid real estate businesses in identifying at-risk customers, preventing churn, increasing retention rates, and improving customer lifetime value. |
| **Fraud Detection** | • FICO Falcon Fraud Manager by Fair Isaac Corporation<br>• SAS Fraud Management by SAS Institute<br>• Fraud.net Platform by Fraud.net, Inc.<br>• DataVisor Fraud Detection Platform by DataVisor, Inc.<br>• Kount Fraud Prevention Platform by Kount, Inc. | • Fraud Detection employs AI to detect and prevent fraudulent activities like identity theft, credit card fraud, insurance fraud, and money laundering.<br>• AI monitors transactions, flags anomalies, scores risk levels, and alerts authorities using data analytics and machine learning.<br>• The solutions assist real estate businesses in reducing fraud losses, protecting customers, and ensuring regulatory compliance. |

## Key Takeaways

- Predictive analytics and forecasting in real estate leverage data and AI to make predictions about the future of the market.

- Property Valuation, Market Trend Analysis, Customer Segmentation, Churn Prediction, and Fraud Detection are key AI applications transforming the real estate industry.

- AI enhances decision-making, risk management, and profitability for real estate businesses and professionals.

- The integration of AI introduces new challenges and opportunities, influencing ethical considerations, business models, and data-driven insights. The transformation is driven by creating value for the real estate industry.

## 11.2. CHATBOTS AND VIRTUAL ASSISTANTS

The chatbot and virtual assistant (CVA) industry utilizes AI for human communication through text or voice. Offering services like information retrieval, customer support, and personal assistance, CVAs operate across diverse platforms, including websites, mobile apps, social media, messaging apps, and smart speakers. Challenges such as natural language understanding, response generation, context retention, handling multiple intents, and ensuring user satisfaction shape the industry. To address these challenges, AI solutions enhance natural language processing, machine learning, conversational AI, and user experience. AI manifests in various forms within CVAs, including natural language understanding, generation, dialogue management, sentiment analysis, and speech recognition.

| AI APPLICATIONS IN CHATBOTS AND VIRTUAL ASSISTANTS | SOLUTIONS PROVIDED BY COMPANIES | SOLUTIONS DESCRIPTIONS |
| --- | --- | --- |
| Natural Language Understanding | • Roof AI by Roof AI, Inc.<br>• CINC AI by CINC, a Fidelity National Financial, Inc. Company<br>• AIVA by Black Knight, Inc.<br>• kvCORE by InsideRE, LLC<br>• Landbot by Landbot<br>• Rasa by Rasa Technologies, Inc.<br>• Structurely by Reinform, Inc.<br>• Medium Relevance by Amazon.com, Inc.<br>• Google Dialogflow by Google LLC<br>• IBM Watson Assistant by IBM Corporation | • AI extracts meaning, intent, and entities from text or speech inputs, improving user understanding and response relevance.<br>• Natural language processing and machine learning parse inputs into structured data for further processing.<br>• Solutions enhance CVA capabilities, providing better user understanding and relevant responses. |

| AI APPLICATIONS IN CHATBOTS AND VIRTUAL ASSISTANTS | SOLUTIONS PROVIDED BY COMPANIES | SOLUTIONS DESCRIPTIONS |
| --- | --- | --- |
| **Natural Language Generation** | • Roof AI by Roof AI, Inc.<br>• Agentology by Verse, Inc.<br>• KS by KAI<br>• Rasa by Rasa Technologies, Inc.<br>• KAI Consumer Banking by Kasisto, Inc.<br>• Landbot by Landbot<br>• Google Dialogflow<br>• IBM Watson Assistant<br>• Microsoft Bot Framework | • AI produces text or speech outputs from structured data or keywords, ensuring coherent, fluent, and contextually appropriate communication.<br>• Natural language processing and machine learning generate outputs suitable for user interaction.<br>• Solutions enable CVAs to communicate naturally with users. |
| **Dialogue Management** | • Roof AI by Roof AI, Inc.<br>• CINC AI by CINC, a Fidelity National Financial, Inc.<br>• kvCORE by InsideRE, LLC<br>• Landbot by Landbot<br>• Rasa by Rasa Technologies, Inc.<br>• Google Dialogflow by Google LLC<br>• IBM Watson Assistant by IBM Corporation<br>• KAI Consumer Banking by Kasisto, Inc.<br>• Microsoft Bot Framework by Microsoft Corporation<br>• Eve by Roostify, Inc.<br>• Dippidi by Dippidi, LLC. | • AI manages conversation flow, handling multiple intents, maintaining context, and resolving ambiguities, providing an engaging user experience.<br>• Natural language processing and machine learning track dialogue state, ensuring smooth interaction and error handling.<br>• Solutions enhance CVA conversational experiences. |

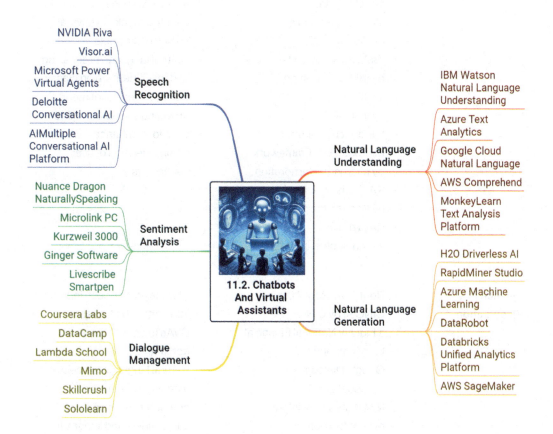

NVIDIA Riva

Visor.ai

Microsoft Power Virtual Agents

Deloitte Conversational AI

AIMultiple Conversational AI Platform

**Speech Recognition**

Nuance Dragon NaturallySpeaking

Microlink PC

Kurzweil 3000

Ginger Software

Livescribe Smartpen

**Sentiment Analysis**

Coursera Labs

DataCamp

Lambda School

Mimo

Skillcrush

Sololearn

**Dialogue Management**

**11.2. Chatbots And Virtual Assistants**

**Natural Language Understanding**

IBM Watson Natural Language Understanding

Azure Text Analytics

Google Cloud Natural Language

AWS Comprehend

MonkeyLearn Text Analysis Platform

**Natural Language Generation**

H2O Driverless AI

RapidMiner Studio

Azure Machine Learning

DataRobot

Databricks Unified Analytics Platform

AWS SageMaker

| AI APPLICATIONS IN CHATBOTS AND VIRTUAL ASSISTANTS | SOLUTIONS PROVIDED BY COMPANIES | SOLUTIONS DESCRIPTIONS |
|---|---|---|
| **Sentiment Analysis** | • Roof AI by Roof AI, Inc.<br>• CINC AI by CINC, a Fidelity National Financial, Inc. Company<br>• Google Dialogflow by Google LLC<br>• IBM Watson Assistant by IBM Corporation<br>• kvCORE by InsideRE, LLC<br>• Landbot by Landbot<br>• Microsoft Bot Framework by Microsoft Corporation<br>• KAI Consumer Banking by Kasisto, Inc.<br>• Rasa by Rasa Technologies, Inc. | • AI extracts and analyzes opinions, emotions, and attitudes from text or speech, aiding CVA understanding of user feedback, reviews, and social media posts.<br>• Natural language processing and machine learning classify text or speech sentiment, providing valuable insights.<br>• Solutions enhance CVA comprehension of user sentiments. |
| **Speech Recognition** | • Roof AI by Roof AI, Inc.<br>• CINC AI by CINC, a Fidelity National Financial, Inc. Company<br>• Google Dialogflow by Google LLC<br>• IBM Watson Assistant by IBM Corporation<br>• kvCORE by InsideRE, LLC<br>• Microsoft Bot Framework by Microsoft Corporation<br>• KAI Consumer Banking by Kasisto, Inc.<br>• Rasa by Rasa Technologies, Inc. | • AI translates speech inputs into written text, enabling CVAs to accept voice commands.<br>• Natural language processing, machine learning, and computer vision analyze audio, video, and images for accurate speech recognition.<br>• Solutions facilitate voice-based user interactions with CVAs. |

## *Key Takeaways*

- AI is integral to the CVA industry, addressing complex challenges and driving innovation.
- Natural Language Understanding improves user understanding and response relevance.
- Natural Language Generation facilitates natural communication between CVAs and users.
- Dialogue Management ensures a smooth and engaging conversational experience.
- Sentiment Analysis enhances CVA comprehension of user sentiments.
- Speech Recognition enables CVAs to accept voice commands, expanding user interaction possibilities.
- Rapid and widespread adoption of AI transforms the CVA industry, delivering value to users and businesses. Leveraging AI is crucial for achieving innovation, excellence, and engagement in CVAs.

## 11.3. CONTENT GENERATION AND PERSONALIZATION

Content generation and personalization create and deliver relevant and engaging content to target audiences in the real estate domain. Content can include text, graphics, audio, and video, and can be used for marketing, education, entertainment, and information. Content generation and personalization are essential for real estate businesses, organizations, and individuals. AI can enhance the efficiency, effectiveness, and innovation of content generation and personalization. AI can automate content creation and optimization, generate content variations and recommendations, detect errors and plagiarism, and provide quality control and feedback. These solutions can help content creators and marketers reduce costs, save time, improve quality, and increase engagement.

| AI APPLICATIONS IN CONTENT GENERATION AND PERSONALIZATION | SOLUTIONS PROVIDED BY COMPANIES | SOLUTIONS DESCRIPTIONS |
| --- | --- | --- |
| **Automated Content Creation** | • Zillow by Zillow Group, Inc.<br>• Trulia by Zillow Group, Inc.<br>• Redfin by Redfin Corporation<br>• HomeLight by HomeLight, Inc.<br>• Opendoor by Opendoor Labs, Inc. | • AI generates content based on property data, images, video, or user feedback.<br>• AI provides fast and scalable content production for property descriptions, reviews, blogs, and video tours.<br>• AI enhances human creativity by providing suggestions, variations, and alternatives. |
| **Content Optimization** | • Lingo by Lingo, Inc.<br>• Phrasee by Phrasee Ltd.<br>• Persado by Persado, Inc.<br>• MarketMuse by MarketMuse, Inc.<br>• Clearscope by Clearscope, Inc. | • AI improves the quality, relevance, and effectiveness of content in the real estate domain.<br>• AI analyzes content for readability, clarity, sentiment, tone, and SEO. |

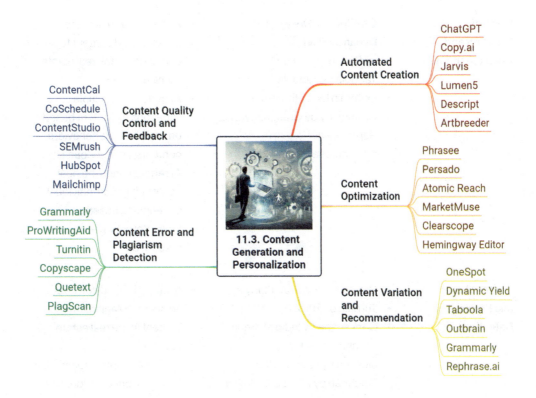

- ContentCal
- CoSchedule
- ContentStudio
- SEMrush
- HubSpot
- Mailchimp

**Content Quality Control and Feedback**

- Grammarly
- ProWritingAid
- Turnitin
- Copyscape
- Quetext
- PlagScan

**Content Error and Plagiarism Detection**

**11.3. Content Generation and Personalization**

**Automated Content Creation**
- ChatGPT
- Copy.ai
- Jarvis
- Lumen5
- Descript
- Artbreeder

**Content Optimization**
- Phrasee
- Persado
- Atomic Reach
- MarketMuse
- Clearscope
- Hemingway Editor

**Content Variation and Recommendation**
- OneSpot
- Dynamic Yield
- Taboola
- Outbrain
- Grammarly
- Rephrase.ai

| AI APPLICATIONS IN CONTENT GENERATION AND PERSONALIZATION | SOLUTIONS PROVIDED BY COMPANIES | SOLUTIONS DESCRIPTIONS |
| --- | --- | --- |
| | • Hemingway App by Hemingway Editor | • AI provides feedback and recommendations to optimize content for goals, audiences, and platforms. |
| **Content Variation and Recommendation** | • OneSpot by OneSpot, Inc.<br>• Dynamic Yield by Dynamic Yield Ltd.<br>• Taboola by Taboola<br>• Outbrain by Outbrain, Inc.<br>• Grammarly by Grammarly, Inc.<br>• Rephrase.ai by Rephrase Corp. | • AI creates and delivers personalized content to target audiences in the real estate domain.<br>• AI generates multiple variations of content based on preferences, behaviors, contexts, and feedback.<br>• AI recommends the best content for each individual or segment, based on their interests, needs, and responses. |
| **Content Error and Plagiarism Detection** | • Grammarly by Grammarly Inc.<br>• Turnitin by Turnitin, LLC<br>• Copyscape by Indigo Stream Technologies, Ltd.<br>• Quetext by Quetext, Inc.<br>• PlagScan by PlagScan GmbH | • AI identifies and corrects errors and plagiarism in content in the real estate domain.<br>• AI checks content for spelling, grammar, punctuation, and style errors.<br>• AI checks content for copy-paste, paraphrasing, and citation plagiarism. |
| **Content Quality Control and Feedback** | • ContentCal by ContentCal.io Ltd.<br>• CoSchedule by CoSchedule, LLC | • AI monitors and evaluates the performance and impact of content in the real estate domain. |

| AI APPLICATIONS IN CONTENT GENERATION AND PERSONALIZATION | SOLUTIONS PROVIDED BY COMPANIES | SOLUTIONS DESCRIPTIONS |
| --- | --- | --- |
| | • ContentStudio by ContentStudio, Inc.<br>• Semrush by Semrush Holdings, Inc.<br>• HubSpot by HubSpot, Inc. | • AI measures content for engagement, reach, conversion, and retention.<br>• AI provides feedback and suggestions to improve content strategy and execution. |

## *Key Takeaways*

- AI revolutionizes content generation and personalization in the real estate domain, enhancing quality, relevance, and engagement.
- AI automates content creation and optimization, generates content variations and recommendations, detects errors and plagiarism, and provides quality control and feedback.
- AI reduces costs, saves time, improves quality, and increases engagement for content creators and marketers in the real estate domain.

## 11.4.  PROPERTY DATA AND ANALYTICS

Property data and analytics collect, process, and analyze data related to properties, such as location, size, condition, features, price, and market trends. The industry covers valuation, appraisal, investment, development, marketing, and management. The industry faces challenges like data quality, availability, and standardization, and data integration, visualization, and interpretation. AI can enhance accuracy, efficiency, relevance, and scalability in property data and analytics. AI can help with automated valuation models, property search and recommendation engines, market analysis and forecasting, property management and optimization, and risk assessment and mitigation. AI can also create new challenges and opportunities, such as ethical and regulatory issues, new business models, and new forms of collaboration and competition. AI is transforming the property data and analytics industry, creating value for various stakeholders.

| AI APPLICATIONS IN PROPERTY DATA AND ANALYTICS | SOLUTIONS PROVIDED BY COMPANIES | SOLUTIONS DESCRIPTIONS |
|---|---|---|
| **Automated Valuation Models** | • CoreLogic Automated Valuation Model by CoreLogic, Inc. <br> • Collateral Analytics Home Price Index by Collateral Analytics, LLC <br> • HouseCanary Value Report by HouseCanary, Inc. <br> • Zillow Zestimate by Zillow Group, Inc. <br> • Redfin Estimate by Redfin Corporation <br> • Realtor.com RealValue by Move, Inc. <br> • Trulia Estimate by Zillow Group, Inc. | • AI estimates property values based on data such as location, size, condition, features, comparable sales, and market trends. <br> • AI uses machine learning and deep learning to analyze data from multiple sources and generate accurate and timely valuations. <br> • AI helps assess property values for various purposes. |

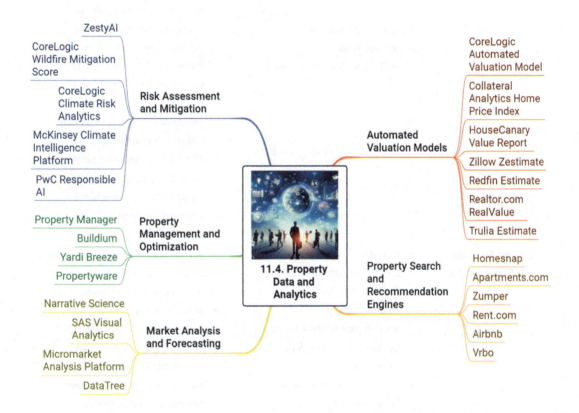

Risk Assessment and Mitigation
- ZestyAI
- CoreLogic Wildfire Mitigation Score
- CoreLogic Climate Risk Analytics
- McKinsey Climate Intelligence Platform
- PwC Responsible AI

Property Management and Optimization
- Property Manager
- Buildium
- Yardi Breeze
- Propertyware

Market Analysis and Forecasting
- Narrative Science
- SAS Visual Analytics
- Micromarket Analysis Platform
- DataTree

11.4. Property Data and Analytics

Automated Valuation Models
- CoreLogic Automated Valuation Model
- Collateral Analytics Home Price Index
- HouseCanary Value Report
- Zillow Zestimate
- Redfin Estimate
- Realtor.com RealValue
- Trulia Estimate

Property Search and Recommendation Engines
- Homesnap
- Apartments.com
- Zumper
- Rent.com
- Airbnb
- Vrbo

| AI APPLICATIONS IN PROPERTY DATA AND ANALYTICS | SOLUTIONS PROVIDED BY COMPANIES | SOLUTIONS DESCRIPTIONS |
| --- | --- | --- |
| **Property Search and Recommendation Engines** | • Homesnap by Homesnap, Inc.<br>• Apartments.com by CoStar Group, Inc.<br>• Zumper by Zumper, Inc.<br>• Rent.com by RentPath, LLC<br>• Airbnb by Airbnb, Inc.<br>• Vrbo by Vrbo, an Expedia Group Company | • AI helps users find properties that match their preferences, needs, and budget.<br>• AI uses natural language processing and computer vision to understand user queries and images. It also uses machine learning and deep learning to learn from user behavior and feedback. It then generates personalized recommendations based on various factors.<br>• AI helps users discover properties for rent or purchase, as well as for short-term stays or home improvement projects. |
| **Market Analysis and Forecasting** | • Narrative Science by Tableau Software, LLC.<br>• SAS Visual Analytics by SAS Institute<br>• Micromarket Analysis Platform by GeoPhy, a Walker & Dunlop Company<br>• DataTree by First American Data Tree LLC | • AI analyzes and predicts the property market, such as supply, demand, prices, trends, etc.<br>• AI processes data from multiple sources using natural language processing, machine learning, deep learning, computer vision, geospatial analysis, etc. It then generates insights, reports, dashboards, visualizations, etc.<br>• AI helps make informed decisions and strategies regarding the property market. |
| **Property Management and Optimization** | • Property Manager by AppFolio, Inc.<br>• Buildium by Buildium, A RealPage Company | • AI helps users manage and optimize their properties, such as maintenance, leasing, rent, tenant, energy, security, etc. |

| AI APPLICATIONS IN PROPERTY DATA AND ANALYTICS | SOLUTIONS PROVIDED BY COMPANIES | SOLUTIONS DESCRIPTIONS |
|---|---|---|
| | • Yardi Breeze by Yardi Systems, Inc.<br>• Propertyware by RealPage, Inc. | • AI uses natural language processing, machine learning, deep learning, computer vision, internet of things, etc., to automate tasks, streamline workflows, monitor performance, detect issues, provide solutions, etc. It also uses data analytics to provide insights and suggestions for improvement.<br>• AI helps reduce costs, increase revenue, enhance customer satisfaction, and improve property value. |
| **Risk Assessment and Mitigation** | • ZestyAI by ZestyAI<br>• CoreLogic Wildfire Mitigation Score by CoreLogic, Inc.<br>• McKinsey Climate Intelligence Platform by McKinsey & Company, Inc.<br>• PwC Responsible AI by PricewaterhouseCoopers LLP<br>• Climate Risk Analytics by CoreLogic, Inc. | • AI helps users identify, measure, and reduce the risks associated with property data and analytics, such as climate change, natural disasters, cyberattacks, ethical issues, etc.<br>• AI uses natural language processing, machine learning, deep learning, computer vision, geospatial analysis, etc., to collect and analyze data from various sources and generate risk scores, reports, dashboards, visualizations, etc.<br>• AI helps manage and mitigate the risks and enhance the resilience of properties and communities. |

### Key Takeaways

- AI boosts accuracy and efficiency in property data analytics, delivering value to stakeholders.
- Using machine learning and deep learning, AI estimates property values for varied purposes.
- AI aids users in discovering properties aligning with preferences, needs, and budgets through advanced technologies.
- AI employs diverse techniques like NLP, machine learning, and computer vision to analyze and forecast property market trends.
- Through various AI technologies, users optimize properties, enhancing revenue, customer satisfaction, and value.
- AI leverages multiple technologies to identify and mitigate risks in property data, fortifying property and community resilience.
- AI presents evolving challenges and opportunities, refining the property data analytics sector with improved metrics and scalability.

## 11.5. PROFESSIONAL SERVICES

The professional services industry provides specialized knowledge, skills, and expertise to clients in the real estate domain. The industry faces challenges like meeting client expectations, delivering high-quality services, maintaining professional standards and ethics, and staying competitive and innovative. AI can enhance productivity, quality, efficiency, and value in professional services, using techniques like natural language processing, data analytics, process automation, and knowledge discovery. AI can also create new challenges and opportunities, such as ethical and regulatory issues, new business models and strategies, and new forms of collaboration and competition. AI is transforming the professional services industry, creating value for service providers, clients, and society.

| AI APPLICATIONS IN PROFESSIONAL SERVICES | SOLUTIONS PROVIDED BY COMPANIES | SOLUTIONS DESCRIPTIONS |
|---|---|---|
| **Engineering Services** | • PlanGrid by Autodesk, Inc.<br>• Arup by Arup Group Limited<br>• KONE by KONE Corporation<br>• Autodesk Construction Cloud by Autodesk, Inc.<br>• Trimble Construction by Trimble Inc.<br>• Bentley iTwin by Bentley Systems, Incorporated<br>• SketchUp by Trimble Inc.<br>• Revit by Autodesk, Inc.<br>• Autodesk Revit by Autodesk, Inc.<br>• Civil 3D by Autodesk, Inc. | • AI performs engineering tasks for clients in the real estate domain.<br>• AI uses computer vision, machine learning, deep learning, etc., to create and manipulate 3D models of properties, and optimize the design, construction, operation, and maintenance of properties.<br>• AI improves quality, efficiency, and innovation in engineering services. |
| **Accounting and Auditing** | • PwC Halo by PricewaterhouseCoopers International Limited | • AI performs accounting and auditing tasks for clients in the real estate domain. |

| AI APPLICATIONS IN PROFESSIONAL SERVICES | SOLUTIONS PROVIDED BY COMPANIES | SOLUTIONS DESCRIPTIONS |
|---|---|---|
| | • Reonomy by Reonomy, an Altus Group Company<br>• Buildium by Buildium, A RealPage Company<br>• KPMG Clara by KPMG International Cooperative<br>• Deloitte AI and Data by Deloitte Touche Tohmatsu Limited<br>• EY Helix by Ernst & Young Global Limited<br>• Botkeeper by Botkeeper, Inc.<br>• Smacc by Smacc GmbH | • AI uses natural language processing and machine learning to understand financial documents, extract information and insights, and generate reports and recommendations.<br>• AI improves accuracy, efficiency, and compliance in accounting and auditing. |
| Consulting and Advisory | • RealPage by RealPage, Inc.<br>• Cushman & Wakefield by Cushman & Wakefield plc<br>• JLL Spark by JLL, Inc.<br>• Bain Vector by Bain & Company, Inc.<br>• BCG Gamma by Boston Consulting Group<br>• IBM Corporation<br>• Microsoft Azure AI by Microsoft Corporation<br>• Google Cloud AI by Google LLC<br>• Amazon Web Services AI by Amazon.com, Inc. | • AI provides consulting and advisory services to clients in the real estate domain.<br>• AI uses various techniques to collect and analyze data, and provide insights, predictions, recommendations, etc., for real estate problems and opportunities.<br>• AI improves decision making, performance, and innovation in the real estate domain. |
| Legal Services | • Dentons by Dentons<br>• DocuSign Agreement Cloud by DocuSign, Inc. | • AI performs legal tasks for clients in the real estate domain. |

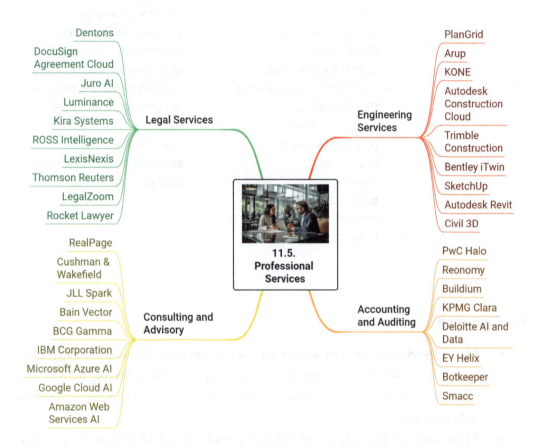

Legal Services
- Dentons
- DocuSign Agreement Cloud
- Juro AI
- Luminance
- Kira Systems
- ROSS Intelligence
- LexisNexis
- Thomson Reuters
- LegalZoom
- Rocket Lawyer

Engineering Services
- PlanGrid
- Arup
- KONE
- Autodesk Construction Cloud
- Trimble Construction
- Bentley iTwin
- SketchUp
- Autodesk Revit
- Civil 3D

11.5. Professional Services

Consulting and Advisory
- RealPage
- Cushman & Wakefield
- JLL Spark
- Bain Vector
- BCG Gamma
- IBM Corporation
- Microsoft Azure AI
- Google Cloud AI
- Amazon Web Services AI

Accounting and Auditing
- PwC Halo
- Reonomy
- Buildium
- KPMG Clara
- Deloitte AI and Data
- EY Helix
- Botkeeper
- Smacc

| AI APPLICATIONS IN PROFESSIONAL SERVICES | SOLUTIONS PROVIDED BY COMPANIES | SOLUTIONS DESCRIPTIONS |
| --- | --- | --- |
| | • Juro AI by Juro<br>• Luminance by Luminance Technologies, Ltd.<br>• Kira Systems by Kira Systems, Inc.<br>• ROSS Intelligence by ROSS Intelligence, Inc.<br>• LexisNexis by LexisNexis, a RELX Company<br>• Thomson Reuters by Thomson Reuters Corporation<br>• LegalZoom by LegalZoom.com, Inc.<br>• Rocket Lawyer by Rocket Lawyer Incorporated | • AI uses natural language processing and machine learning to understand legal documents, extract information and insights, and generate reports and recommendations. It can also create legal documents, such as contracts, leases, deeds, etc.<br>• AI improves accuracy, efficiency, and compliance in legal services. |

### *Key Takeaways*

- AI is enhancing the professional services industry in the real estate domain, providing solutions to challenges like meeting client expectations, delivering high-quality services, maintaining professional standards and ethics, and staying competitive and innovative.
- AI can perform accounting and auditing, consulting and advisory, legal, and engineering tasks for clients in the real estate domain, using techniques like natural language processing, data analytics, process automation, and computer vision.
- AI introduces new challenges and opportunities, shaping the future of the professional services industry with enhanced productivity, quality, efficiency, and value, creating value for service providers, clients, and society in the real estate domain.

## 11.6. INNOVATION AND RESEARCH

The innovation and research industry creates and applies new knowledge, ideas, and technologies to the real estate domain. The industry faces challenges like finding research questions, conducting experiments, disseminating findings, and translating research into practice and policy. AI can enhance creativity, efficiency, quality, and impact in innovation and research, using techniques like natural language processing, data analytics, process automation, and knowledge discovery. AI can also create new challenges and opportunities, such as ethical and regulatory issues, new paradigms and methods, and new forms of collaboration and competition. AI is transforming the innovation and research industry, creating value for researchers, practitioners, policymakers, and society.

| AI APPLICATIONS IN INNOVATION AND RESEARCH | SOLUTIONS PROVIDED BY COMPANIES | SOLUTIONS DESCRIPTIONS |
|---|---|---|
| **Literature Review and Synthesis** | • MIT Center for Real Estate by Massachusetts Institute of Technology<br>• Urban Institute<br>• CREtech Labs by CREtech<br>• REalyse by Realyse, Ltd.<br>• GeoPhy by GeoPhy, a Walker & Dunlop Company<br>• HouseCanary by HouseCanary, Inc. | • AI searches, reviews, and synthesizes literature in the real estate domain.<br>• AI uses natural language processing and machine learning to understand queries and documents, extract information and insights, and generate summaries.<br>• AI helps researchers conduct literature reviews faster and easier. |
| **Hypothesis Generation and Testing** | • MIT Center for Real Estate by Massachusetts Institute of Technology<br>• Urban Institute<br>• CREtech Labs by CREtech<br>• Property Insights by ZestyAI<br>• Cherre by Cherre, Inc.<br>• Remine by Remine, Inc. | • AI generates and tests hypotheses based on data or knowledge in the real estate domain.<br>• AI uses various techniques to create and test hypotheses for validity, reliability, significance, etc. |

| AI APPLICATIONS IN INNOVATION AND RESEARCH | SOLUTIONS PROVIDED BY COMPANIES | SOLUTIONS DESCRIPTIONS |
|---|---|---|
| | • Reonomy by Reonomy, an Altus Group Company<br>• CompStak by CompStak, Inc. | • AI helps researchers discover new patterns, relationships, causes, effects, etc. |
| Data Collection and Analysis | • CoreLogic by CoreLogic, Inc.<br>• CoStar by CoStar Group, Inc.<br>• Reonomy by Reonomy, an Altus Group Company<br>• Realtor.com by Move, Inc.<br>• Zillow by Zillow Group, Inc.<br>• Trulia by Zillow Group, Inc.<br>• Redfin by Redfin Corporation<br>• HomeLight by HomeLight, Inc.<br>• Opendoor by Opendoor Labs, Inc.<br>• Offerpad by Offerpad<br>• Knock by Knock Homes, Inc. | • AI collects and analyzes data from various sources in the real estate domain.<br>• AI uses various techniques to collect and analyze data for patterns, trends, insights, predictions, etc.<br>• AI helps researchers acquire and process data more efficiently and effectively. |
| Research Design and Optimization | • RStudio by Posit, PBC<br>• Jupyter Notebook by Project Jupyter<br>• ScholarlyCommons by University of Pennsylvania<br>• MIT Center for Real Estate by Massachusetts Institute of Technology<br>• REalyse by Realyse<br>• Cherre<br>• Monday.com by Monday.com, Ltd.<br>• Notion by Notion Labs, Inc. | • AI designs and optimizes research processes and workflows in the real estate domain.<br>• AI uses various techniques to automate tasks, streamline workflows, monitor performance, detect issues, provide solutions, etc.<br>• AI helps researchers plan and execute research projects more efficiently and effectively. |

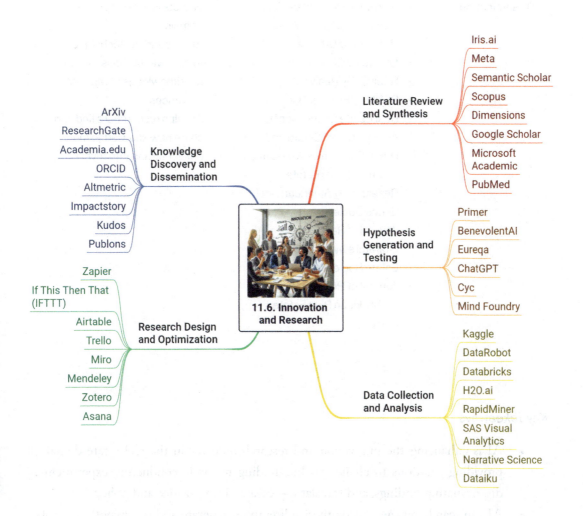

Knowledge Discovery and Dissemination
- ArXiv
- ResearchGate
- Academia.edu
- ORCID
- Altmetric
- Impactstory
- Kudos
- Publons

Research Design and Optimization
- Zapier
- If This Then That (IFTTT)
- Airtable
- Trello
- Miro
- Mendeley
- Zotero
- Asana

11.6. Innovation and Research

Literature Review and Synthesis
- Iris.ai
- Meta
- Semantic Scholar
- Scopus
- Dimensions
- Google Scholar
- Microsoft Academic
- PubMed

Hypothesis Generation and Testing
- Primer
- BenevolentAI
- Eureqa
- ChatGPT
- Cyc
- Mind Foundry

Data Collection and Analysis
- Kaggle
- DataRobot
- Databricks
- H2O.ai
- RapidMiner
- SAS Visual Analytics
- Narrative Science
- Dataiku

| AI APPLICATIONS IN INNOVATION AND RESEARCH | SOLUTIONS PROVIDED BY COMPANIES | SOLUTIONS DESCRIPTIONS |
|---|---|---|
| **Knowledge Discovery and Dissemination** | • Journal of Real Estate Finance and Economics by Springer<br>• "CREtech Real Estate Tech Conference" by CREtech<br>• Urban AI by Urban AI<br>• Cherre by Cherre, Inc.<br>• REalyse by Realyse<br>• SSRN by Elsevier B.V.<br>• Real Estate Economics by American Real Estate and Urban Economics Association<br>• Journal of Real Estate Research by American Real Estate Society<br>• Journal of Real Estate Literature by American Real Estate Society<br>• Journal of Housing Research by American Real Estate Society | • AI discovers and disseminates new knowledge from research outputs in the real estate domain.<br>• AI uses various techniques to discover and disseminate new knowledge to relevant audiences.<br>• AI helps researchers find and share new knowledge more efficiently and effectively. |

## Key Takeaways

- AI is enhancing the innovation and research industry in the real estate domain, providing solutions to challenges like finding research, conducting experiments, disseminating findings, and translating research into practice and policy.
- AI can search, review, and synthesize literature, generate and test hypotheses, collect and analyze data, design and optimize research processes and workflows, and discover and disseminate new knowledge in the real estate domain.
- AI introduces new challenges and opportunities, shaping the future of the innovation and research industry with enhanced creativity, efficiency, quality, and impact, creating value for researchers, practitioners, policymakers, and society in the real estate domain.

## 11.7. SUSTAINABILITY AND SOCIAL IMPACT

The sustainability and social impact industry addresses the environmental, social, and economic challenges and opportunities related to properties. The industry faces challenges like data availability and quality, stakeholder engagement, and impact measurement and reporting. AI can enhance effectiveness, efficiency, innovation, and scalability in sustainability and social impact, as shown below. AI can also create new challenges and opportunities, such as ethical and regulatory issues, new business models, and new forms of collaboration and competition. AI is transforming the sustainability and social impact industry, creating value for property owners, developers, managers, professionals, tenants, customers, and society.

| AI APPLICATIONS IN SUSTAINABILITY AND SOCIAL IMPACT | SOLUTIONS PROVIDED BY COMPANIES | SOLUTIONS DESCRIPTIONS |
|---|---|---|
| **Energy Management and Optimization** | • Honeywell by Honeywell International Inc.<br>• Siemens by Siemens AG<br>• BuildingIQ by BuildingIQ<br>• GridBeyond<br>• Verdigris by Verdigris Technologies, Inc.<br>• Carbon Lighthouse by Carbon Lighthouse, Inc.<br>• BrainBox AI by BrainBox AI, Inc.<br>• Gridium by Gridium, Inc.<br>• Enertiv by Enertiv, Inc.<br>• Aquicore by Aquicore, Inc.<br>• Switch Automation by Switch Automation Pty Ltd<br>• Sense by Sense Labs, Inc. | • AI monitors and controls energy consumption and performance of properties.<br>• AI uses various data sources and techniques to generate insights and optimization.<br>• AI reduces energy costs, improves efficiency, and enhances sustainability. |

| AI APPLICATIONS IN SUSTAINABILITY AND SOCIAL IMPACT | SOLUTIONS PROVIDED BY COMPANIES | SOLUTIONS DESCRIPTIONS |
|---|---|---|
| **Carbon Emission Reduction and Offsetting** | • LanzaTech by LanzaTech<br>• SoFi by Social Finance, Inc.<br>• Rocky Mountain Institute<br>• WattTime by WattTime<br>• CarbonCure by CarbonCure Technologies, Inc.<br>• Carbon Engineering by Carbon Engineering, Ltd.<br>• Climeworks by Climeworks AG<br>• Project Wren by Wren, Inc. | • AI measures and reduces carbon footprint of properties and activities.<br>• AI supports carbon removal or sequestration projects to compensate for emissions.<br>• AI mitigates climate change and achieves carbon neutrality or negativity. |
| **Waste Management and Recycling** | • Waste Robotics by Waste Robotics<br>• RecycleBank by RecycleBank<br>• Zero Waste International Alliance<br>• AMP Robotics by AMP Robotics Corp.<br>• Recycleye by Recycleye, Ltd.<br>• Greyparrot by Greyparrot AI, Ltd.<br>• Bin-e by Bin-e Sp. z o.o.<br>• Compology by Compology, Inc. | • AI monitors and sorts waste generated by properties and activities.<br>• AI facilitates recycling and reuse of materials.<br>• AI reduces waste generation, increases recycling rates, and enhances sustainability. |
| **Water Management and Conservation** | • Netafim by Netafim<br>• WaterSmart by Oracle Corporation<br>• Phyn by Phyn, LLC<br>• Flume by Flume, Inc.<br>• StreamLabs by StreamLabs<br>• Flo by Flo Technologies, Inc.<br>• WaterBit by WaterBit, Inc.<br>• HydroPoint by HydroPoint Data Systems, Inc. | • AI monitors and controls water consumption and performance of properties.<br>• AI detects and prevents water leaks, waste, and damage.<br>• AI reduces water costs, improves efficiency, and enhances sustainability. |

National Low Income Housing Coalition
Center for Community Change
Data for Black Lives
JustFix.nyc
Landlord Watchlist
Eviction Lab
Anti-Eviction Mapping Project
Urban Displacement Project

Social Justice and Inclusion

Honeywell
Siemens
BuildingIQ
GridBeyond
Verdigris
Carbon Lighthouse
BrainBox AI
Gridium
Enertiv
Aquicore
Switch Automation
Sense Labs

Energy Management and Optimization

Community Land Trusts
Neighborly
Code for America
Neighborland
CoUrbanize
Nextdoor
Citymapper
Waze
Moovit

Community Development and Engagement

LanzaTech
SoFi
Rocky Mountain Institute
WattTime
CarbonCure
Carbon Engineering
Climeworks
Project Wren

Carbon Emission Reduction and Offsetting

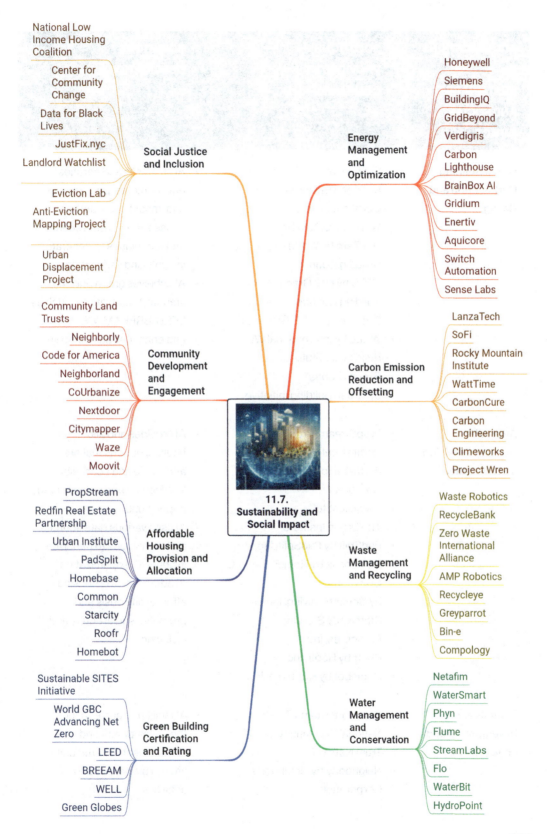

11.7. Sustainability and Social Impact

PropStream
Redfin Real Estate Partnership
Urban Institute
PadSplit
Homebase
Common
Starcity
Roofr
Homebot

Affordable Housing Provision and Allocation

Waste Robotics
RecycleBank
Zero Waste International Alliance
AMP Robotics
Recycleye
Greyparrot
Bin-e
Compology

Waste Management and Recycling

Sustainable SITES Initiative
World GBC Advancing Net Zero
LEED
BREEAM
WELL
Green Globes

Green Building Certification and Rating

Netafim
WaterSmart
Phyn
Flume
StreamLabs
Flo
WaterBit
HydroPoint

Water Management and Conservation

| AI APPLICATIONS IN SUSTAINABILITY AND SOCIAL IMPACT | SOLUTIONS PROVIDED BY COMPANIES | SOLUTIONS DESCRIPTIONS |
|---|---|---|
| **Green Building Certification and Rating** | • Sustainable SITES Initiative by Green Business Certification Inc.<br>• World GBC Advancing Net Zero by World Green Building Council<br>• LEED by U.S. Green Building Council<br>• BREEAM by BRE Global, Ltd.<br>• WELL by International WELL Building Institute<br>• Green Globes by Green Building Initiative | • AI assesses and certifies environmental performance and impact of properties.<br>• AI uses various data sources and techniques to generate insights and verification.<br>• AI achieves green building standards and ratings, such as LEED, BREEAM, WELL, etc., and enhances sustainability. |
| **Affordable Housing Provision and Allocation** | • PropStream: PropStream<br>• Redfin Real Estate Partnership: Redfin Corporation<br>• Urban Institute: The Urban Institute<br>• PadSplit by PadSplit, Inc.<br>• Homebase by Homebase, LLC<br>• Common by Common Living, Inc.<br>• Starcity by Starcity Properties, Inc.<br>• Roofr by Roofr, Inc.<br>• Homebot by Homebot, Inc. | • AI provides and allocates housing options that are affordable and accessible for low-income and underserved populations.<br>• AI uses various data sources and techniques to generate insights and optimization.<br>• AI addresses the housing affordability crisis and promotes social equity and inclusion. |
| **Community Development and Engagement** | • Community Land Trusts: National Community Land Trust Network<br>• Neighborly by Neighborly Corporation | • AI facilitates and enhances the development and engagement of communities around properties and activities. |

| AI APPLICATIONS IN SUSTAINABILITY AND SOCIAL IMPACT | SOLUTIONS PROVIDED BY COMPANIES | SOLUTIONS DESCRIPTIONS |
| --- | --- | --- |
| | • Code for America<br>• Neighborland by Neighborland, Inc.<br>• CoUrbanize by CoUrbanize, Inc.<br>• Nextdoor by Nextdoor, Inc.<br>• Citymapper by Citymapper, Ltd.<br>• Waze by Waze Mobile, Ltd.<br>• Moovit by Moovit App Global, Ltd. | • AI uses various data sources and techniques to generate insights and communication.<br>• AI creates and sustains livable, vibrant, and resilient communities. |
| Social Justice and Inclusion | • National Low Income Housing Coalition by National Low Income Housing Coalition<br>• Center for Community Change by Community Change<br>• Data for Black Lives by Data for Black Lives<br>• JustFix.nyc by JustFix.nyc<br>• Landlord Watchlist by New York City Public Advocate<br>• Eviction Lab by Princeton University<br>• Anti-Eviction Mapping Project by Anti-Eviction Mapping Project<br>• Urban Displacement Project by Urban Displacement Project | • AI addresses and prevents the social injustices and inequalities related to properties and activities, such as discrimination, eviction, displacement, gentrification, segregation, etc.<br>• AI uses various data sources and techniques to generate insights and combat the social injustices and inequalities.<br>• AI promotes and protects the human rights and dignity of all people. |

## Key Takeaways

- AI is enhancing the sustainability and social impact of properties and activities, addressing environmental, social, and economic challenges and opportunities.
- AI facilitates efficient energy, water, waste management, carbon reduction, green building certifications, affordable housing solutions, and community engagement within the real estate sector.
- However, AI also introduces fresh challenges and opportunities like ethical dilemmas, regulatory shifts, novel business frameworks, and evolving collaborative landscapes, reshaping sustainability efforts and value generation for all stakeholders involved.

# CHAPTER 12
# SPECIAL CASE – AI IN SPATIAL APPLICATIONS a.k.a. GeoAI

## 12.1. HOW YOU WILL BENEFIT FROM READING THIS CHAPTER

GeoAI, or Geospatial Artificial Intelligence, is the combination of geographic information systems (GIS), artificial intelligence (AI), and machine learning (ML) to analyze and interpret spatial data. GeoAI is a rapidly growing field that has many applications and benefits for the real estate industry, such as enhancing location intelligence, optimizing site selection, improving risk management, providing market insights, and offering customized property recommendations.

In this chapter, we will explore eleven (11) of the leading GeoAI applications in real estate and thirty-nine (39) companies in the United States and India that are currently transforming the real estate industry with their innovative solutions.

We will also look at forecasts of GeoAI future impacts on the real estate sector, including how GeoAI is evolving as a technology.

As an aside, this "Special Case" chapter has been prepared because the book's authors believe that GeoAI in real estate has received inadequate attention in AI literature. As previously stated in Chapter 2, "GeoAI can be a truly remarkable source of inputs to data-hungry Deep Learning systems… GIS can use *any [emphasis added]* information that includes location." GeoAI thus has the potential to be a greater integrator of innumerable, highly diverse data sets than any other type of AI, thereby facilitating notably superior AI products and services in the real estate industry.

## 12.2. LEADING GEOAI APPLICATIONS AND COMPANIES

### 12.2.1. Geospatial Integration in Real Estate

One of the fundamental applications of GeoAI is to integrate geospatial data with other types of data, such as property attributes, market trends, customer behavior, and environmental factors. This allows for a more holistic and comprehensive understanding of the real estate market and its dynamics.

Some of the companies that are using GeoAI to integrate geospatial data in real estate are:

- *Esri:* Esri is one of the largest software developers in the GIS space, with over 350,000 customers worldwide. Esri provides a range of GeoAI solutions for the real estate industry, such as ArcGIS, which is a platform for analyzing, visualizing, and sharing geospatialdata; Business Analyst, which is a tool for market analysis and site selection; and ArcGIS Indoors, which is a solution for indoor mapping and navigation.
- *Orbital Insight:* Orbital Insight is a company that uses computer vision and machine learning to analyze satellite imagery and geospatial data. Orbital Insight provides insights for various industries, including real estate, where it helps investors, developers, brokers, and retailers to monitor construction activity, assess property values, identify market opportunities, and optimize site selection.
- *Carto:* Carto is a company that provides a cloud-based platform for location intelligence and spatial analysis. Carto enables users to integrate geospatialdata with other sources of data, such as demographics, transactions, social media, and IoT sensors. Carto helps real estate professionals to gain insights into market trends, customer preferences, competitive landscapes, and optimal locations.

### 12.2.2. Predictive Location Analytics

Another important application of GeoAI is to use predictive analytics and machine learning to forecast future outcomes and scenarios based on geospatial data. This can help real estate professionals to make better decisions, reduce uncertainty, and improve performance.

Some of the companies that are using GeoAI to provide predictive location analytics are:

- *Remine:* Remine is a company that provides a platform for real estate agents to access property data and predictive analytics. Remine uses machine learning to analyze millions of property records, transactions, consumer behavior, and geospatial data to generate insights and recommendations for agents. Remine helps agents to identify leads, find opportunities, evaluate properties, and close deals.
- *HouseCanary:* HouseCanary is a company that provides a platform for real estate valuation and forecasting. HouseCanary uses AI and geospatial data to create accurate and transparent valuations for properties across the US. HouseCanary also provides market insights and forecasts for investors, lenders, appraisers, brokers, and homeowners.
- *Cherre:* Cherre is a company that provides a platform for real estate data management and analysis. Cherre uses AI and geospatial data to connect disparate sources of data into a single source of truth. Cherre enables users to access comprehensive property data, perform advanced analytics, generate insights, and automate workflows.

## 12.2.3. Site Selection and Development

One of the key applications of GeoAI is to assist in site selection and development for real estate projects. GeoAI can help developers to find optimal locations based on various criteria, such as market demand, land availability, zoning regulations, environmental impact, and infrastructure accessibility.

Some of the companies that are using GeoAI to facilitate site selection and development are:

- *Land Intelligence:* Land Intelligence is a company that provides a platform for land acquisition and development. Land Intelligence uses AI and geospatial data to analyze the feasibility, profitability, and risk of land parcels across the US. Land Intelligence helps developers to find and evaluate land opportunities, conduct due diligence, and secure financing.
- *SiteZeus:* SiteZeus is a company that provides a platform for location intelligence and site selection. SiteZeus uses AI and geospatial data to create predictive models for various industries, such as retail, restaurant, healthcare, and hospitality. SiteZeus helps users to identify and validate the best locations for their businesses, optimize their portfolios, and maximize their revenues.

- *Skyline AI:* Skyline AI is a company that provides a platform for real estate investment and asset management. Skyline AI uses AI and geospatial data to analyze the performance, potential, and risk of commercial properties across the US. Skyline AI helps investors to source, underwrite, acquire, and manage properties with data-driven insights and recommendations.

## 12.2.4. Risk Assessment and Mitigation

Another vital application of GeoAI is to assess and mitigate the various risks associated with real estate properties and projects. GeoAI can help real estate professionals to identify and quantify the impact of natural disasters, climate change, crime, terrorism, regulatory changes, and other factors that may affect the value, safety, and sustainability of their assets.

Some of the companies that are using GeoAI to provide risk assessment and mitigation are:

- *Cape Analytics:* Cape Analytics is a company that provides a platform for property intelligence and risk management. Cape Analytics uses computer vision and machine learning to extract property attributes and risks from aerial imagery and geospatial data. Cape Analytics helps insurers, reinsurers, brokers, and investors to assess property values, underwrite policies, monitor portfolios, and mitigate losses.
- *One Concern:* One Concern is a company that provides a platform for disaster resilience and recovery. One Concern uses AI and geospatial data to simulate and predict the impact of natural hazards, such as earthquakes, floods, fires, and hurricanes. One Concern helps governments, businesses, and communities to prepare for, respond to, and recover from disasters.
- *HqO:* HqO is a company that provides a platform for tenant experience and building operations. HqO uses AI and geospatial data to enhance the safety, security, comfort, and convenience of tenants in commercial buildings. HqO helps landlords, property managers, and tenants to monitor building conditions, communicate alerts, access amenities, and optimize occupancy.

## 12.2.5. Market Insights and Analytics

One of the main applications of GeoAI is to provide market insights and analytics for real estate professionals. GeoAI can help users to understand the current and future trends, opportunities, challenges, and competition in the real estate market.

Some of the companies that are using GeoAI to offer market insights and analytics are:

- *Reonomy:* Reonomy is a company that provides a platform for commercial real estate data and analytics. Reonomy uses AI and geospatial data to collect, cleanse, enrich, and connect millions of property records across the US. Reonomy helps users to access comprehensive property data, perform market research, identify prospects, and generate leads.

- *GeoPhy:* GeoPhy is a company that provides a platform for real estate valuation and analytics. GeoPhy uses AI and geospatial data to create objective and transparent valuations for commercial properties worldwide. GeoPhy helps users to access reliable property data, benchmark performance, evaluate opportunities, and monitor portfolios.

- *Local Logic:* Local Logic is a company that provides a platform for location intelligence and analytics. Local Logic uses AI and geospatial data to measure the livability and attractiveness of neighborhoods across North America. Local Logic helps users to discover the best places to live, work, and play based on their preferences, lifestyle, and budget.

## 12.2.6. Customized Property Recommendations

One of the most exciting applications of GeoAI in real estate is the ability to provide customized property recommendations based on the preferences and needs of the users. This can be done by using machine learning algorithms to analyze various types of data, such as location, amenities, price, neighborhood, market trends, user behavior, and feedback. By combining these data sources, GeoAI can generate personalized suggestions that match the user's criteria and expectations.

Some of the leading companies that are using GeoA to offer customized property recommendations are:

- *Zillow:* Zillow is one of the largest online real estate platforms in the US, with over 200 million monthly visitors. Zillow uses GeoAI to power its home value estimation tool, Zestimate, which uses computer vision, natural language processing, and deep learning to analyze millions of photos, descriptions, and historical data of properties. Zillow also uses GeoAI to provide personalized home recommendations based on the user's search history, preferences, and feedback.

- *Housing.com*: Housing.com is one of the leading online real estate platforms in India, with over 10 million monthly visitors. Housing.com uses GeoAI to provide customized property suggestions based on the user's location, budget, lifestyle, and preferences. Housing.com also uses GeoAI to create interactive maps that show various aspects of the properties and neighborhoods, such as amenities, connectivity, safety, and livability.

- *Realtor.com*: Realtor.com is another popular online real estate platform in the US, with over 86 million monthly visitors. Realtor.com uses GeoAI to provide personalized home recommendations based on the user's search behavior, preferences, and feedback. Realtor.com also uses GeoAI to create dynamic maps that show various features of the properties and neighborhoods, such as schools, crime, traffic, and market trends.

- *Trulia*: Trulia is another online real estate platform in the US, with over 60 million monthly visitors. Trulia uses GeoAI to provide personalized home suggestions based on the user's preferences, lifestyle, and goals. Trulia also uses GeoAI to create interactive maps that show various aspects of the properties and neighborhoods, such as crime, schools, commute, and amenities.

- *Magicbricks*: Magicbricks is one of the leading online real estate platforms in India, with over 20 million monthly visitors. Magicbricks uses GeoAI to provide customized property recommendations based on the user's location, budget, requirements, and preferences. Magicbricks also uses GeoAI to create interactive maps that show various aspects of the properties and neighborhoods, such as price trends, ratings, reviews, and nearby facilities.

- *Redfin*: Redfin is an online real estate brokerage in the US, with over 40 million monthly visitors. Redfin uses GeoAI to provide personalized home recommendations based on the user's search criteria, preferences, and feedback. Redfin also uses GeoAI to create dynamic maps that show various features of the properties and neighborhoods, such as walk score, transit score, bike score, and market trends.

## 12.2.7. Residential Brokerage

One of the major applications of GeoAI in real estate is to enhance the residential brokerage process and experience. GeoAI can help brokers and agents to find and attract more clients, provide better service and guidance, and close more deals.

Some of the companies that are using GeoAI to improve residential brokerage are:

- *Compass:* Compass is a company that provides a platform for residential real estate brokerage. Compass uses AI and geospatial data to empower agents with data-driven insights, tools, and services. Compass helps agents to market their listings, generate leads, manage transactions, and grow their business.
- *Opendoor:* Opendoor is a company that provides a platform for online home buying and selling. Opendoor uses AI and geospatial data to offer instant offers, valuations, and appraisals for homes across the US. Opendoor helps homeowners to sell their homes quickly, conveniently, and hassle-free.
- *Rex:* Rex is a company that provides a platform for residential real estate brokerage. Rex uses AI and geospatial data to automate the listing, marketing, and selling process for homes. Rex helps homeowners to save on commission fees, reach more buyers, and sell faster.

## 12.2.8. Efficient Project Management

Another significant application of GeoAI in real estate is to enable efficient project management and collaboration. GeoAI can help project managers, contractors, engineers, architects, and other stakeholders to plan, execute, monitor, and control real estate projects with data-driven insights and automation.

Some of the companies that are using GeoAI to facilitate efficient project management are:

- *Procore:* Procore is a company that provides a platform for construction management. Procore uses AI and geospatial data to streamline the workflow, communication, and documentation of construction projects. Procore helps users to manage contracts, budgets, schedules, drawings, quality, safety, and more.
- *Bentley Systems:* Bentley Systems is a company that provides software solutions for infrastructure engineering and design. Bentley Systems uses AI and geospatial data to create digital twins of physical assets, such as buildings, bridges, roads, and

railways. Bentley Systems helps users to design, build, operate, and maintain infrastructure projects with improved efficiency, quality, and sustainability.

- *Autodesk*: Autodesk is a company that provides software solutions for architecture, engineering, and construction. Autodesk uses AI and geospatial data to enhance the design, simulation, and visualization of real estate projects. Autodesk helps users to create innovative and optimized designs, reduce errors and costs, and collaborate effectively.

## 12.2.9. Real-Time Analytics

One of the emerging applications of GeoAI in real estate is to provide real-time analytics and insights for real estate properties and projects. GeoAI can help users to monitor and track the status, performance, and changes of their assets in real time, using various sources of data, such as sensors, cameras, drones, satellites, and mobile devices.

Some of the companies that are using GeoAI to deliver real-time analytics are:

- *Disperse*: Disperse is a company that provides a platform for construction intelligence and automation. Disperse uses computer vision and machine learning to capture and analyze data from construction sites using cameras and drones. Disperse helps users to monitor progress, quality, safety, and productivity in real time, and automate tasks such as reporting, scheduling, and issue resolution.
- *Enertiv*: Enertiv is a company that provides a platform for building operations and maintenance. Enertiv uses AI and geospatial data to collect and analyze data from building systems and equipment using IoT sensors. Enertiv helps users to monitor performance, efficiency, and reliability in real time, and optimize operations, maintenance, and energy consumption.
- *Placense*: Placense is a company that provides a platform for location analytics and insights. Placense uses AI and geospatialdata to collect and analyze data from mobile devices using location-based services. Placense helps users to monitor foot traffic, dwell time, origin, destination, and behavior in real time, and understand the demand, supply, and competition of locations.

## 12.2.10. Compliance and Regulations

One of the critical applications of GeoAI in real estate is to ensure compliance and regulations for real estate properties and projects. GeoAI can help users to comply with the various laws, rules, standards, and codes that govern the real estate industry, such as zoning, building, environmental, tax, and legal regulations.

Some of the companies that are using GeoAI to support compliance and regulations are:

- *Landgrid*: Landgrid is a company that provides a platform for land data and mapping. Landgrid uses AI and geospatial data to collect and organize data from various sources, such as public records, satellite imagery, and crowdsourcing. Landgrid helps users to access accurate and up-to-date land data, such as ownership, boundaries, parcels, zoning, taxes, and assessments.
- *Honest Buildings*: Honest Buildings is a company that provides a platform for project management and procurement for real estate owners and operators. Honest Buildings uses AI and geospatial data to streamline the workflow, communication, and documentation of real estate projects. Honest Buildings helps users to manage contracts, budgets, invoices, payments, and compliance.
- *GeoComply*: GeoComply is a company that provides a platform for geolocation verification and compliance. GeoComply uses AI and geospatial data to verify the location of users and devices using various methods, such as GPS, Wi-Fi, IP address, and cell tower triangulation. GeoComply helps users to comply with the geolocation

## 12.2.11. Global / India Perspectives

GeoAI is not only a global phenomenon, but also a local one. Different regions and countries have different needs, challenges, opportunities, and innovations in the real estate industry. In this section, we will focus on the GeoAI landscape in India, which is one of the largest and fastest-growing real estate markets in the world.

India has a huge potential for GeoAI applications in real estate, as it has a large and diverse population, a vast and varied geography, a dynamic and competitive economy, and a complex and evolving regulatory environment. Some of the benefits of GeoAI for the Indian real estate industry are:

- Improving the quality and availability of property data, which is often scarce, inconsistent, or outdated in India.
- Enhancing the transparency and trust in the real estate transactions, which are often plagued by fraud, corruption, or litigation in India.
- Increasing the efficiency and productivity of the real estate processes, which are often slow, costly, or cumbersome in India.
- Supporting the social and environmental sustainability of the real estate development, which is often challenged by issues such as urbanization, pollution, or climate change in India.

Some of the challenges of GeoAI for the Indian real estate industry are:

- Adapting to the diverse and dynamic needs and preferences of the Indian consumers, who have different cultures, languages, lifestyles, and aspirations.
- Complying with the complex and evolving regulations and policies of the Indian government, which have different levels, authorities, and objectives.
- Competing with the established and emerging players in the Indian real estate market, which have different strategies, capabilities, and resources.
- Collaborating with the various other stakeholders in the Indian real estate ecosystem, which have different interests, roles, and expectations.

Some of the examples of GeoAI applications and companies in the Indian real estate industry are:

- *NoBroker*: NoBroker is a company that provides a platform for online home rental and purchase. NoBroker uses AI and geospatial data to eliminate brokers from the real estate transactions and connect owners and tenants directly. NoBroker helps users to find properties based on their location, budget, preferences, and feedback.
- *Square Yards*: Square Yards is a company that provides a platform for real estate brokerage and advisory. Square Yards uses AI and geospatial data to offer end-to-end services for property buyers and sellers across India and abroad. Square Yards helps users to access property data, market insights, valuation, legal assistance, and financing.
- *Propstack*: Propstack is a company that provides a platform for commercial real estate data and analytics. Propstack uses AI and geospatial data to collect and organize data from various sources, such as public records, satellite imagery, and crowdsourcing. Propstack helps users to access comprehensive property data, perform market research, identify prospects, and generate leads.

- *Bhoomi:* Bhoomi is an online land records management system developed by the government of Karnataka state in India. It uses AI to digitize land records, including ownership certificates, mutation registers, maps, and more. This system facilitates online access and updates for land records, reducing manual paperwork and intermediaries. It also enhances the verification of land records' authenticity and validity, preventing fraud and corruption.

- *Land Conflict Watch:* Land Conflict Watch is a data journalism initiative using AI to map and document land conflicts in India. It aids users in understanding the causes, impacts, and status of land disputes that affect millions of people and thousands of hectares of land in India. The initiative provides access to data and stories on land conflicts, including the parties involved, the issues at stake, legal frameworks, resolutions, and more. It also helps users advocate for the rights and interests of affected communities.

- *Housing.com:* Housing.com is a digital real estate platform based in India that uses GeoAI in streamlining the process of buying, renting, and selling properties. It offers unique features such as 3D modeling for all new projects and 360-degree visualizations for each property listed on the site.

## 12.2.12. Key Takeaways

In this section, we have seen some of the leading GeoAI applications and companies that are transforming the real estate industry with their innovative solutions. We have learned how GeoAI can help real estate professionals to:

- Integrate geospatial data with other types of data to gain a more holistic and comprehensive understanding of the real estate market and its dynamics.

- Use predictive analytics and machine learning to forecast future outcomes and scenarios based on geospatial data and reduce uncertainty and improve performance.

- Assist in site selection and development for real estate projects based on various criteria, such as market demand, land availability, zoning regulations, environmental impact, and infrastructure accessibility.

- Assess and mitigate the various risks associated with real estate properties and projects, such as natural disasters, climate change, crime, terrorism, regulatory changes, and other factors that may affect the value, safety, and sustainability of their assets.

- Provide market insights and analytics for real estate professionals to understand the current and future trends, opportunities, challenges, and competition in the real estate market.
- Offer customized property recommendations based on the preferences and needs of the users by analyzing various types of data, such as location, amenities, price, neighborhood, market trends, user behavior, and feedback.
- Enhance the residential brokerage process and experience by helping brokers and agents to find and attract more clients, provide better service and guidance, and close more deals.
- Enable efficient project management and collaboration by helping project managers, contractors, engineers, architects, and other stakeholders to plan, execute, monitor, and control real estate projects with data-driven insights and automation.
- Provide real-time analytics and insights for real estate properties and projects by monitoring and tracking the status, performance, and changes of their assets in real time using various sources of data, such as sensors, cameras, drones, satellites, and mobile devices.
- Ensure compliance and regulations for real estate properties and projects by complying with the various laws, rules, standards, and codes that govern the real estate industry, such as zoning, building, environmental, tax, and legal regulations.

We have also seen how GeoAI is not only a global phenomenon but also a local one. We have focused on the GeoAI landscape in India, which is one of the largest and fastest-growing real estate markets in the world. We have seen how GeoAI can provide benefits and challenges for the Indian real estate industry, and some of the examples of GeoAI applications and companies in India.

## 12.2.13. References

- Mappital. (n.d.). GIS in real estate: How it can improve your business. Retrieved from [*https://mappitall.com/blog/gis-solutions-for-real-estate*].
- Inoxoft. (n.d.). GIS in real estate: Benefits for property industry. Retrieved from [*https://inoxoft.com/blog/how-to-get-benefits-with-applying-gis-technologies-in-real-estate-industry*].
- USC GIS Online. (2019, November 20). GIS as a platform for real estate. Retrieved from [*https://gis.usc.edu/blog/gis-as-a-tool-for-real-estate*].

- Esri. (2021, January 22). The new analyst: The rise of location in advanced analytics. Forbes. Retrieved from [*https://www.forbes.com/sites/esri/2021/01/22/ the-new-analyst-the-rise-of-location-in-advanced-analytics*].
- G2. (n.d.). Best location intelligence software. Retrieved from [*https://www.g2.com/categories/location-intelligence*].
- KDnuggets. (2020, January 15). Top 7 location intelligence companies in 2020. Retrieved from [*https://www.kdnuggets.com/2020/01/top-7-location-intelligence-companies-2020.html*].
- GoodFirms. (n.d.). Top predictive analytics companies - Reviews 2023. Retrieved from [*https://www.goodfirms.co/big-data-analytics/predictive-analytics*].
- Crunchbase. (n.d.). List of top predictive analytics companies. Retrieved from [*https://www.crunchbase.com/hub/predictive-analytics-companies*].
- eWEEK. (n.d.). Best predictive analytics solutions 2023. Retrieved from [*https://www.eweek.com/big-data-and-analytics/predictive-analytics-solutions*].
- Strategic Development Group. (n.d.). Expert site selection consultants. Retrieved from [*https://strategicdev.com*].
- Hickey & Associates. (n.d.). Global site selection and location strategy consulting services. Retrieved from [*https://www.hickeyandassociates.com*].
- ResearchFDI. (n.d.). Choosing the perfect spot: How site selection powers economic development. Retrieved from [*https://researchfdi.com/resources/articles/ choosing-the-perfect-spot-how-site-selection-powers-economic-development*].
- International Trade Administration. (n.d.). Site selection in the United States. Retrieved from [*https://www.trade.gov/sites/default/files/2021-05/Chapter%20 10%20-%20Site%20Selection.pdf*].
- Global Location Strategies. (n.d.). Corporate site selection & location strategy. Retrieved from [*https://globallocationstrategies.com*].
- Grand View Research. (n.d.). Market research reports & consulting | Grand View Research Inc. Retrieved from [*https://www.grandviewresearch.com*].
- National Association of REALTORS®. (n.d.). Risk management. Retrieved from [*https://www.nar.realtor/risk-management*].
- Embroker. (2019, July 17). A guide to real estate risk management. Retrieved from [*https://www.embroker.com/blog/real-estate-risk-management*].
- Messner Reeves LLP. (2019). Environmental assessments: Three ways they protect companies in corporate real estate transactions | Messner Reeves LLP - JDSupra. JD Supra LLC. Retrieved from [*https://messner.com/environmental-assessments-3-ways-they-protect-companies-in-corporate-real-estate-transactions*].

- Realized Holdings Inc. (2019). Real estate investment risk analysis | How to mitigate risks | Realized Holdings Inc.Retrieved from [*https://www.realized1031. com/blog/8-ways-to-mitigate-risk-in-real-estate-investing*].

- Financial Action Task Force. (2019, June). Guidance for a risk-based approach: The real estate sector. Retrieved from [*https://www.fatf-gafi.org/content/dam/fatf-gafi/guidance/RBA-Real-Estate-Sector.pdf*].

- McKinsey & Company. (2016, September). Getting ahead of the market: How big data is transforming real estate. Retrieved from [*https://www.mckinsey.com/industries/real-estate/our-insights/ getting-ahead-of-the-market-how-big-data-is-transforming-real-estate*].

- Green Street. (n.d.). Definitive leaders in real estate analysis & research. Retrieved from [*https://www.greenstreet.com*].

- Unacast. (2019, August 14). The top real estate analytics companies right now. Retrieved from [*https://www.unacast.com/post/ the-top-real-estate-analytics-companies-right-now*].

- The Close. (2020, December 18). 10 predictive analytics companies transforming real estate. Retrieved from [*https://theclose.com/ best-real-estate-predictive-analytics-companies*].

- StartUs Insights GmbH. (2019, July 25). 5 top AI solutions impacting property & real estate companies. Retrieved from [*https://www.startus-insights.com/ innovators-guide/ai-solutions-property-real-estate-companies*].

- Ascendix Technologies Inc. (2020, December 29). Top 32 proptech companies and startups in the USA in 2023. Retrieved from [*https://ascendixtech.com/ proptech-companies-startups-overview*].

- The Close. (2020, December 18). Best real estate website builder of 2024. Retrieved from [*https://theclose.com/best-real-estate-website-builders*].

- Forbes Advisor. (n.d.). Best CRM for real estate 2023. Retrieved from [*https://www.forbes.com/advisor/business/software/best-real-estate-crm*].

- HomeLight Inc. (n.d.). 10 high-end luxury home real estate companies in the US. Retrieved from [*https://www.homelight.com/blog/high-end-real-estate-companies*].

- Smartsheet Inc. (n.d.). Real estate project management | Smartsheet. Retrieved from [*https://www.smartsheet.com/real-estate-project-management*].

- Avison Young Inc. (n.d.). Real estate development project management | Avison Young US. Retrieved from [*https://www.avisonyoung.us/project-management*].

- FounderJar LLC. (n.d.). Best project management software for real estate in 2023 - FounderJar. Retrieved from [*https://www.founderjar.com/real-estate-project-management*].

- Capterra Inc. (n.d.). Top real estate project management software | Capterra. Retrieved from [*https://www.capterra.com/resources/top-real-estate-project-management-software*].
- Esri Inc. (2018, November 14). Using geospatial technology and analytics to unlock hidden value. Forbes. Retrieved from [*https://www.forbes.com/sites/esri/2018/11/14/using-geospatial-technology-and-analytics-to-unlock-hidden-value*].
- JLL Research Inc. (n.d.). Artificial intelligence - implications for real estate | JLL Research. Retrieved from [*https://www.us.jll.com/en/trends-and-insights/research/artificial-intelligence-and-its-implications-for-real-estate*].
- MIT Technology Review Insights Inc. (2019). Using data , AI , and cloud to transform real estate | MIT Technology Review Insights Inc. Retrieved from [*https://www.technologyreview.com/2023/10/16/1081609/using-data-ai-and-cloud-to-transform-real-estate*].

## 12.3. GEOAI FORECASTS

GeoAI is not only a present reality, but also a future possibility. GeoAI has the potential to revolutionize the real estate industry in the coming years, as it becomes more advanced, accessible, and affordable. In this section, we will explore some of the current and future forecasts of GeoAI and its impact on the real estate sector.

## 12.3.1. The Benefits of GeoAI Forecasts

GeoAI forecasts can provide many benefits for the real estate industry, such as:

- Enhancing the strategic planning and decision making of real estate profession-als, by providing them with reliable and actionable insights into the future trends, opportunities, challenges, and scenarios of the real estate market.
- Improving the performance and profitability of real estate projects and portfolios, by helping them to optimize their location, design, development, operation, and maintenance, all based on predicted future demand, supply, and competition in the real estate market.
- Reducing the uncertainty and risk of real estate investments and transactions, by helping them to anticipate and mitigate the potential impact of various factors,

such as natural disasters, climate change, regulatory changes, and market fluctuations on the value, safety, and sustainability of their assets.

- Supporting the innovation and transformation of the real estate industry, by helping them to discover and adopt new technologies, business models, and solutions that can enhance their efficiency, productivity, quality, and customer satisfaction.

## 12.3.2. Current Forecasts

GeoAI is already making a significant impact on the real estate industry, as evidenced by some of the current forecasts and statistics:

- According to a report by MarketsandMarkets, the global geospatial analytics market size is expected to grow from USD 52.6 billion in 2020 to USD 96.3 billion by 2025, at a Compound Annual Growth Rate (CAGR) of 12.9%.
- According to a report by Grand View Research, the global artificial intelligence in real estate market size is expected to reach USD 12.9 billion by 2025, expanding at a CAGR of 38.4%.
- According to a report by PwC, AI could contribute up to USD 15.7 trillion to the global economy in 2030, with USD 6.6 trillion coming from increased productivity and USD 9.1 trillion coming from consumption effects.
- According to a report by McKinsey, AI could deliver additional economic output of around USD 13 trillion by 2030, boosting global GDP by about 1.2% per year.
- According to a report by CBRE, AI could create up to USD 1.2 trillion in value for the global real estate industry by 2030, with USD 340 billion coming from cost savings and efficiency gains and USD 850 billion coming from new revenue opportunities.

Here are additional trends, focusing on how GeoAI is evolving as a technology.

- Deep learning algorithms have been revolutionized by the field of GeoAI, enabling the development of new and innovative applications. For example, deep learning algorithms are now being used to develop more accurate and efficient methods for image classification, object detection, and land cover mapping.
- The increasing availability of geospatial data from a variety of sources, such as satellites, drones, and sensors, is another major trend in GeoAI. This is fueling the development of new GeoAI applications and enabling more sophisticated analyses.
- Cloud computing and edge computing are enabling new and innovative ways to

develop and deploy GeoAI applications. Cloud computing provides access to powerful computing resources, while edge computing allows GeoAI applications to be deployed near the source of the data.

- New GeoAI algorithms and models are being developed all the time, which are enabling new and innovative applications. For example, new algorithms are being developed for tasks such as point cloud processing, 3D reconstruction, and spatio-temporal analysis.

- Explainable GeoAI is a growing field of research that focuses on developing methods for making GeoAI models more transparent and understandable. This is important for ensuring that GeoAI models are used in a responsible and ethical manner.

- Fair and equitable GeoAI is another growing field of research that focuses on developing methods for ensuring that GeoAI models are not biased or discriminatory. This is important for ensuring that GeoAI benefits everyone, regardless of their race, gender, or other factors.

- Responsible GeoAI is a growing field of research that focuses on developing guidelines and best practices for the development and deployment of GeoAI systems. This is important for ensuring that GeoAI is used in a way that is beneficial to society and does not cause harm.

## 12.3.3. Key Takeaways

- In this section, we have seen some of the current and future forecasts of GeoAI and its impact on the real estate sector.

- We have learned how GeoAI can provide many benefits for the real estate industry, such as:
  - enhancing strategic planning and decision making,
  - improving performance and profitability,
  - reducing uncertainty and risk, and
  - supporting innovation and transformation.

- We have also seen how GeoAI is already making a significant impact on the real estate industry, as evidenced by some of the current forecasts and statistics, such as:
  - the growth and value of the geospatialanalytics and artificial intelligence markets,
  - the contribution and output of AI to the global economy, and
  - the value and opportunities of AI for the global real estate industry.

## 12.3.4. References

- MarketsandMarkets. (2020). Geospatial analytics market - Global forecast to 2028. [Report]. Retrieved from h*ttps://www.marketsandmarkets.com/Market-Reports/geospatial-analytics-market-198354497.html*

- Grand View Research. (2019). Artificial Intelligence Market Size, Share, Trends Analysis Report 2023-2030 [Report]. Retrieved from *https://www.grandviewresearch.com/industry-analysis/artificial-intelligence-ai-market*

- PwC. (2017). The economic impact of artificial intelligence on the UK economy. [Report]. Retrieved from *https://www.pwc.co.uk/economic-services/assets/ai-uk-report-v2.pdf*

- McKinsey. (2018). Notes from the AI frontier: Modeling the impact of AI on the world economy. [Report]. Retrieved from *https://www.mckinsey.com/~/media/McKinsey/Featured%20Insights/Artificial%20Intelligence/Notes%20from%20the%20frontier%20Modeling%20the%20impact%20of%20AI%20on%20the%20world%20economy/MGI-Notes-from-the-AI-frontier-Modeling-the-impact-of-AI-on-the-world-economy-September-2018.ashx*

- CBRE. (2018). [The Rise of the Machine – Impacts and applications of AI in real estate (*https://www.cbre.com/insights/articles/the-rise-of-the-machine-impacts-and-applications-of-ai-in-real-estate*). Retrieved from *https://www.cbre.com/insights/articles/the-rise-of-the-machine-impacts-and-applications-of-ai-in-real-estate*

- Coherent Market Insights. (2020). Geospatial Analytics Market Analysis. [Report]. Retrieved from *https://www.coherentmarketinsights.com/market-insight/geospatial-analytics-market-5874*

- MDPI. (2020). GeoAI for large-scale image analysis and machine vision tasks: A review. [Article]. Retrieved from *https://www.mdpi.com/22*

- Dalumpines, R., Clavijo, J., Buchanan, J., Chacon, R., & Larson, T. (2022, September). Using GeoA in property valuation. FIG Congress, Warsaw, Poland. Retrieved from *https://www.fig.net/resources/proceedings/fig_proceedings/fig2022/papers/ts08a/TS08A_dalumpines_clavijo_et_al_11702.pdf*

- Liu, P., & Biljecki, F. (2022). A review of spatially-explicit GeoAIapplications in urban geography. International Journal of Applied Earth Observation and Geoinformation. Retrieved from *https://www.sciencedirect.com/science/article/pii/S1569843222001339*

- Casali, Y., Aydin, N. Y., & Comes, T. (2022, October). Machine learning for spatial analyses in urban areas: a scoping review. Sustainable Cities and

Society. Retrieved from *https://www.sciencedirect.com/science/article/pii/S2210670722003687*

- Janowicz, K., Gao, S., McKenzie, G., Hu, Y., & Bhaduri, B. (2019). GeoAI: Spatially explicit artificial intelligence techniques for geographic knowledge discovery and beyond. International Journal of Geographical Information Science. Retrieved from *https://www.tandfonline.com/doi/full/10.1080/13658816.2019.1684500*

- Alastal, A. I., & Shaqfa, A. H. (2022, May). GeoAI technologies and their application areas in urban planning and development: Concepts, opportunities and challenges in smart city (Kuwait, study case). Journal of Data Analysis and Information Processing. Retrieved from *https://www.scirp.org/journal/paperinformation.aspx?paperid=116308*

- Mortaheb, R., & Jankowski, P. (2023, March). Smart city re-imagined: City planning and GeoAI in the age of big data. Journal of Urban Management. Retrieved from *https://www.sciencedirect.com/science/article/pii/S2226585622000693*

- Richter, K.-F., & Scheider, S. (2022). Current topics and challenges in GeoAI. KI - Künstliche Intelligenz. Retrieved from *https://link.springer.com/article/10.1007/s13218-022-00796-0*

- Chiappinelli, C. (2022, March 1). Think tank: GeoAI reveals a glimpse of the future. WhereNext Magazine. Retrieved from *https://www.esri.com/about/newsroom/publications/wherenext/think-tank-on-geoai-simulation/*

- PiinPoint. (2023, August 31). Retail real estate executives need new tools. Retrieved from *https://www.piinpoint.com/blog/network-simulations-blog-post-2023*

# PART III

# WHAT DOES THE FUTURE HOLD?

*The best way
to predict the future is
to create it.*

**– Abraham Lincoln**

# CHAPTER 13
# CONTEXT FOR MAKING PREDICTIONS

## 13.1. HOW YOU WILL BENEFIT FROM READING PART III

Sundar Pichai, the CEO of Google a.k.a. Alphabet, in 2018 first asserted that "AI is one of the most important things humanity is working on. It is more profound than, I dunno, electricity or fire." A few months earlier Mark Cuban, self-made billionaire and star investor of the reality show "Shark Tank," predicted that "the world's first trillionaires are going to come from somebody who masters AI and all its derivatives and applies it in ways we never thought of." Even if only a fraction of what these and other Silicon Valley rock stars are saying comes true, the impacts of AI on the world will be profound indeed.

The real estate industry will not be exempt. All industry players are thus well advised to not only monitor current AI developments (i.e., Part II of this book) but also seriously investigate the likely future impacts of AI on real estate (Part III). Without exaggeration, career paths are at stake.

Serious investigations of future AI impacts are hampered by two problems. The first is the sheer number of information sources to be reviewed – not unlike "drinking from a firehose." The second problem is the widely varying reliability of those sources.

We have endeavored to do the legwork for you, at a minimum on a first-pass basis and hopefully well beyond that. As described in the methodology section below, we have diligently searched for a consensus among credible sources on what the future holds – the so-called Notable Observations in section 13.3. Thereafter, in section 13.4 we identify leading AI-centric real estate companies to watch.

That said, a salient caveat is in order: The AI industry is so multi-faceted and is evolving so rapidly that no one can warrant the eventual accuracy of their predictions. Ultimately you remain responsible for reaching your own conclusions.

## 13.2. METHODOLOGY EMPLOYED

The product of our search for a consensus on what the future holds has been a series of "notable observations" that personify the most important AI trends. We provide not only the author but also the verbatim wording of each notable observation.

To assemble "the pieces of the puzzle", our search has focused on four main types of sources:

- General literature on AI as published by news portals, management consulting firms, IT consulting firms, and so on,
- Real estate-specific AI literature, again as published by real estate news portals, consulting firms, leading bloggers, etc.,
- Surveys of what AI investments venture capitalists are making, and
- Academic research studies.

As has been true throughout this book beginning with Chapter 1, all sources cited in the References at the end of this chapter are publicly available via the Internet should any of our readers wish to pursue additional research on any given topic.

## 13.3. NOTABLE OBSERVATIONS FROM THE LITERATURE

Again, keeping up with AI literature is like drinking from a firehouse, while simultaneously being vigilant about the quality of the torrent of information – no small challenge!

Though we are mostly focusing on the real estate industry, we'll begin with a few notable observations about trends in AI generally.

### 13.3.1. AI Generally

The notable overall AI observations below are grouped by:

- Growth forecasts,
- Company Technology Adoption Rates, and
- How to Respond.

#### *Growth Forecast*

AI's impact on the world's Gross Domestic Product (GDP) is projected to be huge.

PwC a.k.a. Price Waterhouse Coopers is the second-largest professional services network in the world, with more than 700 offices in 157 countries. From a March 2023 PwC publication entitled Global Artificial Intelligence Study: Exploiting the AI Revolution:

> "According to the analysis conducted for this PwC report, AI is likely to be a major game changer with a significant amount of value potential. Research indicates that global GDP could be up to 14% higher in 2030 as a result of AI, equivalent to an additional $15.7 trillion. This makes AI the biggest commercial opportunity in today's rapidly changing economy. While some markets, sectors, and individual businesses are more advanced than others, AI is still in its early stages of development overall."

#### *Company Technology Adoption Rates*

AI's huge impact on global GDP will be facilitated in part by nearly ubiquitous corporate adoption rates.

Built In (builtin.com), an online community for over 2 million tech professionals and 75,000 startups, provides information about tech industry news, events, and job opportunities. From a March 2023 Built In posting entitled The Future of AI: How Artificial Intelligence Will Change the World:

> "The field of artificial intelligence is rapidly evolving, with innovations accelerating at a breakneck pace. AI is shaping the future of humanity across nearly every industry and is the driving force behind emerging technologies such as big data, robotics, and IoT. Generative AI tools, such as ChatGPT and AI art generators, are also gaining mainstream attention. Approximately 44% of companies are planning to make significant investments in AI and integrate it into their businesses. The future of AI is indeed a rapidly changing landscape, with the present innovations making it difficult to keep up."

Gartner, Inc. is an American technology research and consulting firm with offices in over 100 countries. From a July 2023 Gartner publication entitled Gartner Identifies Top Trends Shaping the Future of Data Science and Machine Learning:

> "According to a recent Gartner poll of more than 2,500 executive leaders, investment in AI is expected to continue to accelerate. The poll found that 45% of respondents reported that recent hype around ChatGPT prompted them to increase AI investments. Additionally, 70% of respondents said their organization is in investigation and exploration mode with generative AI, while 19% are in pilot or production mode. This suggests that organizations are actively exploring and implementing AI solutions, and that industries are looking to grow through the use of AI technologies and AI-based businesses."

ZDNet (zdnet.com) is a website that provides news and advice on the world's latest innovations; the website has 130 million annual visits worldwide. From a May 2022 ZDNet news story entitled IBM CEO: Artificial Intelligence is Nearing a Key Tipping Point:

> "According to IBM CEO Arvind Krishna, the global market is on the verge of reaching a critical AI tipping point that will unlock significant productivity gains. IBM's Global AI Adoption Index 2022, which surveyed 7,502 senior business decision-makers, supports this claim. The survey found that 35% of companies are currently using AI in their business, up four points from 2021. Additionally, 30% of respondents reported that their employees are already saving time with new AI and automation software and tools. Krishna believes

that these numbers will continue to rise until they reach a *tipping point of around 50%, at which point adoption will quickly increase to 90%* [emphasis added]. This means that we are just before this tipping point, which will unlock a great deal of productivity."

## *How to Respond*

Most organizations will confront substantial challenges in adopting AI technologies.

The Forbes Technology Council is an invitation-only organization for respected CEOs, CIOs, and CTOs, selected for their deep knowledge and diverse experience in the industry. From an April 2023 Forbes Technology Council publication authored by Council member Peter van der Made, entitled The Future Of Artificial Intelligence:

> "The AI revolution is here, and companies must be ready to adapt. To do so, it's important to assess the current skills within the company and identify any additional skills that employees need to learn. Developing an AI strategy that outlines the areas where AI can be most effective, whether in a product or service, is also crucial. Failing to act means falling behind. Training should include an introduction to AI, its capabilities, and its limitations – since AI can only be as good as the data on which it trained."

Mihir A. Desai is an Indian-American economist who is currently a Professor both at the Harvard Business School and the Harvard Law School. From an August 2023 article of his published in the Harvard Business Review, entitled What the Finance Industry Tells Us About the Future of AI:

> "The finance industry, which has long been incorporating data and algorithms, provides a preview of the impact of AI on industries and jobs. The experience of finance suggests that AI will transform some industries, sometimes very quickly, and will particularly benefit larger players. However, the overall system may not be better off. The challenge for the finance industry, and perhaps most industries, is to remember that the *hardest questions facing managers and leaders are not entirely determined by hard data* [emphasis added]. Decisions such as what will allow an enterprise to succeed in 10 years require acts of imagination and conviction. While hard data will inform these decisions, it is unlikely to be the end-all. As the ability to use hard data

becomes cheaper and more efficient through AI, acts of judgment will rise in importance. Acknowledging the primacy of these human questions does not diminish the value of AI; it simply reasserts that AI is a technology and that the greatest rewards for managers and investors lie in fundamentally human endeavors."

This concludes notable observations on AI generally. We now turn to those specific to the real estate industry.

## 13.3.2. Real Estate Specifically

Articles on AI in real estate typically focus on a few high-profile applications such as virtual assistants in residential brokerage, automated property valuation, smart home devices, and so on. However, as Part II has shown, AI applications in the real estate industry are widespread – if not yet ubiquitous.

The notable real estate-centric observations below are grouped by:

- Growth forecasts,
- How the industry will change, and
- Cautionary notes.

### *Growth Forecasts*

Reflecting AI's huge impact on global GDP, the real estate industry can achieve remarkable gains.

JLL a.k.a. Jones Lang LaSalle, a real estate company with offices in 80 countries, provides investment management services, technology products, and venture capital investments. From an August 2023 JLL publication entitled Artificial Intelligence: Real Estate Revolution or Evolution?

"According to JLL research, the use of AI in PropTech is expected to continue to grow. In 2022, the total capital raised to fund AI-powered PropTech reached US$4 billion globally, almost double the amount raised in 2021. Venture capital (VC) is the main driving force behind the development of AI products, with over 70% of all AI-powered PropTech companies being VC-backed. The ecosystem is young and energetic, with about 20% of companies in the very early incubator, angel or seed stage; 25% at early-stage VC rounds; and 15% at late-stage VC rounds."

LeadSquared is a unicorn startup in India that helps sales teams become more efficient with its CRM platform. From a November 2022 LeadSquared publication entitled Top 10 PropTech Startups in India:

> "The PropTech market in India will continue to experience rapid growth, expanding from $120 billion in 2017 to *$1 trillion by 2030* [emphasis added]"

### How the Industry Will Change

Disruptive, revolutionary, transformative, and similar adjectives are frequently encountered in commentaries on how AI will affect the real estate industry.

Co-libry is a Belgium company that provides AI personalization solutions for real estate portals. From a September 2020 Co-libry publication entitled 5 Powerful Ways AI Is Disrupting the Real Estate Sector:

> "Artificial Intelligence (AI) is poised to become one of the most disruptive technologies in history, with the real estate industry being a prime target for its transformative effects. The sector has already seen significant changes due to AI, but this is just the beginning. Historically, the real estate industry has been plagued by inefficient data management and cumbersome processes. However, with the advent of AI, these issues are being addressed. The online real estate sector generates vast amounts of data that can be used to enhance customer experiences and drive sales. As AI continues to evolve, the real estate industry can expect even more exciting developments in the future."

The mission of Property Industry Eye (propertyindustryeye.com) is to provide unbiased, factual, and accurate news coverage on topics relevant to those working in the property market in the United Kingdom and beyond. From a June 2023 commentary written by Richard Murray entitled Unleashing the Power of AI in the Property Industry:

> "The property industry is on the brink of a revolution, as the possible uses of AI are vast. AI has the potential to transform everything from operations to customer interactions, giving estate agents who adopt this technology a significant edge over their competitors."

The American Genius (theamericangenius.com ) is a news website that focuses on technology entrepreneurship. From a May 2023 commentary written by Lisa Wyatt Roe entitled How To Capitalize On AI As It Shifts Real Estate:

> "The real estate industry, particularly commercial real estate, is now all about data. Thanks to AI, vast amounts of data are being processed, organized, and analyzed by AI-powered tools, transforming the way deals are made and the future of the industry. AI's ability to predict future trends with greater accuracy and efficiency, increased productivity, and reduced costs is enormous for both commercial and residential real estate. The pace of innovation and disruption from AI is staggering, and it's crucial for the commercial real estate industry to keep up."

TNT - The Next Tech (the-next-tech.com) is an online platform that provides news and information about technology, including machine learning, natural language processing, robotics, and other types of artificial intelligence. From a July 2023 commentary entitled AI In Real Estate: Revolutionizing The Future Of The Industry:

> "In a rapidly changing world, technology is transforming many industries. AI is now a disruptive force in real estate, bringing innovation and change to traditional practices. From property valuation and customer service to property management, AI has the potential to revolutionize every aspect of the industry. Despite ongoing legal and ethical challenges, the use of AI in real estate shows no signs of slowing down, indicating a future where it becomes an essential tool for industry professionals."

## Cautionary Notes

Innumerable commentators about AI generally as well as AI in real estate have reiterated that "AI won't replace you, but people using AI will." The idea is that AI is not capable of replacing humans, but rather those who know how to effectively use AI can make certain human tasks obsolete. AI is a tool designed to support and enhance human intelligence, not replace it. While AI can automate many routine tasks, it lacks the emotional intelligence, creativity, and ethical judgment that are uniquely human. However, while this may be true today, the commentators rarely address what could happen if AI systems reach the stage of Artificial General Intelligence (AGI) and even Artificial Superintelligence (ASI), as discussed in Chapter 2; AI would then no longer lack humanistic emotional intelligence, creativity, and ethical judgment.

David Bluhm is a technology entrepreneur with over three decades of experience in starting and growing technology companies; he is the co-founder and president of Plunk, an advanced analytics company that uses AI in residential real estate. From an April 2023 publication of his entitled How Artificial Intelligence Will Change Real Estate: Should We Brace For Impact Or Embrace It?:

> "The recent excitement surrounding Artificial Intelligence has largely focused on generative AI, particularly the ability of chatbots to generate informed responses to complex inputs. While AI has the potential to automatically generate property descriptions and marketing content, improve ad targeting, and manage customer service responses, its role in the residential real estate ecosystem will be much broader. Like other significant technological innovations such as the automobile, television, internet, smartphones, and social media, AI presents new opportunities for expression, learning, entertainment, education, and more. However, it also presents significant social and ethical challenges. The power of AI raises more complex and serious concerns than previous innovations. It is important to embrace AI and use it to our advantage while remaining vigilant in recognizing its challenges."

Dr. Philip Seagraves is an Associate Professor of Finance and Real Estate at the Jones College of Business at Middle Tennessee State University. From a July 2023 research paper of his published in the *Journal of Property Investment & Finance* entitled Real Estate Insights: Is the AI Revolution a Real Estate Boon or Bane?

> "In conclusion, AI has had a profound impact on the real estate industry, presenting both significant opportunities and challenges. It is changing the way we buy, sell, manage, and think about property, affecting not only real estate businesses but also homeowners, tenants, and investors. To fully harness its potential, it is important to understand its capabilities, address its limitations, and integrate it responsibly and ethically."

## 13.4. TOP AI COMPANIES IN THE REAL ESTATE INDUSTRY

The evolution of AI in the real estate industry will be largely driven by the leading companies in that space. These are companies that provide real estate-specific AI tools for others to use (for example, Compass), or use AI in offering services to consumers and other businesses (Zillow). These are not companies that provide generic AI tools, such as Microsoft.

The Western and India companies delineated below have been selected on a consensus emerging from our previously described literature search, together with the frequency of companies observed in Part II of this book.

The Appendix provides additional information on these top companies, and on other companies not included in this section but nonetheless worth noting.

## 13.4.1. Western Companies

TABLE 13.1

| NAME & LOCATION | AI ACTIVITIES |
| --- | --- |
| **Apartment Ocean**<br>New York, NY<br>*https://www.*<br>*apartmentocean.com/* | Apartment Ocean is an AI chatbot that helps realtors convert potential customers and reduce acquisition expenses. The chatbot serves as a communication tool on a website, providing instant replies to customer inquiries without requiring effort or time from the realtor. The AI application can answer even the trickiest questions in a human-like manner and is easy to customize and install on a website. This makes it a convenient solution for busy realtors looking to improve their customer conversion rates. |
| **Blackstone**<br>New York, NY<br>*https://www.blackstone.*<br>*com/our-businesses/*<br>*real-estate/* | Blackstone is a global leader in real estate investing, with $326 billion of investor capital under management. Blackstone is the largest owner of commercial real estate globally, owning and operating assets across every major geography and sector, including logistics, residential, office, hospitality, and retail. Among other applications, Blackstone leverages AI technology to find and acquire undermanaged, well-located assets across the world. |
| **Brookfield Asset Management**<br>Toronto, Canada<br>*https://www.brookfield.*<br>*com/our-businesses/*<br>*real-estate* | As one of the world's largest investors in real estate with $272 billion under management, Brookfield Asset Management owns, operates, and develops iconic properties in the world's most dynamic markets. From next-generation logistics facilities and state-of-the-art office buildings to luxury hotels and residential communities, its global portfolio spans five continents and is diversified across every sector of real estate. Brookfield employs AI tools in analyzing market trends, assessing risk, reducing operational costs, as well as making informed investment decisions. |
| **Cherre**<br>New York, NY<br>*https://cherre.com/* | Cherre is an AI startup that offers a data management platform called CoreConnect, which intelligently collects and indexes real estate data from thousands of sources, and thereby provides crucial data insights. Cherre has won multiple awards for its use |

| NAME & LOCATION | AI ACTIVITIES |
| --- | --- |
| | of AI in its real estate products and has partnered with several Fortune 500 companies. Its SaaS system includes several key elements such as CoreAugment, CoreExplore, CoreConnect, and CorePredict, collectively offering features like risk analysis and prevention, ROI modeling, and forecasting. Cherre possesses data on 177 million real estate assets. |
| **CityBldr**<br>Bellevue, WA<br>*https://www.citybldr.com/* | CityBldr is an AI-powered real estate app that helps discover undervalued properties and multi-property parcels. It combines professional expertise to carve out a niche in the property research and analytics industry. CityBldr helps users find the best property by searching for available sites and connecting them with stakeholders. CityBldr also uses AI to determine the best use of land. This involves massive amounts of data to predict the future of land use and measuring the outcomes of different types of land use. |
| **Compass**<br>New York, NY<br>*https://www.compass.com/* | Compass is a real estate brokerage company that uses AI to provide agents with insights into the market, find leads, and close deals. The app is used by more than 14,000 agents across 100 U.S. cities. Compass's customer relationship management platform uses AI to nudge agents to contact clients when they are most likely to buy and auto-drafts emails to speed up outreach. The company hired over 200 engineers and AI professionals in 2019 to power up AI solutions and now has an AI team of over 320 people in New York, Washington, and Seattle. |
| **CoreLogic**<br>Irvine, CA<br>*https://www.corelogic.com/* | CoreLogic is the largest provider of advanced property and ownership information, analytics, and solutions in the US. Their databases cover more than 150 million assessor parcels in 3,000 counties, representing 97% of the nation's real estate transactions. CoreLogic obtains property records, tax assessments, and other information from tax assessors and county recorders offices on a daily basis, and combine it with flood, demographics, crime, and other data from proprietary sources. With over 600,000 users nationwide, CoreLogic's analytics and solutions are used to measure property values, improve customer acquisition and retention, detect fraud, improve mortgage transaction efficiency, identify real estate trends, and increase market share. |

| NAME & LOCATION | AI ACTIVITIES |
| --- | --- |
| **DeepBlocks**<br>Miami, FL<br>*https://www.deepblocks.com/* | Deepblocks is a Miami-based agency that offers a subscription service that uses AI to help real estate developers and investors pick the optimum site for their projects. The platform automates the site selection and feasibility analysis process, allowing users to select a city and development criteria, view potential properties on a parcel grid, and export sites of interest. Users can also see zoning requirements, analyze market trends, and test buildings on the site through a virtual platform that combines 3D modeling with financial analysis. |
| **Divvy Homes**<br>San Francisco, CA<br>*https://www.divvyhomes.com/* | Divvy Homes is a modern rent-to-own program that empowers renters to become homeowners. It was founded with the mission to make homeownership, and all the power and security that comes with it, accessible to everyone. Divvy Homes is clear about their process and fees, but do require a double monthly payment and have the right to evict tenants who miss payments. With Divvy Homes, clients can find a home, move in, and rent with built-in savings for a subsequent down payment. In three years or less, they are ready to buy the home. |
| **Doxel**<br>Redwood City, CA<br>*https://www.doxel.ai/* | Doxel is a real estate technology company that uses AI to create 3D models of properties from drone or satellite imagery. It focuses on projects still under construction, tracking installed items and automatically measuring the earned value for each item. With Doxel, clients can see the construction site in 3D, view an updated progress report, and see the completion stats. Doxel is an example of how artificial intelligence can be used to improve productivity and efficiency in the construction industry. |
| **GeoPhy**<br>Delft, Netherlands<br>*https://geophy.com/* | Founded in 2014, GeoPhy uses an enterprise-scale AVM that relies on AI to estimate values for commercial properties such as office buildings and shopping complexes, based on thousands of data sources. Its smart algorithms feed on countless data points, ranging from hyperlocal data on crime and park proximity to digitized property records. Major real estate enterprises, investors, and lenders can make accurate predictions about upcoming price changes and automate analysis of multiple aspects affecting the final price. |

| NAME & LOCATION | AI ACTIVITIES |
|---|---|
| **HouseCanary**<br>San Francisco, CA<br>*https://www.*<br>*housecanary.com/* | HouseCanary is a company that uses AI to provide cost estimations and predictive analytics for the real estate residential market. Their software evaluates current and near-future house prices by analyzing data from the last 40 years, generating forecasts with a 2.5% margin of error. This allows for wise buying decisions and higher customer conversions. HouseCanary offers analysis tools, data, and continual updates to help customers make informed decisions on properties of interest. Real estate brokers and. lending organizations use this software to build trust with their customers. |
| **Hyro**<br>New York, NY<br>*https://www.hyro.ai/* | Hyro is the world's first Adaptive Communications Platform for real estate. It uses AI to provide round-the-clock assistance to customers through call centers, SMS, and web-based inquiries, capturing every lead even when busy realtors are unavailable. Property management companies can use the fresh conversational insights provided by Hyro to optimize their digital channels and maximize their conversion rate. Hyro is thus a conversational AI platform that helps real estate companies capture and follow up on leads, schedule viewings, and answer customer questions through its AI chat and voice interfaces. |
| **Jointer**<br>Los Altos, CA<br>*https://about.jointer.io/* | Jointer is a startup that brings blockchain technology to real estate, offering a better alternative to commercial, one-time investments by replacing them with tokens that provide diversification to investors and increase ROI for owners. The platform uses an embedded AI engine to analyze thousands of real estate items and identify the best opportunities and most secure investments. Jointer has been called a game-changer in real estate and won the award for best startup in the world in 2018, competing against 4,000 other startups. |
| **Localize**<br>New York, NY<br>*https://signup.localizeos.*<br>*com/about-us* | Localize's Hunter app is a concierge texting service that uses both artificial and human intelligence to engage real estate agents' leads. The app builds a profile of each lead with relevant information such as budget and pre-approval status, and updates users on the progress of their leads. When a buyer is ready to start visiting properties, Hunter alerts the agent. Localize.city is |

| NAME & LOCATION | AI ACTIVITIES |
|---|---|
| | another tool offered by the company that analyzes the amount of sunlight each apartment receives throughout the year, including the sunniest hours of the day and the amount of time sunlight penetrates each room. This provides an alternative to visiting the apartment in person multiple times to determine the amount of sunlight. |
| **Main Street Renewal**<br>Austin, TX<br>*https://www.msrenewal.com/* | Main Street Renewal is a privately owned company that focuses on renovating high-quality homes and leasing them at affordable prices. The company serves residents in dozens of markets across the United States and is expanding to more locations. Main Street Renewal uses a unique AI model to find excellent properties and upgrade them to their standard, then leases and manages the properties long-term. Residents have access to an online portal where they can pay bills, request maintenance, and renew their lease, as well as convenient features like auto-pay. |
| **Mashvisor**<br>Campbell, CA<br>*https://www.mashvisor.com/* | Founded in 2014, Mashvisor is a pioneering platform that equips real estate investors with AI data-driven insights to navigate the complexities of the investment landscape. Its mission is to automate and analyze nationwide real estate data for investors to identify lucrative traditional and Airbnb investment properties and optimize their rental performance. Mashvisor has developed interactive property and neighborhood insights encompassing a comprehensive analysis of traditional and Airbnb pricing, occupancy rates, seasonality trends, revenue potential, cost assumptions, cash flow calculations, and purchase investment analyses. |
| **PGIM Real Estate**<br>Arlington, VA<br>*https://www.pgim.com/real-estate/* | PGIM Real Estate is the global real estate investment arm of the American life insurance company Prudential Financial. PGIM Real Estate is one of the largest real estate managers in the world with professionals in 32 cities worldwide and $182.5 billion in gross assets under management. As of 2021 an announced strategic focus is connecting PGIM Real Estate's data, proprietary market insights and research, with new technological innovations — notably artificial intelligence — to help drive investment decisions. |

| NAME & LOCATION | AI ACTIVITIES |
|---|---|
| **PropStream**<br>Lake Forest, CA<br>*https://www.propstream.com/* | PropStream is a powerful tool for real estate agents and investors, providing access to an extensive property database and MLS integration. With millions of property records, foreclosure data, and neighborhood statistics at their fingertips, professionals can make more informed decisions. PropStream's AI-powered predictive analytics take it a step further by helping users discover opportunities in the market that may not be listed publicly. This data-driven approach can lead to increased success rates and higher returns on investments for agents and investors. |
| **Quantarium**<br>Bellevue, WA<br>*https://www.quantarium.com/* | Quantarium is an AI-powered real estate app that provides accurate valuations of properties for brokers, banks, insurers, and lenders. The app is built on scalable cloud infrastructure and features deep learning algorithms that have processed data on more than 153 million property parcels in the United States. Real estate professionals, including mortgage lenders and construction companies, rely on Quantarium's valuations of commercial and residential properties. The app's predictive analytics can also provide insights into potential risks that could affect an owner's portfolio. |
| **RedFin**<br>Seattle, WA<br>*https://www.redfin.com/* | Redfin is a real estate company that uses AI to augment the work of its agents, rather than replace them. The company has automated the property recommendation process with an AI matchmaking tool that analyzes data to suggest homes to potential buyers. Data suggests that users are four times more likely to click on a Redfin recommendation than on a property that merely fits their search criteria. Redfin also uses AI to calculate the value of houses and advise home sellers on their marketing, all while simplifying the customer search process and requiring only a 1% commission per sale. |
| **Reonomy**<br>New York, NY | Reonomy is a real estate platform that uses AI algorithms to discover new insights about properties and predict the probability of future sales. The platform serves as an enhanced search engine, providing data on owners, previous deals, and debt information to help users make more informed decisions. |

| NAME & LOCATION | AI ACTIVITIES |
| --- | --- |
| | In addition to assembling various types of data, Reonomy uses predictive analytics to provide insights on property maintenance and potential future sales. |
| **Rex Homes**<br>Woodland Hills, CA<br>*https://www.rexhomes.com/* | Rex is a real estate agency that aims to simplify the process of buying and selling a house by using AI to replace traditional agents. The company tracks user behavior on its website and displays ads that match their interests. Rex also uses intelligent algorithms to analyze homeowner history data and determine buying capabilities. Rex charges only a 2% commission instead of the typical 5-6%. In addition to its main platform, Rex owns multiple real estate technology brands, including JobCall, an AI assistant that facilitates communication between property maintenance teams and renters using speech recognition technology. |
| **Skyline AI**<br>New York, NY<br>*https://skyline.ai/* | Skyline AI is a JLL company that offers AI-augmented commercial investment management solutions for real estate investors. Investors use this powerful AI real estate app to find high-reward opportunities and predict market anomalies. The company's tool combines human expertise with AI's ability to analyze large amounts of data, including location, web data, and AI-generated data. This results in a cutting-edge system that helps investors make informed decisions on when to buy and sell properties. Skyline AI also offers an investment calculator and uses deep-dive analysis of past deals to predict market trends such as rental costs and ROI for buyers. The company was heralded as the most innovative AI startup of 2019. |
| **TRIRIGA**<br>Las Vegas, NV<br>*https://www.ibm.com/products/tririga* | IBM® TRIRIGA® is an intelligent asset management solution that helps organizations evolve their facilities management using data and AI. It is an integrated workplace management system (IWMS) that integrates functional models across various areas such as real estate, capital projects, facilities, workplace operations, portfolio data, and environmental and energy management within a single technology platform. TRIRIGA is simple, fast, and flexible, offering the right mix of applications in one modular solution to maximize the building lifecycle while preparing for future needs. |

| NAME & LOCATION | AI ACTIVITIES |
|---|---|
| **Trulia**<br>San Francisco, CA<br>*https://www.trulia.com/* | Trulia is a platform that helps buyers and renters find homes and neighborhoods across the United States. It provides recommendations, local insights, and map overlays with information on commutes, schools, churches, and nearby businesses. Customers can browse original neighborhood photos, drone footage, resident reviews, etc., to find their ideal living place. The app uses intelligent AI algorithms to remember a user's browsing criteria and preferred items, such as construction materials and wall colors from liked photos. With more than 35 filtering parameters and keywords taken into account, the app offers a highly personalized experience for its users. |
| **Veros Real Estate Solutions**<br>Santa Ana, CA<br>*https://www.veros.com/* | Veros Real Estate Solutions is a company that specializes in enterprise risk management and collateral valuation services. It uses predictive technology, data analytics, and industry expertise to provide AI-driven automated decision-making solutions. Veros' products and services are integrated into leading companies in the mortgage industry, helping to optimize millions of profitable decisions from loan origination to servicing and the secondary markets. The company offers solutions to control risk and increase profits, including automated valuations, portfolio analysis, fraud and risk detection. In 2019 the agency added information about natural disasters, forecasting property value changes caused by natural phenomena. |
| **Zillow**<br>Seattle, WA<br>*https://www.zillow.com/*<br>*https://www.zillowgroup.com/* | Zillow is a platform that helps customers sell, buy, rent, or finance their next home with speed, certainty, and ease. Zillow's annual AI budget is estimated to be $100 million or more. As the most-visited real estate website in the United States, Zillow and its affiliates offer an on-demand experience with transparency and nearly seamless end-to-end service. Zillow Home Loans, an affiliate lender, provides customers with an easy option to get pre-approved and secure financing for their next home purchase. Zillow Group's brands, affiliates, and subsidiaries include Zillow Premier Agent, Zillow Closing Services, Zillow Homes Inc., Trulia, Out East, StreetEasy, HotPads, and ShowingTime. |

## 13.4.2. India Companies

TABLE 13.2

| NAME & LOCATION | AI ACTIVITIES |
|---|---|
| **Magicbricks - Noida, India** | Magicbricks.com is a high-end property portal launched in 2006 by Times Group. It quickly became the No. 1 Property Portal in India, with a design based on rigorous research and unique product developments. The portal constantly evaluates and upgrades its features to best serve its users. In March 2023 MagicBricks launched India's first AI-powered marketing solution too -- Project Market Scanner (PMS) -- for developers and real-estate agents. PMS acts as a reach maximizer, predicting results based on customers' previous search histories, taking into account buyers' preferences for specific property attributes and images that they are most likely to respond to. |
| **NestAway - Bengaluru, India** | NestAway is India's fastest-growing "Managed Home Rental Network" attempting to provide better rental solutions via design and technology. The company helps find and book rental homes across Indian cities. They assist with move-in and provide home maintenance services from cleaning to damages to rent payment and even move-out. With NestAway tenants can avoid paying brokerage fees, and homeowners can sub-let rooms in fully furnished houses. |
| **NoBroker - Bengaluru, India** | NoBroker is a platform that uses artificial intelligence and machine learning algorithms to bypass brokers. Customers can buy, sell, and rent houses without paying any broker fees using the NoBroker website or app. The platform offers customized suggestions and supports decision-making with real-time data, allowing individuals to make well-informed and profitable selections. |
| **Propstack - Mumbai, India** | Propstack claims to be the leading source of real estate intelligence in India, leveraging its sizeable datasets to create analytics and insights that help clients make better decisions. Propstack provides AI-driven predictive and prescriptive analytics based on deep data. Its suite of online services enables |

| NAME & LOCATION | AI ACTIVITIES |
| --- | --- |
| | clients to analyze, interpret, and gain unmatched insight into commercial property values, market conditions, and current availabilities. Propstack clients include India's largest funds, investors, corporations, developers, brokers, and lenders. |
| **PropTiger - Delhi, India** | PropTiger.com is a leading online real estate platform in India with a team of over 500 relationship managers. The platform leverages AI technology and data to guide home buyers from search to possession, with a focus on trust, transparency, and expertise. PropTiger assists with home loans and property registrations, and offers a full stack of services from online search to transaction assistance. Since its launch in 2011, PropTiger has expanded to nine cities with 18 offices and has helped over 18,000 customers buy properties worth over US $1.5 billion. |
| **SquareYards - Gurugram, India** | SquareYards is a leading proptech platform that offers comprehensive solutions for buying, selling, and investing in properties. The company simplifies property transactions using cutting-edge AI technology and provides services such as property search, mortgage support, legal assistance, and property management. SquareYards has an extensive inventory of residential and commercial properties. The company recently launched an AI-driven solution called Edge, a Software-as-a-Service (SaaS) offering that aims to empower the sales and distribution functions of real estate players in India and offshore markets. |
| **Zolo Stays - Bengaluru, India** | Zolo is a rapidly growing technology startup in India that specializes in co-living and student housing. Zolo offers fully managed living spaces with a variety of amenities for working professionals and students, with the goal of creating a hassle-free living environment. Zolo employs AI techniques to optimize inventory, provide personalized experiences to customers, and to explore solutions for growing their supply of rooms. |

## 13.5. KEY TAKEAWAYS

***AI Industry Generally:***

- AI's impact on the world's Gross Domestic Product (GDP) is projected to be huge. Global GDP could be up to 14% higher in 2030 as a result of AI, equivalent to an additional $15.7 trillion.

- AI's huge impact on global GDP will be facilitated in part by aggressive corporate adoption rates. Approximately 44% of companies across nearly every industry are planning to make significant investments in AI and integrate it into their businesses.

- Investment in AI is expected to continue to accelerate. In one recent poll 70% of respondents said their organization is in investigation and exploration mode with generative AI, while 19% are in pilot or production mode.

- The global market is on the verge of reaching a critical AI tipping point that will unlock significant productivity gains. An IBM survey found that 35% of companies are currently using AI in their business. IBM's CEO has stated that these numbers will continue to rise until they reach a tipping point of around 50%, at which point adoption will quickly increase to 90%.

- Most organizations will confront substantial challenges in adopting AI technologies and must be ready to adapt. Failing to act means falling behind.

- The hardest questions facing managers and leaders are not entirely determined by hard data. Decisions such as what will allow an enterprise to succeed in 10 years require acts of imagination and conviction. While hard data will inform these decisions, it is unlikely to be the end-all.

- Innumerable commentators have observed that "AI won't replace you, but people using AI will." AI is a tool designed to support and enhance human intelligence, not replace it. While AI can automate many routine tasks, it lacks the emotional intelligence, creativity, and ethical judgment that are uniquely human.

- However, while the above takeaway may be true today, the commentators rarely address what could happen if AI systems reach the stage of Artificial General Intelligence (AGI) and even Artificial Superintelligence (ASI). AI would then no longer lack humanistic emotional intelligence, creativity, and ethical judgment. The stage would then be set for AI to largely or even completely supplant humans in the workplace.

*Real Estate Industry Specifically:*

- Reflecting AI's huge impact on global GDP, the real estate industry can achieve remarkable gains.

- The use of AI in PropTech is expected to continue to grow. In 2022, the total capital raised to fund AI-powered PropTech reached US$4 billion globally, almost double the amount raised in 2021. Venture capital (VC) is the main driving force behind the development of AI products.

- The PropTech market in India will continue to experience rapid growth, expanding from $120 billion in 2017 to $1 trillion by 2030.

- Artificial Intelligence (AI) is poised to become one of the most disruptive technologies in history, with the real estate industry being a prime target for its transformative effects. Historically, the real estate industry has been plagued by inefficient data management and cumbersome processes. With the advent of AI, these issues are being addressed.

- The property industry is on the brink of a revolution, as the possible uses of AI are vast. AI has the potential to transform everything from operations to customer interactions, giving estate agents who adopt this technology a significant edge over their competitors."

- Vast amounts of data are now being processed, organized, and analyzed by AI-powered tools, transforming the way real estate deals are made. AI's ability to predict future trends with greater accuracy and efficiency, increased productivity, and reduced costs is enormous for both commercial and residential real estate.

- Despite ongoing legal and ethical challenges, the use of AI in real estate shows no signs of slowing down, indicating a future where it becomes an essential tool for industry professionals.

- Overall, AI is transforming the real estate industry, bringing both opportunities and challenges. It is changing the way we buy, sell, manage, and think about property, impacting real estate businesses, homeowners, tenants, and investors. To maximize its potential, we must understand its capabilities, address its limitations, and integrate it responsibly and ethically.

## 13.6. REFERENCES

- Catherine Clifford, "Google CEO: A.I. Is More Important Than Fire Or Electricity", CNBC, 2018 *https://www.cnbc.com/2018/02/01/google-ceo-sundar-pichai-ai-is-more-important-than-fire-electricity.html*
- Catherine Clifford, "Mark Cuban: The World's First Trillionaire Will Be An Artificial Intelligence Entrepreneur", CNBC, 2017 *https://www.cnbc.com/2017/03/13/mark-cuban-the-worlds-first-trillionaire-will-be-an-ai-entrepreneur.html*
- PwC, "PwC's Global Artificial Intelligence Study: Exploiting the AI Revolution", 2023 *https://www.pwc.com/gx/en/issues/data-and-analytics/publications/artificial-intelligence-study.html*
- Mike Thomas, "The Future of AI: How Artificial Intelligence Will Change the World", Built In, 2023 *https://builtin.com/artificial-intelligence/artificial-intelligence-future*
- Gartner Inc. "Gartner Identifies Top Trends Shaping the Future of Data Science and Machine Learning", 2023 *https://www.gartner.com/en/newsroom/press-releases/2023-08-01-gartner-identifies-top-trends-shaping-future-of-data-science-and-machine-learning*
- Stephanie Condon, "IBM CEO: Artificial intelligence Is Nearing a Key Tipping Point", ZDNET, 2022 *https://www.zdnet.com/article/ibm-ceo-ai-is-near-a-key-tipping-point-but-generalized-ai-is-still-decades-out/*
- Peter van der Made, "The Future of Artificial Intelligence", Forbes Technology Council, 2023 *https://www.forbes.com/sites/forbestechcouncil/2023/04/10/the-future-of-artificial-intelligence/?sh=231b1d514ac4*
- Mihir A. Desai, "What the Finance Industry Tells Us About the Future of AI", Harvard Business Review, 2023 *https://hbr.org/2023/08/what-the-finance-industry-tells-us-about-the-future-of-ai*
- JLL, "Artificial Intelligence: Real Estate Revolution or Evolution?", 2023 *https://www.joneslanglasalle.co.jp/en/trends-and-insights/research/artificial-intelligence-and-its-implications-for-real-estate*
- LeadSquared, "Top 10 PropTech Startups in India" 2022 *https://www.leadsquared.com/industries/real-estate/proptech-startups-in-india/#:~:text=Proptech%20in%20India%20is%20forecast,most%20successful%20Indian%20Proptech%20startups.*
- Co-libry, "5 Powerful Ways AI Is Disrupting the Real Estate Sector" 2020 *https://co-libry.com/blogs/real-estate-artificial-intelligence-ai/*

- Richard Murray, "Unleashing the Power of AI in the Property Industry", Property Industry Eye, 2023 *https://propertyindustryeye.com/unleashing-the-power-if-ai-in-the-property-industry/*

- Lisa Wyatt Roe, "How to Capitalize on AI as It Shifts Real Estate", American Genius, 2023 *https://theamericangenius.com/housing/big-data/5-major-ways-ai-is-shifting-real-estate-scene-and-how-to-utilize-it/*

- Alan Jackson, "AI in Real Estate: Revolutionizing the Future Of The Industry", TNT-The Next Tech, 2023 *https://www.the-next-tech.com/artificial-intelligence/ai-in-real-estate-revolutionizing-the-future-of-the-industry/#google_vignette*

- David Bluhm, "How Artificial Intelligence Will Change Real Estate: Should We Brace for Impact Or Embrace It?", RISMedia, 2023 *https://www.rismedia.com/2023/04/28/how-artificial-intelligence-will-change-real-estate-should-we-brace-for-impact-or-embrace-ai/*

- Dr. Philip Seagraves, "Real Estate Insights: Is the AI Revolution a Real Estate Boon or Bane?", Journal of Property Investment & Finance, 2023 *https://www.emerald.com/insight/content/doi/10.1108/JPIF-05-2023-0045/full/html#:~:text=Findings%20The%20study%20finds%20that%20AI%20has%20significant,and%20optimisation%20in%20building%20management%20also%20hold%20promise.*

# CHAPTER 14

# THE
# PREDICTIONS

AI is already revolutionizing the real estate industry, with far more changes yet to come. The growth rate of AI in the coming two decades will continue to be very rapid, with nearly all companies adopting the technology in varying ways and degrees. "AI won't replace you, but people using AI will."

Accordingly, all real estate professionals are well advised to closely monitor AI developments; continually evaluate how AI might benefit them; and aggressively implement AI tools when appropriate. Toward that end, this section consolidates salient predictions of how AI will transform the real estate industry in the coming years. Given how extensive and complex AI already is, this is not a complete list of predictions but ideally will prove to be a reliable roadmap.

Thirty-two (32) predictions are grouped by those impacting:

- Residential Real Estate,
- Commercial Real Estate, and
- Both Residential and Commercial Real Estate.

Within each of the three groupings are sub-groupings, e.g., Commercial Real Estate has sub-groupings of Market-Wide Analytics, Property Specific Analytics, and Property Management.

Note that in 2021 the total value of commercial real estate in the United States was $20.7 trillion, the total value of residential real estate was $43.4 trillion, and so AI developments in both sectors are of undeniable importance.

## 14.1. CONSOLIDATED PREDICTIONS

## 14.1.1. Residential Real Estate

*Helping Customers*

### Finding Candidate Properties

1. Chatbots will become even more widely used as virtual assistants that can handle inquiries about buying, selling, and renting properties. Chatbots can also perform various other tasks such as qualifying potential clients and scheduling meetings. This can all be done by using natural language processing to understand search queries and by using machine learning to identify patterns in the customer search queries, in inventories of available properties, and in numerous other relevant databases such as neighborhood quality and potential natural hazards.
2. AI-powered property search engines will become increasingly personalized. AI can determine a buyer's preferences (property features, location, etc.) and financial situation to generate personalized property recommendations. By rapidly and efficiently narrowing down the list of properties that are a good fit, AI can save buyers substantial time and money.

### Visiting Candidate Properties in Person and Virtually

3. AI can already be used to create virtual reality (VR) and augmented reality (AR) experiences that allow buyers to explore properties without having to physically visit them. This will make it easier for people to find properties that meet their needs and make informed decisions about their real estate purchases. This will be especially helpful for homebuyers who live in remote areas or are unable to travel.

### Additionally

4. AI technology has the potential to promote inclusivity and equity in the housing market. By analyzing data on factors such as housing costs, availability, and amenities, AI can help identify affordable housing options for all individuals.
5. AI technology can improve accessibility in the real estate industry for people with

disabilities. By designing AI-powered platforms with accessibility in mind, it can become easier for people with disabilities to search for and purchase homes.

6. AI technology can be utilized to keep track of the condition of homes and detect signs of wear and tear. This enables homeowners to identify and address issues at an early stage, potentially avoiding expensive repairs.

### *Helping Agents*

### Office Functions

7. AI can be used in target marketing campaigns and to measure the effectiveness of marketing efforts.
8. AI can analyze properties in extreme detail, including information often not included in the metadata in the past such as aerial photos of property conditions
9. AI will help real estate agents find homes that are most likely to sell in the next 12 months.
10. AI can be used to create personalized continuing education programs, enabling real estate professionals to stay up-to-date on the latest industry trends and to improve their skills.

### Customer Relationship Management (CRM)

11. By streamlining communication and delivering timely and relevant content, chatbots and machine learning interfaces will enhance lead generation and content marketing. Generative AI can be employed to produce more precise and detailed property listings, giving prospective buyers a clearer picture of the properties they're considering.
12. AI-powered real estate agents are emerging, to provide personalized service to buyers and sellers. AI will be able to access and analyze a vast amount of data to find the best properties tailored to each client's tastes, and then negotiate the best deals. This will free up real estate agents to focus on more complex tasks and provide better service to their clients.

## 14.1.2. Commercial Real Estate

### Market-Wide Analytics

13. AI-powered real estate market analytics will become ever more sophisticated. AI can analyze data on historical market trends, current market conditions, sources of risk, and likely future demand to efficiently identify the most promising investment opportunities.

### Property-Specific Analytics

14. AI can soon become a one-stop solution for providing all real estate industry players the ability to gather comprehensive, timely, and accurate information about properties of interest.
15. AI-enabled procedures will facilitate quicker transactions and a more effective comprehension of markets and properties worldwide, spurring greater investment in real estate on a global level.
16. By tracking, analyzing, and instantly publishing ever more comprehensive real estate data, AI will enhance the transparency of the real estate industry while also minimizing the risk of fraud.
17. AI is being increasingly utilized in sophisticated ways across the real estate industry, with "Scenario and Sensitivity Analysis" being a prime example. This analysis concentrates on evaluating a property's financial and operational performance to facilitate informed and lucrative investment choices. Data analysis can uncover a range of unexpected findings that may have otherwise gone unnoticed.

### Property Management

18. The use of AI-driven property management platforms will increase as they offer significant time and cost savings for property managers. These platforms employ AI to automate various tasks, including collecting rent, scheduling maintenance, and screening tenants. Further, property managers are responsible for monitoring tenant applications, rental listings, maintenance requests, inspections, finances, and more on a daily basis. This can be overwhelming, but with the help of AI, property managers can proactively address issues before they arise.

## 14.1.3. Both Residential and Commercial Real Estate

### Repetitive Tasks, Efficiency, Productivity

19. AI will continue to enhance the effectiveness and output of real estate professionals by taking over mundane tasks. For instance, AI can facilitate the creation of smart contracts, streamlining the real estate transaction process. Additionally, AI can automate homebuying tasks such as responding to inquiries from potential buyers and sellers, arranging property viewings, and negotiating deals through chatbots. In administrative work, AI can handle routine documentation and produce reports automatically.

### Property Valuation

20. AI automation of property valuations will continue to save ever more time and money for all parties in a real estate transaction -- real estate agents, brokers, mortgage underwriters buyers, sellers, etc.

21. AI-powered property valuations are becoming increasingly the norm, with models already proving to be more accurate than human-based valuations. This trend is expected to continue, making it easier for buyers and sellers to get a fair price for their properties.

22. AI, with its ability to analyze patterns in large amounts of data, will anticipate evolving real estate market conditions and then make accurate predictions about the future value of specific properties.

### Mortgage Underwriting

23. AI will continue to simplify the data-intensive and time-consuming process of both residential and commercial mortgage lending, making it easier and faster for borrowers to get approved for loans. Moreover, AI will be used to determine the best loan types for borrowers and help borrowers save money by building an optimal budgeting model for their particular circumstances.

### Smart Buildings

24. The birth of the 'real intelligent building' is imminent. AI-compliant infrastructure will become the default.

25. AI will be used to create smart homes that can automatically adjust to the needs of the occupants, to make homes more comfortable, convenient, and energy-efficient.

AI can be used to automate such tasks as adjusting the thermostat, turning on the lights, locking the doors, personalizing home maintenance schedules, and sounding real-time alerts about potential hazards.

## Sustainable Buildings

26. AI will be used to make real estate more sustainable by designing and building more energy-efficient homes and buildings. For example, AI can optimize energy use by automatically adjusting HVAC systems, lighting, and other systems based on occupancy and weather conditions. Collectively these AI advancements will help to reduce the environmental impact of the real estate industry.

## Additionally

27. AI will assist real estate professionals in complying with regulations, reducing the risk of fines and penalties. This not only benefits the professionals but also helps protect consumers.
28. AI is revolutionizing the home insurance industry by more accurately and efficiently assessing the risk of insuring a property, pricing policies, and handling claims. This can lead to improved home insurance operations and reduced costs for homeowners.
29. AI has the potential to revolutionize the home improvement industry by recommending projects, providing estimates, and connecting homeowners with contractors. This can help homeowners make informed decisions about their home improvement opportunities.
30. AI can reduce discrimination in the real estate industry by screening potential buyers and sellers without bias based on factors such as race, gender, or ethnicity.
31. AI will make real estate more accessible to everyone, including those living in rural areas, people with disabilities, and those who are not fluent in the local language.
32. AI will revolutionize the way we think about and interact with real estate -- by making the real estate market more accessible, efficient, and personalized.

## 14.2. POSITIVE AND NEGATIVE CONSEQUENCES

Reflecting on all the above-detailed predictions, the authors will conclude this book with:

- Balancing the pros and cons,
- Reliance on AI as new types come into play, and
- Our take on the bottom line.

### 14.2.1. Balancing the Pros and Cons

Chapter 3, entitled "AI – Friend or Foe?" delineated potential AI Advantages, Threats, and Disasters. These are reproduced in Exhibit 14.1.

EXHIBIT 14.1

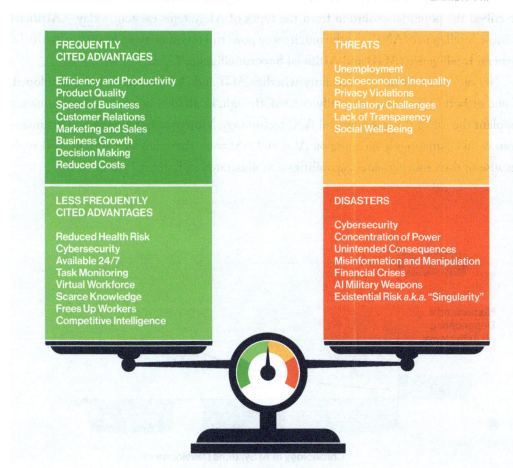

**FREQUENTLY CITED ADVANTAGES**

Efficiency and Productivity
Product Quality
Speed of Business
Customer Relations
Marketing and Sales
Business Growth
Decision Making
Reduced Costs

**LESS FREQUENTLY CITED ADVANTAGES**

Reduced Health Risk
Cybersecurity
Available 24/7
Task Monitoring
Virtual Workforce
Scarce Knowledge
Frees Up Workers
Competitive Intelligence

**THREATS**

Unemployment
Socioeconomic Inequality
Privacy Violations
Regulatory Challenges
Lack of Transparency
Social Well-Being

**DISASTERS**

Cybersecurity
Concentration of Power
Unintended Consequences
Misinformation and Manipulation
Financial Crises
AI Military Weapons
Existential Risk *a.k.a.* "Singularity"

We believe that most real estate professionals who are either considering or already implementing AI tools are focusing on AI Advantages. Relatively little thought is given to the AI Threats, beyond the possibility of jobs being lost. We further believe that few real estate professionals are seriously contemplating AI Disasters. Consequently, on balance AI's positives are perceived as outweighing the negatives.

This circumstance is generally true of all industries, not just real estate. Not surprisingly, then, the adoption of AI technologies is charging ahead worldwide and will continue to do so.

Time will tell whether far more attention should have been given to the potential AI Threats and Disaster.

## 14.2.2. Dependence on AI as New Types Come into Play

Chapter 2, entitled "Types of AI from the Beginning Years (1950s) to the Present", described the potential evolution from the types of AI systems existent today – Artificial Narrow Intelligence (ANI) – to the much more powerful theoretic types known as Artificial General Intelligence (AGI) and Artificial Superintelligence (ASI).

Nobody knows with any certainty whether AGI and ASI can actually be developed. If one or both types are successfully created, though, in all likelihood they would quickly supplant the use of the less powerful ANI technology. Moreover, individuals and organizations would come to rely far more on AGI and ASI tools than they ever did on ANI tools because of their much greater capabilities – as illustrated in Exhibit 14.2.

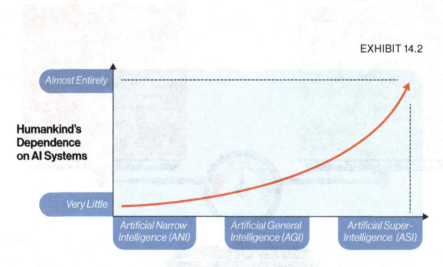

EXHIBIT 14.2

**Chronology of AI Systems Development**

Foreshadowing cases in point are the explosive adoption rates of ChatGPT, Dall-E, and other Generative AI apps. ChatGPT, for example, had one million users within the first five days of its launching in November 2022; by April 2023 it had 173 million users in a broad spectrum of industries. Such unprecedented growth will likely pale in comparison to the adoption rates of AGI and ASI technologies, should those become available.

## 14.2.3. Our Take on the Bottom Line

The potential upside is that humankind will benefit enormously from AI, perhaps more so than from any previous technological development. The potential downside is the increased possibility of AI Threats and AI Disasters materializing – including the risk of machines doing away with humankind altogether.

To date humankind has failed to effectively address the clear and present dangers of climate change, despite credible predictions that continued failure could be catastrophic. Little evidence suggests that humankind would do any better in effectively addressing the potential dangers and even catastrophes posed by AI technological advancements.

Accordingly, we best all keep our fingers crossed that AI Threats and AI Disasters do not become overwhelming.

## 14.3. REFERENCES

The predictions in this chapter have been drawn from many sources, notably from the 99 cited in the Bibliography. As has been our journalistic confirmation practice throughout this book, we have looked for redundancies in the predictions from multiple sources.

We are not going to essentially footnote all the many sources for all the above 32 predictions here. We would like to leave you, however, with three citations for three books that are widely regarded as "must reads". Though not specifically focused on the real estate industry, they provide invaluable insights on where AI will take us – for better or for worse.

- Martin Ford, "Rise of the Robots – Technology and the Threat of a Jobless Future", Basic Books, New York NY, 2015.
- Nick Bostrom, "Superintelligence – Paths, Dangers, Strategies", Oxford University Press, Oxford UK, 2014.
- Pedro Domingos, "The Master Algorithm – How the Quest for the Ultimate Learning Machine Will Remake Our World", Basic Books, New York NY, 2015.

# EPILOGUE
## ARE YOU READY?

# BUCKLE UP, EVERYONE, IT'S GOING TO BE A WILD RIDE!

The future ain't what it used to be.

**– Yogi Berra**

EPILOGUE

ARE YOU READY?

BUCKLE UP,
EVERYONE.
IT'S GOING
TO BE A
WILD RIDE

# APPENDIX
# ADDITIONAL ARTIFICIAL INTELLIGENCE RESOURCES

**A.** CROSS INDEX OF 52 AI APPLICATIONS, 800 COMPANIES AND 1,000 AI PRODUCTS/SERVICES

**B.** EDUCATIONAL OPPORTUNITIES

**C.** THIS BOOK'S WEBSITES AT *RealEstateBook.ai* AND *RealEstateIndustry.ai*

# CROSS INDEX OF 52 AI APPLICATIONS, 800 COMPANIES AND 1,000 AI PRODUCTS/SERVICES

The extensive table beginning on the next page provides an alphabetical listing of more than 800 companies previously identified in the AI applications detailed in Part II

of this book. Each company's listing includes AI products offered, the chapter number(s) in Part II that cite the company, and the corresponding Broad Categories and AI Applications. Readers can thereby quickly located any company of interest and see at a glance the company's AI focus within the real estate industry. As a corollary, at a glance the reader can determine which companies have a narrow AI focus and which address numerous AI Applications.

Note that in the interests of saving space and increasing legibility, the table employs abbreviations for some of the Broad Category and AI Application names, as shown below. Broad Categories and AI Applications not needing an abbreviation have been excluded (for example, the Broad Categories of "7. Manage the Property" and "10. Education").

| CH. | BROAD CATEGORY | INDEX ABBREVIATION |
| --- | --- | --- |
| 5 | Search for and Acquire a Property for Purchase or Lease | Property Search |
| 6 | Modify the Property as Needed for Occupancy | Modify the Property |
| 8 | Dispose of the Owned or Leased Property | Dispose of Property |
| 9 | Public Sector (Industry Regulators, Courtroom Officials, Etc.) | Public Sector |
| 11 | AI's Multifaceted Influence Across Real Estate | Multifaceted Influence |

| CH. | AI APPLICATION | INDEX ABBREVIATION |
| --- | --- | --- |
| 5.1 | Home Buying and Selling | Home Sales |
| 5.2 | Real Estate Mortgage Automation | Mortgage Automation |
| 5.3 | Commercial Real Estate Investment | Commercial Investment |
| 5.4 | Real Estate Agent Management | Agent Management |
| 5.5 | Investment Property Analysis | Investment Analysis |
| 5.9 | Lead Generation and Management | Lead Generation |
| 5.10 | Optimized Advertising Campaigns | Optimized Advertising |
| 5.11 | 3D Modeling and Augmented Reality | 3D Modeling and AR |
| 5.16 | Property Financing and Mortgage | Financing and Mortgage |
| 7.3 | Real Estate Portfolio Management | Portfolio Management |
| 8.1 | Title and Closing Services | Title Services |
| 11.1 | Predictive Analytics and Forecasting | Predictive Analytics |
| 11.2 | Chatbots And Virtual Assistants | Chatbots |
| 11.4 | Property Data and Analytics | Data and Analytics |
| 11.7 | Sustainability and Social Impact | Sustainability |

| COMPANY | PRODUCT | BROAD CATEGORY | AI APPLICATION |
|---|---|---|---|
| 75F, LLC https://www.75f.io/ | 75F | Chapter 6. Modify the Property | Smart Buildings |
| Aave, Ltd. https://www.aave.com/ | Aave | Chapter 6. Modify the Property | Real Estate Development |
| Abode Systems, Inc. https://www.goabode.com/ | Abode | Chapter 6. Modify the Property | Smart Homes |
| ACI Worldwide, Inc. https://www.aciworldwide.com/ | ACI Sky Review | Chapter 5. Property Search | Appraisal Management |
| Actovia https://actovia.com/ | Actovia | Chapter 5. Property Search | Commercial Investment |
| | | Chapter 5. Property Search | Investment Analysis |
| | | Chapter 5. Property Search | Real Estate Leasing |
| Adobe Inc. https://www.adobe.com/ | Behance https://www.behance.net/ | Chapter 6. Modify the Property | Architecture and Design |
| Adwerx, Inc. https://www.adwerx.com/ | Adwerx | Chapter 5. Property Search | Agent Management |
| | | Chapter 5. Property Search | Optimized Advertising |
| | | Chapter 8. Dispose of the Property | Sales and Marketing |
| AI21 Labs Ltd. https://www.ai21.com/ | Wordtune | Chapter 10. Education | Education and Training |
| Airbnb, Inc. https://www.airbnb.com/ | Airbnb | Chapter 11. Multifaceted Influence | Data and Analytics |
| AirDNA, LLC https://www.airdna.co/ | AirDNA | Chapter 6. Modify the Property | Real Estate Development |
| | AirDNA MarketMinder | Chapter 5. Property Search | Real Estate Leasing |

| COMPANY | PRODUCT | BROAD CATEGORY | AI APPLICATION |
|---|---|---|---|
| Aire Labs Ltd. https://www.aire.io/ | Aire | Chapter 5. Property Search | Mortgage Automation |
| | | Chapter 5. Property Search | Agent Management |
| Airex, Inc. https://www.airexmarket.com/ | Airex | Chapter 5. Property Search | Lead Generation |
| Airthings AS https://www.airthings.com/ | Airthings | Chapter 6. Modify the Property | Smart Buildings |
| AirWorks Solutions https://www.airworks.io/ | AirWorks Solutions | Chapter 6. Modify the Property | Construction |
| Aiva Labs, Inc. https://www.aivalabs.com/ | Aiva | Chapter 5. Property Search | Financing and Mortgage |
| Alanna.ai https://www.alanna.ai/ | Alanna | Chapter 8. Dispose of the Property | Title Services |
| Alder Holdings, LLC https://www.alder.com/ | Alder Security | Chapter 7. Manage the Property | Real Estate Security and Safety |
| Alesco Data, LLC https://alescodata.com/ | Alesco Data | Chapter 5. Property Search | Mortgages |
| Alexa Internet, Inc. https://www.alexa.com/ | Alexa Site Comparisons | Chapter 5. Property Search | Competitive Analysis |
| ALICE Technologies, Inc. https://www.alicetechnologies.com/ | ALICE | Chapter 6. Modify the Property | Construction Management |
| | | Chapter 6. Modify the Property | Construction |
| Alpha Realty Capital https://www.arealtycapital.com/ | Real Estate Investment | Chapter 5. Property Search | Investment Analysis |

| COMPANY | PRODUCT | BROAD CATEGORY | AI APPLICATION |
|---|---|---|---|
| AlphaChat https://www.alphachat.ai/ | AlphaChat | Chapter 8. Dispose of the Property | Brokerage |
| AlphaSense, Inc. https://www.alpha-sense.com/ | AlphaSense | Chapter 8. Dispose of the Property | Brokerage |
| Altos Research LLC https://www.altosresearch.com/ | Altos Research | Chapter 11. Multifaceted Influence | Predictive Analytics |
| Altus Group Limited https://www.altusgroup.com/ | Argus Enterprise | Chapter 7. Manage the Property | Portfolio Management |
| | | Chapter 7. Manage the Property | Asset Management |
| Amazon.com, Inc. https://www.amazon.com/ | Alexa https://www.alexa.com/ | Chapter 6. Modify the Property | Smart Homes |
| | Alexa for Residential https://www.amazon.com/alexaresidential/ | Chapter 7. Manage the Property | Property Management |
| | | Chapter 7. Manage the Property | Tenant Management |
| | Amazon Lex https://aws.amazon.com/lex/ | Chapter 7. Manage the Property | Asset Management |
| | Amazon Web Services AI https://aws.amazon.com/ai/ | Chapter 11. Multifaceted Influence | Professional Services |
| | Blink Camera https://www.blinkforhome.com/ | Chapter 6. Modify the Property | Smart Homes |
| | | Chapter 7. Manage the Property | Real Estate Security and Safety |
| | Fire TV https://www.amazon.com/b/?node=8521791011 | Chapter 6. Modify the Property | Smart Homes |

| COMPANY | PRODUCT | BROAD CATEGORY | AI APPLICATION |
|---|---|---|---|
| | Medium Relevance https://mediumrelevance.com/ | Chapter 11. Multifaceted Influence | Chatbots |
| | Ring Alarm https://ring.com/security-system | Chapter 6. Modify the Property | Smart Homes |
| | Ring Doorbell https://ring.com/security-system | Chapter 6. Modify the Property | Smart Homes |
| | | Chapter 7. Manage the Property | Real Estate Security and Safety |
| AMC Bridge, Inc. https://www.amcbridge.com/ | AMC Bridge | Chapter 6. Modify the Property | Architecture and Design |
| American Real Estate and Urban Economics Association https://www.areuearj.org/ | Journal of Real Estate Economics https://www.areuearj.org/content/real-estate-economics/ | Chapter 11. Multifaceted Influence | Innovation and Research |
| | Journal of Housing Research https://www.ares.org/journals/journal-of-housing-research/ | Chapter 11. Multifaceted Influence | Innovation and Research |
| American Real Estate Society https://www.ares.org/ | Journal of Real Estate Literature https://www.ares.org/journals/journal-of-real-estate-literature/ | Chapter 11. Multifaceted Influence | Innovation and Research |
| | Journal of Real Estate Research https://www.ares.org/journals/journal-of-real-estate-research/ | Chapter 11. Multifaceted Influence | Innovation and Research |
| AMP Robotics Corp. https://www.amprobotics.com/ | AMP Robotics | Chapter 11. Multifaceted Influence | Sustainability |

| COMPANY | PRODUCT | BROAD CATEGORY | AI APPLICATION |
|---|---|---|---|
| Anaplan, Inc. https://www.anaplan.com/ | Anaplan | Chapter 5. Property Search | Competitive Analysis |
| Anker Innovations Co., Limited https://www.eufylife.com/ | Eufy | Chapter 6. Modify the Property | Smart Homes |
| | Eufy Security | Chapter 7. Manage the Property | Real Estate Security and Safety |
| Anow Software, Inc. https://www.anow.com/ | Anow Nexus | Chapter 5. Property Search | Appraisal Management |
| Ansys Inc. https://www.ansys.com/ | Ansys Twin Builder | Chapter 6. Modify the Property | Construction |
| Anti-Eviction Mapping Project https://www.antievictionmap.com/ | Anti-Eviction Mapping Project | Chapter 11. Multifaceted Influence | Sustainability |
| Apartment List, Inc. https://www.apartmentlist.com/ | Apartment List | Chapter 5. Property Search | Rental Property Search |
| | | Chapter 5. Property Search | Real Estate Leasing |
| Apartment Ocean, Inc. https://www.apartmentocean.com/ | Apartment Ocean | Chapter 11. Multifaceted Influence | Predictive Analytics |
| AppFolio, Inc. https://www.appfolio.com/ | Investment Manager | Chapter 5. Property Search | Investment Analysis |
| | Property Manager | Chapter 5. Property Search | Rental Property Search |
| | | Chapter 5. Property Search | Real Estate Investment |
| | | Chapter 7. Manage the Property | Property Management |

| COMPANY | PRODUCT | BROAD CATEGORY | AI APPLICATION |
|---|---|---|---|
| | | Chapter 7. Manage the Property | Tenant Management |
| | | Chapter 11. Multifaceted Influence | Data and Analytics |
| Apple Inc. https://www.apple.com/ | Apple TV | Chapter 6. Modify the Property | Smart Homes |
| | Apple Vision Pro | Chapter 5. Property Search | 3D Modeling and AR |
| | Siri | Chapter 6. Modify the Property | Smart Homes |
| Appraisal Scope https://www.appraisalscope.com/ | Appraisal Scope | Chapter 8. Dispose of the Property | Valuation and Appraisal |
| Appraiser Dashboard, Inc. https://www.appraiserdash.com/ | Spark | Chapter 5. Property Search | Appraisal Management |
| Aquantify, Inc. https://www.aquantify.com/ | Aquantify | Chapter 5. Property Search | Real Estate Investment |
| Aquicore, Inc. https://www.aquicore.com/ | Aquicore | Chapter 7. Manage the Property | Property Management |
| | | Chapter 11. Multifaceted Influence | Sustainability |
| ArchDaily, Inc. https://www.archdaily.com/ | ArchDaily | Chapter 6. Modify the Property | Architecture and Design |
| Archilogic AG https://www.archilogic.com/ | Archilogic Platform | Chapter 5. Property Search | 3D Modeling and AR |
| Archilovers S.r.l. https://www.archilovers.com/ | Archilovers | Chapter 6. Modify the Property | Architecture and Design |

| COMPANY | PRODUCT | BROAD CATEGORY | AI APPLICATION |
| --- | --- | --- | --- |
| Architizer, Inc. https://architizer.com/ | Architizer | Chapter 6. Modify the Property | Architecture and Design |
| ArcSite https://www.arcsite.com/ | ArcSite | Chapter 6. Modify the Property | Construction Management |
| | | Chapter 6. Modify the Property | Construction |
| Area9 Lyceum A/S https://www.area9lyceum.com/ | Newton | Chapter 10. Education | Education and Training |
| Arlo Technologies, Inc. https://www.arlo.com/ | Arlo Smart | Chapter 6. Modify the Property | Smart Homes |
| Arup Group Limited https://www.arup.com/ | Arup | Chapter 11. Multifaceted Influence | Professional Services |
| Ascent Technologies, Inc. https://www.ascentregtech.com/ | Ascent | Chapter 9. Public Sector | Law and Compliance |
| Assemble Systems Inc. https://www.assemblesystems.com/ | Assemble Systems | Chapter 6. Modify the Property | Construction Management |
| Asteroom, Inc. https://www.asteroom.com/ | Asteroom | Chapter 5. Property Search | Real Estate Leasing |
| Asurity Technologies, LLC https://www.asurity.com/ | Asurity Technologies | Chapter 5. Property Search | Mortgages |
| Athena Security, Inc. https://www.athena-security.com/ | Athena Security | Chapter 7. Manage the Property | Real Estate Security and Safety |

| COMPANY | PRODUCT | BROAD CATEGORY | AI APPLICATION |
|---|---|---|---|
| ATTOM https://www. attomdata.com/ | Property Data | Chapter 5. Property Search | Lead Generation |
| | Property Valuation Data | Chapter 5. Property Search | Appraisal Management |
| Augury Systems, Inc. https://www.augury. com/ | Augury | Chapter 6. Modify the Property | Smart Buildings |
| Autodesk, Inc. https://www. autodesk.com/ | Arnold https://www. autodesk.com/ products/arnold/ | Chapter 5. Property Search | 3D Modeling and AR |
| | Autodesk BIM 360 https://www. autodesk.com/ bim-360/ | Chapter 6. Modify the Property | Construction Management |
| | | Chapter 6. Modify the Property | Architecture and Design |
| | | Chapter 6. Modify the Property | Construction |
| | Autodesk Construction Cloud https://acc.autodesk. com/ | Chapter 11. Multifaceted Influence | Professional Services |
| | Autodesk Platform https://www. autodesk.com/ | Chapter 12. GeoAI | Efficient Project Management |
| | | Chapter 6. Modify the Property | Construction |
| | Autodesk Revit https://www. autodesk.com/ products/revit/ | Chapter 11. Multifaceted Influence | Professional Services |
| | | Chapter 11. Multifaceted Influence | Professional Services |
| | Civil 3D https://www. autodesk.com/ products/civil-3d/ | Chapter 11. Multifaceted Influence | Professional Services |

| COMPANY | PRODUCT | BROAD CATEGORY | AI APPLICATION |
|---|---|---|---|
| | Dreamcatcher https://www.research.autodesk.com/projects/project-dreamcatcher/ | Chapter 6. Modify the Property | Architecture and Design |
| | Dynamo Studio https://www.autodesk.com/products/dynamo-studio/ | Chapter 6. Modify the Property | Architecture and Design |
| | Fusion 360 https://www.autodesk.com/products/fusion-360/ | Chapter 5. Property Search | 3D Modeling and AR |
| | | Chapter 6. Modify the Property | Construction Management |
| | Maya https://www.autodesk.com/products/maya/ | Chapter 5. Property Search | 3D Modeling and AR |
| | PlanGrid https://construction.autodesk.com/products/plangrid/ | Chapter 11. Multifaceted Influence | Professional Services |
| | Project Refinery https://www.autodesk.com/campaigns/refinery-beta/ | Chapter 6. Modify the Property | Architecture and Design |
| Automation Hero, Inc. https://www.automationhero.ai/ | Automation Hero | Chapter 5. Property Search | Mortgage Automation |
| | | Chapter 5. Property Search | Agent Management |
| Avail Software, LLC https://www.avail.co/ | Avail | Chapter 5. Property Search | Rental Property Search |
| | | Chapter 7. Manage the Property | Property Management |
| | | Chapter 7. Manage the Property | Tenant Management |

| COMPANY | PRODUCT | BROAD CATEGORY | AI APPLICATION |
|---|---|---|---|
| Avvir, Inc. https://www.avvir.io/ | Avvir | Chapter 6. Modify the Property | Construction Management |
| | | Chapter 7. Manage the Property | Real Estate Security and Safety |
| Awair Inc. https://www.getawair.com/ | Awair | Chapter 6. Modify the Property | Smart Buildings |
| Axioma, Inc. (now part of Qontigo) https://www.axioma.com/ | Axioma Portfolio Optimizer | Chapter 7. Manage the Property | Asset Management |
| Bain & Company, Inc. https://www.bain.com/ | Bain Vector | Chapter 11. Multifaceted Influence | Professional Services |
| Bang the Table Pty Ltd. https://www.bangthetable.com/ | Bang the Table | Chapter 9. Public Sector | Ethics and Regulations |
| Benchmarking Report Tool https://www.benchmarking.com/ | Benchmarking Report Tool | Chapter 5. Property Search | Competitive Analysis |
| Bentley Systems, Incorporated https://www.bentley.com/ | Bentley iTwin | Chapter 11. Multifaceted Influence | Professional Services |
| | Bentley Systems iTwin Services | Chapter 6. Modify the Property | Construction |
| | Bentley Systems Platform | Chapter 12. GeoAI | Efficient Project Management |
| | Bentley Systems SYNCHRO XR | Chapter 6. Modify the Property | Construction |
| | GenerativeComponents | Chapter 6. Modify the Property | Architecture and Design |

| COMPANY | PRODUCT | BROAD CATEGORY | AI APPLICATION |
|---|---|---|---|
| Berkman Klein Center for Internet & Society by Harvard University https://www.cyber.harvard.edu/ | Berkman Klein Center for Internet & Society | Chapter 9. Public Sector | Ethics and Regulations |
| Better Mortgage Corporation https://www.better.com/ | Better Mortgage | Chapter 5. Property Search | Home Sales |
| | | Chapter 5. Property Search | Mortgage Automation |
| Betterment Holdings, Inc. https://www.betterment.com/ | Betterment | Chapter 7. Manage the Property | Asset Management |
| Beyond Pricing, Inc. https://www.beyondpricing.com/ | Beyond Pricing | Chapter 5. Property Search | Lead Generation |
| | Beyond Pricing Insights Dashboard | Chapter 5. Property Search | Real Estate Leasing |
| Bhoomi Online - Land Records System of Karnataka https://landrecords.karnataka.gov.in/Service2/ | Bhoomi Online | Chapter 12. GeoAI | Global / India Perspectives |
| Bidtracer https://www.bidtracer.com/ | Bidtracer | Chapter 6. Modify the Property | Construction |
| BIM Track, Inc. https://www.bimtrack.co/ | BIM Track | Chapter 6. Modify the Property | Architecture and Design |
| Bin-e Sp. z o.o. https://www.bin-e.com/ | Bin-e | Chapter 11. Multifaceted Influence | Sustainability |
| BirdDogHR https://www.birddoghr.com/ | BirdDogHR | Chapter 6. Modify the Property | Construction |

| COMPANY | PRODUCT | BROAD CATEGORY | AI APPLICATION |
|---|---|---|---|
| BizMiner https://www.bizminer.com/ | BizMiner | Chapter 5. Property Search | Competitive Analysis |
| BizStats https://www.bizstats.com/ | BizStats | Chapter 5. Property Search | Competitive Analysis |
| Black Knight, Inc. https://www.blackknightinc.com/ | AIVA | Chapter 5. Property Search | Mortgages |
| | AIVA | Chapter 11. Multifaceted Influence | Chatbots |
| | Mortgage MarketSmart | Chapter 5. Property Search | Mortgages |
| Blend Labs, Inc. https://www.blend.com/ | Blend | Chapter 5. Property Search | Financing and Mortgage |
| | Blend Intelligence Engine | Chapter 5. Property Search | Mortgages |
| Blender Foundation https://www.blender.org/ | Blender | Chapter 5. Property Search | 3D Modeling and AR |
| Bloomberg L.P. https://www.bloomberg.com/ | Bloomberg PORT | Chapter 7. Manage the Property | Portfolio Management |
| | Bloomberg PORT | Chapter 7. Manage the Property | Asset Management |
| Bluebeam Software Inc. https://www.bluebeam.com/ | Bluebeam Revu | Chapter 6. Modify the Property | Construction Management |
| Board International SA https://www.board.com/ | Board | Chapter 5. Property Search | Competitive Analysis |

| COMPANY | PRODUCT | BROAD CATEGORY | AI APPLICATION |
|---|---|---|---|
| BoldLeads https://boldleads.com/ | BoldLeads | Chapter 5. Property Search | Home Sales |
| | | Chapter 5. Property Search | Mortgage Automation |
| | | Chapter 5. Property Search | Agent Management |
| | | Chapter 5. Property Search | Lead Generation |
| | | Chapter 8. Dispose of the Property | Sales and Marketing |
| | | Chapter 8. Dispose of the Property | Brokerage |
| BoomTown ROI https://www.boomtownroi.com/ | BoomTown | Chapter 5. Property Search | Home Sales |
| | | Chapter 5. Property Search | Agent Management |
| | | Chapter 8. Dispose of the Property | Sales and Marketing |
| | | Chapter 8. Dispose of the Property | Brokerage |
| Bose Corporation https://www.bose.com/ | Bose | Chapter 6. Modify the Property | Smart Homes |
| Boston Consulting Group https://www.bcg.com/ | BCG Gamma | Chapter 11. Multifaceted Influence | Professional Services |
| Botkeeper, Inc. https://botkeeper.com/ | Botkeeper | Chapter 11. Multifaceted Influence | Professional Services |
| Botmock, Inc. https://www.botmock.com/ | Botmock | Chapter 5. Property Search | Agent Management |
| Botsify https://botsify.com/ | Botsify | Chapter 8. Dispose of the Property | Brokerage |

| COMPANY | PRODUCT | BROAD CATEGORY | AI APPLICATION |
|---|---|---|---|
| Bowery Valuation, Inc. https://www. boweryvaluation. com/ | Bowery Valuation | Chapter 5. Property Search | Commercial Investment |
| | | Chapter 5. Property Search | Investment Analysis |
| | | Chapter 5. Property Search | Financing and Mortgage |
| Boxabl Inc. https://www.boxabl. com/ | Boxabl | Chapter 6. Modify the Property | Construction |
| BoxBrownie.com Pty Ltd. https://www. boxbrownie.com/ | BoxBrownie | Chapter 5. Property Search | Virtual Staging |
| Bradford Technologies https://www. bradfordsoftware. com/ | Bradford Technologies | Chapter 8. Dispose of the Property | Valuation and Appraisal |
| Bradford Technologies, Inc. https://www. bradfordsoftware. com/ | ClickFORMS | Chapter 5. Property Search | Appraisal Management |
| BrainBox AI, Inc. https://brainboxai. com/ | BrainBox AI | Chapter 6. Modify the Property | Smart Buildings |
| | | Chapter 11. Multifaceted Influence | Sustainability |
| BRE Global, Ltd. https://www. bregroup.com/ | BREEAM | Chapter 11. Multifaceted Influence | Sustainability |
| Brevitas, LLC https://www.brevitas. com/ | Brevitas | Chapter 5. Property Search | Commercial Investment |
| | | Chapter 5. Property Search | Investment Analysis |

| COMPANY | PRODUCT | BROAD CATEGORY | AI APPLICATION |
|---|---|---|---|
| Brickchain Ltd. https://www.brickchain.com/ | Brickchain | Chapter 6. Modify the Property | Construction Management |
| Bridgit https://www.gobridgit.com/ | Bridgit Bench | Chapter 6. Modify the Property | Construction Management |
| | Bridgit Bench | Chapter 6. Modify the Property | Construction |
| | Bridgit Field | Chapter 6. Modify the Property | Construction |
| Bright Power, Inc. https://www.brightpower.com/ | Bright Power | Chapter 7. Manage the Property | Property Management |
| BrightSight https://www.brightsight.com/ | BrightSight | Chapter 9. Public Sector | Dispute Resolution |
| Bsafe AS https://www.getbsafe.com/ | Bsafe | Chapter 7. Manage the Property | Real Estate Security and Safety |
| Building Engines, Inc. https://www.buildingengines.com/ | Building Engines | Chapter 5. Property Search | Commercial Investment |
| | Tenant Engagement Platform | Chapter 7. Manage the Property | Tenant Management |
| BuildingIQ https://www.buildingiq.com/ | BuildingIQ | Chapter 11. Multifaceted Influence | Sustainability |
| Buildium, A RealPage Company https://www.buildium.com/ | Buildium | Chapter 5. Property Search | Investment Analysis |
| | | Chapter 5. Property Search | Rental Property Search |
| | | Chapter 5. Property Search | Real Estate Investment |
| | | Chapter 7. Manage the Property | Property Management |

| COMPANY | PRODUCT | BROAD CATEGORY | AI APPLICATION |
|---|---|---|---|
| | | Chapter 11. Multifaceted Influence | Data and Analytics |
| | | Chapter 11. Multifaceted Influence | Professional Services |
| | Resident Center | Chapter 7. Manage the Property | Tenant Management |
| Buildots Ltd. https://www.buildots.com/ | Buildots | Chapter 6. Modify the Property | Construction Management |
| | | Chapter 7. Manage the Property | Real Estate Security and Safety |
| Builtspace Technologies Corp. https://www.builtspace.com/ | Builtspace Technologies Corp. | Chapter 7. Manage the Property | Property Management |
| BuiltWith Pty Ltd https://www.builtwith.com/ | BuiltWith | Chapter 5. Property Search | Competitive Analysis |
| Buxton Company https://www.buxtonco.com/ | Buxton Analytics Platform | Chapter 5. Property Search | Competitive Analysis |
| C3.ai, Inc. https://c3.ai/ | C3 AI Property Appraisal | Chapter 5. Property Search | Appraisal Management |
| Caidio https://www.caidio.io/ | Caidio | Chapter 6. Modify the Property | Construction |
| Calyx Software, Inc. https://www.calyxsoftware.com/ | Calyx AUS | Chapter 5. Property Search | Appraisal Management |
| Camio, Inc. https://www.camio.com/ | Camio | Chapter 7. Manage the Property | Real Estate Security and Safety |
| Capacity, LLC https://www.capacity.com/ | Capacity | Chapter 5. Property Search | Mortgages |

| COMPANY | PRODUCT | BROAD CATEGORY | AI APPLICATION |
|---|---|---|---|
| Cape Analytics, Inc. https://capeanalytics.com/ | Cape Analytics Platform | Chapter 12. GeoAI | Risk Assessment and Mitigation |
| CaptureFast, Inc. https://www.capturefast.com/ | CaptureFast | Chapter 5. Property Search | Agent Management |
| Carbon Engineering, Ltd. https://carbonengineering.com/ | Carbon Engineering | Chapter 11. Multifaceted Influence | Sustainability |
| Carbon Lighthouse, Inc. https://www.carbonlighthouse.com/ | Carbon Lighthouse | Chapter 6. Modify the Property / Chapter 11. Multifaceted Influence | Smart Buildings / Sustainability |
| CarbonCure Technologies, Inc. https://www.carboncure.com/ | CarbonCure | Chapter 11. Multifaceted Influence | Sustainability |
| Carnegie Endowment for International Peace https://www.carnegieendowment.org/ | Carnegie Endowment for International Peace | Chapter 9. Public Sector | Ethics and Regulations |
| CARTO, Inc. https://www.carto.com/ | CARTO | Chapter 5. Property Search | Real Estate Investment |
| Casalova Realty, Inc. https://www.casalova.com/ | Casalova | Chapter 5. Property Search | Lead Generation |
| CaseMetrix https://www.casemetrix.com/ | CaseMetrix | Chapter 9. Public Sector | Dispute Resolution |

| COMPANY | PRODUCT | BROAD CATEGORY | AI APPLICATION |
|---|---|---|---|
| Casepoint LLC https://www.casepoint.com/ | Casepoint | Chapter 9. Public Sector | Law and Compliance |
| Casetext, Inc. https://casetext.com/ | Casetext | Chapter 9. Public Sector | Law and Compliance |
| CB Insights https://www.cbinsights.com/ | CBI Insights | Chapter 5. Property Search | Competitive Analysis |
| CBRE Group, Inc. https://www.cbre.com/ | CBRE Econometric Advisors | Chapter 11. Multifaceted Influence | Predictive Analytics |
| CertifID, LLC https://www.certifid.com/ | WireSafe | Chapter 8. Dispose of the Property | Title Services |
| Chainlink Labs https://www.chain.link/ | Chainlink | Chapter 6. Modify the Property | Real Estate Development |
| Chatfuel, Inc. https://www.chatfuel.com/ | Chatfuel | Chapter 5. Property Search | Agent Management |
| Cherre, Inc. https://cherre.com/ | Cherre | Chapter 5. Property Search | Commercial Investment |
| | | Chapter 5. Property Search | Investment Analysis |
| | | Chapter 5. Property Search | Real Estate Investment |
| | | Chapter 6. Modify the Property | Real Estate Development |
| | | Chapter 7. Manage the Property | Property Management |
| | | Chapter 7. Manage the Property | Portfolio Management |
| | | Chapter 11. Multifaceted Influence | Innovation and Research |

| COMPANY | PRODUCT | BROAD CATEGORY | AI APPLICATION |
|---|---|---|---|
| | | Chapter 12. GeoAI | Geospatial Integration |
| | | Chapter 12. GeoAI | Predictive Location Analytics |
| ChurnBee, Inc. https://www. churnbee.com/ | ChurnBee | Chapter 11. Multifaceted Influence | Predictive Analytics |
| ChurnKit, Inc. https://www.churnkit. com/ | ChurnKit | Chapter 11. Multifaceted Influence | Predictive Analytics |
| ChurnSpotter SAS https://www. churnspotter.com/ | ChurnSpotter | Chapter 11. Multifaceted Influence | Predictive Analytics |
| ChurnZero, Inc. https://www. churnzero.com/ | ChurnZero | Chapter 11. Multifaceted Influence | Predictive Analytics |
| CIM Enviro Pty Ltd https://www. buildingiq.com/ | BuildingIQ | Chapter 6. Modify the Property | Smart Buildings |
| | CINC AI | Chapter 8. Dispose of the Property | Sales and Marketing |
| | | Chapter 11. Multifaceted Influence | Chatbots |
| CINC, a Fidelity National Financial, Inc. Company https://www.cincpro. com/ | CINC Pro | Chapter 5. Property Search | Home Sales |
| | | Chapter 5. Property Search | Mortgage Automation |
| | | Chapter 5. Property Search | Agent Management |
| | | Chapter 5. Property Search | Optimized Advertising |
| | | Chapter 8. Dispose of the Property | Sales and Marketing |

| COMPANY | PRODUCT | BROAD CATEGORY | AI APPLICATION |
|---|---|---|---|
| CircuitMeter Inc. https://www.circuitmeter.com/ | CircuitMeter Inc. | Chapter 7. Manage the Property | Property Management |
| CitizenLab NV https://www.citizenlab.co/ | CitizenLab | Chapter 9. Public Sector | Ethics and Regulations |
| CityBldr, Inc. https://www.citybldr.com/ | CityBldr | Chapter 5. Property Search | Real Estate Investment |
| | | Chapter 6. Modify the Property | Real Estate Development |
| Citymapper, Ltd. https://citymapper.com/ | Citymapper | Chapter 11. Multifaceted Influence | Sustainability |
| Claritas, LLC https://www.claritas.com/ | Claritas | Chapter 5. Property Search | Competitive Analysis |
| Clause, Inc. https://clause.io/ | Clause | Chapter 9. Public Sector | Law and Compliance |
| Clausehound Inc. https://clausehound.com/ | Clausehound | Chapter 9. Public Sector | Dispute Resolution |
| Clear Blockchain Technologies LTD https://www.clearx.io/ | Blockchain Platform | Chapter 8. Dispose of the Property | Title Services |
| ClearCapital.com, Inc. https://www.clearcapital.com/ | Clear Capital | Chapter 5. Property Search | Financing and Mortgage |
| | | Chapter 8. Dispose of the Property | Valuation and Appraisal |
| Clearscope, Inc. https://www.clearscope.io/ | Clearscope | Chapter 11. Multifaceted Influence | Content Generation |
| Climeworks AG https://climeworks.com/ | Climeworks | Chapter 11. Multifaceted Influence | Sustainability |

| COMPANY | PRODUCT | BROAD CATEGORY | AI APPLICATION |
|---|---|---|---|
| Cloe, Inc. https://www.cloe.ai/ | Cloe | Chapter 5. Property Search | Financing and Mortgage |
| CloseSimple, LLC https://www.closesimple.com/ | CloseSimple | Chapter 8. Dispose of the Property | Title Services |
| Closinglock, Inc. https://www.closinglock.com/ | Closinglock | Chapter 8. Dispose of the Property | Title Services |
| CloudLex https://www.cloudlex.com/ | CloudLex Real Estate Suite | Chapter 9. Public Sector | Dispute Resolution |
| Cloudvirga, Inc. https://www.cloudvirga.com/ | Cloudvirga | Chapter 5. Property Search | Financing and Mortgage |
| | Mia | Chapter 5. Property Search | Mortgages |
| Co-libry https://co-libry.com/ | Co-libry | Chapter 8. Dispose of the Property | Brokerage |
| Cobalt Robotics, Inc. https://www.cobaltrobotics.com/ | Cobalt Robotics | Chapter 7. Manage the Property | Real Estate Security and Safety |
| Code for America https://www.codeforamerica.org/ | Code for America | Chapter 11. Multifaceted Influence | Sustainability |
| Codoxo https://www.codoxo.com/ | Codoxo | Chapter 5. Property Search | Financing and Mortgage |
| | Fraud Scope | Chapter 5. Property Search | Mortgage Automation |
| | | Chapter 5. Property Search | Real Estate Investment |
| CogBooks Ltd. https://www.cogbooks.com/ | CogBooks | Chapter 10. Education | Education and Training |
| Cognii, Inc. https://www.cognii.com/ | Cognii | Chapter 10. Education | Education and Training |

| COMPANY | PRODUCT | BROAD CATEGORY | AI APPLICATION |
|---|---|---|---|
| Collateral Analytics, LLC https://www.collateralanalytics.com/ | Collateral Analytics | Chapter 5. Property Search | Financing and Mortgage |
| | Collateral Analytics Home Price Index | Chapter 11. Multifaceted Influence | Data and Analytics |
| Comfy, Inc. https://www.comfyapp.com/ | Comfy | Chapter 5. Property Search | Commercial Investment |
| Common Living, Inc. https://common.com/ | Common | Chapter 11. Multifaceted Influence | Sustainability |
| Community Change https://communitychange.org/ | Center for Community Change | Chapter 11. Multifaceted Influence | Sustainability |
| Compass, Inc. https://www.compass.com/ | Compass | Chapter 5. Property Search | Home Sales |
| | | Chapter 8. Dispose of the Property | Brokerage |
| | | Chapter 12. GeoAI | Residential Brokerage |
| Compliance.ai https://www.compliance.ai/ | Compliance.ai | Chapter 9. Public Sector | Law and Compliance |
| ComplyAdvantage https://complyadvantage.com/ | ComplyAdvantage | Chapter 9. Public Sector | Law and Compliance |
| Compology, Inc. https://www.compology.com/ | Compology | Chapter 11. Multifaceted Influence | Sustainability |
| Compound Labs, Inc. https://www.compound.finance/ | Compound | Chapter 6. Modify the Property | Real Estate Development |

| COMPANY | PRODUCT | BROAD CATEGORY | AI APPLICATION |
|---|---|---|---|
| CompStak, Inc. https://www. compstak.com/ | CompStak | Chapter 7. Manage the Property | Property Management |
| | | Chapter 7. Manage the Property | Portfolio Management |
| | | Chapter 11. Multifaceted Influence | Innovation and Research |
| Concord Legal https://www. concordnow.com/ | Legal AI for Real Estate Disputes | Chapter 9. Public Sector | Dispute Resolution |
| ConstructConnect https://www. constructconnect. com/ | SmartBid | Chapter 6. Modify the Property | Construction |
| ContentCal.io Ltd. https://www. contentcal.io/ | ContentCal | Chapter 11. Multifaceted Influence | Content Generation |
| ContentStudio, Inc. https://contentstudio. io/ | ContentStudio | Chapter 11. Multifaceted Influence | Content Generation |
| Contify, Inc. https://www.contify. com/ | Contify | Chapter 5. Property Search | Competitive Analysis |
| ContractPod Technologies Ltd. https://contractpodai. com/ | ContractPodAi | Chapter 8. Dispose of the Property | Brokerage |
| | | Chapter 9. Public Sector | Law and Compliance |
| Converge https://www. converge.io/ | Mix AI | Chapter 6. Modify the Property | Construction Management |
| CoreLogic, Inc. https://www. corelogic.com/ | a la mode | Chapter 5. Property Search | Appraisal Management |
| | Automated Appraisal Review | Chapter 5. Property Search | Appraisal Management |

| COMPANY | PRODUCT | BROAD CATEGORY | AI APPLICATION |
|---|---|---|---|
| | Climate Risk Analytics | Chapter 11. Multifaceted Influence | Data and Analytics |
| | CoreLogic | Chapter 5. Property Search | Financing and Mortgage |
| | | Chapter 8. Dispose of the Property | Valuation and Appraisal |
| | | Chapter 11. Multifaceted Influence | Innovation and Research |
| | CoreLogic Automated Valuation Model | Chapter 11. Multifaceted Influence | Predictive Analytics |
| | | Chapter 11. Multifaceted Influence | Data and Analytics |
| | CoreLogic AVMs | Chapter 5. Property Search | Appraisal Management |
| | CoreLogic Growth Solutions | Chapter 6. Modify the Property | Real Estate Development |
| | CoreLogic Wildfire Mitigation Score | Chapter 11. Multifaceted Influence | Data and Analytics |
| | LoanSafe | Chapter 5. Property Search | Investment Analysis |
| | Property Analytics and Discovery Platform | Chapter 5. Property Search | Rental Property Search |
| | NeighborhoodScout | Chapter 5. Property Search | Home Sales |
| | Realist | Chapter 5. Property Search | Agent Management |
| | | Chapter 5. Property Search | Agent Management |

| COMPANY | PRODUCT | BROAD CATEGORY | AI APPLICATION |
|---|---|---|---|
| | RiskMeter | Chapter 7. Manage the Property | Portfolio Management |
| | WinTOTAL Aurora | Chapter 5. Property Search | Appraisal Management |
| CoSchedule, LLC https://coschedule.com/ | CoSchedule | Chapter 11. Multifaceted Influence | Content Generation |
| | Apartments.com https://www.apartments.com/ | Chapter 5. Property Search | Rental Property Search |
| | | Chapter 5. Property Search | Real Estate Leasing |
| | | Chapter 11. Multifaceted Influence | Data and Analytics |
| | | Chapter 5. Property Search | Commercial Investment |
| CoStar Group, Inc. https://www.costar.com/ | CoStar | Chapter 5. Property Search | Investment Analysis |
| | | Chapter 5. Property Search | Rental Property Search |
| | | Chapter 8. Dispose of the Property | Valuation and Appraisal |
| | CoStar Group | Chapter 11. Multifaceted Influence | Innovation and Research |
| | CoStar Market Analytics | Chapter 11. Multifaceted Influence | Predictive Analytics |
| CoUrbanize, Inc. https://co-urbanize.com/ | CoUrbanize | Chapter 11. Multifaceted Influence | Sustainability |
| Coursera, Inc. https://www.coursera.org/ | Coursera | Chapter 10. Education | Education and Training |

| COMPANY | PRODUCT | BROAD CATEGORY | AI APPLICATION |
|---|---|---|---|
| Cove Smart, LLC https://www.covesmart.com/ | Cove Security | Chapter 7. Manage the Property | Real Estate Security and Safety |
| CoworkIntel, LLC https://www.coworkintel.com/ | CoworkIntel | Chapter 5. Property Search | Real Estate Leasing |
| Cozy Services, Ltd. https://www.cozy.co/ | Cozy | Chapter 5. Property Search | Rental Property Search |
| | | Chapter 7. Manage the Property | Property Management |
| | | Chapter 7. Manage the Property | Tenant Management |
| Crayon, Inc. https://www.crayon.co/ | Crayon | Chapter 5. Property Search | Competitive Analysis |
| CrediFi Corp. https://www.credifi.com/ | CrediFi | Chapter 7. Manage the Property | Portfolio Management |
| CreditVidya Technologies Pvt Ltd https://www.creditvidya.com/ | CreditVidya | Chapter 5. Property Search | Financing and Mortgage |
| CreditXpert, Inc. https://www.creditxpert.com/ | CreditXpert Compliance Tools | Chapter 5. Property Search | Appraisal Management |
| CREtech https://www.cretech.com/ | CREtech Labs | Chapter 11. Multifaceted Influence | Innovation and Research |
| | CREtech Real Estate Tech Conference | Chapter 11. Multifaceted Influence | Innovation and Research |
| CrisisGo, Inc. https://www.crisisgo.com/ | CrisisGo | Chapter 7. Manage the Property | Real Estate Security and Safety |

| COMPANY | PRODUCT | BROAD CATEGORY | AI APPLICATION |
|---|---|---|---|
| CrowdComfort, Inc. https://www.crowdcomfort.com/ | CrowdComfort | Chapter 6. Modify the Property | Smart Buildings |
| CrowdStreet, Inc. https://www.crowdstreet.com/ | CrowdStreet | Chapter 6. Modify the Property | Real Estate Development |
| Crytek GmbH https://www.crytek.com/ | CryEngine | Chapter 5. Property Search | 3D Modeling and AR |
| CS Disco, Inc. https://www.csdisco.com/ | DISCO | Chapter 9. Public Sector | Dispute Resolution |
| | | Chapter 9. Public Sector | Law and Compliance |
| Curaytor, LLC https://www.curaytor.com/ | Curaytor | Chapter 5. Property Search | Home Sales |
| | | Chapter 5. Property Search | Agent Management |
| | | Chapter 8. Dispose of the Property | Sales and Marketing |
| Cushman & Wakefield plc https://www.cushmanwakefield.com/ | Cushman & Wakefield | Chapter 11. Multifaceted Influence | Professional Services |
| | Cushman & Wakefield Recovery Readiness Dashboard | Chapter 5. Property Search | Real Estate Leasing |
| CyStack.,JSC https://cystack.net/ | SafeChain | Chapter 8. Dispose of the Property | Title Services |
| Cyxtera Technologies https://www.cyxtera.com/ | Brainspace | Chapter 9. Public Sector | Law and Compliance |
| D-CENT https://www.dcentproject.eu/ | D-CENT | Chapter 9. Public Sector | Ethics and Regulations |

| COMPANY | PRODUCT | BROAD CATEGORY | AI APPLICATION |
|---|---|---|---|
| DarwinAI Corp. https://www.darwinai.com/ | DarwinAI | Chapter 6. Modify the Property | Construction Management |
| Dassault Systèmes SE https://www.3ds.com/ | CATIA | Chapter 6. Modify the Property | Architecture and Design |
| Data for Black Lives https://d4bl.org/ | Data for Black Lives | Chapter 11. Multifaceted Influence | Sustainability |
| Datacomp Sp. z o.o. https://www.bimvision.eu/ | BIM Vision | Chapter 6. Modify the Property | Architecture and Design |
| DataMaster, LLC https://www.datamasterusa.com/ | DataMaster | Chapter 5. Property Search | Appraisal Management |
| Dataminr, Inc. https://www.dataminr.com/ | Dataminr | Chapter 5. Property Search | Lead Generation |
| Datanyze, LLC https://www.datanyze.com/ | Datanyze | Chapter 5. Property Search | Competitive Analysis |
| DataRobot, Inc. https://www.datarobot.com/ | DataRobot | Chapter 5. Property Search | Mortgage Automation |
| | DataRobot AI Platform | Chapter 7. Manage the Property | Asset Management |
| DataTrace Information Services, LLC https://www.datatracetitle.com/ | DataTrace | Chapter 5. Property Search | Lead Generation |
| | Title Search | Chapter 8. Dispose of the Property | Title Services |
| | TitleFlex https://www.titleflex.com/ | Chapter 8. Dispose of the Property | Title Services |

| COMPANY | PRODUCT | BROAD CATEGORY | AI APPLICATION |
|---|---|---|---|
| DataVisor, Inc. https://www.datavisor.com/ | DataVisor Fraud Detection Platform | Chapter 5. Property Search | Investment Analysis |
| | | Chapter 11. Multifaceted Influence | Predictive Analytics |
| Dealpath, Inc. https://www.dealpath.com/ | Dealpath | Chapter 5. Property Search | Real Estate Investment |
| | | Chapter 7. Manage the Property | Portfolio Management |
| | | Chapter 7. Manage the Property | Asset Management |
| Deep Sentinel Corp. https://www.deepsentinel.com/ | Deep Sentinel | Chapter 6. Modify the Property | Smart Buildings |
| | | Chapter 7. Manage the Property | Real Estate Security and Safety |
| DeepBlocks, Inc. https://www.deepblocks.com/ | DeepBlocks | Chapter 5. Property Search | Virtual Staging |
| | | Chapter 6. Modify the Property | Architecture and Design |
| Deloitte Touche Tohmatsu Limited https://www.deloitte.com/ | Deloitte AI and Data https://www.deloitte.com/global/en/services/consulting/services/artificial-intelligence-and-data.html | Chapter 11. Multifaceted Influence | Professional Services |
| Density, Inc. https://www.density.io/ | Density | Chapter 6. Modify the Property | Smart Buildings |
| Dentons https://www.nextlawlabs.com/ | NextLaw Labs | Chapter 11. Multifaceted Influence | Professional Services |
| Dezeen Limited https://www.dezeen.com/ | Dezeen | Chapter 6. Modify the Property | Architecture and Design |

| COMPANY | PRODUCT | BROAD CATEGORY | AI APPLICATION |
|---|---|---|---|
| DiligenceVault, Inc. https://www. diligencevault.com/ | DiligenceVault | Chapter 5. Property Search | Real Estate Investment |
| Dippidi, LLC. https://dippidi.com/ | Dippidi | Chapter 8. Dispose of the Property | Sales and Marketing |
| | | Chapter 8. Dispose of the Property | Brokerage |
| | | Chapter 11. Multifaceted Influence | Chatbots |
| Disperse https://www.disperse. io/ | Disperse | Chapter 6. Modify the Property | Construction Management |
| | | Chapter 6. Modify the Property | Construction |
| | | Chapter 12. GeoAI | Real-Time Analytics |
| DocuSign, Inc. https://www. docusign.com/ | DocuSign Agreement Cloud | Chapter 5. Property Search | Home Sales |
| | | Chapter 5. Property Search | Mortgages |
| | | Chapter 5. Property Search | Real Estate Leasing |
| | | Chapter 11. Multifaceted Influence | Professional Services |
| Donnelley Financial Solutions, Inc. https://www. dfinsolutions.com/ | eBrevia | Chapter 6. Modify the Property | Real Estate Development |
| | | Chapter 9. Public Sector | Ethics and Regulations |
| DoubleVerify, Inc. https://www. doubleverify.com/ | DoubleVerify | Chapter 5. Property Search | Optimized Advertising |
| Doxel https://www.doxel.ai/ | Doxel | Chapter 6. Modify the Property | Construction |

| COMPANY | PRODUCT | BROAD CATEGORY | AI APPLICATION |
|---|---|---|---|
| DreamBox Learning, Inc. https://www.dreambox.com/ | DreamBox Learning | Chapter 10. Education | Education and Training |
| Dynamic Yield Ltd. https://www.dynamicyield.com/ | Dynamic Yield | Chapter 11. Multifaceted Influence | Content Generation |
| Dyson Ltd. https://www.dyson.com/ | Dyson | Chapter 6. Modify the Property | Smart Homes |
| Eagle Eye Networks, Inc. https://www.een.com/ | Eagle Eye Networks | Chapter 7. Manage the Property | Real Estate Security and Safety |
| Earnix https://www.earnix.com/ | Earnix | Chapter 5. Property Search | Mortgage Automation |
| | | Chapter 5. Property Search | Agent Management |
| Ebi https://www.ebi.ai/ | Ebi | Chapter 8. Dispose of the Property | Brokerage |
| eBrevia https://www.ebrevia.com/ | eBrevia Case Analysis | Chapter 9. Public Sector | Dispute Resolution |
| Ecobee Inc. https://www.ecobee.com/ | Ecobee SmartThermostat | Chapter 6. Modify the Property | Smart Homes |
| EcoEnergy Insights, a part of Carrier Global Corporation https://www.ecoenergyinsights.com/ | EcoEnergy Insights | Chapter 7. Manage the Property | Property Management |
| Ecovacs Robotics https://www.ecovacs.com/ | Ecovacs | Chapter 6. Modify the Property | Smart Homes |
| | | Chapter 6. Modify the Property | Smart Buildings |

| COMPANY | PRODUCT | BROAD CATEGORY | AI APPLICATION |
|---|---|---|---|
| edX, Inc. https://www.edx.org/ | edX | Chapter 10. Education | Education and Training |
| eFront SA (now part of BlackRock) https://www.efront.com/ | eFront Insight LP | Chapter 7. Manage the Property | Asset Management |
| Elevate https://elevate.law/ | Analyse Documents | Chapter 8. Dispose of the Property | Brokerage |
| | | Chapter 9. Public Sector | Law and Compliance |
| Ellie Mae, Inc. https://www.elliemae.com/ | Ellie Mae | Chapter 5. Property Search | Financing and Mortgage |
| | Encompass Data Connect | Chapter 5. Property Search | Mortgages |
| | Mavent Compliance Service | Chapter 5. Property Search | Appraisal Management |
| Elsevier B.V. https://www.elsevier.com/ | SSRN | Chapter 11. Multifaceted Influence | Innovation and Research |
| Emerson Electric Co. https://www.emerson.com/ | Sensi Smart Thermostat | Chapter 6. Modify the Property | Smart Homes |
| Enel X North America, Inc. https://www.enelx.com/n-a/ | Enel X | Chapter 7. Manage the Property | Property Management |
| Enerbrain Srl https://www.enerbrain.com/ | Enerbrain Srl | Chapter 7. Manage the Property | Property Management |
| Enertiv, Inc. https://www.enertiv.com/ | Enertiv | Chapter 6. Modify the Property | Smart Buildings |
| | | Chapter 7. Manage the Property | Real Estate Security and Safety |

| COMPANY | PRODUCT | BROAD CATEGORY | AI APPLICATION |
|---|---|---|---|
| | | Chapter 11. Multifaceted Influence | Sustainability |
| | | Chapter 12. GeoAI | Real-Time Analytics |
| Enodo, Inc., a Walker & Dunlop Company https://www.enodoinc.com/ | Enodo | Chapter 5. Property Search | Commercial Investment |
| | | Chapter 5. Property Search | Investment Analysis |
| | | Chapter 7. Manage the Property | Property Management |
| | | Chapter 7. Manage the Property | Portfolio Management |
| Environics Analytics Inc. https://www.environicsanalytics.com/ | Environics Analytics | Chapter 5. Property Search | Competitive Analysis |
| Environmental Systems Research Institute, Inc. (ESRI) https://www.esri.com/ | ArcGIS | Chapter 5. Property Search | Real Estate Investment |
| | | Chapter 12. GeoAI | Geospatial Integration |
| Envoy, Inc. https://www.envoy.com/ | Envoy | Chapter 5. Property Search | Commercial Investment |
| | | Chapter 6. Modify the Property | Smart Buildings |
| Epic Games Inc. https://www.epicgames.com/site/ | Unreal Engine https://www.unrealengine.com/ | Chapter 5. Property Search | 3D Modeling and AR |
| Epiq Legal Solutions https://www.epiqglobal.com/ | Epiq Legal Solutions | Chapter 9. Public Sector | Dispute Resolution |
| Epique https://www.epique.ai/ | Epique | Chapter 8. Dispose of the Property | Sales and Marketing |

| COMPANY | PRODUCT | BROAD CATEGORY | AI APPLICATION |
|---|---|---|---|
| Equiem Services Pty Ltd. https://www.getequiem.com/ | Equiem | Chapter 5. Property Search | Commercial Investment |
| EquipmentShare.com Inc. https://www.equipmentshare.com/ | EquipmentShare | Chapter 6. Modify the Property | Construction Management |
| Ernst & Young Global Limited https://www.ey.com/ | EY Helix https://www.ey.com/gl/en/services/assurance/ey-helix/ | Chapter 11. Multifaceted Influence | Professional Services |
| Ethelo Decisions Inc. https://www.ethelo.com/ | Ethelo Decisions | Chapter 9. Public Sector | Ethics and Regulations |
| Ethereum Foundation https://www.ethereum.org/ | Ethereum | Chapter 6. Modify the Property | Real Estate Development |
| Ethica Data Services, Inc. https://www.ethicadata.com/ | Ethica | Chapter 9. Public Sector | Ethics and Regulations |
| Ethical Intelligence Associates Ltd. https://www.ethicalintelligence.co/ | Ethical Intelligence | Chapter 9. Public Sector | Ethics and Regulations |
| Ethics Canvas https://www.ethicscanvas.org/ | Ethics Canvas | Chapter 9. Public Sector | Ethics and Regulations |
| Ethics Litmus Test https://www.ethicslitmustest.com/ | Ethics Litmus Test | Chapter 9. Public Sector | Ethics and Regulations |

| COMPANY | PRODUCT | BROAD CATEGORY | AI APPLICATION |
|---|---|---|---|
| EthicsAI Ltd. https://www.ethicsai.co.uk/ | EthicsAI | Chapter 9. Public Sector | Ethics and Regulations |
| Ethixbase Pte. Ltd. https://www.ethixbase.com/ | Ethixbase | Chapter 9. Public Sector | Ethics and Regulations |
| Everlaw https://www.everlaw.com/ | Everlaw | Chapter 9. Public Sector | Dispute Resolution |
| | | Chapter 9. Public Sector | Law and Compliance |
| EyeSpy360, Ltd. https://www.eyespy360.com/ | EyeSpy360 | Chapter 5. Property Search | Real Estate Leasing |
| Facilio, Inc. https://www.facilio.com/ | Facilio | Chapter 5. Property Search | Commercial Investment |
| Factory_OS https://factoryos.com/ | Factory_OS | Chapter 6. Modify the Property | Construction |
| Fair Isaac Corporation https://www.fico.com/ | FICO Falcon Fraud Manager | Chapter 5. Property Search | Investment Analysis |
| | | Chapter 11. Multifaceted Influence | Predictive Analytics |
| | FICO Falcon Platform | Chapter 5. Property Search | Mortgage Automation |
| | FICO Score XD | Chapter 5. Property Search | Mortgages |
| | FICO Xpress Optimization Suite | Chapter 7. Manage the Property | Portfolio Management |
| | | Chapter 7. Manage the Property | Asset Management |

| COMPANY | PRODUCT | BROAD CATEGORY | AI APPLICATION |
|---|---|---|---|
| FARO Technologies, Inc. https://www.faro.com/ | HoloBuilder | Chapter 6. Modify the Property | Construction Management |
| | | Chapter 6. Modify the Property | Construction |
| Fastcase, Inc. https://www.fastcase.com/ | Fastcase | Chapter 9. Public Sector | Law and Compliance |
| Feedzai, Inc. https://www.feedzai.com/ | Feedzai Fraud Prevention Platform | Chapter 5. Property Search | Investment Analysis |
| Fidelity National Financial, Inc. https://fnf.com/ | Real Geeks https://www.realgeeks.com/ | Chapter 5. Property Search | Home Sales |
| | | Chapter 5. Property Search | Agent Management |
| | | Chapter 5. Property Search | Lead Generation |
| Fieldwire https://www.fieldwire.com/ | Fieldwire | Chapter 6. Modify the Property | Construction Management |
| | | Chapter 6. Modify the Property | Construction |
| Finastra https://www.finastra.com/ | Mortgagebot | Chapter 5. Property Search | Financing and Mortgage |
| Finicity Corporation https://www.finicity.com/ | Finicity Mortgage Verification Service | Chapter 5. Property Search | Mortgages |
| First American Data Tree LLC https://dna.firstam.com/ | DataTree | Chapter 5. Property Search | Commercial Investment |
| | | Chapter 5. Property Search | Investment Analysis |
| | | Chapter 5. Property Search | Lead Generation |
| | | Chapter 5. Property Search | Real Estate Investment |

| COMPANY | PRODUCT | BROAD CATEGORY | AI APPLICATION |
|---|---|---|---|
|  |  | Chapter 11. Multifaceted Influence | Data and Analytics |
|  | FraudGuard | Chapter 5. Property Search | Mortgages |
|  |  | Chapter 5. Property Search | Financing and Mortgage |
| Flo Technologies, Inc. https://www.getflo.com/ | Flo | Chapter 11. Multifaceted Influence | Sustainability |
| FloatChat https://www.floatchat.ai/ | FloatChat | Chapter 8. Dispose of the Property | Brokerage |
| Florida Realtors https://www.floridarealtors.org/ | Form Simplicity | Chapter 5. Property Search | Home Sales |
| Flume, Inc. https://www.flume.com/ | Flume | Chapter 11. Multifaceted Influence | Sustainability |
| Follow Up Boss https://www.followupboss.com/ | Follow Up Boss | Chapter 8. Dispose of the Property | Sales and Marketing |
|  |  | Chapter 8. Dispose of the Property | Brokerage |
|  | Real Estate Team OS | Chapter 5. Property Search | Agent Management |
|  |  | Chapter 5. Property Search | Optimized Advertising |
| FormFree Holdings Corporation https://www.formfree.com/ | FormFree | Chapter 5. Property Search | Mortgages |
| Fraud.net, Inc. https://www.fraud.net/ | Fraud.net Platform | Chapter 5. Property Search | Mortgage Automation |

| COMPANY | PRODUCT | BROAD CATEGORY | AI APPLICATION |
|---|---|---|---|
| | | Chapter 5. Property Search | Real Estate Investment |
| | | Chapter 5. Property Search | Financing and Mortgage |
| | | Chapter 11. Multifaceted Influence | Predictive Analytics |
| FraudFix, Inc. https://www.fraudfix.com/ | FraudFix | Chapter 5. Property Search | Real Estate Investment |
| FraudGuard, LLC https://www.fraudguard.io/ | FraudGuard | Chapter 5. Property Search | Real Estate Investment |
| FraudLabs Pro, Inc. https://www.fraudlabspro.com/ | FraudLabs Pro | Chapter 5. Property Search | Real Estate Investment |
| FullStack Modular LLC https://www.fullstackmodular.com/ | FullStack Modular | Chapter 6. Modify the Property | Construction |
| Fundbox Ltd. https://www.fundbox.com/ | Fundbox | Chapter 5. Property Search | Mortgage Automation |
| Fundrise, LLC https://www.fundrise.com/ | Fundrise | Chapter 6. Modify the Property | Real Estate Development |
| General Electric https://www.geappliances.com/ | GE Appliances | Chapter 6. Modify the Property | Smart Homes |
| Gensler https://www.gensler.com/ | Wisp | Chapter 6. Modify the Property | Smart Buildings |

| COMPANY | PRODUCT | BROAD CATEGORY | AI APPLICATION |
|---|---|---|---|
| GeoComply Solutions, Inc. https://www.geocomply.com/ | GeoGuard | Chapter 12. GeoAI | Compliance and Regulations |
| GeoPhy, a Walker & Dunlop Company https://geophy.com/ | GeoPhy | Chapter 5. Property Search | Financing and Mortgage |
| | | Chapter 12. GeoAI | Market Insights and Analytics |
| | | Chapter 5. Property Search | Commercial Investment |
| | | Chapter 5. Property Search | Investment Analysis |
| | | Chapter 7. Manage the Property | Property Management |
| | | Chapter 7. Manage the Property | Portfolio Management |
| | | Chapter 11. Multifaceted Influence | Innovation and Research |
| | GeoPhy AVM | Chapter 5. Property Search | Appraisal Management |
| | Micromarket Analysis Platform | Chapter 11. Multifaceted Influence | Data and Analytics |
| Getfloorplan https://getfloorplan.com/ | Getfloorplan | Chapter 8. Dispose of the Property | Sales and Marketing |
| Ghotit Ltd. https://www.ghotit.com/ | Ghotit Real Writer & Reader | Chapter 10. Education | Education and Training |
| Google LLC https://www.google.com/ | Chromecast https://www.google.com/chromecast/ | Chapter 6. Modify the Property | Smart Homes |
| | Dynamically Creative Optimization (DCO) | Chapter 5. Property Search | Optimized Advertising |

| COMPANY | PRODUCT | BROAD CATEGORY | AI APPLICATION |
|---|---|---|---|
| | Google Analytics https:// marketingplatform. google.com/about/ analytics/ | Chapter 5. Property Search | Home Sales |
| | Google Assistant https://assistant. google.com/ | Chapter 6. Modify the Property | Smart Homes |
| | Google Cloud AI https://cloud.google. com/ai-platform/ | Chapter 11. Multifaceted Influence | Professional Services |
| | Google Contract DocAI https://cloud.google. com/document-ai/ | Chapter 8. Dispose of the Property | Brokerage |
| | Google Dialogflow https://cloud.google. com/dialogflow/ docs/ | Chapter 7. Manage the Property | Asset Management |
| | | Chapter 11. Multifaceted Influence | Chatbots |
| | Google Marketing Platform https:// marketingplatform. google.com/ | Chapter 5. Property Search | Optimized Advertising |
| | Nest Cam https://store.google. com/us/category/ nest_cams/ | Chapter 6. Modify the Property | Smart Homes |
| | | Chapter 7. Manage the Property | Real Estate Security and Safety |
| | Nest Doorbell https://store.google. com/us/product/ nest_doorbell/ | Chapter 6. Modify the Property | Smart Homes |

| COMPANY | PRODUCT | BROAD CATEGORY | AI APPLICATION |
|---|---|---|---|
| | Nest Learning Thermostat https://store.google.com/us/product/nest_learning_thermostat/ | Chapter 6. Modify the Property | Smart Homes |
| Grammarly, Inc. https://www.grammarly.com/ | Grammarly | Chapter 10. Education<br><br>Chapter 11. Multifaceted Influence | Education and Training<br><br>Content Generation |
| Graphisoft https://www.graphisoft.com/ | ArchiCAD | Chapter 6. Modify the Property | Architecture and Design |
| Green Building Initiative https://thegbi.org/ | Green Globes | Chapter 11. Multifaceted Influence | Sustainability |
| Green Business Certification Inc. https://www.sustainablesites.org/ | Sustainable SITES Initiative | Chapter 11. Multifaceted Influence | Sustainability |
| Greyparrot AI, Ltd. https://www.greyparrot.ai/ | Greyparrot | Chapter 11. Multifaceted Influence | Sustainability |
| GridBeyond https://gridbeyond.com/ | GridBeyond | Chapter 11. Multifaceted Influence | Sustainability |
| Gridium, Inc. https://gridium.com/ | Gridium | Chapter 6. Modify the Property<br><br>Chapter 11. Multifaceted Influence | Smart Buildings<br><br>Sustainability |
| Grooper, Inc. https://www.grooper.com/ | Grooper | Chapter 5. Property Search | Mortgage Automation |
| | | Chapter 5. Property Search | Agent Management |

| COMPANY | PRODUCT | BROAD CATEGORY | AI APPLICATION |
|---|---|---|---|
| Groundfloor Finance, Inc. https://www.groundfloor.us/ | Groundfloor | Chapter 6. Modify the Property | Real Estate Development |
| GumGum, Inc. https://www.gumgum.com/ | GumGum Verity | Chapter 5. Property Search | Optimized Advertising |
| H2O.ai, Inc. https://www.h2o.ai/ | H2O.ai | Chapter 5. Property Search | Commercial Investment |
| HappyCo https://www.happy.co/ | HappyCo | Chapter 5. Property Search | Commercial Investment |
| | | Chapter 7. Manage the Property | Tenant Management |
| Havenly, Inc. https://www.havenly.com/ | Havenly | Chapter 5. Property Search | Virtual Staging |
| Hemingway Editor https://www.hemingwayapp.com/ | Hemingway App | Chapter 10. Education | Education and Training |
| | | Chapter 11. Multifaceted Influence | Content Generation |
| Hemlane, Inc. https://www.hemlane.com/ | Hemlane | Chapter 5. Property Search | Rental Property Search |
| | | Chapter 5. Property Search | Real Estate Investment |
| | | Chapter 7. Manage the Property | Property Management |
| | | Chapter 7. Manage the Property | Tenant Management |
| Home Value by Opendoor Labs https://www.opendoor.com/ | Home Value | Chapter 8. Dispose of the Property | Valuation and Appraisal |

| COMPANY | PRODUCT | BROAD CATEGORY | AI APPLICATION |
|---------|---------|----------------|----------------|
| Homebase, LLC https://homebase.com/ | Homebase | Chapter 11. Multifaceted Influence | Sustainability |
| Homebot, Inc. https://homebot.ai/ | Homebot | Chapter 11. Multifaceted Influence | Predictive Analytics |
| | | Chapter 11. Multifaceted Influence | Sustainability |
| HomeLight, Inc. https://www.homelight.com/ | HomeLight | Chapter 5. Property Search | Agent Management |
| | | Chapter 8. Dispose of the Property | Valuation and Appraisal |
| | | Chapter 11. Multifaceted Influence | Content Generation |
| | | Chapter 11. Multifaceted Influence | Innovation and Research |
| Homesnap, Inc. https://www.homesnap.com/ | Homesnap | Chapter 5. Property Search | Home Sales |
| | | Chapter 8. Dispose of the Property | Brokerage |
| | | Chapter 11. Multifaceted Influence | Data and Analytics |
| HomeZada, Inc. https://www.homezada.com/ | HomeZada | Chapter 11. Multifaceted Influence | Predictive Analytics |
| Honeywell International Inc. https://www.honeywell.com/ | Honeywell | Chapter 11. Multifaceted Influence | Sustainability |

| COMPANY | PRODUCT | BROAD CATEGORY | AI APPLICATION |
|---|---|---|---|
| | | Chapter 5. Property Search | Commercial Investment |
| | | Chapter 5. Property Search | Investment Analysis |
| | | Chapter 5. Property Search | Real Estate Investment |
| | | Chapter 5. Property Search | Financing and Mortgage |
| | | Chapter 6. Modify the Property | Real Estate Development |
| | HouseCanary | Chapter 7. Manage the Property | Property Management |
| | | Chapter 7. Manage the Property | Portfolio Management |
| HouseCanary, Inc. https://www. housecanary.com/ | | Chapter 8. Dispose of the Property | Valuation and Appraisal |
| | | Chapter 11. Multifaceted Influence | Innovation and Research |
| | | Chapter 12. GeoAI | Predictive Location Analytics |
| | | Chapter 5. Property Search | Appraisal Management |
| | | Chapter 5. Property Search | Lead Generation |
| | HouseCanary Value Report | Chapter 11. Multifaceted Influence | Predictive Analytics |
| | | Chapter 11. Multifaceted Influence | Data and Analytics |
| Houzz, Inc. https://www.houzz. com/ | Houzz | Chapter 6. Modify the Property | Architecture and Design |

| COMPANY | PRODUCT | BROAD CATEGORY | AI APPLICATION |
|---|---|---|---|
| HqO, Inc. https://www.hqo.com/ | HqO | Chapter 5. Property Search | Commercial Investment |
| | | Chapter 12. GeoAI | Risk Assessment and Mitigation |
| | Tenant Experience Platform | Chapter 7. Manage the Property | Tenant Management |
| HubSpot, Inc. https://www.hubspot.com/ | HubSpot | Chapter 8. Dispose of the Property | Sales and Marketing |
| | | Chapter 11. Multifaceted Influence | Content Generation |
| Humanyze Analytics, Inc. https://www.humanyze.com/ | Humanyze | Chapter 6. Modify the Property | Smart Buildings |
| Husqvarna AB https://www.husqvarna.com/ | Gardena | Chapter 6. Modify the Property | Smart Homes |
| | Husqvarna Automower | Chapter 6. Modify the Property | Smart Homes |
| HydroPoint Data Systems, Inc. https://www.hydropoint.com/ | HydroPoint | Chapter 11. Multifaceted Influence | Sustainability |
| Hyperscience, Inc. https://www.hyperscience.com/ | Hyperscience | Chapter 5. Property Search | Agent Management |
| Hyro, Inc. https://hyro.ai/ | Hyro | Chapter 5. Property Search | Agent Management |
| | | Chapter 5. Property Search | Lead Generation |
| | | Chapter 8. Dispose of the Property | Brokerage |
| IBM Corporation https://cloud.ibm.com/docs/assistant/ | IBM Watson Assistant | Chapter 11. Multifaceted Influence | Chatbots |

| COMPANY | PRODUCT | BROAD CATEGORY | AI APPLICATION |
|---|---|---|---|
| IBM Corporation https://www.ibm.com/ | IBM Maximo Application Suite https://www.ibm.com/products/maximo/ | Chapter 6. Modify the Property | Construction |
| | IBM Planning Analytics https://www.ibm.com/products/planning-analytics/ | Chapter 5. Property Search | Competitive Analysis |
| | IBM TRIRIGA https://www.ibm.com/products/tririga | Chapter 7. Manage the Property | Property Management |
| | | Chapter 7. Manage the Property | Portfolio Management |
| | IBM Watson https://www.ibm.com/watson/ | Chapter 11. Multifaceted Influence | Professional Services |
| | IBM Watson Assistant https://www.ibm.com/products/watsonx-assistant | Chapter 7. Manage the Property | Asset Management |
| | IBM Watson Discovery https://www.ibm.com/products/watson-discovery | Chapter 5. Property Search | Real Estate Investment |
| iCan Systems Inc. https://www.smartsettle.com/ | Smartsettle | Chapter 9. Public Sector | Law and Compliance |
| Ideal.com https://www.ideal.com/ | Ideal | Chapter 5. Property Search | Agent Management |
| iHOUSEweb, Inc. https://www.ihouseweb.com/ | TurboLeads CRM | Chapter 5. Property Search | Home Sales |
| | | Chapter 5. Property Search | Agent Management |

| COMPANY | PRODUCT | BROAD CATEGORY | AI APPLICATION |
| --- | --- | --- | --- |
| Indeed, Inc. https://www.indeed.com/ | Indeed | Chapter 5. Property Search | Agent Management |
| Indigo Stream Technologies, Ltd. https://www.copyscape.com/ | Copyscape | Chapter 11. Multifaceted Influence | Content Generation |
| Indus.ai, Inc. https://www.indus.ai/ | Indus.ai | Chapter 6. Modify the Property | Construction Management |
| | | Chapter 7. Manage the Property | Real Estate Security and Safety |
| InEight Inc. https://www.ineight.com/ | InEight Schedule | Chapter 6. Modify the Property | Construction Management |
| | | Chapter 6. Modify the Property | Construction |
| InsideRE, LLC https://www.insiderealestate.com/ | kvCore | Chapter 5. Property Search | Home Sales |
| | | Chapter 5. Property Search | Mortgage Automation |
| | | Chapter 5. Property Search | Agent Management |
| | | Chapter 8. Dispose of the Property | Sales and Marketing |
| | | Chapter 8. Dispose of the Property | Brokerage |
| | | Chapter 11. Multifaceted Influence | Chatbots |
| Institute for the Future https://www.iftf.org/ | Ethical OS | Chapter 9. Public Sector | Ethics and Regulations |
| Integral Ad Science, Inc. https://www.integralads.com/ | Integral Ad Science | Chapter 5. Property Search | Optimized Advertising |

| COMPANY | PRODUCT | BROAD CATEGORY | AI APPLICATION |
|---|---|---|---|
| Inter IKEA Systems B.V. https://www.ikea.com/ | Ikea Tradfri | Chapter 6. Modify the Property | Smart Homes |
| Interaktive Demokratie e.V. https://www.liquidfeedback.org/ | LiquidFeedback | Chapter 9. Public Sector | Ethics and Regulations |
| International WELL Building Institute https://wellcertified.com/ | WELL | Chapter 11. Multifaceted Influence | Sustainability |
| Investor Management Services, LLC https://www.imscre.com/ | Investor Management Services | Chapter 7. Manage the Property | Portfolio Management |
| | | Chapter 7. Manage the Property | Asset Management |
| iRobot Corporation https://www.irobot.com/ | iRobot | Chapter 6. Modify the Property | Smart Buildings |
| | Roomba | Chapter 6. Modify the Property | Smart Homes |
| iStaging Corp. https://www.istaging.com/ | 3D Staging | Chapter 5. Property Search | 3D Modeling and AR |
| IXACT Contact Solutions, Inc. https://www.ixactcontact.com/ | IXACT Contact | Chapter 8. Dispose of the Property | Sales and Marketing |
| | | Chapter 8. Dispose of the Property | Brokerage |
| Jasper AI, Inc. https://jasper.ai/ | Jasper.ai | Chapter 8. Dispose of the Property | Sales and Marketing |
| | | Chapter 8. Dispose of the Property | Brokerage |

| COMPANY | PRODUCT | BROAD CATEGORY | AI APPLICATION |
|---------|---------|----------------|----------------|
| JLL, Inc. https://www.jll.com/ | JLL Azara https://www.jllt.com/blog/jll-azara-cre-data-platform/ | Chapter 5. Property Search | Real Estate Leasing |
| | JLL Spark https://spark.jllt.com/ | Chapter 11. Multifaceted Influence | Professional Services |
| Jointer.io https://www.jointer.io/ | Jointer | Chapter 5. Property Search | Investment Analysis |
| | | Chapter 5. Property Search | Real Estate Investment |
| Juniper Square, Inc. https://www.junipersquare.com/ | Juniper Square | Chapter 5. Property Search | Real Estate Investment |
| | | Chapter 7. Manage the Property | Portfolio Management |
| | | Chapter 7. Manage the Property | Asset Management |
| Juro https://juro.com/ | Juro AI | Chapter 6. Modify the Property | Real Estate Development |
| | | Chapter 9. Public Sector | Ethics and Regulations |
| | | Chapter 11. Multifaceted Influence | Professional Services |
| JustFix.nyc https://www.justfix.nyc/ | JustFix.nyc | Chapter 11. Multifaceted Influence | Sustainability |
| Kabbage, Inc. https://www.kabbage.com/ | Kabbage | Chapter 5. Property Search | Mortgage Automation |
| Kalibrate Technologies Ltd https://kalibrate.com/ | Location Intelligence | Chapter 6. Modify the Property | Real Estate Development |

| COMPANY | PRODUCT | BROAD CATEGORY | AI APPLICATION |
|---|---|---|---|
| Kasisto, Inc. https://www.kasisto.com/ | Digital Mortgage Assistant | Chapter 5. Property Search | Financing and Mortgage |
| | KAI Consumer Banking | Chapter 5. Property Search | Mortgages |
| | | Chapter 11. Multifaceted Influence | Chatbots |
| | KS | Chapter 11. Multifaceted Influence | Chatbots |
| Keeper Security, Inc. https://www.keepersecurity.com/ | Keeper | Chapter 7. Manage the Property | Property Management |
| | | Chapter 7. Manage the Property | Tenant Management |
| Kelvin, Inc. https://www.kelvin.com/ | Kelvin Home Value Estimator | Chapter 6. Modify the Property | Real Estate Development |
| Kenshoo Ltd. https://www.kenshoo.com/ | Kenshoo Ecommerce | Chapter 5. Property Search | Optimized Advertising |
| Kira Systems https://kirasystems.com/ | Kira | Chapter 9. Public Sector | Law and Compliance |
| Kira Systems, Inc. https://www.kirasystems.com/ | Kira Systems | Chapter 6. Modify the Property | Real Estate Development |
| | | Chapter 9. Public Sector | Ethics and Regulations |
| | | Chapter 11. Multifaceted Influence | Professional Services |
| Kleros https://kleros.io/ | Kleros | Chapter 9. Public Sector | Law and Compliance |
| Klue Labs, Inc. https://www.klue.com/ | Klue | Chapter 5. Property Search | Competitive Analysis |

| COMPANY | PRODUCT | BROAD CATEGORY | AI APPLICATION |
|---|---|---|---|
| Knewton, Inc. https://www.knewton.com/ | Knewton | Chapter 10. Education | Education and Training |
| KnightScope, Inc. https://www.knightscope.com/ | KnightScope | Chapter 7. Manage the Property | Real Estate Security and Safety |
| Knock Homes, Inc. https://www.knock.com/ | Knock | Chapter 5. Property Search | Home Sales |
| | | Chapter 11. Multifaceted Influence | Innovation and Research |
| Kogniz, Inc. https://www.kogniz.ai/ | Kogniz | Chapter 6. Modify the Property | Smart Buildings |
| Kompyte, Inc. https://www.kompyte.com/ | Kompyte | Chapter 5. Property Search | Competitive Analysis |
| KONE Corporation https://www.kone.com/ | KONE | Chapter 11. Multifaceted Influence | Professional Services |
| Konstru, Inc. https://www.konstru.com/ | Konstru | Chapter 6. Modify the Property | Architecture and Design |
| Kount, Inc. https://www.kount.com/ | Kount | Chapter 5. Property Search | Mortgage Automation |
| | Kount Fraud Prevention Platform | Chapter 11. Multifaceted Influence | Predictive Analytics |
| KPMG International Cooperative https://www.kpmg.com/ | KPMG Clara | Chapter 11. Multifaceted Influence | Professional Services |
| Kreo Software Ltd. https://www.kreo.net/ | Kreo | Chapter 6. Modify the Property | Architecture and Design |

| COMPANY | PRODUCT | BROAD CATEGORY | AI APPLICATION |
|---|---|---|---|
| Kurzweil Education, Inc. https://www.kurzweiledu.com/ | Kurzweil 3000 | Chapter 10. Education | Education and Training |
| Kwant.ai https://www.kwant.ai/ | Kwant.ai | Chapter 6. Modify the Property | Construction |
| Land Conflict Watch https://www.landconflictwatch.org/ | Land Conflict Watch Database | Chapter 12. GeoAI | Global / India Perspectives |
| Land Intelligence, Inc. https://www.landintelligence.net/ | Land Intelligence | Chapter 6. Modify the Property | Real Estate Development |
| | | Chapter 12. GeoAI | Site Selection and Development |
| Landbot https://landbot.io/ | Landbot | Chapter 5. Property Search | Agent Management |
| | | Chapter 11. Multifaceted Influence | Chatbots |
| LanzaTech https://www.lanzatech.com/ | LanzaTech | Chapter 11. Multifaceted Influence | Sustainability |
| Latchel, Inc. https://latchel.com/ | Latchel | Chapter 7. Manage the Property | Property Management |
| | | Chapter 7. Manage the Property | Tenant Management |
| Laurel & Wolf, Inc. https://www.laurelandwolf.com/ | Laurel & Wolf | Chapter 5. Property Search | Virtual Staging |
| LAWCLERK.Legal https://www.lawclerk.legal/ | LAWCLERK | Chapter 6. Modify the Property | Real Estate Development |
| | | Chapter 9. Public Sector | Ethics and Regulations |

| COMPANY | PRODUCT | BROAD CATEGORY | AI APPLICATION |
|---|---|---|---|
| LawGeex https://www.lawgeex.com/ | LawGeex | Chapter 9. Public Sector | Law and Compliance |
| LeaseAbstraction, LLC https://www.leaseabstraction.com/ | LeaseAbstraction | Chapter 5. Property Search | Real Estate Leasing |
| Leasecake, Inc. https://www.leasecake.com/ | Leasecake | Chapter 5. Property Search | Real Estate Leasing |
| LeaseHawk, LLC https://www.leasehawk.com/ | LeaseHawk | Chapter 5. Property Search | Rental Property Search |
| LeasePilot, Inc. https://www.leasepilot.co/ | LeasePilot | Chapter 5. Property Search | Real Estate Leasing |
| LeaseQuery, LLC https://www.leasequery.com/ | LeaseQuery | Chapter 5. Property Search | Real Estate Leasing |
| LeaseRunner, Inc. https://www.leaserunner.com/ | LeaseRunner | Chapter 7. Manage the Property | Property Management |
| | | Chapter 7. Manage the Property | Tenant Management |
| LegalSifter, Inc. https://www.legalsifter.com/ | Legalsifter | Chapter 9. Public Sector | Law and Compliance |
| LegalZoom.com, Inc. https://www.legalzoom.com/ | LegalZoom | Chapter 11. Multifaceted Influence | Professional Services |
| Lenda, Inc. https://www.lenda.com/ | Lenda | Chapter 5. Property Search | Home Sales |
| LenddoEFL https://www.lenddoefl.com/ | LenddoEFL | Chapter 5. Property Search | Financing and Mortgage |

| COMPANY | PRODUCT | BROAD CATEGORY | AI APPLICATION |
|---|---|---|---|
| LenderX, LLC https://www.lenderx.com/ | LenderX | Chapter 5. Property Search | Appraisal Management |
| Lendesk Technologies, Inc. https://www.lendesk.com/ | Lara | Chapter 5. Property Search | Financing and Mortgage |
| LendingHome Corporation https://www.lendinghome.com/ | LendingHome | Chapter 5. Property Search | Home Sales |
| | | Chapter 5. Property Search | Mortgage Automation |
| | | Chapter 5. Property Search | Financing and Mortgage |
| | LendingHome Bridge Pro | Chapter 5. Property Search | Mortgages |
| LendingTree, LLC https://www.lendingtree.com/ | LendingTree | Chapter 5. Property Search | Home Sales |
| | | Chapter 5. Property Search | Mortgages |
| | | Chapter 5. Property Search | Financing and Mortgage |
| Lendio, Inc. https://www.lendio.com/ | Lendio | Chapter 5. Property Search | Home Sales |
| | | Chapter 5. Property Search | Mortgage Automation |
| Lessonly, Inc. https://www.lessonly.com/ | Lessonly | Chapter 5. Property Search | Agent Management |
| LexisNexis, a RELX Company https://www.lexisnexis.com/ | Lex Machina https://lexmachina.com/ | Chapter 9. Public Sector | Law and Compliance |
| | Lex Machina Legal Analytics https://lexmachina.com/legal-analytics/ | Chapter 9. Public Sector | Dispute Resolution |

| COMPANY | PRODUCT | BROAD CATEGORY | AI APPLICATION |
|---|---|---|---|
| | LexisNexis | Chapter 9. Public Sector | Law and Compliance |
| | | Chapter 11. Multifaceted Influence | Professional Services |
| Lifeline Response, LLC https://www.llresponse.com/ | Lifeline Response | Chapter 7. Manage the Property | Real Estate Security and Safety |
| Lifi Labs, Inc. https://www.lifx.com/ | LIFX | Chapter 6. Modify the Property | Smart Homes |
| Lightbox Holdings LP https://www.lightboxre.com/ | LandVision | Chapter 6. Modify the Property | Real Estate Development |
| Likely.AI https://likely.ai/ | Likely.AI | Chapter 8. Dispose of the Property | Brokerage |
| Lingo, Inc. https://www.lingo.com/ | Lingo | Chapter 11. Multifaceted Influence | Content Generation |
| LinkedIn Corporation https://www.linkedin.com/ | LinkedIn Learning | Chapter 5. Property Search | Agent Management |
| | LinkedIn Talent Solutions | Chapter 5. Property Search | Agent Management |
| LionDesk, LLC. https://liondesk.com/ | LionDesk CRM | Chapter 5. Property Search | Home Sales |
| | | Chapter 5. Property Search | Mortgage Automation |
| | | Chapter 5. Property Search | Agent Management |
| | | Chapter 5. Property Search | Lead Generation |
| | | Chapter 8. Dispose of the Property | Sales and Marketing |
| | | Chapter 8. Dispose of the Property | Brokerage |

| COMPANY | PRODUCT | BROAD CATEGORY | AI APPLICATION |
|---|---|---|---|
| Litigation Analytics https://www.litigationanalytics.com/ | Litigation Analytics | Chapter 9. Public Sector | Dispute Resolution |
| Livly, Inc. https://www.livly.io/ | Livly Pricing Engine | Chapter 6. Modify the Property | Real Estate Development |
| Livv.ai https://www.livv.ai/ | Livv.ai | Chapter 8. Dispose of the Property | Brokerage |
| LoanDepot.com, LLC https://www.loandepot.com/ | LoanDepot | Chapter 5. Property Search | Home Sales |
| Loanpal, LLC https://www.loanpal.com/ | Amy | Chapter 5. Property Search | Financing and Mortgage |
| LoanSnap, Inc. https://www.goloansnap.com/ | LoanSnap | Chapter 5. Property Search | Mortgage Automation |
| Local Logic Inc. https://www.locallogic.co/ | Local Logic | Chapter 5. Property Search | Real Estate Investment |
| | | Chapter 12. GeoAI | Market Insights and Analytics |
| LocalizeOS https://localizeos.com/ | LocalizeAI | Chapter 5. Property Search | Home Sales |
| | | Chapter 5. Property Search | Lead Generation |
| | LocalizeOS | Chapter 8. Dispose of the Property | Brokerage |
| Locatee AG https://www.locatee.com/ | Locatee | Chapter 6. Modify the Property | Smart Buildings |
| Locon Solutions Private Limited (Housing.com) https://housing.com/ | Housing.com Platform | Chapter 12. GeoAI | Customized Recommendations |
| | | Chapter 12. GeoAI | Global / India Perspectives |

| COMPANY | PRODUCT | BROAD CATEGORY | AI APPLICATION |
|---|---|---|---|
| Lofty, Inc. https://lofty.com/ | Lofty | Chapter 5. Property Search | Agent Management |
| | | Chapter 8. Dispose of the Property | Sales and Marketing |
| | | Chapter 8. Dispose of the Property | Brokerage |
| LogicEase Solutions Inc. https://www.complianceease.com/ | ComplianceEase | Chapter 5. Property Search | Mortgages |
| LogicGate, Inc. https://www.logicgate.com/ | LogicGate | Chapter 9. Public Sector | Law and Compliance |
| Logikcull https://www.logikcull.com/ | Logikcull | Chapter 9. Public Sector | Dispute Resolution |
| | | Chapter 9. Public Sector | Law and Compliance |
| London Computer Systems, Inc. https://www.rentmanager.com/ | Rent Manager | Chapter 5. Property Search | Rental Property Search |
| Lone Wolf Technologies https://www.lwolf.com/ | Lone Wolf Transactions (zipForm Edition) | Chapter 5. Property Search | Home Sales |
| Luminance Technologies Ltd. https://www.luminance.com/ | Luminance | Chapter 6. Modify the Property | Real Estate Development |
| | | Chapter 9. Public Sector | Ethics and Regulations |
| | | Chapter 9. Public Sector | Law and Compliance |
| | | Chapter 11. Multifaceted Influence | Professional Services |

| COMPANY | PRODUCT | BROAD CATEGORY | AI APPLICATION |
|---|---|---|---|
| Magicbricks Realty Services Limited https://www. magicbricks.com/ | Magicbricks | Chapter 5. Property Search | Optimized Advertising |
| | | Chapter 12. GeoAI | Customized Recommendations |
| | Smart Search | Chapter 5. Property Search | Lead Generation |
| Maintenance Care https://www. maintenancecare. com/ | CMMS | Chapter 7. Manage the Property | Property Management |
| | | Chapter 7. Manage the Property | Tenant Management |
| ManyChat, Inc. https://www. manychat.com/ | ManyChat | Chapter 5. Property Search | Agent Management |
| MarketMuse, Inc. https://www. marketmuse.com/ | MarketMuse | Chapter 11. Multifaceted Influence | Content Generation |
| Mashvisor, Inc. https://www. mashvisor.com/ | Mashvisor | Chapter 5. Property Search | Investment Analysis |
| | | Chapter 5. Property Search | Real Estate Investment |
| | | Chapter 6. Modify the Property | Real Estate Development |
| Massachusetts Institute of Technology https://mitcre.mit. edu/ | MIT Center for Real Estate | Chapter 10. Education | Education and Training |
| | | Chapter 11. Multifaceted Influence | Innovation and Research |
| MatchWare A/S https://www. matchware.com/ | MindView AT | Chapter 10. Education | Education and Training |
| Materialize.X Ltd. https://www. materializex.com/ | Materialize.X | Chapter 6. Modify the Property | Construction Management |

| COMPANY | PRODUCT | BROAD CATEGORY | AI APPLICATION |
|---|---|---|---|
| Matic Network https://www.matic.network/ | Matic Network | Chapter 6. Modify the Property | Real Estate Development |
| Matterport, Inc. https://www.matterport.com/ | Matterport | Chapter 5. Property Search<br><br>Chapter 5. Property Search | 3D Modeling and AR<br><br>Real Estate Leasing |
| McGraw Hill Education, Inc. https://www.mheducation.com/ | ALEKS https://www.aleks.com/ | Chapter 10. Education | Education and Training |
| McKinsey & Company, Inc. https://www.mckinsey.com/ | McKinsey Climate Intelligence Platform | Chapter 11. Multifaceted Influence | Data and Analytics |
| MediaMath, Inc. https://www.mediamath.com/ | MediaMath | Chapter 5. Property Search | Optimized Advertising |
| Meltwater US News Inc. https://www.meltwater.com/ | Owler https://www.owler.com/ | Chapter 5. Property Search | Competitive Analysis |
| Mercado Labs, Inc. https://www.mercadolabs.com/ | Mercado | Chapter 5. Property Search | Lead Generation |
| Mercury Network, LLC https://www.mercuryvmp.com/ | Collateral QC | Chapter 5. Property Search | Appraisal Management |
| MeridianLink, Inc. https://www.meridianlink.com/ | LendingQB | Chapter 5. Property Search | Mortgages |
| Meridio https://www.meridio.co/ | Meridio | Chapter 6. Modify the Property | Real Estate Development |

| COMPANY | PRODUCT | BROAD CATEGORY | AI APPLICATION |
|---|---|---|---|
| Meta https://www.meta.com/ | Meta Business Suite https://www.facebook.com/business/tools/meta-business-suite | Chapter 5. Property Search | Optimized Advertising |
| | Meta Quest https://www.oculus.com/ | Chapter 5. Property Search | 3D Modeling and AR |
| | Meta Smart Glasses https://www.meta.com/us/smart-glasses/ | Chapter 5. Property Search | 3D Modeling and AR |
| Meya https://www.meya.ai/ | Meya | Chapter 8. Dispose of the Property | Brokerage |
| Microsoft Corporation https://www.microsoft.com/ | Microsoft Azure AI https://azure.microsoft.com/en-us/solutions/ai/ | Chapter 11. Multifaceted Influence | Professional Services |
| | Microsoft Azure Digital Twins https://azure.microsoft.com/en-us/products/digital-twins/ | Chapter 6. Modify the Property | Construction |
| | Microsoft Bot Framework https://dev.botframework.com/ | Chapter 7. Manage the Property | Asset Management |
| | | Chapter 11. Multifaceted Influence | Chatbots |
| Mobile Monkey https://mobilemonkey.com/ | Mobile Monkey | Chapter 8. Dispose of the Property | Brokerage |
| Modsy, Inc. https://www.modsy.com/ | Modsy | Chapter 5. Property Search | Virtual Staging |

| COMPANY | PRODUCT | BROAD CATEGORY | AI APPLICATION |
|---|---|---|---|
| Module Housing Inc. https://www. modulehousing.com/ | Module | Chapter 6. Modify the Property | Construction |
| Mojang Studios AB https://www. minecraft.net/ | Minecraft Earth | Chapter 5. Property Search | 3D Modeling and AR |
| Monevo Inc. https://www.monevo. com/ | Monevo | Chapter 5. Property Search | Mortgages |
| Moody's Analytics, Inc. https://cre. moodysanalytics. com/ | REIS | Chapter 5. Property Search | Rental Property Search |
| Moovit App Global, Ltd. https://moovit.com/ | Moovit | Chapter 11. Multifaceted Influence | Sustainability |
| Morningstar, Inc. https://www. morningstar.com/ | Morningstar Direct | Chapter 7. Manage the Property | Asset Management |
| Mortgage Cadence, an Accenture Company https://www. mortgagecadence. com/ | Mortgage Cadence | Chapter 5. Property Search | Financing and Mortgage |
| Mortgage Coach, Inc. https://www. mortgagecoach.com/ | Mortgage Coach | Chapter 5. Property Search | Financing and Mortgage |
| Mortgage Harmony Corp. https://www. mortgageharmony. com/ | Mortgage Harmony | Chapter 5. Property Search | Financing and Mortgage |

| COMPANY | PRODUCT | BROAD CATEGORY | AI APPLICATION |
|---|---|---|---|
| MortgageHippo, Inc. https://www. mortgagehippo.com/ | MortgageHippo | Chapter 5. Property Search | Mortgages |
| | | Chapter 5. Property Search | Financing and Mortgage |
| Morty, Inc. https://www.himorty. com/ | Morty | Chapter 5. Property Search | Home Sales |
| Move, Inc. https://www.move. com/ | Realtor.com https://www.realtor. com/ | Chapter 5. Property Search | Home Sales |
| | | Chapter 8. Dispose of the Property | Valuation and Appraisal |
| | | Chapter 8. Dispose of the Property | Brokerage |
| | | Chapter 11. Multifaceted Influence | Innovation and Research |
| | | Chapter 12. GeoAI | Customized Recommendations |
| | Realtor.com RealValue https://www.realtor. com/myhome/ | Chapter 11. Multifaceted Influence | Predictive Analytics |
| | | Chapter 11. Multifaceted Influence | Data and Analytics |
| MRI Software, LLC https://www. mrisoftware.com/ | Leverton | Chapter 5. Property Search | Appraisal Management |
| | | Chapter 5. Property Search | Real Estate Leasing |
| | | Chapter 6. Modify the Property | Real Estate Development |
| | | Chapter 9. Public Sector | Ethics and Regulations |

| COMPANY | PRODUCT | BROAD CATEGORY | AI APPLICATION |
|---|---|---|---|
| MSCI, Inc. https://www.msci.com/ | MSCI Barra Portfolio Manager | Chapter 7. Manage the Property | Asset Management |
| | RiskMetrics RiskManager | Chapter 7. Manage the Property | Portfolio Management |
| Mysa Smart Thermostat https://www.getmysa.com/ | Mysa | Chapter 6. Modify the Property | Smart Homes |
| Nanoleaf BV https://www.nanoleaf.me/ | Nanoleaf | Chapter 6. Modify the Property | Smart Homes |
| National Association of REALTORS® https://www.nar.realtor/ | NAR's AI for REALTORS https://www.nar.realtor/artificial-intelligence-real-estate/ | Chapter 8. Dispose of the Property | Sales and Marketing |
| National Community Land Trust Network https://www.cltnetwork.org/ | Community Land Trusts | Chapter 11. Multifaceted Influence | Sustainability |
| National Low Income Housing Coalition https://nlihc.org/ | National Low Income Housing Coalition | Chapter 11. Multifaceted Influence | Sustainability |
| Nationstar Mortgage LLC https://www.mrcooper.com/ | Google Assistant Action for Mr. Cooper | Chapter 5. Property Search | Mortgages |
| Neato Robotics, Inc. https://www.neatorobotics.com/ | Neato | Chapter 6. Modify the Property | Smart Homes |
| Neighborland, Inc. https://www.neighborland.com/ | Neighborland | Chapter 11. Multifaceted Influence | Sustainability |

| COMPANY | PRODUCT | BROAD CATEGORY | AI APPLICATION |
|---|---|---|---|
| Neighborly Corporation https://www.neighborly.com/ | Neighborly | Chapter 11. Multifaceted Influence | Sustainability |
| Nesta https://www.nesta.org.uk/ | Nesta | Chapter 9. Public Sector | Ethics and Regulations |
| NestAway Technologies Private Limited https://www.nestaway.com/ | NestAway | Chapter 5. Property Search | Real Estate Leasing |
| | Nestie | Chapter 5. Property Search | Lead Generation |
| NestEgg https://nestegg.rent/ | NestEgg | Chapter 7. Manage the Property | Property Management |
| | | Chapter 7. Manage the Property | Tenant Management |
| Netafim https://www.netafim.com/ | Netafim | Chapter 11. Multifaceted Influence | Sustainability |
| Netatmo SA https://www.netatmo.com/ | Netatmo Smart Thermostat | Chapter 6. Modify the Property | Smart Homes |
| | Netatmo Smart Video Doorbell | Chapter 6. Modify the Property | Smart Homes |
| Netro Inc. https://www.netrohome.com/ | Netro | Chapter 6. Modify the Property | Smart Homes |
| New York City Public Advocate https://pubadvocate.nyc.gov/ | Landlord Watchlist https://advocate.nyc.gov/landlord-watchlist/ | Chapter 11. Multifaceted Influence | Sustainability |
| Newmetrix https://www.newmetrix.com/ | Newmetrix | Chapter 6. Modify the Property | Construction Management |
| | | Chapter 6. Modify the Property | Construction |
| | | Chapter 7. Manage the Property | Real Estate Security and Safety |

| COMPANY | PRODUCT | BROAD CATEGORY | AI APPLICATION |
|---|---|---|---|
| Nextdoor, Inc. https://nextdoor.com/ | Nextdoor | Chapter 11. Multifaceted Influence | Sustainability |
| Nextpoint, Inc. https://www.nextpoint.com/ | Nextpoint | Chapter 9. Public Sector | Law and Compliance |
| Niantic, Inc. https://www.nianticlabs.com/ | Pokémon Go | Chapter 5. Property Search | 3D Modeling and AR |
| Nielsen Holdings plc https://www.nielsen.com/ | Nielsen Segmentation & Market Solutions | Chapter 5. Property Search | Competitive Analysis |
| Nike, Inc. https://www.nike.com/ | Nike Fit | Chapter 5. Property Search | 3D Modeling and AR |
| NoBroker Technologies Solutions Private Limited https://www.nobroker.in/ | NoBroker | Chapter 5. Property Search | Home Sales |
| | | Chapter 12. GeoAI | Global / India Perspectives |
| Nomis Solutions, Inc. https://www.nomissolutions.com/ | Nomis Mortgage Suite | Chapter 5. Property Search | Mortgages |
| | Nomis Solutions | Chapter 5. Property Search | Mortgage Automation |
| | | Chapter 5. Property Search | Agent Management |
| Noonlight, Inc. https://www.noonlight.com/ | Noonlight | Chapter 7. Manage the Property | Real Estate Security and Safety |
| nPlan Ltd. https://www.nplan.io/ | nPlan | Chapter 6. Modify the Property | Construction Management |
| Nuance Communications, Inc. https://www.nuance.com/ | Nuance Dragon NaturallySpeaking | Chapter 10. Education | Education and Training |

| COMPANY | PRODUCT | BROAD CATEGORY | AI APPLICATION |
|---|---|---|---|
| Nyfty.ai https://www.nyfty.ai/ | Nyfty.ai | Chapter 6. Modify the Property | Construction |
| Ocrolus, Inc. https://www.ocrolus.com/ | Ocrolus | Chapter 5. Property Search | Agent Management |
| Offerpad https://www.offerpad.com/ | Instant Cash Offer | Chapter 8. Dispose of the Property | Valuation and Appraisal |
| | Offerpad | Chapter 8. Dispose of the Property | Valuation and Appraisal |
| | | Chapter 11. Multifaceted Influence | Innovation and Research |
| One Concern, Inc. https://oneconcern.com/ | One Concern Platform | Chapter 12. GeoAI | Risk Assessment and Mitigation |
| OneSpot, Inc. https://www.onespot.com/ | OneSpot | Chapter 11. Multifaceted Influence | Content Generation |
| OneTrust LLC https://www.onetrust.com/ | OneTrust | Chapter 9. Public Sector | Law and Compliance |
| Onna Technologies, Inc. https://onna.com/ | Onna | Chapter 9. Public Sector | Law and Compliance |
| Onshape https://www.onshape.com/ | Modern CAD | Chapter 5. Property Search | 3D Modeling and AR |
| OnSiteIQ Inc. https://www.onsiteiq.com/ | OnSiteIQ | Chapter 6. Modify the Property | Construction Management |
| Oosto https://oosto.com/ | OnWatch | Chapter 6. Modify the Property | Smart Buildings |
| | | Chapter 7. Manage the Property | Real Estate Security and Safety |

| COMPANY | PRODUCT | BROAD CATEGORY | AI APPLICATION |
|---|---|---|---|
| OpenAI https://openai.com/ | ChatGPT | Chapter 10. Education | Education and Training |
| Opendoor Labs, Inc. https://www. opendoor.com/ | Opendoor | Chapter 5. Property Search | Home Sales |
| | | Chapter 6. Modify the Property | Real Estate Development |
| | | Chapter 7. Manage the Property | Portfolio Management |
| | | Chapter 8. Dispose of the Property | Valuation and Appraisal |
| | | Chapter 11. Multifaceted Influence | Content Generation |
| | | Chapter 11. Multifaceted Influence | Innovation and Research |
| | | Chapter 12. GeoAI | Residential Brokerage |
| Openpath Security, Inc. https://www. openpath.com/ | Openpath | Chapter 6. Modify the Property | Smart Buildings |
| OpenSpace https://www. openspace.ai/ | OpenSpace | Chapter 6. Modify the Property | Construction |
| Optimizely, Inc. https://www. optimizely.com/ | Optimizely | Chapter 8. Dispose of the Property | Sales and Marketing |
| Oracle Corporation https://www.oracle. com/ | MOAT Analytics | Chapter 5. Property Search | Optimized Advertising |
| | Oracle Hyperion Planning | Chapter 5. Property Search | Competitive Analysis |
| | Oracle Internet of Things Cloud Service | Chapter 6. Modify the Property | Construction |

| COMPANY | PRODUCT | BROAD CATEGORY | AI APPLICATION |
|---|---|---|---|
| | WaterSmart | Chapter 11. Multifaceted Influence | Sustainability |
| Orbit Irrigation Products, LLC https://www.orbitonline.com/ | Orbit B-hyve | Chapter 6. Modify the Property | Smart Homes |
| Orbital Insight, Inc. https://orbitalinsight.com/ | GO Platform | Chapter 12. GeoAI | Geospatial Integration |
| Oso Technologies, Inc. https://www.osotechnologies.com/ | PlantLink | Chapter 6. Modify the Property | Smart Homes |
| Outbrain, Inc. https://www.outbrain.com/ | Outbrain | Chapter 11. Multifaceted Influence | Content Generation |
| Outgrow https://outgrow.co/ | Outgrow | Chapter 8. Dispose of the Property | Brokerage |
| Pacvue, LLC https://www.pacvue.com/ | Pacvue | Chapter 5. Property Search | Optimized Advertising |
| PadSplit, Inc. https://padsplit.com/ | PadSplit | Chapter 11. Multifaceted Influence | Sustainability |
| PadStyler, LLC https://www.padstyler.com/ | PadStyler | Chapter 5. Property Search | Virtual Staging |
| Pametan AI https://www.pametan.ai/ | Self Supervised AI | Chapter 6. Modify the Property | Smart Buildings |
| Paperless Pipeline, LLC https://www.paperlesspipeline.com/ | Paperless Pipeline | Chapter 5. Property Search | Home Sales |

| COMPANY | PRODUCT | BROAD CATEGORY | AI APPLICATION |
|---|---|---|---|
| Parrot SA https://www.parrot.com/ | Parrot | Chapter 6. Modify the Property | Smart Homes |
| PayRent, LLC https://www.payrent.com/ | PayRent | Chapter 7. Manage the Property | Property Management |
| | | Chapter 7. Manage the Property | Tenant Management |
| PB Network UK https://www.pbnetwork.org.uk/ | PB Network UK | Chapter 9. Public Sector | Ethics and Regulations |
| Pearson Education, Inc. https://www.pearson.com/ | Aida | Chapter 10. Education | Education and Training |
| PeerStreet, Inc. https://www.peerstreet.com/ | PeerStreet | Chapter 6. Modify the Property | Real Estate Development |
| Pendo.io, Inc. https://www.Pendo.io/ | Pendo.io | Chapter 5. Property Search | Lead Generation |
| Persado, Inc. https://www.persado.com/ | Persado | Chapter 11. Multifaceted Influence | Content Generation |
| PhotoUp, Inc. https://www.photoup.net/ | PhotoUp | Chapter 5. Property Search | Virtual Staging |
| Phrasee Ltd. https://phrasee.co/ | Phrasee | Chapter 11. Multifaceted Influence | Content Generation |
| Phyn, LLC https://www.phyn.com/ | Phyn | Chapter 11. Multifaceted Influence | Sustainability |
| Picture It Settled, LLC https://pictureitsettled.com/ | Picture It Settled | Chapter 9. Public Sector | Law and Compliance |

| COMPANY | PRODUCT | BROAD CATEGORY | AI APPLICATION |
|---|---|---|---|
| Pillar Technologies Inc. https://www.pillartech.co/ | Pillar Technologies Pillar Technologies Inc. | Chapter 6. Modify the Property | Construction |
| Pinterest, Inc. https://www.pinterest.com/ | Pinterest | Chapter 6. Modify the Property | Architecture and Design |
| Pioneer Holding Inc. https://pioneertitleco.com/ | Pioneer Title | Chapter 8. Dispose of the Property | Title Services |
| Placer Labs, Inc. https://www.placer.ai/ | Placer.ai | Chapter 5. Property Search | Appraisal Management |
| | | Chapter 8. Dispose of the Property | Sales and Marketing |
| Placester, Inc. https://www.placester.com/ | Placester | Chapter 5. Property Search | Home Sales |
| | | Chapter 5. Property Search | Agent Management |
| | | Chapter 8. Dispose of the Property | Sales and Marketing |
| | | Chapter 12. GeoAI | Real-Time Analytics |
| PlagScan GmbH https://www.plagscan.com/en/ | PlagScan | Chapter 11. Multifaceted Influence | Content Generation |
| Planner 5D, UAB https://www.planner5d.com/ | Planner 5D | Chapter 5. Property Search | Virtual Staging |
| PlanRadar https://www.planradar.com/ | PlanRadar | Chapter 6. Modify the Property | Construction Management |
| | | Chapter 6. Modify the Property | Construction |
| PointGrab Ltd https://www.pointgrab.com/ | PointGrab | Chapter 6. Modify the Property | Smart Buildings |

| COMPANY | PRODUCT | BROAD CATEGORY | AI APPLICATION |
|---------|---------|----------------|----------------|
| PointPredictive, Inc. https://www.pointpredictive.com/ | PointPredictive | Chapter 5. Property Search | Mortgages |
| PointServ Technologies, Inc. https://www.pointserv.com/ | PointServ | Chapter 5. Property Search | Mortgages |
| Poli Technologies, Inc. https://www.politech.io/ | Poli | Chapter 9. Public Sector | Ethics and Regulations |
| Posit, PBC https://posit.co/ | RStudio | Chapter 11. Multifaceted Influence | Innovation and Research |
| Precisely Holdings, LLC https://www.precisely.com/ | Precisely | Chapter 5. Property Search | |
| | | Chapter 5. Property Search | |
| Preclose, Inc. https://www.preclose.com/ | Preclose | Chapter 5. Property Search | Lead Generation |
| Predictive Solutions Corporation https://www.predictivesolutions.com/ | Predictive Solutions | Chapter 6. Modify the Property | Construction Management |
| Prescient Co Inc. https://www.prescientco.com/ | Prescient | Chapter 6. Modify the Property | Construction |
| Presenso https://www.presenso.com/ | Presenso | Chapter 6. Modify the Property | Smart Buildings |
| Pricefx AG https://www.pricefx.com/ | Pricefx | Chapter 5. Property Search | Mortgage Automation |

| COMPANY | PRODUCT | BROAD CATEGORY | AI APPLICATION |
|---|---|---|---|
| Pricewaterhouse Coopers International Limited https://www.pwc.com/ | PwC Halo https://www.pwc.com/mu/en/services/assurance/risk-assurance/tech-assurance/general-ledger-audit.html | Chapter 11. Multifaceted Influence | Professional Services |
| | PwC Responsible AI https://www.pwc.com/gx/en/issues/data-and-analytics/artificial-intelligence/what-is-responsible-ai/pwc-responsible-ai-maturing-from-theory-to-practice.pdf | Chapter 11. Multifaceted Influence | Data and Analytics |
| Princeton University https://www.princeton.edu/ | Eviction Lab https://evictionlab.org/ | Chapter 11. Multifaceted Influence | Sustainability |
| Procore Technologies, Inc. https://www.procore.com/ | Procore | Chapter 6. Modify the Property | Construction Management |
| | | Chapter 12. GeoAI | Efficient Project Management |
| | | Chapter 12. GeoAI | Compliance and Regulations |
| Project Jupyter https://jupyter.org/ | Jupyter Notebook | Chapter 11. Multifaceted Influence | Innovation and Research |
| Property Base, Inc. https://www.propertybase.com/ | Property Base | Chapter 8. Dispose of the Property | Sales and Marketing |
| Property Radar https://www.propertyradar.com/ | Property Radar | Chapter 5. Property Search | Appraisal Management |

| COMPANY | PRODUCT | BROAD CATEGORY | AI APPLICATION |
|---|---|---|---|
| Propertybase https://www.propertybase.com/ | Propertybase | Chapter 8. Dispose of the Property | Brokerage |
| Propstack Services Private Limited https://www.propstack.com/ | Propstack | Chapter 5. Property Search | Competitive Analysis |
| | | Chapter 12. GeoAI | Global / India Perspectives |
| PropStream https://www.propstream.com/ | PropStream | Chapter 5. Property Search | Commercial Investment |
| | | Chapter 5. Property Search | Investment Analysis |
| | | Chapter 10. Education | Education and Training |
| | | Chapter 11. Multifaceted Influence | Sustainability |
| PropTech School https://proptechschool.com/ | PropTech School | Chapter 10. Education | Education and Training |
| PropTiger.com https://www.proptiger.com/ | PropTiger | Chapter 5. Property Search | Home Sales |
| | | Chapter 5. Property Search | Mortgage Automation |
| Propy, Inc. https://propy.com/ | Propy | Chapter 6. Modify the Property | Real Estate Development |
| Proxy, Inc. https://www.proxy.com/ | Proxy | Chapter 6. Modify the Property | Smart Buildings |
| PTC Inc. https://www.ptc.com/ | Vuforia Engine | Chapter 5. Property Search | 3D Modeling and AR |
| Qualia Labs, Inc. https://www.qualia.com/ | Qualia Assurance | Chapter 8. Dispose of the Property | Title Services |
| | Qualia Data | Chapter 8. Dispose of the Property | Title Services |

| COMPANY | PRODUCT | BROAD CATEGORY | AI APPLICATION |
|---|---|---|---|
| Quantarium, LLC https://www. quantarium.com/ | Quantarium Valuation Model (QVM) | Chapter 5. Property Search | Home Sales |
| | | Chapter 5. Property Search | Appraisal Management |
| | | Chapter 5. Property Search | Real Estate Investment |
| | | Chapter 5. Property Search | Financing and Mortgage |
| | TerraLook | Chapter 5. Property Search | 3D Modeling and AR |
| | | Chapter 5. Property Search | Real Estate Investment |
| Quetext, Inc. https://www.quetext. com/ | Quetext | Chapter 11. Multifaceted Influence | Content Generation |
| Quicken Loans https://www. quickenloans.com/ | Alexa, Pay My Rocket Mortgage https://alexa. rocketmortgage.com | Chapter 5. Property Search | Mortgages |
| | Pathfinder Rocket Mortgage https://www. rocketprotpo. com/resources/ pathfindertm-by- rocket/ | Chapter 5. Property Search | Home Sales |
| QuillBot, Inc. https://www.quillbot. com/ | QuillBot | Chapter 10. Education | Education and Training |
| Rachio, Inc. https://www.rachio. com/ | Rachio | Chapter 6. Modify the Property | Smart Homes |
| RapidMiner, Inc. https://www. rapidminer.com/ | RapidMiner | Chapter 5. Property Search | Commercial Investment |

| COMPANY | PRODUCT | BROAD CATEGORY | AI APPLICATION |
|---|---|---|---|
| RapidSOS, Inc. https://www.rapidsos.com/ | RapidSOS | Chapter 7. Manage the Property | Real Estate Security and Safety |
| Rasa Technologies, Inc. https://rasa.com/ | Rasa | Chapter 7. Manage the Property | Asset Management |
| | | Chapter 11. Multifaceted Influence | Chatbots |
| RateSpot https://www.ratespot.io/ | RateSpot | Chapter 5. Property Search | Mortgages |
| Real Capital Analytics, A MSCI Company https://www.rcanalytics.com/ | RCA Analytics | Chapter 5. Property Search | Commercial Investment |
| | | Chapter 5. Property Search | Investment Analysis |
| | | Chapter 11. Multifaceted Influence | Predictive Analytics |
| Real Estate Technology Institute https://reti.us/ | RETI | Chapter 10. Education | Education and Training |
| Real Geeks, LLC https://www.realgeeks.com/ | Real Geeks | Chapter 8. Dispose of the Property | Sales and Marketing |
| Reali, Inc. https://reali.com/ | Reali | Chapter 8. Dispose of the Property | Brokerage |
| RealNex, LLC https://realnex.com/ | Asset Management | Chapter 5. Property Search | Investment Analysis |
| RealPage, Inc. https://realpage.com/ | Axiometrics | Chapter 5. Property Search | Commercial Investment |
| | | Chapter 5. Property Search | Rental Property Search |
| | Propertyware | Chapter 11. Multifaceted Influence | Data and Analytics |

| COMPANY | PRODUCT | BROAD CATEGORY | AI APPLICATION |
|---|---|---|---|
| | RealPage | Chapter 5. Property Search | Investment Analysis |
| | | Chapter 11. Multifaceted Influence | Professional Services |
| | RealPage Investment Accounting | Chapter 7. Manage the Property | Asset Management |
| | | Chapter 5. Property Search | Lead Generation |
| | | Chapter 5. Property Search | Real Estate Leasing |
| | Rentlytics | Chapter 6. Modify the Property | Real Estate Development |
| | | Chapter 7. Manage the Property | Portfolio Management |
| Realtor.com https://www.realtor.com/ | Home Value | Chapter 8. Dispose of the Property | Valuation and Appraisal |
| | Realtor.com | Chapter 8. Dispose of the Property | Valuation and Appraisal |
| RealtyMogul.com, LLC https://www.realtymogul.com/ | RealtyMogul | Chapter 6. Modify the Property | Real Estate Development |
| RealtyShares, Inc. https://www.realtyshares.com/ | RealtyShares | Chapter 6. Modify the Property | Real Estate Development |
| RealtyTrac https://www.realtytrac.com/ | RealtyTrac | Chapter 11. Multifaceted Influence | Predictive Analytics |
| Realvolve, LLC https://www.realvolve.com/ | Realvolve | Chapter 8. Dispose of the Property | Sales and Marketing |
| ReaLync Corporation https://www.realync.com/ | ReaLync | Chapter 5. Property Search | Real Estate Investment |

| COMPANY | PRODUCT | BROAD CATEGORY | AI APPLICATION |
|---|---|---|---|
| Realyse https://www.realyse.com/ | REalyse | Chapter 11. Multifaceted Influence | Innovation and Research |
| Rechat, Inc. https://www.rechat.com/ | Rechat | Chapter 8. Dispose of the Property | Sales and Marketing |
| RECON Dynamics https://www.recondynamics.com/ | Pillar https://pillar.tech/ | Chapter 6. Modify the Property | Construction Management |
| RecycleBank https://recyclebank.com/ | RecycleBank | Chapter 11. Multifaceted Influence | Sustainability |
| Recycleye, Ltd. https://recycleye.com/ | Recycleye | Chapter 11. Multifaceted Influence | Sustainability |
| Redfin Corporation https://www.redfin.com/ | Redfin | Chapter 5. Property Search | Home Sales |
| | | Chapter 8. Dispose of the Property | Valuation and Appraisal |
| | | Chapter 11. Multifaceted Influence | Content Generation |
| | | Chapter 11. Multifaceted Influence | Innovation and Research |
| | | Chapter 12. GeoAI | Customized Recommendations |
| | | Chapter 7. Manage the Property | Portfolio Management |
| | Redfin Estimate | Chapter 8. Dispose of the Property | Valuation and Appraisal |
| | | Chapter 11. Multifaceted Influence | Predictive Analytics |

| COMPANY | PRODUCT | BROAD CATEGORY | AI APPLICATION |
| --- | --- | --- | --- |
| | | Chapter 11. Multifaceted Influence | Data and Analytics |
| | Redfin Real Estate Partnership | Chapter 11. Multifaceted Influence | Sustainability |
| Reggora, Inc. https://www.reggora.com/ | Reggora | Chapter 5. Property Search | Mortgages |
| Regrid https://regrid.com/ | Regrid | Chapter 6. Modify the Property | Real Estate Development |
| | | Chapter 12. GeoAI | Compliance and Regulations |
| Rehearsal VRP, Inc. https://www.rehearsal.com/ | Rehearsal | Chapter 5. Property Search | Agent Management |
| REimagineHome https://reimaginehome.com/ | REimagineHome | Chapter 8. Dispose of the Property | Sales and Marketing |
| Reinform, Inc. https://www.structurely.com/ | Structurely | Chapter 5. Property Search | Agent Management |
| | | Chapter 5. Property Search | Lead Generation |
| | | Chapter 8. Dispose of the Property | Sales and Marketing |
| | | Chapter 11. Multifaceted Influence | Predictive Analytics |
| | | Chapter 11. Multifaceted Influence | Chatbots |
| Relativity ODA LLC https://www.relativity.com/ | Relativity | Chapter 9. Public Sector | Law and Compliance |

| COMPANY | PRODUCT | BROAD CATEGORY | AI APPLICATION |
|---|---|---|---|
| Remine, Inc. https://www.remine.com/ | Remine | Chapter 11. Multifaceted Influence | Innovation and Research |
| | | Chapter 12. GeoAI | Predictive Location Analytics |
| Rent Manager, LLC https://www.rentmanager.com/ | Resident App by Rent Manager | Chapter 7. Manage the Property | Tenant Management |
| Rentberry, Inc. https://rentberry.com/ | Rentberry | Chapter 5. Property Search | Real Estate Leasing |
| | | Chapter 7. Manage the Property | Property Management |
| | | Chapter 7. Manage the Property | Tenant Management |
| Rentec Direct, LLC https://www.rentecdirect.com/ | Rentec Direct | Chapter 5. Property Search | Rental Property Search |
| | | Chapter 7. Manage the Property | Property Management |
| | | Chapter 7. Manage the Property | Tenant Management |
| Renthop.com https://www.renthop.com/ | RentHop | Chapter 5. Property Search | Rental Property Search |
| | Rentometer Pro | Chapter 5. Property Search | Rental Property Search |
| RentHub https://www.renthub.com/ | RentHub | Chapter 5. Property Search | Real Estate Leasing |
| Rentler, Inc. https://www.rentler.com/ | Rentler | Chapter 7. Manage the Property | Property Management |
| | | Chapter 7. Manage the Property | Tenant Management |
| Rentlogic, Inc. https://www.rentlogic.com/ | Rentlogic | Chapter 5. Property Search | Real Estate Leasing |

| COMPANY | PRODUCT | BROAD CATEGORY | AI APPLICATION |
|---|---|---|---|
| Rentometer, Inc. https://www. rentometer.com/ | Rent Estimate | Chapter 5. Property Search | Rental Property Search |
| | Rentometer | Chapter 6. Modify the Property | Real Estate Development |
| | Rentometer Pro | Chapter 5. Property Search | Real Estate Leasing |
| RentPath, LLC https://www.rentpath. com/ | Rent.com | Chapter 5. Property Search | Rental Property Search |
| | | Chapter 5. Property Search | Real Estate Leasing |
| | | Chapter 11. Multifaceted Influence | Data and Analytics |
| RentPrep, a Roofstock Company https://rentprep.com/ | RentPrep | Chapter 5. Property Search | Real Estate Leasing |
| | | Chapter 7. Manage the Property | Property Management |
| | | Chapter 7. Manage the Property | Tenant Management |
| RentRange, LLC https://www. rentrange.com/ | RentRange | Chapter 5. Property Search | Rental Property Search |
| | | Chapter 5. Property Search | Real Estate Leasing |
| RentRedi, Inc. https://rentredi.com/ | RentRedi | Chapter 7. Manage the Property | Property Management |
| | | Chapter 7. Manage the Property | Tenant Management |
| RentSpree, LLC https://www. rentspree.com/ | RentSpree | Chapter 5. Property Search | Real Estate Leasing |
| Reonomy, an Altus Group Company https://www.reonomy. com/ | Reonomy | Chapter 5. Property Search | Commercial Investment |
| | | Chapter 5. Property Search | Investment Analysis |

| COMPANY | PRODUCT | BROAD CATEGORY | AI APPLICATION |
|---|---|---|---|
| | | Chapter 5. Property Search | Appraisal Management |
| | | Chapter 5. Property Search | Lead Generation |
| | | Chapter 5. Property Search | Real Estate Investment |
| | | Chapter 5. Property Search | Real Estate Leasing |
| | | Chapter 6. Modify the Property | Real Estate Development |
| | | Chapter 7. Manage the Property | Property Management |
| | | Chapter 7. Manage the Property | Portfolio Management |
| | | Chapter 8. Dispose of the Property | Sales and Marketing |
| | | Chapter 11. Multifaceted Influence | Predictive Analytics |
| | | Chapter 11. Multifaceted Influence | Professional Services |
| | | Chapter 11. Multifaceted Influence | Innovation and Research |
| | | Chapter 12. GeoAI | Market Insights and Analytics |
| Rephrase Corp. https://www.rephrase.ai/ | Rephrase.ai | Chapter 11. Multifaceted Influence | Content Generation |
| Resident, Inc. https://www.residenthome.com/ | Resident | Chapter 7. Manage the Property | Tenant Management |

| COMPANY | PRODUCT | BROAD CATEGORY | AI APPLICATION |
|---|---|---|---|
| Resideo Technologies, Inc. https://www.resideo.com/ | Honeywell Home | Chapter 6. Modify the Property | Smart Homes |
| Restb.ai https://restb.ai/ | Restb.ai | Chapter 8. Dispose of the Property | Sales and Marketing |
| | Restb.ai | Chapter 8. Dispose of the Property | Brokerage |
| | Restb.ai Appraisal Suite | Chapter 5. Property Search | Appraisal Management |
| Retain.ai, Inc. https://www.retain.ai/ | Retain.ai | Chapter 11. Multifaceted Influence | Predictive Analytics |
| Revaluate, Inc. https://revaluate.com/ | Revaluate | Chapter 5. Property Search | Real Estate Investment |
| | Revaluate | Chapter 8. Dispose of the Property | Sales and Marketing |
| | Revaluate | Chapter 8. Dispose of the Property | Brokerage |
| | Revaluate | Chapter 11. Multifaceted Influence | Predictive Analytics |
| Reveal Data Corporation https://www.revealdata.com/ | Reveal | Chapter 9. Public Sector | Law and Compliance |
| REX - Real Estate Exchange, Inc. https://www.rexhomes.com/ | Rex Platform | Chapter 12. GeoAI | Residential Brokerage |
| | TitleGenius | Chapter 8. Dispose of the Property | Title Services |
| Rhombus Systems, Inc. https://www.rhombussystems.com/ | Rhombus Systems | Chapter 7. Manage the Property | Real Estate Security and Safety |

| COMPANY | PRODUCT | BROAD CATEGORY | AI APPLICATION |
|---|---|---|---|
| Ricoh Company, Ltd. https://www. ricoh360.com/ | RICOH360 Tours | Chapter 5. Property Search | Real Estate Leasing |
| Rifiniti, Inc. https://www.rifiniti. com/ | Rifiniti | Chapter 6. Modify the Property | Smart Buildings |
| Riskalyze, Inc. https://www.riskalyze. com/ | Riskalyze | Chapter 7. Manage the Property | Portfolio Management |
| | | Chapter 7. Manage the Property | Asset Management |
| Riskcast Solutions Inc. https://www.riskcast. com/ | Riskcast | Chapter 6. Modify the Property | Construction Management |
| RiskFirst Group Limited https://www.riskfirst. com/ | RiskFirst PFaroe DB Solution Suite | Chapter 7. Manage the Property | Portfolio Management |
| | | Chapter 7. Manage the Property | Asset Management |
| RiskSpan, Inc. https://www.riskspan. com/ | RiskSpan Edge Platform | Chapter 7. Manage the Property | Portfolio Management |
| | | Chapter 7. Manage the Property | Asset Management |
| Rival IQ Corporation https://www.rivaliq. com/ | Rival IQ | Chapter 5. Property Search | Competitive Analysis |
| Robert Bosch GmbH https://www.bosch. com/ | Bosch Connected Control | Chapter 6. Modify the Property | Smart Homes |
| Robert McNeel & Associates https://www.rhino3d. com/ | Grasshopper | Chapter 6. Modify the Property | Architecture and Design |
| | Rhino.Inside.Revit | Chapter 6. Modify the Property | Architecture and Design |
| | Rhino3D | Chapter 6. Modify the Property | Architecture and Design |

| COMPANY | PRODUCT | BROAD CATEGORY | AI APPLICATION |
|---|---|---|---|
| Roborock Technology Co., Ltd. https://www.roborock.com/ | Roborock | Chapter 6. Modify the Property | Smart Homes |
| Robot Lawyer LISA https://www.robotlawyerlisa.com/ | LISA | Chapter 9. Public Sector | Ethics and Regulations |
| | LISA's Property Tools | Chapter 6. Modify the Property | Real Estate Development |
| Rocket Lawyer Incorporated https://www.rocketlawyer.com/ | Rocket Lawyer | Chapter 11. Multifaceted Influence | Professional Services |
| Rocky Mountain Institute https://rmi.org/ | Rocky Mountain Institute | Chapter 11. Multifaceted Influence | Sustainability |
| Roku, Inc. https://www.roku.com/ | Roku | Chapter 6. Modify the Property | Smart Homes |
| Roof AI, Inc. https://www.roof.ai/ | Roof AI | Chapter 5. Property Search | Agent Management |
| | | Chapter 11. Multifaceted Influence | Predictive Analytics |
| | | Chapter 11. Multifaceted Influence | Chatbots |
| Roofr, Inc. https://roofr.com/ | Roofr | Chapter 11. Multifaceted Influence | Sustainability |
| Roofstock, Inc. https://www.roofstock.com/ | Roofstock | Chapter 6. Modify the Property | Real Estate Development |
| | | Chapter 8. Dispose of the Property | Brokerage |
| Roomstyler, BV https://www.roomstyler.com/ | Roomstyler | Chapter 5. Property Search | Virtual Staging |

| COMPANY | PRODUCT | BROAD CATEGORY | AI APPLICATION |
|---|---|---|---|
| Rooomy, Inc. https://www.rooomy.com/ | Rooomy | Chapter 5. Property Search | Virtual Staging |
| | | Chapter 5. Property Search | Real Estate Leasing |
| Roostify, Inc. https://www.roostify.com/ | Eve | Chapter 5. Property Search | Mortgages |
| | | Chapter 11. Multifaceted Influence | Chatbots |
| | Roostify | Chapter 5. Property Search | Financing and Mortgage |
| ROSS Intelligence, Inc. https://rossintelligence.com/ | ROSS Intelligence | Chapter 9. Public Sector | Law and Compliance |
| | | Chapter 11. Multifaceted Influence | Professional Services |
| Rulai https://www.rul.ai/ | Rulai | Chapter 8. Dispose of the Property | Brokerage |
| Safesite https://www.safesitehq.com/ | Safesite | Chapter 6. Modify the Property | Construction Management |
| | | Chapter 6. Modify the Property | Construction |
| SafetyApp, LLC https://www.safetyapp.com/ | SafetyApp | Chapter 7. Manage the Property | Real Estate Security and Safety |
| SafetyCulture https://www.safetyculture.com/ | SafetyCulture | Chapter 6. Modify the Property | Construction |
| Salesforce.com, Inc. https://www.salesforce.com/ | Ethical Explorer | Chapter 9. Public Sector | Ethics and Regulations |
| Samsung Electronics Co., Ltd. https://www.samsung.com/ | Bixby | Chapter 6. Modify the Property | Smart Homes |
| | SmartThings | Chapter 6. Modify the Property | Smart Homes |

| COMPANY | PRODUCT | BROAD CATEGORY | AI APPLICATION |
|---------|---------|----------------|----------------|
| SAP SE https://www.sap.com/ | SAP Marketing Cloud | Chapter 5. Property Search | Competitive Analysis |
| | SAP Risk Management | Chapter 7. Manage the Property | Portfolio Management |
| | | Chapter 7. Manage the Property | Asset Management |
| SAS Institute https://www.sas.com/ | SAS Customer Intelligence 360 | Chapter 5. Property Search | Competitive Analysis |
| | SAS Fraud Management | Chapter 5. Property Search | Mortgage Automation |
| | | Chapter 11. Multifaceted Influence | Predictive Analytics |
| | SAS Risk Management for Banking | Chapter 7. Manage the Property | Portfolio Management |
| | SAS Risk Management Software | Chapter 7. Manage the Property | Asset Management |
| | SAS Visual Analytics | Chapter 11. Multifaceted Influence | Data and Analytics |
| Scienaptic Systems, Inc. https://www.scienaptic.ai/ | Scienaptic | Chapter 5. Property Search | Financing and Mortgage |
| Sellozo, Inc. https://www.sellozo.com/ | Sellozo | Chapter 5. Property Search | Optimized Advertising |
| Semrush Holdings, Inc. https://www.semrush.com/ | Semrush | Chapter 11. Multifaceted Influence | Content Generation |

| COMPANY | PRODUCT | BROAD CATEGORY | AI APPLICATION |
|---|---|---|---|
| Sengled Optoelectronics Co., Ltd. https://www.sengled.com/ | Sengled | Chapter 6. Modify the Property | Smart Homes |
| Sense Labs, Inc. https://sense.com/ | Sense | Chapter 11. Multifaceted Influence | Sustainability |
| Senseye Ltd https://www.senseye.io/ | Senseye | Chapter 6. Modify the Property | Smart Buildings |
| Sensopia Inc. https://www.magicplan.app/ | MagicPlan | Chapter 6. Modify the Property | Construction Management |
| Sentieo, Inc. https://www.sentieo.com/ | Sentieo | Chapter 8. Dispose of the Property | Brokerage |
| Sephora USA, Inc. https://www.sephora.com/ | Sephora Virtual Artist | Chapter 5. Property Search | 3D Modeling and AR |
| SFREP, Inc. https://www.sfrep.com/ | Appraise-It Pro | Chapter 5. Property Search | Appraisal Management |
| SharperLending Solutions, LLC https://sharperlending.co/ | Appraisal Firewall | Chapter 5. Property Search  Chapter 8. Dispose of the Property | Appraisal Management  Valuation and Appraisal |
| | Comfy | Chapter 6. Modify the Property | Smart Buildings |
| Siemens AG https://www.siemens.com/ | Siemens | Chapter 11. Multifaceted Influence | Sustainability |
| | Siemens Digital Enterprise Suite | Chapter 6. Modify the Property | Construction |

| COMPANY | PRODUCT | BROAD CATEGORY | AI APPLICATION |
|---|---|---|---|
| Sift Science, Inc. https://www.sift.com/ | Sift | Chapter 5. Property Search | Mortgage Automation |
| Sightly Enterprises, Inc. https://www.sightly.com/ | Sightly Brand Safety Intelligence (BSI) | Chapter 5. Property Search | Optimized Advertising |
| Signify Holding https://www.signify.com/ | Philips Hue | Chapter 6. Modify the Property | Smart Homes |
| Silent Beacon, LLC https://www.silentbeacon.com/ | Silent Beacon | Chapter 7. Manage the Property | Real Estate Security and Safety |
| SimilarWeb Ltd. https://www.similarweb.com/ | SimilarWeb | Chapter 5. Property Search | Competitive Analysis |
| SimpliSafe, Inc. https://www.simplisafe.com/ | SimpliSafe | Chapter 6. Modify the Property | Smart Homes |
| | | Chapter 7. Manage the Property | Real Estate Security and Safety |
| Sisu, Inc. https://www.sisu.co/ | Sisu | Chapter 5. Property Search | Agent Management |
| SiteAware, Inc. https://www.siteaware.com/ | SiteAware | Chapter 6. Modify the Property | Construction Management |
| | | Chapter 6. Modify the Property | Construction |
| | | Chapter 7. Manage the Property | Real Estate Security and Safety |
| Sitely, LLC https://www.sitely.ai/ | Sitely | Chapter 6. Modify the Property | Real Estate Development |
| SiteSeer https://www.siteseer.com/ | SiteSeer Pro | Chapter 6. Modify the Property | Real Estate Development |
| SiteZeus, Inc. https://sitezeus.com/ | SiteZeus Platform | Chapter 12. GeoAI | Site Selection and Development |

| COMPANY | PRODUCT | BROAD CATEGORY | AI APPLICATION |
|---|---|---|---|
| Sketchfab Inc. https://www. sketchfab.com/ | Sketchfab | Chapter 5. Property Search | 3D Modeling and AR |
| Skillshare, Inc. https://www. skillshare.com/ | Skillshare | Chapter 10. Education | Education and Training |
| Skyline AI Ltd. https://www.skyline. ai/ | Skyline AI | Chapter 5. Property Search | Commercial Investment |
| | | Chapter 5. Property Search | Investment Analysis |
| | | Chapter 12. GeoAI | Site Selection and Development |
| SkySlope, Inc. https://www. skyslope.com/ | SkySlope | Chapter 5. Property Search | Home Sales |
| Smacc GmbH https://www.smacc. com/ | Smacc | Chapter 11. Multifaceted Influence | Professional Services |
| Small Change, LLC https://www. smallchange.com/ | Small Change | Chapter 6. Modify the Property | Real Estate Development |
| Smart Sparrow Pty Ltd. https://www. smartsparrow.com/ | Smart Sparrow | Chapter 10. Education | Education and Training |
| SmartPM Technologies, Inc. https://www. smartpmtech.com/ | SmartPM | Chapter 6. Modify the Property | Construction Management |
| SmartTek, LLC https://smarttek. solutions/ | VR/AR Solutions | Chapter 5. Property Search | 3D Modeling and AR |
| SmartZip Analytics, Inc. https://www.smartzip. com/ | SmartZip | Chapter 5. Property Search | Home Sales |

| COMPANY | PRODUCT | BROAD CATEGORY | AI APPLICATION |
|---|---|---|---|
| | | Chapter 5. Property Search | Agent Management |
| | | Chapter 8. Dispose of the Property | Sales and Marketing |
| | | Chapter 8. Dispose of the Property | Brokerage |
| Snap Inc. https://www.snap.com/ | Snapchat Lenses | Chapter 5. Property Search | 3D Modeling and AR |
| Snapdocs, Inc. https://www.snapdocs.com/ | eClosing | Chapter 8. Dispose of the Property | Title Services |
| SnapEngage https://snapengage.com/ | SnapEngage | Chapter 8. Dispose of the Property | Brokerage |
| Social Finance, Inc. https://www.sofi.com/ | SoFi | Chapter 11. Multifaceted Influence | Sustainability |
| SocialBee https://socialbee.com/ | SocialBee | Chapter 8. Dispose of the Property | Brokerage |
| Solibri, Inc. https://www.solibri.com/ | Solibri | Chapter 6. Modify the Property | Architecture and Design |
| SolidWorks Corporation, Dassault Systèmes SE Company https://www.solidworks.com/ | SolidWorks | Chapter 6. Modify the Property | Construction Management |
| | | Chapter 6. Modify the Property | Architecture and Design |
| Sonos, Inc. https://www.sonos.com/ | Sonos | Chapter 6. Modify the Property | Smart Homes |
| SpaceIQ, Inc. https://www.spaceiq.com/ | SpaceIQ | Chapter 6. Modify the Property | Smart Buildings |

| COMPANY | PRODUCT | BROAD CATEGORY | AI APPLICATION |
|---|---|---|---|
| Spaceti s.r.o. https://www.spaceti.com/ | Spaceti | Chapter 6. Modify the Property | Smart Buildings |
| Spacewell NV https://www.spacewell.com/ | Spacewell | Chapter 6. Modify the Property | Smart Buildings |
| SparkCognition, Inc. https://www.sparkcognition.com/ | SparkCognition | Chapter 6. Modify the Property | Smart Buildings |
| Spotify AB https://www.spotify.com/ | Spotify | Chapter 6. Modify the Property | Smart Homes |
| Spotless Agency, LLC https://www.spotlessagency.com/ | Spotless Agency | Chapter 5. Property Search | Virtual Staging |
| Springer https://link.springer.com/ | Journal of Real Estate Finance and Economics https://link.springer.com/journal/11146 | Chapter 11. Multifaceted Influence | Innovation and Research |
| Spruce Holdings, Inc. https://www.spruce.co/ | Title Report | Chapter 8. Dispose of the Property | Title Services |
| Square Yards Consulting Private Limited https://www.squareyards.com/ | Edge | Chapter 5. Property Search | Real Estate Investment |
| Squirrel AI Learning by Yixue Group https://www.squirrelai.com/ | Squirrel AI | Chapter 10. Education | Education and Training |
| Starcity Properties, Inc. https://www.starcity.com/ | Starcity | Chapter 11. Multifaceted Influence | Sustainability |

| COMPANY | PRODUCT | BROAD CATEGORY | AI APPLICATION |
|---|---|---|---|
| StarTex Software https://www.startexsoftware.com/ | EHS Insight | Chapter 6. Modify the Property | Construction |
| States Title https://statestitle.com/ | States Title | Chapter 8. Dispose of the Property | Title Services |
| States Title Holding, Inc. https://www.statestitle.com/ | Title Report | Chapter 8. Dispose of the Property | Title Services |
| StreamLabs https://streamlabs.com/ | StreamLabs | Chapter 11. Multifaceted Influence | Sustainability |
| StructionSite https://www.structionsite.com/ | StructionSite | Chapter 6. Modify the Property | Construction |
| SurveyMonkey, Inc. https://www.surveymonkey.com/ | Tenant Satisfaction Survey | Chapter 7. Manage the Property | Tenant Management |
| Switch Automation Pty Ltd https://www.switchautomation.com/ | Switch Automation | Chapter 6. Modify the Property | Smart Buildings |
| | | Chapter 11. Multifaceted Influence | Sustainability |
| Sygno https://www.sygno.com/ | Sygno | Chapter 5. Property Search | Financing and Mortgage |
| Tableau Software, LLC. https://www.tableau.com/ | Narrative Science | Chapter 11. Multifaceted Influence | Data and Analytics |
| Taboola https://www.taboola.com/ | Taboola | Chapter 11. Multifaceted Influence | Content Generation |

| COMPANY | PRODUCT | BROAD CATEGORY | AI APPLICATION |
|---|---|---|---|
| Tado GmbH https://www.tado.com/ | Tado Smart Thermostat | Chapter 6. Modify the Property | Smart Homes |
| Tango https://www.tangoanalytics.com/ | Tango | Chapter 6. Modify the Property | Smart Buildings |
| | | Chapter 6. Modify the Property | Real Estate Development |
| Ten-X, LLC https://www.ten-x.com/ | Ten-X Commercial | Chapter 5. Property Search | Commercial Investment |
| | | Chapter 5. Property Search | Investment Analysis |
| Tenant Turner, Inc. https://www.tenantturner.com/ | Tenant Turner | Chapter 5. Property Search | Rental Property Search |
| | | Chapter 7. Manage the Property | Tenant Management |
| TenantBase, Inc. https://www.tenantbase.com/ | TenantBase | Chapter 7. Manage the Property | Tenant Management |
| TenantCloud, LLC https://www.tenantcloud.com/ | TenantCloud | Chapter 5. Property Search | Rental Property Search |
| | | Chapter 5. Property Search | Real Estate Investment |
| | | Chapter 5. Property Search | Real Estate Leasing |
| | | Chapter 7. Manage the Property | Property Management |
| | | Chapter 7. Manage the Property | Tenant Management |
| TenantLoop, LLC https://www.tenantloop.com/ | TenantLoop | Chapter 7. Manage the Property | Tenant Management |
| The Alan Turing Institute https://www.turing.ac.uk/ | The Alan Turing Institute | Chapter 9. Public Sector | Ethics and Regulations |

| COMPANY | PRODUCT | BROAD CATEGORY | AI APPLICATION |
|---|---|---|---|
| The GovLab https://www.thegovlab.org/ | The GovLab | Chapter 9. Public Sector | Ethics and Regulations |
| The IEEE Global Initiative on Ethics of Autonomous and Intelligent Systems https://www.ethicsinaction.ieee.org/ | The IEEE Global Initiative on Ethics of Autonomous and Intelligent Systems | Chapter 9. Public Sector | Ethics and Regulations |
| The Partnership on AI https://www.partnershiponai.org/ | The Partnership on AI | Chapter 9. Public Sector | Ethics and Regulations |
| The Trade Desk, Inc. https://www.thetradedesk.com/ | The Trade Desk | Chapter 5. Property Search | Optimized Advertising |
| The Urban Institute https://www.urban.org/ | Urban Institute | Chapter 11. Multifaceted Influence | Sustainability |
| The Wise Agent https://wiseagent.com/ | Wise Agent | Chapter 5. Property Search | Lead Generation |
| | | Chapter 5. Property Search | Mortgages |
| Thinkster Math https://www.hellothinkster.com/ | Thinkster Math | Chapter 10. Education | Education and Training |
| Thomson Reuters https://legal.thomsonreuters.com/ | Westlaw | Chapter 9. Public Sector | Dispute Resolution |
| | | Chapter 9. Public Sector | Law and Compliance |
| Thomson Reuters Corporation https://www.thomsonreuters.com/ | Thomson Reuters | Chapter 11. Multifaceted Influence | Professional Services |

| COMPANY | PRODUCT | BROAD CATEGORY | AI APPLICATION |
|---|---|---|---|
| ThoughtTrace https://www.thoughttrace.com/ | ThoughtTrace | Chapter 8. Dispose of the Property | Brokerage |
| Tinuiti, Inc. https://www.tinuiti.com/ | Tinuiti Amazon Marketing Services (AMS) | Chapter 5. Property Search | Optimized Advertising |
| Title Forward, LLC https://www.titleforward.com/ | Title Report | Chapter 8. Dispose of the Property | Title Services |
| TitleCapture, LLC https://www.titlecapture.com/ | Title Search | Chapter 8. Dispose of the Property | Title Services |
| TitleWave Real Estate Solutions https://www.titlewave.com/ | TitleWave | Chapter 8. Dispose of the Property | Title Services |
| Tobii Dynavox LLC https://www.tobiidynavox.com/ | Tobii Dynavox Snap Core First | Chapter 10. Education | Education and Training |
| TopHap, Inc. https://www.tophap.com/ | TopHap | Chapter 8. Dispose of the Property | Brokerage |
| TotallyMoney Limited https://www.totallymoney.com/ | TotallyMoney | Chapter 5. Property Search | Mortgages |
| TP-Link Technologies Co., Ltd. https://www.tp-link.com/ | TP-Link Kasa | Chapter 6. Modify the Property | Smart Homes |
| TracFlo Inc. https://www.tracfloapp.com/ | TracFlo | Chapter 6. Modify the Property | Construction Management |
| Trackunit A/S https://www.trackunit.com/ | Trackunit | Chapter 6. Modify the Property | Construction Management |

| COMPANY | PRODUCT | BROAD CATEGORY | AI APPLICATION |
|---|---|---|---|
| Trimble Inc. https://www.trimble.com/ | SketchUp https://www.sketchup.com/ | Chapter 6. Modify the Property | Construction |
| | | Chapter 11. Multifaceted Influence | Professional Services |
| | Trimble Connect https://connect.trimble.com/ | Chapter 6. Modify the Property | Construction Management |
| | Trimble Construction https://construction.trimble.com/ | Chapter 11. Multifaceted Influence | Professional Services |
| Trulia, LLC https://www.trulia.com/ | Trulia | Chapter 8. Dispose of the Property | Brokerage |
| TurboTenant, Inc. https://turbotenant.com/ | TurboTenant | Chapter 5. Property Search | Rental Property Search |
| | | Chapter 5. Property Search | Real Estate Leasing |
| | | Chapter 7. Manage the Property | Property Management |
| | | Chapter 7. Manage the Property | Tenant Management |
| Turnitin, LLC https://www.turnitin.com/ | Turnitin | Chapter 11. Multifaceted Influence | Content Generation |
| TurnKey Lender Pte Ltd https://www.turnkey-lender.com/ | TurnKey Lender | Chapter 5. Property Search | Financing and Mortgage |
| Tyler Technologies, Inc. https://www.tylertech.com/ | Modria | Chapter 9. Public Sector | Law and Compliance |

| COMPANY | PRODUCT | BROAD CATEGORY | AI APPLICATION |
|---|---|---|---|
| U.S. Department of Energy https://www.energy.gov/ | Better Buildings Initiative | Chapter 7. Manage the Property | Property Management |
| U.S. Green Building Council https://www.usgbc.org/ | LEED | Chapter 11. Multifaceted Influence | Sustainability |
| Ubitquity, LLC https://ubitquity.io/ | Ubitquity | Chapter 6. Modify the Property | Real Estate Development |
| Udacity, Inc. https://www.udacity.com/ | Udacity | Chapter 10. Education | Education and Training |
| Udemy, Inc. https://www.udemy.com/ | Udemy | Chapter 10. Education | Education and Training |
| Umbo Computer Vision, Inc. https://www.umbocv.com/ | Umbo AiCameras | Chapter 7. Manage the Property | Real Estate Security and Safety |
| Unbounce Marketing Solutions, Inc. https://unbounce.com/ | Unbounce | Chapter 8. Dispose of the Property | Sales and Marketing |
| Unity Technologies ApS https://www.unity.com/ | Unity | Chapter 5. Property Search | 3D Modeling and AR |
| University of Oxford https://www.oii.ox.ac.uk/ | Oxford Internet Institute | Chapter 9. Public Sector | Ethics and Regulations |
| University of Pennsylvania https://www.upenn.edu/ | ScholarlyCommons https://www.library.upenn.edu/services/scholarlycommons/ | Chapter 11. Multifaceted Influence | Innovation and Research |

| COMPANY | PRODUCT | BROAD CATEGORY | AI APPLICATION |
|---|---|---|---|
| Upstart Network, Inc. https://www.upstart.com/ | Upstart | Chapter 5. Property Search | Financing and Mortgage |
| Uptake Technologies, Inc. https://www.uptake.com/ | Uptake | Chapter 6. Modify the Property | Construction Management |
| | | Chapter 6. Modify the Property | Smart Buildings |
| Urban AI https://urbanai.fr/ | Urban AI | Chapter 11. Multifaceted Influence | Innovation and Research |
| Urban Displacement Project https://www.urbandisplacement.org/ | Urban Displacement Project | Chapter 11. Multifaceted Influence | Sustainability |
| Urban Institute https://www.urban.org/ | Urban Institute | Chapter 11. Multifaceted Influence | Innovation and Research |
| Valcre, LLC https://www.valcre.com/ | Valcre | Chapter 5. Property Search | Commercial Investment |
| | | Chapter 5. Property Search | Investment Analysis |
| ValPal https://valpal.com/ | ValPal | Chapter 8. Dispose of the Property | Sales and Marketing |
| ValueLink Software https://valuelinksoftware.com/ | CrossCheck | Chapter 5. Property Search | Appraisal Management |
| | ValueLink QC | Chapter 5. Property Search | Appraisal Management |
| ValuTrac Software, Inc. https://www.valutracsoftware.com/ | ValuTrac | Chapter 5. Property Search | Appraisal Management |

| COMPANY | PRODUCT | BROAD CATEGORY | AI APPLICATION |
|---|---|---|---|
| VantageScore Solutions, LLC https://www.vantagescore.com/ | VantageScore | Chapter 5. Property Search | Mortgages |
| Verdigris Technologies, Inc. https://www.verdigris.co/ | Verdigris | Chapter 6. Modify the Property | Smart Buildings |
| | | Chapter 11. Multifaceted Influence | Sustainability |
| VergeSense https://www.vergesense.com/ | VergeSense | Chapter 6. Modify the Property | Smart Buildings |
| | | Chapter 6. Modify the Property | Construction |
| Veritone, Inc. https://www.veritone.com/ | Veritone | Chapter 9. Public Sector | Law and Compliance |
| Verkada, Inc. https://www.verkada.com/ | Verkada | Chapter 6. Modify the Property | Smart Buildings |
| | | Chapter 7. Manage the Property | Real Estate Security and Safety |
| Veros Real Estate Solutions, LLC. https://www.veros.com/ | Veros PATHWAY | Chapter 5. Property Search | Appraisal Management |
| | VeroVALUE | Chapter 5. Property Search | Appraisal Management |
| | | Chapter 5. Property Search | Lead Generation |
| Verse, Inc. https://agentology.verse.io/ | Agentology | Chapter 8. Dispose of the Property | Sales and Marketing |
| | | Chapter 11. Multifaceted Influence | Chatbots |
| VHT Studios, Inc. https://www.vht.com/ | VHT Studios | Chapter 5. Property Search | Virtual Staging |

| COMPANY | PRODUCT | BROAD CATEGORY | AI APPLICATION |
|---|---|---|---|
| Vintra, Inc. https://www.vintra.io/ | Vintra | Chapter 6. Modify the Property | Smart Buildings |
| | | Chapter 7. Manage the Property | Real Estate Security and Safety |
| Virtual Staging AI https://www. virtualstagingai.app/ | Virtual Staging AI | Chapter 5. Property Search | Virtual Staging |
| Virtual Staging Lab https://www. virtualstaginglab. com/ | Virtual Staging Lab | Chapter 5. Property Search | Virtual Staging |
| Virtual Staging Solutions https://www. virtualstaging solutions.com/ | Virtual Staging Solutions | Chapter 5. Property Search | Virtual Staging |
| Virtually Staging Properties https://www. virtuallystaging properties.com/ | Virtually Staging Properties | Chapter 5. Property Search | Virtual Staging |
| Virtuance, LLC https://www. virtuance.com/ | Virtuance | Chapter 5. Property Search | Virtual Staging |
| Vistaar Technologies, Inc. https://www.vistaar. com/ | Vistaar Technologies | Chapter 5. Property Search | Mortgage Automation |
| | | Chapter 5. Property Search | Agent Management |
| Vivint https://www.vivint. com/ | Vivint Smart Home | Chapter 7. Manage the Property | Real Estate Security and Safety |
| VocalEyes Digital Democracy Ltd. https://www. vocaleyes.org/ | VocalEyes | Chapter 9. Public Sector | Ethics and Regulations |

| COMPANY | PRODUCT | BROAD CATEGORY | AI APPLICATION |
|---|---|---|---|
| Voyanta, Ltd. https://www.voyanta.com/ | Voyanta | Chapter 5. Property Search | Real Estate Investment |
| Vrbo, an Expedia Group Company https://www.vrbo.com/ | Vrbo | Chapter 11. Multifaceted Influence | Data and Analytics |
| VRX Media Group, LLC https://www.vrxstaging.com/ | VRX Staging | Chapter 5. Property Search | Virtual Staging |
| VTS, Inc. https://www.vts.com/ | VTS | Chapter 5. Property Search | Commercial Investment |
| | VTS | Chapter 5. Property Search | Investment Analysis |
| | VTS MarketView | Chapter 5. Property Search | Real Estate Leasing |
| | VTS Value | Chapter 7. Manage the Property | Portfolio Management |
| Wallacei https://www.wallacei.com/ | Wallacei | Chapter 6. Modify the Property | Architecture and Design |
| Warby Parker https://www.warbyparker.com/ | Warby Parker Virtual Try-On | Chapter 5. Property Search | 3D Modeling and AR |
| Waste Robotics https://wasterobotic.com/ | Waste Robotics | Chapter 11. Multifaceted Influence | Sustainability |
| WaterBit, Inc. https://www.waterbit.com/ | WaterBit | Chapter 11. Multifaceted Influence | Sustainability |
| WattTime https://www.watttime.org/ | WattTime | Chapter 11. Multifaceted Influence | Sustainability |

| COMPANY | PRODUCT | BROAD CATEGORY | AI APPLICATION |
|---|---|---|---|
| Waze Mobile, Ltd. https://waze.com/ | Waze | Chapter 11. Multifaceted Influence | Sustainability |
| Wealthfront Corporation https://www.wealthfront.com/ | Wealthfront | Chapter 7. Manage the Property | Asset Management |
| WiseBanyan, Inc. https://www.wisebanyan.com/ | WiseBanyan | Chapter 7. Manage the Property | Asset Management |
| Wiz Connected Lighting Company Limited https://www.wizconnected.com/ | Wiz | Chapter 6. Modify the Property | Smart Homes |
| WizeHire, LLC https://www.wizehire.com/ | WizeHire | Chapter 5. Property Search | Agent Management |
| Wolfram Alpha LLC https://www.wolframalpha.com/ | Wolfram Alpha | Chapter 10. Education | Education and Training |
| Workday, Inc. https://www.workday.com/ | Adaptive Insights | Chapter 5. Property Search | Competitive Analysis |
| World Green Building Council https://worldgbc.org/advancing-net-zero/ | World GBC Advancing Net Zero | Chapter 11. Multifaceted Influence | Sustainability |
| World Wide Web Consortium https://www.w3.org/WAI/ | W3C Web Accessibility Initiative (WAI) | Chapter 10. Education | Education and Training |
| Wren, Inc. https://www.wren.co/ | Project Wren | Chapter 11. Multifaceted Influence | Sustainability |

| COMPANY | PRODUCT | BROAD CATEGORY | AI APPLICATION |
|---|---|---|---|
| Write.Homes https://writehomes.com/ | Write.Homes | Chapter 8. Dispose of the Property | Sales and Marketing |
| Wyze Labs, Inc. https://www.wyze.com/ | Wyze Cam | Chapter 6. Modify the Property | Smart Homes |
| Xandr by AT&T Inc. https://www.xandr.com/ | Xandr | Chapter 5. Property Search | Optimized Advertising |
| Xara Technologies https://www.xara.com/ | Xara | Chapter 8. Dispose of the Property | Sales and Marketing |
| | | Chapter 8. Dispose of the Property | Brokerage |
| Xome Holdings, LLC https://www.xome.com/ | Xome Valuations | Chapter 5. Property Search | Appraisal Management |
| Yardi Systems, Inc. https://www.yardi.com/ | Resident Services by Yardi | Chapter 7. Manage the Property | Tenant Management |
| | Voyager | Chapter 5. Property Search | Investment Analysis |
| | | Chapter 5. Property Search | Rental Property Search |
| | | Chapter 5. Property Search | Rental Property Search |
| | Yardi Breeze | Chapter 5. Property Search | Real Estate Investment |
| | | Chapter 11. Multifaceted Influence | Data and Analytics |
| | Yardi Investment Management | Chapter 7. Manage the Property | Portfolio Management |
| | | Chapter 7. Manage the Property | Asset Management |

| COMPANY | PRODUCT | BROAD CATEGORY | AI APPLICATION |
|---|---|---|---|
| Yeelight Technology Co., Ltd. https://www.yeelight.com/ | Yeelight | Chapter 6. Modify the Property | Smart Homes |
| YieldMo https://www.yieldmo.com/ | Smart Curation Engine | Chapter 5. Property Search | Optimized Advertising |
| YieldStreet, Inc. https://www.yieldstreet.com/ | Cadre | Chapter 5. Property Search | Investment Analysis |
| Ylopo, LLC https://ylopo.com/ | Ylopo | Chapter 5. Property Search | Home Sales |
| | | Chapter 5. Property Search | Agent Management |
| | | Chapter 5. Property Search | Optimized Advertising |
| | | Chapter 8. Dispose of the Property | Sales and Marketing |
| Yseop, Inc. https://yseop.com/ | Yseop | Chapter 8. Dispose of the Property | Brokerage |
| Zefr, Inc. https://www.zefr.com/ | Brand Safety Suite (BSS) | Chapter 5. Property Search | Optimized Advertising |
| Zenplace, Inc. https://www.zenplace.com/ | Zenplace | Chapter 7. Manage the Property | Property Management |
| | | Chapter 7. Manage the Property | Tenant Management |
| Zero Waste International Alliance https://zwia.org/ | Zero Waste International Alliance | Chapter 11. Multifaceted Influence | Sustainability |
| Zest AI https://www.zest.ai/ | Zest AI | Chapter 5. Property Search | Mortgage Automation |
| | | Chapter 5. Property Search | Rental Property Search |

| COMPANY | PRODUCT | BROAD CATEGORY | AI APPLICATION |
|---|---|---|---|
| | | Chapter 5. Property Search | Mortgages |
| | | Chapter 5. Property Search | Financing and Mortgage |
| Zesty.ai https://zesty.ai/ | Property Insights | Chapter 11. Multifaceted Influence | Data and Analytics |
| | | Chapter 11. Multifaceted Influence | Innovation and Research |
| Zilliant, Inc. https://www.zilliant.com/ | Zilliant | Chapter 5. Property Search | Mortgage Automation |
| | Dotloop https://www.dotloop.com/ | Chapter 5. Property Search | Home Sales |
| | HotPads https://hotpads.com/ | Chapter 5. Property Search | Rental Property Search |
| | | Chapter 5. Property Search | Real Estate Leasing |
| | Rent Zestimate https://www.zillow.com/rental-manager/price-my-rental/ | Chapter 5. Property Search | Rental Property Search |
| | | Chapter 5. Property Search | Real Estate Leasing |
| Zillow Group, Inc. https://www.zillowgroup.com/ | | Chapter 5. Property Search | Home Sales |
| | | Chapter 5. Property Search | Rental Property Search |
| | Trulia https://www.trulia.com/ | Chapter 5. Property Search | Real Estate Leasing |
| | | Chapter 8. Dispose of the Property | Valuation and Appraisal |
| | | Chapter 11. Multifaceted Influence | Content Generation |

| COMPANY | PRODUCT | BROAD CATEGORY | AI APPLICATION |
|---|---|---|---|
| | | Chapter 11. Multifaceted Influence | Innovation and Research |
| | | Chapter 12. GeoAI | Customized Recommendations |
| | | Chapter 5. Property Search | Rental Property Search |
| | Trulia Estimate https://www. trulia.com/info/ trulia-estimates/ | Chapter 8. Dispose of the Property | Valuation and Appraisal |
| | | Chapter 11. Multifaceted Influence | Predictive Analytics |
| | | Chapter 11. Multifaceted Influence | Data and Analytics |
| | | Chapter 5. Property Search | Home Sales |
| | | Chapter 5. Property Search | Rental Property Search |
| | | Chapter 5. Property Search | Real Estate Leasing |
| | Zillow https://www.zillow. com/ | Chapter 8. Dispose of the Property | Valuation and Appraisal |
| | | Chapter 8. Dispose of the Property | Brokerage |
| | | Chapter 11. Multifaceted Influence | Content Generation |
| | | Chapter 11. Multifaceted Influence | Innovation and Research |
| | Zillow 3D Home https://www.zillow. com/z/3d-home/ | Chapter 5. Property Search | Real Estate Leasing |

| COMPANY | PRODUCT | BROAD CATEGORY | AI APPLICATION |
|---|---|---|---|
| | Zillow Premier Agent https://www.zillow.com/premier-agent/ | Chapter 5. Property Search | Home Sales |
| | | Chapter 5. Property Search | Agent Management |
| | | Chapter 5. Property Search | Lead Generation |
| | | Chapter 5. Property Search | Optimized Advertising |
| | | Chapter 8. Dispose of the Property | Sales and Marketing |
| | | Chapter 8. Dispose of the Property | Brokerage |
| | Zillow Zestimate https://www.zillow.com/z/zestimate/ | Chapter 5. Property Search | Rental Property Search |
| | | Chapter 5. Property Search | Appraisal Management |
| | | Chapter 6. Modify the Property | Real Estate Development |
| | | Chapter 7. Manage the Property | Portfolio Management |
| | | Chapter 8. Dispose of the Property | Valuation and Appraisal |
| | | Chapter 11. Multifaceted Influence | Predictive Analytics |
| | | Chapter 11. Multifaceted Influence | Data and Analytics |
| | | Chapter 12. GeoAI | Customized Recommendations |
| ZipRecruiter, Inc. https://www.ziprecruiter.com/ | ZipRecruiter | Chapter 5. Property Search | Agent Management |

| COMPANY | PRODUCT | BROAD CATEGORY | AI APPLICATION |
|---------|---------|----------------|----------------|
| Zolo Stays Property Solutions Pvt Ltd https://www.zolo.in/ | Zolo | Chapter 5. Property Search | Real Estate Leasing |
| Zonda, LLC https://www.zondahome.com/ | Zonda Market Intelligence Platform | Chapter 5. Property Search | Investment Analysis |
| Zumper, Inc. https://www.zumper.com/ | PadMapper https://www.padmapper.com/ | Chapter 5. Property Search | Real Estate Leasing |
| | | Chapter 5. Property Search | Rental Property Search |
| | | Chapter 5. Property Search | Real Estate Leasing |
| | Zumper | Chapter 7. Manage the Property | Property Management |
| | | Chapter 7. Manage the Property | Tenant Management |
| | | Chapter 11. Multifaceted Influence | Data and Analytics |
| | Zumper Pro | Chapter 5. Property Search | Rental Property Search |
| Zurple, a Constellation Real Estate Group Company https://www.zurple.com/ | Zurple | Chapter 5. Property Search | Home Sales |
| | | Chapter 5. Property Search | Mortgage Automation |
| | | Chapter 5. Property Search | Agent Management |
| Zuva https://zuva.ai/ | Zuva DocAI | Chapter 8. Dispose of the Property | Brokerage |

# APPENDIX B
# EDUCATIONAL OPPORTUNITIES

Whether you are a real estate student, junior estate professional, senior professional, or other interested party, ample educational opportunities exist to expand your knowledge of artificial intelligence in the real estate industry. This appendix organizes the opportunities into eight categories, with worldwide examples for each:

1. University Courses
2. Continuing Education Unit (CEU) Courses and Certificate Programs
3. Online Courses Not for Credit
4. Professional Events
5. Online Communities and Social Media Groups
6. On-the-Job Training, and
7. Coaching and Mentoring Programs
8. Independent Studies and Research.

| CATEGORY | EXAMPLES WORLDWIDE |
| --- | --- |

### 1. University Courses

**United States:**

At the time of this book's publication, a few universities offer graduate degrees focusing on artificial intelligence in the real estate industry. Numerous other universities offer courses on AI in real estate as part of other graduate degree programs.

Additionally, hundreds of universities around the world offer undergraduate and graduate degrees in AI. Many AI programs offer the flexibility to apply your learning to specific industries, including real estate. It might be beneficial to pursue an AI degree and apply that knowledge to real estate through internships, projects, and real-world experience. You could also consider taking real estate courses alongside your AI degree to gain industry-specific knowledge.

- MIT School of Architecture and Planning offers a Master of Science in Real Estate Development with a concentration in Data Science. This program teaches students how to use AI and data science to make better decisions in the real estate industry.
- Columbia University Graduate School of Business offers a Master of Science in Real Estate Development with a specialization in Artificial Intelligence. This program prepares students for careers in real estate development and investment, with a focus on using AI to make better decisions.
- New York University School of Professional Studies offers a Master of Science in Real Estate with a specialization in Artificial Intelligence. This program teaches students how to use AI to improve the efficiency and effectiveness of real estate transactions and decision-making.

**India**

- Amrita Vishwa Vidyapeetham in Coimbatore, Tamil Nadu offers a Master of Science in Artificial Intelligence for Real Estate (MSAIRE).
- Indian Institute of Technology Madras in Chennai, Tamil Nadu offers an elective course in Artificial Intelligence for Real Estate as part of their Master of Science in Real Estate Management (MSREM) program.
- Indian Institute of Technology Bombay in Mumbai, Maharashtra offers a course on Artificial Intelligence for Real Estate as part of their Master of Science in Civil Engineering (MSCE) program.
- RICS School of Built Environment in Gurgaon, Haryana offers a Postgraduate Diploma in Artificial Intelligence for Real Estate (PGDAI-RE).

In addition to these universities, there are also a few private institutes that offer degrees and courses in artificial

| CATEGORY | EXAMPLES WORLDWIDE |
|---|---|

intelligence in real estate. For example, the Institute of Technology and Management in Mumbai, Maharashtra offers a Master of Business Administration in Real Estate with specialization in Artificial Intelligence (MBA-RE-AI):

**Rest of the World:**

- University of Amsterdam (Netherlands): Master of Science in Real Estate with a specialization in Data Science and Artificial Intelligence
- University of Technology Sydney (Australia): Master of Science in Property Economics and Development with a specialization in Artificial Intelligence and Machine Learning.
- University College London (UK): Master of Science in Real Estate with a specialization in Big Data and Analytics

*Here are some additional examples of universities that offer courses but not degrees in AI and real estate:*

**United States:**

- Stanford University
- Harvard University
- University of California, Berkeley
- University of Pennsylvania
- Carnegie Mellon University
- University of Michigan
- University of Southern California
- Cornell University
- Northwestern University
- University of Texas at Austin
- University of Washington

**Rest of the World:**

- Imperial College London (UK)
- University of Manchester (UK)
- University of Cambridge (UK)

| CATEGORY | EXAMPLES WORLDWIDE |
|---|---|
| | • University of Edinburgh (UK)<br>• National University of Singapore (Singapore)<br>• University of Melbourne (Australia)<br>• University of Sydney (Australia)<br>• University of Toronto (Canada)<br>• University of British Columbia (Canada)<br>• École Polytechnique Fédérale de Lausanne (Switzerland)<br>• Technical University of Delft (Netherlands)<br>• TU München (Germany) |
| **2. Continuing Education Unit (CEU) Courses and Certificate Programs**<br><br>Continuing education unit (CEU) courses in real estate are educational programs designed to help real estate professionals maintain their skills and knowledge in their field. CEUs are typically awarded for attending workshops, seminars, conferences, and online courses. Academic institutions, real estate associations, and private companies offer CEU courses.<br>Certificate education programs in real estate are short-term programs that are designed to provide students with the knowledge and skills they need to start a career in real estate or advance their existing career. Certificate | **United States:**<br><br>• National Association of Realtors (NAR): NAR offers a variety of CEU courses on real estate-related topics, including a course on artificial intelligence in real estate.<br>• Real Estate Institute: The Real Estate Institute offers a CEU course called "Artificial Intelligence for Real Estate Professionals."<br>• Champions School of Real Estate: Champions School of Real Estate offers a CEU course called "Introduction to Artificial Intelligence."<br>• Fast Track Realty School: Fast Track Realty School offers a CEU course called "Artificial Intelligence in Real Estate."<br><br>In addition to these organizations, there are also a number of state and local real estate associations that offer CEU courses on artificial intelligence in real estate. For example, the California Association of Realtors (CAR) offers a CEU course called "Artificial Intelligence in Real Estate."<br><br>**India**<br><br>• Amrita Vishwa Vidyapeetham: Amrita Vishwa Vidyapeetham offers a Master of Science in Artificial Intelligence for Real Estate (MSAIRE) program, which includes CEU courses.<br>• Indian Institute of Technology Madras (IIT Madras): IIT Madras offers an elective course in Artificial Intelligence |

| CATEGORY | EXAMPLES WORLDWIDE |
|---|---|
| programs typically cover topics such as real estate finance, marketing, sales, and technologies. Certificate programs in real estate are offered by a variety of institutions, including universities, colleges, and professional associations. Programs typically range in length from a few weeks to a few months, and can be completed online or in person. | for Real Estate as part of its Master of Science in Real Estate Management (MSREM) program. This course is also available as a CEU course for professionals. <br> • RICS School of Built Environment: RICS School of Built Environment in Gurgaon, Haryana offers a Postgraduate Diploma in Artificial Intelligence for Real Estate (PGDAI-RE). <br> • Institute of Technology and Management (ITM): ITM in Mumbai, Maharashtra offers a Master of Business Administration in Real Estate with specialization in Artificial Intelligence (MBA-RE-AI). |

**Rest of the World:**

- Australian Institute of Real Estate (AIRE): AIRE offers a CEU course called "Artificial Intelligence for Real Estate."
- Canadian Real Estate Association (CREA): CREA offers a CEU course called "Artificial Intelligence in Real Estate."
- UK Property Academy: The UK Property Academy offers a CEU course called "Artificial Intelligence for Property Professionals."
- Royal Institution of Chartered Surveyors (RICS): RICS offers a CEU course called "Artificial Intelligence for Real Estate.".
- Real Estate Institute of New Zealand (REINZ): REINZ offers a CEU course called "Artificial Intelligence for Real Estate."

Additionally, various private companies offer CEU courses and certificate programs on artificial intelligence in real estate in other countries. For example, the company XAI for Real Estate (Seoul, South Korea) offers a variety of CEU courses on this topic to students all over the world.

When choosing a CEU course on artificial intelligence in real estate, it is important to make sure that the course is accredited by a recognized organization, such as the International Association for Continuing Education and Training (IACET). You should also consider the cost of the course, the length of the course, and the topics that are covered.

| CATEGORY | EXAMPLES WORLDWIDE |
|---|---|
| **3. Online Courses Not for Credit**<br><br>Online courses not for credit are courses that are taken for personal or professional development but do not offer university degrees or CEU credits. These courses can be a great way to learn new skills, expand your knowledge, or explore your interests. Online courses not for credit can be offered by a variety of organizations, including universities, colleges, businesses, and non-profit organizations. Many of these courses are free to take, while others may charge a fee. The courses can be in the format of lectures, podcasts, webinars, textbooks, etc. Some of the benefits of taking online courses not for credit include flexibility, affordability, convenience, and variety. | **United States:**<br><br>• Artificial Intelligence for Real Estate by DataCamp<br>• AI in Real Estate by Udemy<br>• Real Estate AI: Emerging Technologies by Skillshare<br>• Real Estate AI: The Future of Real Estate by LinkedIn Learning<br>• Application of AI, InsurTech, and Real Estate Technology by the University of Pennsylvania on Coursera<br>• AI for Real Estate Sales by Udemy<br>• AI for Real Estate Investing by Udemy<br>• AI for Real Estate Marketing by Udemy<br>• AI for Real Estate Valuation by Udemy<br>• AI for Real Estate Asset Management by Udemy<br><br>**India:**<br><br>• AI for Real Estate by Great Learning Academy<br>• AI in Real Estate: The Future of Real Estate in India by Simplilearn<br>• Real Estate AI: Emerging Technologies and Applications by Jigsaw Academy<br>• AI for Real Estate in India by Coursera<br><br>**Rest of the World:**<br><br>• Artificial Intelligence for Real Estate by Real Estate Academy (Australia)<br>• AI for Real Estate in Australia by Coursera (Australia)<br>• Artificial Intelligence for Real Estate in the UK by Property Academy (United Kingdom)<br>• AI in Real Estate: The Future of Real Estate in Canada by RE/MAX Canada (Canada)<br>• AI for Real Estate Sales by Udemy (Global)<br>• AI for Real Estate Professionals by LinkedIn Learning (Global)<br><br>All of these courses are offered by reputable organizations and are designed to help students learn about AI in real |

| CATEGORY | EXAMPLES WORLDWIDE |
|---|---|
| | estate and how to use it to improve their businesses. Some of the courses also offer hands-on projects and exercises to help students apply what they learn to real-world situations. |
| **4. Professional Events** <br><br> Professional workshops, industry conferences, and trade shows are valuable resources for staying competitive and informed on new products and services that can benefit your career. These events often include featured speakers, lectures, panel discussions, hands-on activities, tours of relevant nearby facilities, and social events. Networking with other real estate professionals at these events can also be highly beneficial. | **United States:** <br><br> • PropTech Breakthrough (San Francisco, CA) <br> • RealShare PropTech (Austin, TX) <br> • Inman Connect (New York, NY) <br> • CREtech (New York, NY) <br> • Connected Real Estate (Las Vegas, NV) <br> • AI for Real Estate Summit (San Francisco, CA) <br> • National Association of Realtors Conference & Expo (various locations) <br> • American Real Estate Society Conference (various locations) <br> • Urban Land Institute Fall Meeting (various locations) <br> • RealShare Conference (various locations) <br><br> **India:** <br><br> • PropTech India (Mumbai, Maharashtra) <br> • Real Estate Summit India (New Delhi, Delhi) <br> • CREtech India (Mumbai, Maharashtra) <br> • India AI & VR Summit (various locations) <br> • AI for Real Estate India Summit (Mumbai, Maharashtra) <br> • Confederation of Real Estate Developers' Associations of India (CREDAI) National Convention (various locations) <br> • Indian Property Congress (IPC) Annual Convention (various locations) <br> • National Real Estate Development Council (NAREDCO) Convention (various locations) <br> • ASSOCHAM National Real Estate Summit (various locations) <br> • FICCI Real Estate Summit (various locations) |

| CATEGORY | EXAMPLES WORLDWIDE |
|---|---|
| | **Rest of the World:**<br><br>• PropTech Summit (London, UK)<br>• MIPIM Proptech (Cannes, France)<br>• EXPO REAL (Munich, Germany)<br>• Barcelona Meeting Point (Barcelona, Spain)<br>• Futurebuilt (Sydney, Australia)<br>• Proptech Festival (Paris, France)<br>• BuildTech Asia (Singapore)<br>• RealTech Asia (Hong Kong)<br>• PROPTECH Middle East (Dubai, UAE)<br>• AFRICA PropTech Congress (Johannesburg, South Africa)<br>• PropTech Latam (Mexico City, Mexico)<br>• RE-TECH (Tel Aviv, Israel) |
| **5. Online Communities and Social Media Groups**<br><br>Online communities and social media groups offer valuable platforms for real estate professionals to connect, ask questions, and share ideas. These platforms provide opportunities to learn from peers, stay updated on the latest AI industry trends and developments, and expand one's professional network. | **United States:**<br><br>• LinkedIn Groups:<br>  • AI in Real Estate<br>  • Proptech<br>  • Real Estate Technology<br>• YouTube Channels<br>  • AI in Real Estate<br>  • Real Estate Technology<br>  • PropTech News<br>  • The Real Estate Channel<br>  • Inman News<br>• Facebook Groups:<br>  • AI for Real Estate<br>  • Real Estate AI<br>  • Proptech Community<br>• X (formerly Twitter):<br>  • #AIinRealEstate<br>  • #RealEstateAI<br>  • #Proptech<br>• Reddit:<br>  • r/AIinRealEstate<br>  • r/Proptech |

| CATEGORY | EXAMPLES WORLDWIDE |
|---|---|
| | **India:**<br><br>• LinkedIn Groups:<br>  • AI in Real Estate India<br>  • Proptech India<br>  • Real Estate Technology India<br>• YouTube Channels<br>  • PropTech India<br>  • Real Estate Technology India<br>  • Startup Central<br>• Facebook Groups:<br>  • AI for Real Estate India<br>  • Real Estate AI India<br>  • Proptech Community India<br>• X (formerly Twitter):<br>  • #AIinRealEstateIndia<br>  • #RealEstateAIIndia<br>  • #ProptechIndia<br>• Reddit:<br>  • r/AIinRealEstateIndia<br>  • r/ProptechIndia<br><br>**Rest of the World:**<br><br>• LinkedIn Groups:<br>  • AI in Real Estate Global<br>  • Proptech Global<br>  • Real Estate Technology Global<br>• YouTube Channels<br>  • CRETech (Global)<br>  • RealShare (Global)<br>  • Real Estate Tech Startup (Global)<br>  • Real Estate Disruptors (Global)<br>  • Real Estate Webmasters (Global)<br>  • Real Estate Technology Review (Global)<br>  • Real Estate Tech Hub (Global)<br>• Facebook Groups:<br>  • AI for Real Estate Global<br>  • Real Estate AI Global<br>  • Proptech Community Global |

| CATEGORY | EXAMPLES WORLDWIDE |
|---|---|
| | • X (formerly Twitter):<br>  • #AIinRealEstateGlobal<br>  • #RealEstateAIGlobal<br>  • #ProptechGlobal<br>• Reddit:<br>  • r/AIinRealEstateGlobal<br>  • r/ProptechGlobal<br><br>There are also many regional and country-specific communities and groups on AI in real estate in addition to the above global communities and groups. For example, LinkedIn groups for AI in real estate are active in the United Kingdom, Australia, Canada, and France, among numerous others. |
| **6. On-the-Job Training**<br><br>On-the-job training (OJT) is a type of training that is conducted in the workplace. It is a hands-on approach to learning new skills and knowledge that are necessary to perform a job. OJT is typically provided by a supervisor, manager, or more experienced colleague. OJT can be used to train new employees on the specific tasks and procedures needed to be successful in their roles. It can also be used to train existing employees on new skills and technologies or to help them prepare for a new promotion. | **United States:**<br><br>• Keyway offers on-the-job training to its employees on how to use its AI platform to identify and evaluate potential investment properties.<br>• Reali is a real estate brokerage that offers on-the-job training to its agents on how to use its AI platform to generate leads, qualify buyers, and close deals.<br>• Zillow offers on-the-job training to its employees on how to use its AI platform to develop and maintain its products and services, including providing its users with information on property values, market trends, and other real estate-related topics<br>• Redfin offers on-the-job training to its employees on how to use its AI platform to help clients find homes that meet their needs and budget.<br>• Compass is a real estate brokerage that offers AI on-the-job training to help its agents be more efficient and effective. |

| CATEGORY | EXAMPLES WORLDWIDE |
|---|---|
| Some of the benefits of on-the-job training are that OJT is immediate, cost-effective, flexible, practical, and directly relevant. | **India:**<br><br>• NoBroker, India's largest residential real estate transaction platform, offers on-the-job training to its employees on how to use its AI platform to help sellers and buyers connect and finalize deals.<br>• Housing.com offers on-the-job training to its employees on how to use its AI platform to help users find properties that meet their needs and budget.<br>• PropTiger.com offers on-the-job training to its agents on how to better use its AI platform in real estate brokerage.<br>• MagicBricks is a real estate website that offers on-the-job training to its employees on how to use its AI platform to better provide its clients with information on property values and market conditions.<br>• Square Yards offers on-the-job training to its employees on how to use its AI platform to better assist its real estate brokerage clients.<br><br>**Rest of the World:**<br><br>• PropTech Australia (Australia)<br>• REA Group (Australia)<br>• Domain Holdings (Australia)<br>• PropertyGuru (Singapore)<br>• 99.co (Singapore)<br>• FazWaz (Thailand)<br>• Property Finder (United Arab Emirates)<br>• Bayut.com (United Arab Emirates)<br>• Zoopla (United Kingdom)<br>• Rightmove (United Kingdom)<br>• OnTheMarket (United Kingdom)<br>• Nested (United Kingdom)<br>• OpenRent (United Kingdom)<br>• Keller Williams (United Kingdom)<br>• RE/MAX (United Kingdom)<br><br>These are just a few examples of the ever more numerous companies that offer on-the-job training on artificial intelligence in real estate. |

| CATEGORY | EXAMPLES WORLDWIDE |
|---|---|
| **7. Coaching and Mentoring Programs**<br><br>Real estate coaching programs offer a comprehensive approach to professional development, including training in business skills, marketing, and lead generation. Some real estate associations and companies offer mentoring programs that match you with an experienced mentor who can provide guidance and support on your career development. | **United States:**<br>• AI Real Estate Academy (Ricky Carruth) offers a combination of online courses and live coaching to help real estate agents learn how to use AI to grow their businesses.<br>• AI Real Estate Coaching (David Osborn) provides one-on-one coaching to help real estate agents learn how to use AI to improve their productivity and profitability.<br>• RETech Academy (several coaches) makes available a variety of online courses on AI, machine learning, and other real estate technology topics.<br>• The Real Estate AI Edge (Nick Krem) delivers a combination of online courses and live coaching to help real estate agents learn how to use AI to win more listings and clients.<br>• The AI Agent Academy (Nick Krem) is a more intensive version of The Real Estate AI Edge, offering one-on-one coaching and support to help real estate agents become experts in using AI.<br><br>**India**<br>• PropTech India<br>• AI for Real Estate India<br><br>**Rest of the World:**<br>• Zoopla Academy (United Kingdom)<br>• Rightmove Academy (United Kingdom)<br>• OnTheMarket Academy (United Kingdom)<br>• PropTech Association of Australia (Australia)<br>• Real Estate Institute of New South Wales (Australia)<br>• Real Estate Institute of Victoria (Australia)<br>• PropertyGuru Academy (Singapore)<br>• 99.co Academy (Singapore):<br>• FazWaz Academy (Thailand)<br>• Property Finder Academy (United Arab Emirates)<br>• Bayut.com Academy (United Arab Emirates) |

| CATEGORY | EXAMPLES WORLDWIDE |
|---|---|
| **8. Independent Studies and Research**<br><br>Independent studies allow you to create courses specifically tailored to your interests and goals. Conducting research related to your career and specialties can both deepen your understanding of your specialty and enhance your credentials. | There are many different information sources available for independent studies on artificial intelligence in real estate, including the following (with examples):<br><br>• Academic journals:<br>  • Artificial Intelligence for Real Estate (Elsevier)<br>  • Journal of Real Estate Research (Wiley)<br>  • Journal of Property Investment & Finance (Emerald)<br>  • Urban Studies (Sage)<br>  • International Journal of Artificial Intelligence (CESER)<br>  • Journal of the Indian Institute of Science (ISI)<br><br>• Industry reports and white papers:<br>  • AI in Real Estate: The Next Frontier (CBRE)<br>  • Artificial Intelligence: Real Estate Revolution or Evolution? (JLL)<br>  • The Future of Real Estate with AI (PwC)<br>  • AI in Real Estate: A Market Overview (KPMG)<br>  • AI in Real Estate: Opportunities and Challenges (Deloitte)<br>  • The Impact of AI on the Real Estate Industry (McKinsey & Company)<br>  • AI in Real Estate: A Guide for Brokers (NAR Research)<br>  • AI in Real Estate: A Guide for Homebuyers (Zillow)<br>  • AI in Real Estate: The Future of the Indian Market (PropTech Association of India)<br>  • AI in Real Estate: Opportunities and Challenges for India (CBRE India)<br><br>• Government publications:<br>  • Artificial Intelligence for Real Estate: A Guide for Governments (World Economic Forum)<br>  • AI in Real Estate: A Discussion Paper (UK Government)<br>  • AI in Real Estate: A Scoping Study (Australian Government)<br>  • AI in Real Estate: A Report to the Government (New Zealand Government) |

| CATEGORY | EXAMPLES WORLDWIDE |
|---|---|
| | • AI in Real Estate: A Policy Framework (Singapore Government)<br>• Report of the Committee on Real Estate Technology (India Government) |
| | • Nonprofit organizations:<br>• World Economic Forum (Switzerland)<br>• PropTech for Good (United Kingdom)<br>• Urban Land Institute (ULI) (United States)<br>• BuildingSMART International (Netherlands)<br>• PropTech Association of India (PAI) (India)<br>• India Urban Infrastructure Foundation (IUIF) (India) |
| | • Professional association conferences:<br>• Real Estate Technology Conference (RETEC) (United States)<br>• Construction Management Conference (CMC) (United States)<br>• Urban Land Institute (ULI) Fall Meeting (United States)<br>• National Association of Realtors (NAR) (United States)<br>• PropTech India Conference (India)<br>• International Conference on AI in Real Estate (ICAIRE) (Global)<br>• Urban Analytics and City Science Conference (UACSC) (Global)<br>• Smart Cities Conference (SCC) (Global) |
| | • Open databases:<br>• AI in Real Estate Database (World Economic Forum)<br>• PropTech for Good Database (PropTech for Good)<br>• Urban Land Institute (ULI) Knowledge Finder (Urban Land Institute)<br>• National Association of Realtors (NAR) Research Library (National Association of Realtors)<br>• Semantic Scholar (Allen Institute for AI)<br>• OpenAI API (OpenAI)<br>• Indian Institute of Human Settlements (IIHS) Research Library |

| CATEGORY | EXAMPLES WORLDWIDE |
|---|---|
| | • Books:<br>  • Artificial Intelligence in Real Estate Investing by Bob Mather (2023)<br>  • AI for Real Estate: How Artificial Intelligence is Changing the Way We Buy, Sell, and Manage Property by Daniel D. Holt (2022)<br>  • The AI-Powered Real Estate Agent: How to Use Artificial Intelligence to Win More Listings and Sell More Homes by Craig C. Proctor (2023)<br>  • Artificial Intelligence and the Future of Real Estate by David L. Smith (2021)<br>  • Real Estate in the Age of Artificial Intelligence by Aaron Block and Zach Aarons (2021)<br>  • Artificial Intelligence in Real Estate Marketing by Tim Savage (2021)<br>  • Artificial Intelligence in Real Estate Appraisal by John A. Griffin (2021)<br><br>• News Portals:<br>  • PropTech News: A leading news source for the property technology industry, covering news, analysis, and trends related to AI and other emerging technologies.<br>  • Real Estate Technology Roundup: A daily newsletter that covers the latest news and trends in real estate technology, including AI.<br>  • RETech News: A daily newsletter that covers the latest news and trends in real estate technology, including AI.<br>  • Built In: A technology news and job website that covers the latest news and trends in the tech industry, including real estate tech and AI.<br>  • TechCrunch: A technology news website that covers the latest news and trends in the tech industry, including AI and other emerging technologies.<br>  • Wired: A technology news website and magazine that covers the latest news and trends in the tech industry, including AI and other emerging technologies. |

491

| CATEGORY | EXAMPLES WORLDWIDE |
|---|---|
| | • Forbes: A business magazine and website that covers a wide range of topics, including AI and other emerging technologies in the real estate industry.<br>• PropTiger.com: India's leading property portal, covering a wide range of real estate news and insights, including AI-related news.<br>• The Times of India: A leading newspaper and website in India, covering a wide range of news and insights, including AI-related news in the real estate industry.<br><br>• Scholarly search engines:<br>  • Google Scholar (Google)<br>  • Semantic Scholar (Allen Institute for AI)<br>  • arXiv (Cornell University)<br>  • Microsoft Academic (Microsoft)<br>  • Scopus (Elsevier)<br><br>• Digital Libraries:<br>  • The Association for Computing Machinery (ACM) Digital Library: The ACM Digital Library is a comprehensive collection of computer science literature, including papers on AI in real estate.<br>  • The IEEE Xplore Digital Library: The IEEE Xplore Digital Library is another comprehensive collection of computer science literature, including papers on AI in real estate.<br>  • The Knowledge Graph: The Knowledge Graph is a digital knowledge base developed by Google AI. It contains information on a wide range of topics, including AI in real estate.<br>  • The Real Estate Standards Organization (RESO): The RESO maintains a variety of digital resources related to real estate technology, including some on AI in real estate. |

| CATEGORY | EXAMPLES WORLDWIDE |
|---|---|
| | • HathiTrust Digital Library: The largest digitized collection of knowledge allowable by copyright law, this digital library contains over 18 million books, articles, and research papers on a wide range of topics, including AI in real estate.<br>• The National Digital Library of India (NDLI): The NDLI is a digital library that contains a wide range of digital resources, including books, articles, and research papers on a wide range of topics, including AI in real estate.<br><br>• Interviews with experts: Experts (identified by reviewing the authors of the information sources contained in this Appendix) can provide you with unique insights and perspectives on the topic, and they can also help identify potential research questions.<br><br>When conducting your independent study, it is important to use a variety of sources to get a well-rounded perspective on the topic. You should also be critical of the information that you find and evaluate it carefully. |

# THIS BOOK'S WEBSITES AT REALESTATEBOOK.AI AND REALESTATEINDUSTRY.AI

## REALESTATEBOOK.AI

The purpose of RealEstateBook.ai is to provide potential buyers of this book – *Artificial Intelligence Applications in the Real Estate Industry* – with information to make an informed purchase decision. At the time of this writing, the website has these sections:

- Frequently Asked Questions
  - o   What Is in the Book?
  - o   Why Should You Read the Book?
  - o   Who Wrote the Book?
- Table of Contents
- Biographies of the Co-Authors and Technical Advisory Panel
- Questions?
  - o   Contact the Authors Directly by Email
  - o   Review Sample Pages, Reader Testimonials, Price Options, Etc.
  - o   Purchase the Book at the Most Convenient Amazon Kindle Website Worldwide

Future website enhancements will include reader reviews, a link to a YouTube description of the book, and other information sources.

## REALESTATEINDUSTRY.AI

Currently under construction, RealEstateIndustry.ai will provide comprehensive, continually updated information on artificial intelligence in real estate. Among the website's components will be the following:

- Important news stories (similar to websites like TechCrunch, TechRadar, Builtin, Wired, etc.)
- An interactive catalogue of AI products and services – expanding on this book's Appendix A
- Critical reviews of specific AI products and services
- Interviews with the CEOs of leading real estate AI companies and other industry leaders
- Blogs by the co-authors of this book as well as guest bloggers
- Online seminars and other continuing education opportunities

The goal is for RealEstateIndustry.ai to be the leading go-to portal for staying current on notable AI developments in the real estate industry.

# BIBLIOGRAPHY

## THIS IS AN ALPHABETICAL COMPILATION OF 100+ CITATIONS FOUND IN ALL THE "REFERENCES" SECTIONS OF THIS BOOK.

Alastal, A. I., & Shaqfa, A. H. (2022, May). GeoAI technologies and their application areas in urban planning and development: Concepts, opportunities and challenges in smart city (Kuwait, study case). Journal of Data Analysis and Information Processing. Retrieved from *https://www.scirp.org/journal/paperinformation.aspx?paperid=116308*

Arena, C. (2022, June 14). 7 disadvantages of artificial intelligence everyone should know about. Civil Liberties Union for Europe (Liberties). Retrieved from *https://www.liberties.*

*eu/en/stories/disadvantages-of-artificial-intelligence/44289*

Ascendix Technologies Inc. (2023, November 14). Top 35 proptech companies and startups in the USA in 2023. Retrieved from *https://ascendixtech.com/ proptech-companies-startups-overview/*

Ascendix. (2023, July 7). AI in real estate: Top companies revolutionizing real estate with AI solutions. Retrieved from *https://ascendixtech.com/ai-real-estate-solutions/*

Avison Young Inc. (n.d.). Real estate development project management for commercial real estate. Retrieved from *https://www.avisonyoung.us/project-management*

Bluhm, D. (2023, April 28). How artificial intelligence will change real estate: Should we brace for impact or embrace it? RISMedia. Retrieved from *https://www.rismedia.com/2023/04/28/how-artificial-intelligence-will-change-real-estate-should-we-brace-for-impact-or-embrace-ai/*

Bostrom, N. (2014). Superintelligence – Paths, dangers, strategies. Oxford University Press.

Cape Analytics (2023, January 6). 5 ways computer vision is revolutionizing the real estate industry. Retrieved from *https://capeanalytics.com/blog/computer-vision-real-estate/*

Capterra Inc. (2022, August 3). Top 5 real estate project management software. Retrieved from *https://www.capterra.com/resources/top-real-estate-project-management-software*

Casali, Y., Aydin, N. Y., & Comes, T. (2022, October). Machine learning for spatial analyses in urban areas: a scoping review. Sustainable Cities and Society. Retrieved from *https://www.sciencedirect.com/science/article/pii/S2210670722003687*

CBRE. (2020, July 20). The rise of the machine – Impacts and applications of AI in real estate. Retrieved from *https://www.cbre.com/insights/articles/ the-rise-of-the-machine-impacts-and-applications-of-ai-in-real-estate*

Chiappinelli, C. (2022, March 1). Think tank: GeoAI reveals a glimpse of the future. WhereNext Magazine. Retrieved from *https://www.esri.com/about/newsroom/publications/ wherenext/think-tank-on-geoai-simulation/*

Clifford, C. (2017, March 13). Mark Cuban: The world's first trillionaire will be an artificial intelligence entrepreneur. CNBC. Retrieved from *https://www.cnbc. com/2017/03/13/mark-cuban-the-worlds-first-trillionaire-will-be-an-ai-entrepreneur.html*

Clifford, C. (2018, February 1). Google CEO: A.I. is more important than fire or electricity. CNBC. Retrieved from *https://www.cnbc.com/2018/02/01/google-ceo-sundar-pichai-ai-is-more-important-than-fire-electricity.html*

Coherent Market Insights (2023, June). Geospatial analytics market analysis. [Report]. Retrieved from *https://www.coherentmarketinsights.com/market-insight/ geospatial-analytics-market-5874*

Co-libry. (2020, September 30). 5 powerful ways AI is disrupting the real estate sector. Retrieved from *https://co-libry.com/blogs/real-estate-artificial-intelligence-ai/*

Condon, S. (2022, May 10). IBM CEO: Artificial intelligence is nearing a key tipping point. ZDNET. Retrieved from *https://www.zdnet.com/article/ ibm-ceo-ai-is-near-a-key-tipping-point-but-generalized-ai-is-still-decades-out/*

Crunchbase. (n.d.). List of top predictive analytics companies. Retrieved from *https://www.crunchbase.com/hub/predictive-analytics-companies*

Dalumpines, R., Clavijo, J., Buchanan, J., Chacon, R., & Larson, T. (2022, September). Using GeoAI in property valuation. FIG Congress, Warsaw, Poland. Retrieved from *https://www.fig.net/resources/proceedings/fig_proceedings/fig2022/papers/ts08a/TS08A_ dalumpines_clavijo_et_al_11702.pdf*

Dardas, A. (2020, July 10). GeoAI series #2: The birth and evolution of GeoAI ESRI Canada. Retrieved from *https://resources.esri.ca/education-and-research/ geoai-series-2-the-birth-and-evolution-of-geoai*

Dataconomy. (2022, April 23). Artificial intelligence terms: AI glossary. Retrieved from *https://dataconomy.com/2022/04/23/artificial-intelligence-terms-ai-glossary/*

Desai, M. A. (2023, August 9). What the finance industry tells us about the future of AI. Harvard Business Review. Retrieved from *https://hbr.org/2023/08/ what-the-finance-industry-tells-us-about-the-future-of-ai*

Domingos, P. (2015). The master algorithm – How the quest for the ultimate learning machine will remake our world. Basic Books, New York NY. Retrieved from *https://psycnet.apa.org/record/2015-43168-000*

Embroker. (2023, March 13). A guide to real estate risk management. Retrieved from *https://www.embroker.com/blog/real-estate-risk-management*

Esri Inc. (2022, November 14). Using geospatial technology and analytics to unlock hidden value. Forbes. Retrieved from *https://www.forbes.com/sites/esri/2022/11/14/using-geospatial-technology-and-analytics-to-unlock-hidden-value*

Esri. (2020, December 10). ArcGIS for real estate. Retrieved from *https://storymaps.arcgis.com/stories/db95cc7ba50d4846952f144b65515f9e*

Esri. (2021, January 22). The new analyst: The rise of location in advanced analytics. Forbes. Retrieved from *https://www.forbes.com/sites/esri/2021/01/22/the-new-analyst-the-rise-of-location-in-advanced-analytics*

Esri. (n.d.). GIS for real estate: Precise real estate insight. Retrieved from *https://www.esri.com/en-us/industries/real-estate/overview*

European Commission Joint Research Centre. (2020). Defining artificial intelligence: Towards an operational definition and taxonomy of artificial intelligence. Retrieved from *https://op.europa.eu/en/publication-detail/-/publication/6cc0f1b6-59dd-11ea-8b81-01aa75ed71a1/language-en*

eWEEK. (2023, February 16 22). Best predictive analytics solutions 2023. Retrieved from *https://www.eweek.com/big-data-and-analytics/predictive-analytics-solutions*

Expert.ai. (n.d.). Glossary of AI terms. Retrieved from *https://www.expert.ai/glossary-of-ai-terms/*

Financial Action Task Force. (2022, July). Guidance for a risk-based approach: The real estate sector. Retrieved from *https://www.fatf-gafi.org/content/dam/fatf-gafi/guidance/RBA-Real-Estate-Sector.pdf*

Forbes Advisor. (2023, November 22). Best CRM for real estate 2023. Retrieved from *https://www.forbes.com/advisor/business/software/best-real-estate-crm*

Ford, M. (2015). Rise of the robots – Technology and the threat of a jobless future. Basic Books, New York NY. Retrieved from *https://www.ft.com/content/21fea1ae-f3e7-11e4-a9f3-00144feab7de*

FounderJar LLC. (2023 July 17). Best project management. software for real estate in 2023. Retrieved from *https://www.founderjar.com/real-estate-project-management*

G2. (n.d.). Best location intelligence software. Retrieved from *https://www.g2.com/categories/location-intelligence*

Galvis, N. (2021, April 9). How robotics are being used in real estate businesses. Retrieved from *https://www.robotlab.com/group/blog/how-robotics-are-being-used-in-real-estate-businesses*

Gartner Inc. (2023, August 1). Gartner identifies top trends shaping the future of data science and machine learning. Retrieved from *https://www.gartner.com/en/newsroom/press-releases/2023-08-01-gartner-identifies-top-trends-shaping-future-of-data-science-and-machine-learning*

GeoSpatial Analytics (n.d.). Strategic real estate management software. Retrieved from *https://www.geospatialanalytics.com*

GIS Lounge. (2014, November 11). How GIS is being used in real estate. Retrieved from *https://www.gislounge.com/gis-used-real-estate/*

Global Location Strategies. (n.d.). Corporate site selection. & location strategy. Retrieved from *https://globallocationstrategies.com*

Gonzalez, A. J., & Laureano-Ortiz, R. (1992). A case-based reasoning approach to real estate property appraisal. Expert Systems with Applications, 4(2), 229-246. Retrieved from *https://www.sciencedirect.com/science/article/abs/pii/0957417492901159?via%3Dihub*

GoodFirms. (n.d.). Top predictive analytics companies - Reviews 2023. Retrieved from *https://www.goodfirms.co/big-data-analytics/predictive-analytics*

Google for Developers. (n.d.). Machine learning glossary. Retrieved from *https://developers.google.com/machine-learning/glossary*

Grand View Research. (n.d.). Market research reports & consulting | Grand View Research Inc. Retrieved from *https://www.grandviewresearch.com*

Green Street. (n.d.). Definitive leaders in real estate analysis & research. Retrieved from *https://www.greenstreet.com*

Haan, K. (2023, January 4). 24 top AI statistics and trends in 2023. Forbes Advisor. Retrieved from *https://www.forbes.com/advisor/business/ai-statistics/*

Hickey & Associates. (n.d.). Global site selection. and location strategy consulting services. Retrieved from *https://www.hickeyandassociates.com*

Hintze, A. (2016, November 13). Understanding the four types of AI, from reactive robots to self-aware beings. The Conversation. Retrieved from *https://theconversation.com/ understanding-the-four-types-of-ai-from-reactive-robots-to-self-aware-beings-67616*

HomeLight Inc. (n.d.). 10 high-end luxury home real estate companies in the US. Retrieved from *https://www.homelight.com/blog/high-end-real-estate-companies*

IBM Corporation. (n.d.). What is artificial intelligence (AI)? Retrieved from *https://www.ibm.com/topics/artificial-intelligence*

Inoxoft. (2022, October 26). GIS in real estate: Benefits for property industry. Retrieved from *https://inoxoft.com/blog/how-to-get-benefits-with-applying-gis-technologies-in-real-estate-industry*

International Association of Assessing Officers. (2022). A review of the methods, applications, and challenges of adopting artificial intelligence in the property assessment office. Retrieved from *https://www.iaao.org/media/pubs/Review-of-AI-in-Property-Assessment_v2.pdf*

International Trade Administration. (n.d.). Site selection in the United States. Retrieved from *https://www.trade.gov/sites/default/files/2021-05/Chapter%2010%20-%20 Site%20Selection.pdf*

Jackson, A. (2023). AI in real estate: Revolutionizing the future of the industry. TNT-The Next Tech. Retrieved from *https://www.the-next-tech.com/artificial-intelligence/ ai-in-real-estate-revolutionizing-the-future-of-the-industry/*

Janowicz, K., Gao, S., McKenzie, G., Hu, Y., & Bhaduri, B. (2019). GeoAI: Spatially explicit artificial intelligence techniques for geographic knowledge discovery and beyond. International Journal of Geographical Information Science. Retrieved from *https://www. tandfonline.com/doi/full/10.1080/13658816.2019.1684500*

JLL Research Inc. (n.d.). Artificial intelligence - implications for real estate | JLL Research. Retrieved from *https://www.us.jll.com/en/trends-and-insights/research/ artificial-intelligence-and-its-implications-for-real-estate*

JLL. (2023). Artificial intelligence: Real estate revolution or evolution? Retrieved from *https://www.joneslanglasalle.co.jp/en/trends-and-insights/research/ artificial-intelligence-and-its-implications-for-real-estate*

KDnuggets. (2020, January 15). Top 7 location intelligence companies in 2020. Retrieved from *https://www.kdnuggets.com/2020/01/top-7-location-intelligence-companies-2020.html*

LeadSquared. (2022, November 18). Top 10 proptech startups in India. Retrieved from *https://www.leadsquared.com/industries/real-estate/proptech-startups-in-india/*

Liu, P., & Biljecki, F. (2022). A review of spatially-explicit GeoAI applications in urban geography. International Journal of Applied Earth Observation and Geoinformation. Retrieved from *https://www.sciencedirect.com/science/article/pii/S1569843222001339*

MacLean, P. D. (1990). The triune brain in evolution. Role in paleocerebral functions. Plenum. Retrieved from *https://pubmed.ncbi.nlm.nih.gov/17797318/*

Mappital. (2022, July 19). GIS in real estate: How it can improve your business. Retrieved from *https://mappitall.com/blog/gis-solutions-for-real-estate*

MarketsandMarkets. (2020). Geospatialanalytics market - Global forecast to 2028. [Report]. Retrieved from *https://www.marketsandmarkets.com/Market-Reports/geospatial- analytics-market-198354497.html*

McCarthy, J. (2007). What is artificial intelligence? Retrieved from *https://www-formal. stanford.edu/jmc/whatisai.pdf*

McKinsey & Company. (2016, September). Getting ahead of the market: How big data is transforming real estate. Retrieved from *https://www.mckinsey.com/industries/real-estate/ our-insights/getting-ahead-of-the-market-how-big-data-is-transforming-real-estate*

McKinsey & Company. (2018). Notes from the AI frontier: Modeling the impact of AI on the world economy. [Report]. Retrieved from *https://www.mckinsey.com/~/media/McKinsey/ Featured%20Insights/Artificial%20Intelligence/Notes%20from%20the%20frontier%20Modeling %20the%20impact%20of%20AI%20on%20the%20world%20economy/MGI-Notes-from-the-AI- frontier-Modeling-the-impact-of-AI-on-the-world-economy-September-2018.ashx*

MDPI. (2020). GeoAI for large-scale image analysis and machine vision tasks: A review. [Article]. Retrieved from *https://www.mdpi.com/2220-9964/11/7/385*

Messner Reeves LLP. (2023, October 20). Environmental assessments: Three ways they protect companies in corporate real estate transactions. JD Supra LLC. Retrieved from *https://messner.com/environmental-assessments-3-ways-they-protect-companies-in-corporate- real-estate-transactions*

Miller, Elizabeth & Steward, Ben & Witkower, Zak & Sutherland, Clare & Krumhuber, Eva & Dawel, Amy. (2023). AI Hyperrealism: Why AI Faces Are Perceived as More Real Than Human Ones. Psychological Science. Retrieved from *https://doi.org/10.1177/09567976231207095*

Mijwil, M. M. (2015, April). History of artificial intelligence. ResearchGate. Retrieved from *https://www.researchgate.net/publication/322234922_History_of_Artificial_Intelligence*

MIT Technology Review Insights Inc. (2023, October 16). Using data, AI, and cloud to transform real estate. Retrieved from *https://www.technologyreview. com/2023/10/16/1081609/using-data-ai-and-cloud-to-transform-real-estate*

Mortaheb, R., & Jankowski, P. (2023, March). Smart city re-imagined: City planning and GeoAI in the age of big data. Journal of Urban Management. Retrieved from *https://www.sciencedirect.com/science/article/pii/S2226585622000693*

Murray, R. (2023, June 29). Unleashing the power of AI in the property industry. Property Industry Eye. Retrieved from *https://propertyindustryeye.com/unleashing-the-power-if-ai-in-the-property-industry/*

National Association of REALTORS®. (n.d.). Risk management. Retrieved from *https://www.nar.realtor/risk-management*

Nedelkoska, L., & Quintini, G. (2018). Automation, skills use and training. OECD Social, Employment and Migration Working Papers, No. 202. Retrieved from *https://www.oecd-ilibrary.org/employment/automation-skills-use-and-training_2e2f4eea-en*

Pedersen, M. (2022, July 7). The use of artificial intelligence in real estate. InData Labs. Retrieved from *https://indatalabs.com/blog/artificial-intelligence-real-estate*

PiinPoint. (2023, August 31). Retail real estate executives need new tools. Retrieved from *https://www.piinpoint.com/blog/network-simulations-blog-post-2023*

Press, G. (2021, May 19). 114 milestones in the history of artificial intelligence (AI). Forbes. Retrieved from *https://www.forbes.com/sites/gilpress/2021/05/19/114-milestones-in-the-history-of-artificial-intelligence-ai/?sh=469a97b974bf*

PwC. (2017). The economic impact of artificial intelligence on the UK economy. [Report]. Retrieved from *https://www.pwc.co.uk/economic-services/assets/ai-uk-report-v2.pdf*

PwC. (2023). PwC's global artificial intelligence study: Exploiting the AI revolution. Retrieved from *https://www.pwc.com/gx/en/issues/data-and-analytics/publications/artificial-intelligence-study.html*

Realized Holdings Inc. (2017, March 10). 8 ways to mitigate risk in real estate investing. Retrieved from *https://www.realized1031.com/blog/8-ways-to-mitigate-risk-in-real-estate-investing*

ResearchFDI. (2023, October 18). Choosing the perfect spot: How site selection. powers economic development. Retrieved from *https://researchfdi.com/resources/articles/choosing-the-perfect-spot-how-site-selection-powers-economic-development*

Richter, K.-F., & Scheider, S. (2022). Current topics and challenges in GeoAI. KI - Künstliche Intelligenz. Retrieved from *https://link.springer.com/article/10.1007/s13218-022-00796-0*

Reim, Wiebke & Åström, Josef & Eriksson, Oliver. (2020). Implementation of Artificial Intelligence (AI): A Roadmap for Business Model Innovation. AI. 1. 180-191. Retrieved from DOI: *10.3390/ai1020011*

Roe, L. W. (2023, September 1). How to capitalize on AI as it shifts real estate. American Genius. Retrieved from *https://theamericangenius.com/housing/big-data/5-major-ways-ai-is-shifting-real-estate-scene-and-how-to-utilize-it/*

Seagraves, P. (2023, July 5). Real estate insights: Is the AI revolution a real estate boon or bane? Journal of Property Investment & Finance, 41(1), 1-9. Retrieved from *https://www.emerald.com/insight/content/doi/10.1108/JPIF-05-2023-0045/full/html*

Shakya, H. B., & Christakis, N. A. (2017, April 10). A new, more rigorous study confirms: The more you use Facebook, the worse you feel. Harvard Business Review. Retrieved from *https://hbr.org/2017/04/a-new-more-rigorous-study-confirms-the-more-you-use-facebook-the-worse-you-feel*

Smartsheet Inc. (n.d.). Real estate project management. Retrieved from *https://www.smartsheet.com/real-estate-project-management*

StartUs Insights GmbH. (2019, July 25). 5 top AI solutions impacting property & real estate companies. Retrieved from *https://www.startus-insights.com/innovators-guide/ai-solutions-property-real-estate-companies*

Strategic Development Group. (n.d.). Expert site selection. consultants. Retrieved from *https://strategicdev.com*

The Close. (2023, May 3). 10 predictive analytics companies real estate agents need to know about. Retrieved from *https://theclose.com/best-real-estate-predictive-analytics-companies*

The Close. (2023, October 9). Best 7 real estate website builders of 2023. Retrieved from *https://theclose.com/best-real-estate-website-builders*

Thomas, M. (2023, March 3). The future of AI: How artificial intelligence will change the world. Built In. Retrieved from *https://builtin.com/artificial-intelligence/artificial-intelligence-future*

U.S. News & World Report. (2023, April 11). Housing market predictions for the next 5 years promise lots of opportunities for buyers and sellers. Retrieved from *https://realestate.usnews.com/real-estate/housing-market-index/articles/housing-market-predictions-for-the-next-5-years*

Unacast. (2021, June 7). The top real estate analytics companies right now. Retrieved from *https://www.unacast.com/post/the-top-real-estate-analytics-companies-right-now*

USC GIS Online. (2021, January 18). GIS as a platform for real estate. Retrieved from *https://gis.usc.edu/blog/gis-as-a-tool-for-real-estate*

van der Made, P. (2023, April 10). The future of artificial intelligence. Forbes Technology Council. Retrieved from *https://www.forbes.com/sites/forbestechcouncil/2023/04/10/the-future-of-artificial-intelligence/*

Wikipedia. (n.d.). Glossary of artificial intelligence. Retrieved from *https://en.wikipedia.org/wiki/Glossary_of_artificial_intelligence*

Wikipedia. (n.d.). Timeline of artificial intelligence. Retrieved from *https://en.wikipedia.org/wiki/Timeline_of_artificial_intelligence*

Zuboff, S. (2019). The age of surveillance capitalism: The fight for a human future at the new frontier of power. Public Affairs. Retrieved from *https://www.tandfonline.com/doi/abs/10.1080/17530350.2019.1639068*

# CO-AUTHORS' BIOGRAPHIES AND CONTACT INFORMATION

General Information:
Info@RealEstateBook.ai

# GILBERT H. CASTLE, III

Gil@RealEstateBook.ai

Gilbert Castle first became interested in artificial intelligence in the late 1980s. In the early 1990s he taught conference workshops on expert systems. During the 1990s he also developed an expert system for predicting which U.S. real estate markets offered the best investment potential.

Mr. Castle's career focus has been on Geographic Information Systems (GIS) in real estate since 1978, including serving several years as a multi-state Regional Director of the Roulac Group of Deloitte & Touche (the real estate consulting division of the Big Four accounting firm). Mr. Castle was the originator and editor of the book *GIS in Real Estate: Integrating, Analyzing and Presenting Locational Information* published by the Appraisal Institute, and taught the Appraisal Institute's continuing education seminar on GIS in appraisal to a dozen Appraisal Institute chapters around the nation. He was also the originator and editor of the 400-page book *Profiting from a Geographic Information System*, the seminal text on GIS applications in the private sector. Mr. Castle has more than one hundred professional articles and conference presentations to his credit; for example, for several years he wrote the real estate column for "Business Geographics" magazine.

Mr. Castle is a past president of the Urban and Regional Information Systems Association (URISA), North America's oldest and largest professional association for GIS practitioners. He has lectured at numerous universities nationwide, including the Massachusetts Institute of Technology, the University of Pennsylvania, Texas Tech University, Stanford University, and the University of California at Berkeley.

He holds a Bachelor of Science degree in Economics, Cum Laude, from Harvard University, and a Master of City Planning degree from the University of Pennsylvania.

# SRIKANT "STEVE" HEMMADY

Steve@RealEstateBook.ai

Over the past two decades, Steve Hemmady has forged an impressive career path marked by achievements in business entrepreneurship, real estate development, and technological innovation. As a founding partner and investor at CalClinics, Steve has played a pivotal role in revolutionizing medical facilities to align with contemporary healthcare requirements.

His proficiency in Geographic Information Systems (GIS) and geospatial technology has significantly enhanced the process of selecting optimal locations for medical offices, thereby amplifying their attractiveness for investment. CalClinics boasts a prestigious clientele including the Veteran Administration, Quest Diagnostics Labs, QTC Health, and Fremont Natural Dentistry, underscoring Steve's dependable leadership and the company's state-of-the-art solutions.

Steve's professional journey commenced in the technology sector, where he held prominent positions at industry giants such as Apple, Cisco, and SAP. At Apple, he spearheaded projects related to corporate real estate, showcasing adeptness in navigating complex challenges. His tenure at Cisco was highlighted by his instrumental role in the LifeConnections Health Center, where he contributed to transformative solutions that reshaped healthcare delivery. At SAP, he led the conceptualization of the Onepage Enterprise Portal, further exemplifying his strategic acumen and technical expertise.

Steve's academic background, featuring a Master's degree in Environmental Engineering from the University of Cincinnati and a Bachelor's degree in Civil Engineering from IIT Bombay (consistently ranked as one of the top IITs in India and globally), has served as a cornerstone of his professional success.

In essence, Steve's professional trajectory embodies a fusion of entrepreneurial drive, technological prowess, and real estate acumen. His innovative approach is driving forward the evolution of healthcare infrastructure, setting new benchmarks within the industry.

# TECHNICAL ADVISORY PANEL BIOGRAPHIES

## JOE FRANCICA

Joe Francica has over 40 years of experience in location intelligence and geospatial information technology having worked for major corporations, start-ups, and government organizations. Mr. Francica has authored several hundred articles and blogs and has broadcast numerous podcasts and webinars as the former editor-in-chief of *Directions Magazine*. He was the founding chairman of the Location Intelligence Conference from 2004-2014, the first such event to focus on the intersection of business intelligence and geospatial technology. In 2012, he founded GEOHuntsville, a 501c6 non-profit, to support geospatial technology

in workforce development in Huntsville, Alabama, and in 2014 founded Exemplar City, Inc., a 501c3 organization to support GIS knowledge transfer to local governments. Mr. Francica developed the *Location Intelligence for Business* course curriculum with colleagues at Penn State University and was a featured speaker in *The Geospatial Revolution*, a documentary produced by Penn State Public Broadcasting. He currently works for CoreLogic utilizing location-based data and data science models for new product development. Mr. Francica holds degrees from Rutgers (BA), Dartmouth (MA), and Southern Methodist University (MBA).

## PROFESSOR MURALI KRISHNA GURRAM

Professor Murali Krishna Gurram, with over 27 years of experience, is a distinguished authority in Spatial Information Technology, Geoinformatics, GeoAI and applications. He currently serves at Andhra University and has previously held roles at the prestigious National University of Singapore, Universiti Sains Malaysia and prominent organizations in Corporate sector. Professor Murali Krishna is renowned for his diverse teaching portfolio, spanning subjects from Spatial Data Science to Location Intelligence and for his significant contributions to areas such as urban sustainability, disaster management, public health, coastal zone and natural resource management. With a Ph.D. in Spatial Information Technology, he has earned prestigious awards and fellowships, highlighting his leadership in academia and industry. Committed to driving positive change, Professor Murali Krishna focuses on environmental and micro-climate understanding and urban well-being through his scholarly pursuits.

## DR. NOOKA RATNAM KINTHADA

Dr. Nooka Ratnam Kinthada, a seasoned expert in Geospatial Information Technology and Civil and Environmental Engineering, brings 23 years of practical experience to resolving challenges in geosciences and civil engineering domains. With a Ph.D. in Water Resource Management, she has successfully managed diverse projects and received prestigious awards such as the Senior Research Fellowship (SRF) from the Council of Scientific and Industrial Research (CSIR), India. Dr. Nooka Ratnam has transitioned from roles in industry to academia, currently serving as an Associate Professor at AdiKavi Nannaya University, Rajamahendravaram, Andhra Pradesh. In addition to her teaching responsibilities, she holds administrative roles including University Engineer, Coordinator for the Women's Empowerment and Grievances Cell, and Executive Council Member. Previously, she served as the Head of the Department of GeoSciences.

## DR. GRANT IAN THRALL

Dr. Grant Thrall was the elected President of the American Real Estate Society in 2012-2013 in addition to serving on the Board of Directors for 15 years. ARES is the world's largest and most prestigious publisher of real estate and land economics scholarly research. He has been on the faculty of several universities including McMaster University in Canada, San Diego State University, and the University of Florida, holding titles ranging from Assistant through Distinguished Professor. Dr. Thrall has been a leading contributor to the practice and scholarship of geospatial analysis for business. His book *Business Geography and New Real Estate Market Analysis* (Oxford University Press) encom-

passes his pioneering scholarly contributions of a quarter century. Another landmark book is *his Land Use and Urban Form: The Consumption Theory of Land Rent* (Routledge), first published in 1987 with a second edition published in 2017. All told, Dr. Thrall has written or edited over a dozen books, and over 150 professional articles. As the Owner of www.BusinessGeography.com, he has executed real estate market analysis for over $1B in development. He has also been an expert witness in over $100M in litigation and has been a consultant with global real estate advisory firms including PwC. Dr. Thrall holds a Ph.D. in Geography and Economics, an MA in Economics from The Ohio State University, and a BA in Business & Economics from California State University at Los Angeles.

# ACKNOWLEDGEMENTS

The co-authors would like to thank the four members of the Technical Advisory Panel for taking time to review and critique the book's entire manuscript. Their collective recommendations for revisions and additions have proven invaluable.

Next, the co-authors would like to thank Ms. Ankita Hemmady, an undergraduate student in Architecture at the University of California, Berkeley. Her interest in AI applied to architecture inspired her father, Steve Hemmady, to consider writing a book on AI applications in real estate and to recruit long-term AI enthusiast Gilbert Castle to be his co-author. Moreover, Ms. Hemmady actively participated in research for the book, especially in utilizing state-of-the-art Generative AI tools for ensuring comprehensive and efficient information assembly.

Finally, the co-authors would like to thank two contributing consultants retained through Upwork.com. Nada Orlic (*erelis.design@gmail.com*) designed the book's cover. Luca Funari (*funariediting@gmail.com*) enhanced the book's exhibits, optimized the layout and typesetting, and ensured complete compliance with Amazon Kindle's publishing standards.

Published — July, 2024

Made in the USA
Monee, IL
19 October 2024

67335807R00286